AS THE DUST OF THE EARTH

JEWS IN EASTERN EUROPE

Jeffrey Veidlinger
Mikhail Krutikov
Geneviève Zubrzycki

Editors

AS THE DUST OF THE EARTH

THE LITERATURE OF ABANDONMENT IN REVOLUTIONARY RUSSIA AND UKRAINE

HARRIET MURAV

INDIANA UNIVERSITY PRESS

This book is a publication of

Indiana University Press
Office of Scholarly Publishing
Herman B Wells Library 350
1320 East 10th Street
Bloomington, Indiana 47405 USA

iupress.org

© 2024 by Harriet Murav

All rights reserved
No part of this book may be reproduced or utilized in any form or by any means, electronic or mechanical, including photocopying and recording, or by any information storage and retrieval system, without permission in writing from the publisher. The paper used in this publication meets the minimum requirements of the American National Standard for Information Sciences—Permanence of Paper for Printed Library Materials, ANSI Z39.48–1992.

Chapter 2 is an expanded version of the article "David Hofshteyn's Poetry of Listening" first published in *Lyre: Studies in Poetry and Lyric*. Volume 1. 2022. https://www.biupress.co.il/index.php?dir=site&page=catalog&op=category&cs=5184&language=eng
Chapter 3 is an expanded version of the chapter, "Leyb Kvitko's Poetry of Abandonment" first published in *Building Modern Jewish Culture: The Yiddish Kultur-Lige*, ed. Harriet Murav, Gennady Estraikh, and Myroslav Shkadrij. *Legenda: Studies in Yiddish* 20, Modern Research Association, 2023.

Manufactured in the United States of America

First Printing 2024

Cataloging Information is available from the Library of Congress.

978-0-253-06879-8 (hdbk.)
978-0-253-06880-4 (pbk.)
978-0-253-06881-1 (web PDF)

For Bruce Rosenstock (1951–2023)
and
Lillian Schwartz (1922–2022)

CONTENTS

Acknowledgments ix
Note on Transliteration and Abbreviations xi

Introduction 1

PART I — POETRY

1. Hefker and Abandonment 23
2. David Hofshteyn Listening 45
3. Leyb Kvitko's Poetry of Abandonment 73
4. Enfleshment 99

PART II — DOCUMENTATION

5. Chronicling a Hefker World: Itsik Kipnis's *Months and Days* 125
6. Victor Shklovsky's Archive of Abandonment 150
7. Counting 178
8. Children 205

   Conclusion 229

   Notes 237
   Works Cited 283
   Index 307

ACKNOWLEDGMENTS

The University of Illinois at Urbana-Champaign provided numerous opportunities for intellectual and financial support, including fellowships and teaching release from the Humanities Research Institute and an Arnold Beckmann Research Board Award; lively discussion with the Russian Reading Circle; world-class research assistance from the Slavic Reference Service, ably led by Joe Lenkart; wonderful conversations with my colleagues in comparative and world literature, the Department of Slavic Languages and Literatures, the staff at *Slavic Review* (especially Dmitry Tartakovsky), and the many brilliant graduate students whom I have been lucky enough to study with, particularly LeiAnna Hamel, Daria Semenova, Tyler Dolan, and Nobuto Sato. A University of Michigan Frankel Center for Judaic Studies Fellowship gave me the opportunity to interact with scholars of Yiddish and Jewish history, from whom I learned a great deal and whose friendship I treasure. The late Efim Melamed was an invaluable guide and mentor in the archives in Kyiv and Zhitomir, and I am so sorry not to be able to share the results of this research with him. Numerous other colleagues and friends asked just the right question at the right moment and allowed me to ask innumerable questions of them. Gene Avrutin, Sergey Dolgopolski, Gennady Estraikh, Dov-Ber Kerler, Misha Krutikov, and Jeff Veidlinger were incredibly generous, encouraging, and helpful. I am grateful to the Artists Rights Society New York for granting permission to use an image by Marc Chagall. My beloved husband Bruce Rosenstock died before this book could be published; I miss him more than I can possibly say. He listened to everything, and explained everything he knew about all that went into this book, from the Talmud to the workings of Microsoft word. An earlier version of chapter 2 was published as "David Hofshteyn's Poetry of Listening" in *Lyre: Studies in Poetry and Lyric*, vol. 1 (2022). A previous version of chapter 3 was published in *The Kyiv Kultur-Lige: Building Modern Jewish Culture*, edited by Harriet Murav, Gennady Estraikh, and Myroslav Skhandrij, published by Legenda (2023).

NOTE ON TRANSLITERATION AND ABBREVIATIONS

Transliteration of Russian follows Library of Congress style without diacritics. Transliteration of Yiddish follows YIVO guidelines. Transliteration of Hebrew follows SBL general use.

I refer to place-names using a transliteration of the Yiddish and indicate current usage.

Abbreviations

DAKO	Derzhavnyi arkhiv Kyïvs'koï oblasti
GAZHO	Gosudarstvennyi arkhiv Zhitomirskoi oblasti
RGALI	Rossiiskii gosudarstvennyi arkhiv literatury i iskusstva
YIVO	Institute for Jewish Research

AS THE DUST OF THE EARTH

Introduction

Simon Frug, a Jewish poet who wrote mostly in Russian, turned to Yiddish in "Sand and Stars" ("Zamd un shtern"). Composed at a time of heightened anti-Jewish violence in czarist Russia, the poem comments bitterly on God's promise that the Jewish people would become as numerous as the sand on the seashore and the stars in the sky. The divine promise had been fulfilled but only negatively: Jews had become like "sand, which is *hefker*, / which everyone tramples with their feet."[1] Originating in Jewish property law, the term hefker refers to unclaimed, ownerless objects. Property can be deliberately abandoned (made hefker) by means of an explicit statement of renunciation uttered in the presence of witnesses. Other objects are presumed to be unclaimed, naturally ownerless, including the oceans, wild animals, and sand.[2] Frug employed a term that first emerged in property law to make a point about politics and history. Jews had become like sand not because they had grown more numerous, but because their lives had no value. They were expendable and could be abused with impunity.

Frug's use of the term hefker ramifies throughout the history of anti-Jewish violence in the twentieth century. This study focuses on one crucial period: the years immediately following the 1917 Russian Revolution, from 1918 to 1922, during which as many as forty thousand Jews were killed in pogroms.[3] Hefker is the key term. I examine the use of hefker in poetry, narrative fiction, memoirs, newspaper articles, and documentary reports written in response to the mass public violence of the time. While a number of books on the history of the civil war–era pogroms have been published in the past ten years, *As the Dust of the Earth* is the only book that focuses on the literature of this cataclysmic period, and it is the only one that examines both artistic literature (the subject of part I) and documentary fiction and nonfiction (topics covered in part II), including documentary accounts found in the archives of relief agencies. Poets and pogrom investigators were doing more than chronicling violence and expressing emotions. They were interrogating what was taking place using a term familiar from their everyday lifeworld.

Chapter 1 provides a history of the hefker concept, but a working definition at this point will be helpful. In addition to its use in Jewish property law, hefker entered everyday Yiddish as a term of opprobrium, referring to licentious and immoral behavior. Although the correspondence is not exact, in English as well as in Yiddish you can abandon an object, claim ownership of an object that is abandoned, and act with abandon. Before World War I, Yiddish poets transformed the term into a principle of aesthetic and personal freedom. At the same time, as Frug's "Stars and Sand" shows, Jewish poets, intellectuals, and journalists began using hefker to indicate the degraded status of Jews and their vulnerability to untrammeled violence. Hefker thus spans an array of meanings. It pertains to objects that are up for grabs; it signals freedom and enjoyment, a departure from norms, and indicates a condition of political abandonment, akin to rightlessness and dispossession. I explore the multivalence of the hefker concept as a legal, poetic, existential, and political/social term in the Jewish world in the first quarter of the twentieth century.

Hefker has significance beyond the Jewish world, however. My exploration of *hefker* in the sense of political and social abandonment contributes to a broader discussion. Abandonment has emerged as a central tool for the analysis of the experience of those thrust beyond the realm of governmental care. Abandonment is a global phenomenon in the first part of the twenty-first century, as evidenced by scholarship on inequality, neglect, precarity, dispossession, and violence, including Noam Leshem on Israel/Palestine, Veena Das on India, João Biehl on Brazil, and Elizabeth Povinelli on Australia.[4]

The current use of abandonment derives from biopolitics, which, as the term suggests, emphasizes the importance of the body and life in the domain of politics. Chapter 1 provides more detail, but some preliminary remarks will indicate the parallel between hefker and abandonment.

Introduced by historian Michel Foucault and developed by political theorist Giorgio Agamben, proponents of biopolitics argue that the chief concern of governments is the health and biological vitality of the population. Vaccination mandates are an example. Agamben maintains that the very formation of governmental power depends not on providing care but on withholding it, categorizing some part of the population as outside the realm of care. Abandonment is the first order of business in the establishment of governmental power. Governments distribute rights and protections with one hand and withhold them with the other, leaving the persons and property of some groups abandoned and up for grabs. In revolutionary Russia and Ukraine, nearly everyone was left in a state of abandonment, but Jews were particularly victimized.

Jewish rabbinic authorities did not administer power in the manner of a nation-state. Rabbinic authorities, however, could use the hefker mechanism in a form of eminent domain to confiscate property and in other ways exert arbitrary power. Hefker reveals how abandonment can take place below the level of the state, dispersed across an array of social contexts.[5] Both the hefker concept and biopolitical abandonment reveal the nebulous areas that blur categories and distinctions, destabilizing law and creating border zones of vulnerability. In Hebrew, "no-man's-land" is *sheteh hefker*.[6] My primary concern is the manifold expressions and states of the hefker condition from the perspective of those experiencing it, sometimes because they were pushed into the no-man's-land and sometimes because they embraced it. The poets, prose authors, pogrom investigators, and memoirists whose work I examine dwell on the fissures and gray areas, delighting in the openness and freedom they provide and lamenting the pain of exposure and vulnerability.

As I will show, one layer of the hefker term overlaps with biopolitical abandonment, but other layers are distinct. Maximum overlap occurs when hefker is used to describe political and social dispossession and powerlessness. Working with the two concepts provides for a richer approach to the study of violence against Jews in the former Russian Empire and other minority populations elsewhere and at other times. This book is about the literary archive and the documentary record of destruction and care, the poetry of catastrophe and the documentation of catastrophe. The overlap between hefker and abandonment frames its two parts, the artistic literature that both celebrates and laments the hefker condition in part I—what

I call the literature of abandonment—and the documentation of violence and care in part II. The Jewish social scientists who led the relief effort sought to remove victims of pogroms from the space of abandonment (the hefker condition) by counting and classifying the pogroms and their victims and providing them with material assistance. They and the aid workers and medical and legal professionals with whom they worked attempted to demonstrate the vitality of the Jewish population and they acted as agents of Jewish biopolitics, the subject of chapter 7.[7]

The period from 1918 to 1922 was one of unprecedented violence, and Yiddish poets responded with a series of major works, including Peretz Markish's "The Mound" ("Di kupe"), Arn Kushnirov's "Memorial Prayer" ("Azkore," 1922), Leyb Kvitko's *1919*, and Hofshteyn's *Sorrow* (*Troyer*). The year 1919 was a peak year of pogroms.[8] The protagonists of this study were directly touched by them: Hofshteyn (the subject of chap. 2) and the poet Kadya Molodowsky were in Kyiv in 1919; Kvitko, discussed in chapters 3 and 4, was in Uman; and the prose writer Itsik Kipnis (the focus of chap. 5) was in Slovechno (Slovechne), a small shtetl in northern Ukraine, during the July 1919 pogrom. Victor Shklovsky (chap. 6) traveled throughout the collapsing Russian empire, tracing violence and "abandonment" (using a Russian term) everywhere he went. He discusses the 1919 Elisavetgrad pogrom and tried to stop a pogrom in northern Iran. The Russian-language author Doyvber Levin interviewed children orphaned by pogroms, and Dr. Fischel Shneersohn—a scion of the Lubavitch Hasidic dynasty who became a psychologist—cared for them.

This selection of authors may surprise some readers.[9] I focus on Hofshteyn and Kvitko not only because they are extraordinary but also because they are woefully neglected. Molodowsky did not write a major pogrom work, but her poetry, which sheds light on abandonment beyond anti-Jewish violence, provides a woman's voice. Kipnis's pogrom novel was widely read in its time, and his fascinating use of documentary techniques remains unexamined in the literature. Each of these figures engaged with the hefker condition, both positive and negative. Shklovsky, who explicitly discusses antisemitism in Russia, links pogroms committed against Jews in the Pale of Settlement with pogroms committed against other minority groups elsewhere in the disintegrating Russian empire.[10] Doyvber Levin is a minor Russian Jewish literary figure, and Fischel Schneersohn is virtually unknown; however, both worked with children who had been victimized by the pogroms, and their writings from the 1920s and '30s provide a fascinating counterpart to the testimonies of children found in historical archives. Schneersohn's belief, furthermore, in the hidden creative potential of these children pushes against what might be understood only as a scenario of disaster. Creating a dialogue between literary authors, pogrom investigators, and medical professionals working in different languages, genres, and fields produces a multifaceted picture of abandonment and care, the two themes of this study.

Pogroms: History and Historiography

Pogrom, a Russian word, is an elastic term used to describe destruction of property, mass violence, and ethnic violence, sometimes with deadly results and not necessarily against Jews.[11] A prominent twenty-first-century example is the Gujarat pogrom of 2002, which lasted for three days and during which hundreds of people were killed, mostly Muslims. The 1880s, when Frug wrote "Sand and Stars," and the early 1900s were significant periods of anti-Jewish violence in czarist Russia. These pogroms were usually linked to Easter on the Orthodox calendar, fueled by alcohol, economic rivalry, and the false claim that Jews committed ritual murder. They were facilitated by the printing press and the railroad. Scholars have established that local and imperial government officials, while incompetent, were not complicit.[12] The assassination of Czar Alexander II provoked pogroms in several cities, including Elisavetgrad, also a major pogrom site in 1919. The Kishinev pogrom of 1903, during which approximately forty-five Jews were killed, was a pivotal event. World War I changed the picture, because the military was given complete control, and "for the first time, Jews were targeted for persecution, and sometimes, complete annihilation."[13] The anti-Jewish sentiments and policies of the czarist army that deported thousands of Jews paved the way for the brutality in the same region in the immediate aftermath.[14] Even though World War I marked the turning point to utter and complete abandonment in the biopolitical sense discussed earlier, Jews used the term hefker to describe their condition throughout the period leading up to World War I, as Frug's poem shows. What this difference reveals, is that the government's various reactions to mass violence may not matter to those who experience or witness it.

The temporal and geographical scope, as well as the scale of destruction of the pogroms that followed the Russian Revolution, increased dramatically. Some regions saw the complete decimation of their Jewish populations. Warring state and nonstate armies, gangs, and individuals perpetrated violence in a free for all "shatterzone of empires."[15] From the first declaration of Ukraine's independence in 1918 and throughout the period of the Ukrainian Revolution, 1917–1920, which included the Rada, the Hetmanate, and the Directory, problems beset the central Ukrainian authorities from all sides. The provisional government and then the Bolshevik government were opposed to Ukrainian independence, and the Soviets fought against the Ukrainian army. Local leaders carved out separate republics and peasant insurgent groups mushroomed.[16] The rapid succession of different governments and the brief gain and loss of independence created conditions for total lawlessness, allowing for violence on an unprecedented scale. Rape was an instrument of terror.[17] Anti-Bolshevik sentiment, and the incorrect belief that Jews were necessarily Bolsheviks, the desire for land, the availability of weapons, and the "prolonged absence of a central authority in Ukraine" were among the most important factors leading to the pogroms.[18]

Long overshadowed by the Holocaust, recent years have seen the publication of important new work on the history of pogroms in czarist and revolutionary Ukraine and Russia, Poland, and Hungary, including studies by Steven Zipperstein, Irina Astashkevich, William Hagen, Elissa Bemporad, and Jeffrey Veidlinger, among others.[19] Zipperstein explains how the 1903 Kishinev pogrom became the Jewish story of the time and beyond. Astashkevich examines rape as a tool of terror largely neglected in the scholarship. Hagen's study of Poland finds the myth of Judeo-Bolshevism an inadequate explanation for the anti-Jewish violence of 1914–20.[20] Veidlinger's comprehensive account includes detailed discussions of pogroms across Ukraine, as well as in-depth portraits of individual warlords and group portraits of the various armies involved. Veidlinger sees the 1918–22 pogroms as the precedent that made the Holocaust possible.[21] Other scholars place the anti-Jewish violence of the Russian Civil War in the context of paramilitary violence of the period more broadly.[22]

Although I rely on some of the same sources used by historians, including the archives of the Jewish Public Committee to Aid Victims of Pogroms (Evobshchestkom), the story I tell is less about perpetrators, their attitudes, and actions and more about Jewish responses to violence. I focus on the ways in which pogroms were described and understood by those who experienced, witnessed, poetically reimagined, and investigated them in their immediate aftermath. It is not only first-person accounts of survivors that compel attention but also, more importantly for my purposes, the self-consciousness of investigators at pogrom sites, impossibly tasked with producing comprehensive reports of chaos. I examine the gaps between the instructions pogrom investigators received and the narratives they created, the sudden jumps in time and space in poetry, and the haunting sense of failure in both the poetry and the documentary reports. A common thread shared by both is the extraordinary strangeness of the violence of the revolutionary period, the strange transformations in behavior that witnesses observed. I am interested in what made these acts, both of violence and care, unpredictable, lacking in rationale to all involved.

Abandonment for All

The literary authors and relief workers who are the subject of this study understood the Jews' hefker condition to be the consequence of specific circumstances, not pinned to their age-old destiny. Some, however, articulated another perspective: Jews suffered abandonment because they lacked a national homeland. The socialist Zionist Ber Borokhov (1881–1917), founder of the Po'ale Tsiyon Party, for example, wrote that the blood spilled in Drohobych (in western Galicia), a reference to the pogrom of May 1919, was directly tied to the collective weakness of the Jews as a people, in contrast to the strength and energy of Jewish individuals. The lack of a national homeland and the subsequent weakness of the Jews as a people led energetic and forward-looking Jews as individuals to "abandon" Jews as a community. The term hefker appears in the original Yiddish phrase; the agents perpetuating the abandonment of Jews were Jews. The "exemplary weakness" of the collective was thus the source of internal conflict among Jews in exile (*goles*).[23]

Leyb Kvitko, David Hofshteyn, Itsik Kipnis, and David Bergelson, in contrast, did not link the pogroms of revolutionary Ukraine and Russia to the great chain of Jewish national disaster that stretched back to the biblical exile. Not particularly committed politically in the early 1920s, these authors aligned their sympathies less with Jewish national redemption in Palestine and more with the new socialist society being constructed in the Soviet Union. Socialism was a form of hope. There are other considerations as well, beyond political allegiances. Kvitko, for example, depicts himself as having always been abandoned, not because he was a Jew, and not because of mass public violence, but because of some unknown and incomprehensible force that determined that he should be shunted aside and neglected. Hefker thus appears as the name for a generalized condition, not having access to the decisive moment that shaped one's own life. The fact that artists and intellectuals as different in their convictions and life stories as the figures I have mentioned all used the term hefker to refer to themselves and to Jews and others collectively attests to the importance and multivalence of the term.

By focusing on a Jewish concept, I do not mean to suggest that Jews were the only population subject to violence with impunity in this period or this region, as Yiddish writers themselves, Shklovsky's memoirs, and other sources show.[24] Historian Laura Engelstein characterizes the Russian Civil War as "extraordinarily brutal." The total number of deaths, including the civilian population and military forces, amounted to 9 percent of the population of the former Russian dmpire. All sides of the conflict used "hostage-taking, reprisals against civilians, summary executions, rape and torture, and the targeting of ethnic communities."[25] Characterizing this period in Ukraine, Stephen Velychenko writes, "all civilians faced the threat of plundering, the destruction of property, malnutrition, arbitrary summary execution, torture, and mutilation."[26] Acts perpetrated against Jews by warring state and nonstate armies, gangs, and individuals took place in a larger context of violence—"the practices of total war" conducted internally and externally by the Bolsheviks, including not only military combat but also the forced appropriation of material goods and summary executions conducted by different branches of the new government as it struggled to establish power.[27]

Writing about Russia in 1918–19, Nobel Prize–winning Russian author Ivan Bunin observed that the new "existence" created by the revolution was one of "causeless revelry and an unnatural freedom from everything human society had lived by."[28] The conditions of the new life deprived everyone of the protection granted by laws and rights, subjecting them to torment and mockery. Bunin's description captures the licentiousness and anarchy of what a Yiddish author would call a hefker world. Bunin, who was not Jewish, included anti-Jewish pogroms among the phenomena of the new revolutionary conditions that he abhorred. Valerian Pidmohylnyi's

1921 Ukrainian novella *The Third Revolution* depicts the pillage, rape, and looting that befalls the entire non-Jewish urban population when a detachment from the anarchist army of Nestor Makhno takes over a town. The structures that had previously ordered the world of the town collapse, and the inhabitants become exposed, vulnerable, undifferentiated from one another—"naked," as the author writes.[29] This was a hefker world or a world of abandonment, even though Pidmohylnyi does not use either term.

The pogroms of the Russian Civil War were part of a global phenomenon of ethnic and racial violence, which also included the Armenian genocide and the lesser-known genocide of Assyrian Christians in northern Iran, which Shklovsky discusses at length. On the other side of the Atlantic, Black communities were the targets of racial violence. Chicago's Red Summer and the "anti-Black pogrom" in Tulsa, Oklahoma, are but two examples of racial violence and abandonment from the same time.[30] The Tulsa race riot left hundreds of Blacks dead and destroyed the Greenwood neighborhood known as "Black Wall Street." White officials and the National Guard blamed Blacks for their supposed "uprising," because armed Black veterans attempted to protect Black property and lives, including that of the young man, Dick Rowlands, wrongfully accused of attempting to rape a White woman. The term hefker resonates here as well: Black property and lives were destroyed with impunity; Black citizenship was forfeited. No one was held accountable. There are distinctions to be made, of course, between the two episodes of mass violence on the two sides of the Atlantic, and it is beyond the scope of this book to provide a detailed comparison. My point is to acknowledge a part of history that has been neglected and to avoid contributing to an image of Jews as unique and quintessential victims.[31] One of the factors that distinguishes the civil war pogroms and the anti-Black violence of the same period in the United States is that whereas the former were documented and broadly reported, in the case of Tulsa, evidence was destroyed and relief prevented.[32] The first official report on Tulsa was published in 2001.

The study of interwar abandonment has implications beyond eastern Europe and Jews then and today. Kvitko and Molodowsky understood the potential for political and social dispossession that could unfold in ordinary daily life, apart from catastrophic mass violence. According to Shklovsky, wartime exposes conditions of abandonment and violence obscured during peacetime. The Yiddish authors used the hefker concept to engage these issues beyond their immediate lifeworld. Molodowsky wrote a poem about an Argentinian internment ship that was not permitted to dock in any port, leaving its prisoners abandoned. One of Kvitko's pogrom poems explicitly refers to the condition of Africans "enslaved" to European colonizers.[33] The violence of abandonment is not merely a Jewish or Russian problem for these authors; it is global.

Poetry and Disaster

The image of the person taking notes, writing lists, and collecting metrical data recurs in Yiddish poetry and fiction written in response to the pogroms of the Russian Civil War. Relief workers did not only gather data, however. Pogrom investigators were also instructed to collect poems, stories, and proverbs. Hofshteyn proposed that relief organizations should dispatch literary artists to their native shtetls to record what happened. The proceeds from his own pogrom lament were used to support an orphanage for pogrom victims. The psychologist Dr. Fischel Schneersohn argued that artistic creativity was important in diagnosing and curing the lingering effects of pogroms in children. The literary authors, activists, researchers, and caregivers who are the subject of this study linked artistic work, relief efforts, and care, and this study does as well.

The origin story of the most famous pogrom poem, "In the City of the Slaughter," provides a fascinating case of the interaction between poetry and documentation. As Zipperstein explains, Simon Dubnow and Ahad Ha'am sent Hayim Nachman Bialik to Kishinev to collect data about the 1903 pogrom. Bialik spent weeks interviewing survivors, translating their Yiddish testimony into Hebrew, and filling five notebooks. He then abandoned his notes and, instead of producing a report, created a poem, "In the City of the Slaughter." The outcome did not disappoint Dubnow, according to Zipperstein. "Curiously," as Zipperstein says, Dubnow saw "no substantive difference between the tasks of a chronicler and those of a poet."[34] The question, however, of "how the witness accounts ... informed his poem has long bedeviled his readers."[35]

The writers I discuss were all familiar with Bialik's poem. Unlike Bialik, however, they did not gather witness accounts after the fact; they were at the scene of pogroms. Zipperstein's question nonetheless pertains with this modification: how does the experience of violence inform literary creativity? One answer comes from Kvitko's remarkable preface to *1919*, his pogrom volume. Kvitko observed that time and space were different in Uman in 1919. As he puts it, "the moments were different."[36] A poem is an interlude of time, a moment. Reading or listening to a poem changes the experience of time. Kvitko responds to the catastrophe of the pogroms in Uman by re-creating its strange moments in the form of poems, thus bringing readers to the very edge of ordered time or, to put it another way, to the hefker threshold. The poem registers the horror of experience at right angles to normal life and through its use of sound, rhythm, and imagery draws readers into a moment that is different, experienced otherwise.

The Holocaust has given rise to a paradigmatic body of theoretical and artistic literature about the relation between witness accounts, or testimony, and artistic literature. There are important distinctions, however, between the earlier artistic work and literature written in response to the Nazi genocide, even though the term hefker was used at both times. The epistemological conditions of the postrevolutionary and post–World War II period were different. Holocaust testimony had to prove that the impossible had happened. The Nazi genocide attempted to exterminate all witnesses and thus silence the possibility of speech about the extermination. Testimony confronted the challenge of incredulity. The accumulated weight of philosophical interventions on the topic of witnessing and testimony produced a witness who embodies loss and trauma, and the crisis of representation.[37] The best witnesses cannot speak, and thus the witness who does "must speak solely in the name of the incapacity to speak."[38]

The circumstances that prompted philosophers, historians, and literary scholars to posit a crisis of representation after World War II, however, did not dominate the literary, philosophical, and legal milieu of postrevolutionary Russia and Europe. Jews in both periods were hefker, but in the 1920s, perpetrators were put on trial. Pogrom testimony was used to press legal cases against perpetrators in the Soviet Union. Pogrom testimony from Ukraine was used in the Paris trial of Shlomo Schwartzbard, the confessed assassin of Symon Petliura, former head of the Ukrainian government; the assassin was acquitted.[39] The postwar witness and poet is distinct from the pogrom witness and poet. Hefker was the watchword of poetic experimentation in the first part of the twentieth century but not in the postwar period.

Instead of a crisis of representation, embodied by the Holocaust witness, Russia in the 1920s saw an explosion of new forms of representation, imagination, and meaning making generally. Proponents of the "literature of fact" argued for a citizen-activist approach to literature and for a broader understanding of what counted as belles lettres. Newspaper reporting, memoirs, diaries, and travelogues were recontextualized as new type of literature, oriented to the fact and immediate, ongoing reality. Established literary forms, including poetry, expanded to absorb reportage, lists, street signs, and biometric data. Molodowsky uses the latter in her poem about tuberculosis; Kipnis incorporated factual reportage into his novel about the Slovechno pogrom; Shklovsky's memoir is factographic; and Doyvber Levin relied on factographic methods in his literary refashioning of children's testimonies.

There are parallels, nonetheless, between the literary work created in response to the catastrophic events of both the Russian Civil War and World War II. Literary scholar James Young describes the fundamental tension between the overwhelming form-destroying violence of the Holocaust and the necessity of ordered form in literary narrative. Pogrom poets were intensely aware of this contradiction in their hefker poetry, which tread the tightrope between chaos and ordered form. Young also points out that Holocaust witnesses and authors took pains to establish their immediate connection to the events they described. While Kvitko and Kipnis similarly insist on the fact of their physical presence during specific days and times when pogroms took place, Kvitko's poetry rejects documentarism as a style.

The authenticity of literary works and documentary accounts is not of central concern in the chapters that follow; the register of experience and the activity of care are. I examine abandonment from two ends of the telescope: the poetic works of those who experienced it and the paper trail left by relief agencies who tried to mitigate it. I trace hefker abandonment as the key marker of the experience of mass anti-Jewish violence, explore how poets created new, hefker literary forms to embody it, and examine how relief workers and poets attempted to lessen its consequences.

The question of how literature responds to historical violence has engaged literary authors and scholars working on a broad array of events across the globe, including the Atlantic slave trade, conflict in Ireland, the World War II Leningrad siege, and the civil war in El Salvador. Helen

Vendler characterizes William Butler Yeats's poetic sequence "Nineteen Hundred and Nineteen," published in 1928, as a response to mass public violence, in the aftermath of both World War I and conflicts in Ireland in 1919 and 1920. The "ingenious lovely things" fabricated by human beings have no permanence, artists and intellectuals are but "weasels fighting in a hole," and whether there is "any comfort to be found" remains an open question.[40] Comfort is Hofshteyn's key theme; the poet offers his own work as a gesture of comfort.

The Objectivist poet Charles Reznikoff spent decades reworking decades of transcribed courtroom testimony—the stuff of mundane, everyday violence in American life—into poetry, and the result was his monumental volume, *Testimony: The United States (1885–1915): Recitative*. He used similar methods to reframe testimony from the Nuremberg and Eichmann trials in his later work *Holocaust*. Reznikoff might be considered an heir of the factography of the 1920s. Reliance on documentary methods cannot succeed in other cases, however. Marlene Nourbese Philip's 2008 *Zong!* is an example. Approximately 130 slaves were thrown overboard from the *Zong* slave ship in 1781. The murderous episode abounds with instances of abandonment. The slave owners pursued an insurance claim for the value of their property and were successful. The court ignored the murder of human beings, regarding them as property, and did not punish the perpetrators. Slavery is abandonment: the ownership of human beings, deprived of personality, community, and family and reduced to killable bodies.[41] The court allowed that owners could abandon virtually destroyed property (as long as they were not negligent) and still claim its value.[42] That this provision extended to human beings is yet another dimension of abandonment. Nourbese Philip created an antinarrative poem out of the absence of documentation about the murdered slaves. Looking at the page, at letters that fail to coalesce into words, and words that do not form sentences, "one seems to be looking at bodies in the ocean."[43]

Documentary methods fail when violence confounds those who experience, witness, and write about it. Catastrophe prompts a sense of failure and confusion in poets as well as relief workers. Carolyn Forché's memoir and documentary poetry about the civil war in El Salvador express her disorientation: "I couldn't distinguish between literal and figurative language: Were the guitar player's hands, mangled by ax, a metaphor? What about wingless birds, and the dead waving their arms?"[44] Not confronting atrocity directly, but only reading about it, I was similarly confused about was literally true in pogrom poetry. Sometimes I thought that the poets' description of a scene of violence was the result of exaggeration or metaphor, but I was wrong. What they said was, in many instances, unadorned. In Kvitko's pogrom poetry, the phrase *mise-meshune* does not mean only "unnatural death" but literally "strange death," with emphasis on grotesque strangeness. This was not figurative language.

To return to the question of poetry, documentation, and catastrophe in the broadest possible terms, systems of knowledge, including archives and poems, impose rules.[45] Poems and archives create rules determining what can be said, and both poems and documentary materials may lead to forgetting and remembering, increased attention, silencing, and giving voice. How poets attend to violence requires an expanded definition of what violence is.

Listening to Violence

Violence is typically understood as force—the infliction of physical or psychic injury or the threat of so doing—used by state or nonstate actors, including individuals, to gain or demonstrate power in order to maintain or disrupt order, in the context of law or to disrupt it. While scholars agree that violence can be systemic and structural, they also argue that context and contingency matter.[46] Local contexts and contingencies certainly mattered during the pogroms of the Russian Civil War, as I show in discussions of specific events, but I also show how abandonment worked as a trigger to make other forms of violence possible. The use of the term hefker in sources from the time reveals how pogrom victims conceptualized their experience as fundamentally linked to abandonment.

How they depicted the experience of violence is another matter. To be sure, the literary, documentary, and medical sources describe cutting, hacking, shooting, and other forms of attack against the body, and I must warn readers about scenes of violence in later chapters. What the sources all additionally emphasize, however, are the consequences of violence: the loss of the ability to make sense of the world. To examine this additional dimension of violence, I rely on the approach shared by literary scholar Elaine Scarry and the phenomenologist Michael Staudigl. In her groundbreaking 1985 study *The Body in Pain: The Making and Unmaking of the World*, Scarry demonstrates that the point of the pain inflicted in torture is not to produce information from victims but, instead, to destroy their relation to the external world, "unmaking" the categories by which they previously understood their surrounding environment in relation to themselves. A chair is no longer a place to sit but an object that inflicts pain. The torturer's goal is the deprivation of self and voice in the victim, whose sentience is reengineered according to the torturer's purposes.[47] Staudigl similarly argues that "violence is destructive of pre-given sense structures, but correlatively of the very foundational ways we are able to make sense of the world."[48] In literary works and documentary reports, violence is not only a matter of attacks against bodies but also the attack on meaning, coherence, boundaries, and distinctions between subject and object, human beings and things, and the experiencing body and the stimulus. The focus is on the taste, smell, and feel of the moments that were "different," as Kvitko says. Attending to the immediate phenomena of experience without historicizing, narrativizing, or providing any other framework of explanation is a common feature of poetry and phenomenology.[49] The concept of abandonment, derived from the analysis of sovereign power, cannot account for the ways that abandoned individuals inhabit and express their *hefker* condition. The composite meaning of hefker that emerges from the literary and documentary sources expands beyond an abstract legal notion to encompass a broad psychical, physiological, and kinesthetic experience. I trace both the common conceptual category and the unique specifity and concreteness of the literary forms used to express the experience.

Yiddish Modernism

Yiddish modernism was the perfect vehicle for the articulation of the manifold dimensions of exposure to violence. Yiddish poetic language of this time could shriek and howl, engage in prosaic conversation, quietly reflect in a lyrical style, and orate in an exalted biblical and prophetic register. Yiddish poetry was young and new in the 1920s, and while some writers emphasized their own mood, emotion, memory, and melody, others embraced cacophony, chaos, and the body. Instead of interpreting violence as the wellspring of new literary forms, I trace how literary authors modified language and forms they had already developed in their previous work. This is why I discuss poetry by Hofshteyn and Kvitko that has no obvious relation to the civil war–era pogroms but does have substantial engagement with the hefker theme. The extraordinary violence suffered by Jews in 1919 was coupled with an extraordinary burst of literary creativity in Yiddish.[50] In more than one case, pogrom volumes immediately followed the publication of debut volumes. David Hofshteyn and Leyb Kvitko responded to anti-Jewish violence, but they called upon emotions and prior experiences that on the surface had little to do with mass public violence. I trace their use of the term hefker in both their earliest lyric and subsequent pogrom poetry. Only a short time passes between these two moments, however.

Yiddish modernism, like other modernisms, included an array of movements whose fundamental premises could contradict each other. The clash between Yiddish expressionism and instrospectivism is an example. Yiddish introspectivists insisted on the importance of their own individual experience, memory, and emotions; their inward turn, however, did not preclude an engagement with the larger forces of history. An introspectivist manifesto of 1920 declared that pogroms, Protestantism, and the Buddha could be intensely personal for instrospectivist poets, and whether they wrote about these things depended on what moved them.[51]

In contrast, in his uncharacteristically expressionist literary manifesto of 1922, David Bergelson excoriated individualism in poetry, declaring that the new verse forms had left behind the shattered remains of individual worlds, like so much "abandoned" (hefker) rubble.[52] Yiddish expressionist writers defined their historic moment as one of chaos, revolution, destruction out of which their new, "naked" poetry was created. The bookshelf of Yiddish modernism, so to speak, held volumes by writers as different as the American poets Edgar Allen Poe and Walt Whitman; the Russian poets Alexander Blok, Sergei Esenin, and Vladimir Mayakovsky; and the Ukrainian Pavel Tychyna. This is far from a complete list. A 1920 expressionist manifesto by the Yiddish poet Melekh Ravitsh singles out Whitman as the most important poet.[53] In stanza 24 of *Song of Myself*, Whitman describes himself as "turbulent, fleshy, sensual, eating, drinking, and breeding."[54] He calls seeing, hearing, and feeling "miracles." The Yiddish poetic affinity for Whitman makes sense, given that Yiddish expressionists embraced embodied fleshiness, and yet Whitman's language also points to the problem with *-isms*. No one would call Molodowsky or Hofshteyn expressionists; yet their poetry brims over with palpable delight in seeing, hearing, and feeling, and they, too, listen with their bodies.

Ravitsh cites the same stanza from which I have already quoted, providing a Yiddish translation. The lines are worth dwelling on because they underscore the duality of the hefker condition. I begin with the English original:

> Unscrew the locks from the doors!
> Unscrew the doors themselves from their jambs![55]

The Yiddish translation:

> Reyst di shleser fun di tirn
> Reyst di gantse tirn fun di anglen.[56]

Note the unmelodious and thus seemingly unpoetic qualities of Whitman's repeated word *unscrew*. The poet removes the doors from his house because he wants to be with people, Ravitsh explains. I add that in this space without barriers, precisely in a moment of freedom and openness, there is also a terrible risk of exposure. Anyone could enter the space left open by the missing door. These are the contradictions of the hefker condition.

Modernist Yiddish poetry is "screaming, absurd, grotesque, visionary, utopian."[57] Yet Hofshteyn and Kvitko do not scream; instead, they listen. Kvitko says he listens to the point of deafness. Listening, as opposed to seeing, is a hallmark of modernism generally. Artists and philosophers in the first part of the twentieth century were vitally interested in sound, and they explored how sound connected individuals to the surrounding world, to previous historical eras, and to each other.[58] The poets examined in this study understood sound as a sensation and listening as a fleshy, emotional process. They were listening to the violence of 1919.

The chapters that follow examine abandonment as a form of violence and show how the violence of abandonment demands the reimagination of human creativity in both literature and life. Poetry and the invention of new forms of literary art are part and parcel of remaking the world. The terms *creative* and *creativity* also appear in discussions of how to design care for victims of violence. The chronicle of the world's unmaking is thus also the record of attempts relieve the suffering. Poetry is not merely a register of experience; it is a part of the remaking of worlds unmade by violence, not by restoring what has been destroyed, but by providing an opening to other possibilities.[59] Poetry offers an interlude of order in the chaos of ongoing experience.

This book falls roughly into two parts: artistic literature and documentary texts. Chapter 1 provides the theoretical framework by tracing the intersection between the Jewish concept and the biopolitical concept of abandonment. It offers a history of the term hefker, beginning with Jewish property law, and focusing on the broader use of the term in response to anti-Jewish violence in the first part of the twentieth century, as evidenced in newspaper articles, memoirs, and poetry.

Chapter 2 examines Hofshteyn's sensory experience of joy and pleasure, as well as his encounter with the catastrophe of 1919, through the lens of the hefker concept in its multiple dimensions and across a series of works published in 1919 and the early 1920s. I begin with Hofshteyn's debut volume and trace the continuity of his poetic process from his early poetry through his 1922 pogrom lament. Leyb Kvitko is the subject of chapters 3 and 4. For Kvitko, hefker names an existential condition, theme, and stylistic point of departure. The poetic world of terror and abandonment that he had already created in his first volume prepared the way for his pogrom cycle *1919*. I focus on his use of sound and his evocation of the bodily sensorium. Chapter 4 emphasizes the role of the body and flesh in Kvitko's poetry.

I introduce the problem of documentation in chapters 5 and 6 by analyzing fiction and nonfiction prose work that use documentary strategies. Chapter 5, "Chronicling a Hefker World," examines Itsik Kipnis's 1926 prose narrative *Months and Days*, devoted to the 1919 pogrom in Slovechno. Hefker as both abandonment and transgression is the catalyst for Kipnis's depiction of the strange, off-kilter world of love and violence in *Months and Days*. Shklovsky's memoir *Sentimental Journey*, the subject of chapter 6, is a record of both abandonment and care. Using the Russian word for abandonment, Shklovsky probes the larger political and social context of dispossession and rightlessness in the revolutionary period. Both Kipnis and Shklovsky use the factographic methods that I described earlier.

Chapter 7 turns to the massive record left by aid workers and pogrom investigators, with particular attention to their understanding of their own mission. On the one side, the instructions they were given insisted on the importance of precise biopolitical instruments to assess damage and demonstrate the potential for recovery. The local, emotional, memory oriented, and catastrophe narratives of the investigators, however, pulled against the instructions from the center by showing the unmeasurable dimensions of the catastrophe.

The civil war pogroms created a substantial population of orphaned children, the subject of chapter 8. The Russian-language Jewish writer Doyvber Levin (1904–41), created a volume of children's testimonies of violence in fictitious form, titled *Ten Wagons* (*Desiat' vagonov*), first published in 1931. It was based on his visits to a Jewish orphanage in Leningrad. Fischel Schneersohn (1887–1958), an ordained Hasidic rabbi, was also a novelist and a psychologist who took special interest in the influence of pogroms on young people. In his Yiddish-language study, *Catastrophic Times and Growing Generations*, published in Berlin in 1923, Schneersohn used the word hefker to characterize the "great army of children" growing up without supervision.[60] He used the same word to describe the haphazard state of care available to these children. In *Catastrophic Times*, nonetheless, Schneersohn wrests a vision of a future out of the bleak conditions threatening the younger generation and thus Jews as a people.

PART I ~ POETRY

1

Hefker and Abandonment

Preparing for the Passover holiday, during which leavened foods are forbidden, Jewish householders disavow ownership of any leavened products remaining after the cleaning of their homes. They state, "May all leaven in my possession ... be counted as null and be hefker [ownerless], even as the dust of the earth."[1] In Jewish property law generally, owners may abandon possessions by renouncing ownership—in this case bread and other prohibited foodstuffs. The pre-Passover declaration, however, also suggests what hefker can mean beyond property law: being alive but counted as null, having a human existence but not one that matters, enduring the process of becoming nullified while still retaining life, and thus being treated as the dust of the earth. To be counted as null as the dust of the earth captures the human experience of political and social abandonment.

This chapter examines the Jewish concept of hefker in comparison to biopolitics. The first section expands the preliminary overview given in the introduction by showing how Michel Foucault and Giorgio Agamben differ. For Agamben, abandonment is the foundational political act. Achille Mbembe's critique of Agamben provides an important modification of biopolitics that is directly pertinent to revolutionary Russia and Ukraine. Excerpts from Yiddish literature and archival documents from the Russian Civil War illustrate key theoretical points about biopolitics. I discuss specific forms of abandonment during this period and suggest how it might serve as a touchstone for the analysis of war and occupation in Ukraine in the early twenty-first century.

The second section traces the development of the hefker concept in Jewish legal and religious contexts. I show how a term originating in property law became synonymous with lawlessness. The discussion is weighted heavily toward Russia in the first quarter of the twentieth century, when Jewish intellectuals began to apply the term hefker to the political and social condition of the Jewish population. The final section of the chapter is devoted to hefker poetics and aesthetics. In addition to Peretz Markish and David Bergelson, the poets Uri Tsvi Grinberg and Kadya Molodowsky expand the political and aesthetic implications of the hefker concept in their Yiddish interwar poetry. Grinberg's intensely embodied language and Molodowsky's description of the hefker condition in daily life contexts provide important points of comparison for subsequent chapters. While I attempt in this chapter to provide a framework for the rest of the study, it will become clear, however, that hefker is the kind of term that undermines the possibility of groundwork because it shifts the ground under your feet, creating fissures between apparently stable meanings.

Abandonment and Agamben

Although abandonment in the sense that I am using it is not limited to governments and the actions of states, it is helpful to begin with biopolitics, the theory that the life and health of the population is the primary concern of governmental power. Agamben's analysis of political power rests on a fundamental split in the way that life is conceptualized: the distinction between a specific and socially recognizable way of life and the mere fact of not being dead.[2] Greek distinguishes between the two, using the terms *zoe* and *bios*—hence the term *biopolitics*. Politics, according to Agamben, separates mere life, in which bodies are undifferentiated, from a mode of differentiated, ordered existence. Foucault showed that modern forms of power distinguish those who are to be the recipient of care ("making live") and those who are not ("letting die"). Agamben, in contrast, emphasizes the latter. Sovereign power produces and depends on the production of bare life. For Foucault, biopower arises in the political transition from the power of the sovereign to the sovereignty of the people in the form of the modern administrative state. Agamben brings together the legal and "biopolitical" dimensions of power to argue that the "production of the biopolitical body is the original activity of sovereign power."[3] The sovereign determines the state of exception, the suspension of the normal juridical order for some part of the population. While Agamben thinks beyond the biopolitical machine, looking for ways to stop dividing life into bare life and political life, other scholars are recuperating the positive side—the pastoral care—of biopolitics.[4] Chapter 7 will show in detail how Jewish relief organizations of the 1920s used biopolitical instruments in a positive sense to assess and care for the pogromed Jewish population.

To illustrate the dichotomy between the provision and withholding of care I turn to the Yiddish author Itsik Kipnis, whose 1926 novel *Months and Days* was the point of departure for this study. The novel describes the 1919 pogrom in the author's native shtetl, Slovechno (Slovechne). After a day of violence, it was difficult to decide whether to remain at home or flee. Kipnis writes, "Now we were like animals, which at nightfall would become utterly abandoned [hefker] and helpless."[5] Foucault draws a parallel between the Christian model of pastoral care and modern political sovereignty. The pastor cares for his congregation the way a shepherd cares for his flock, ministering to each one separately and to the whole herd. The shepherd may cull the flock; the biopolitical sovereign, responsible for the well-being of the population, decides who will and who will not receive care.[6] Kipnis compares people to livestock whose owner removes them from care, depriving them of food, shelter, and security. Notice he does not say that the Jews of Slovechno were like animals sent for slaughter; he says they were like animals who were abandoned made hefker. The pivotal moment is abandonment.

The use of biopolitical concepts may seem to present difficulties when it comes to failed states, and states in the process of formation, as was the case for Ukraine and Russia in the immediate postrevolutionary period. Abandoning certain populations to violence—consigning them to the state of exception—is something a state does.[7] This view, however, neglects Agamben's fundamental point about the nature of political order. Establishing political life calls bare life into being. Political life does not come first, and bare life second. Instead, "the originary relation of law to life is not application but Abandonment."[8] Civil war and warlordism—the conditions of revolutionary Russia and Ukraine—show the process of sovereignty in formation. Agamben maintains that the analysis of civil war provides a "paradigm" for the workings of politics.[9]

Sovereignty is made by the decision to exclude and abandon, and this "foundation is not an event achieved once and for all" but is instead an ever-present possibility, with shifting contours.[10] The lives of ordinary citizens are temporarily clothed in rights, norms, limits, and entitlements. This clothing can be stripped away at numerous moments of daily life. Agamben writes, "He who has been banned is not, in fact, simply set outside the law and made indifferent to it but rather *abandoned* by it" [emphasis in original].[11] To be abandoned is to be "open to all," available without limit, denied all social recognition, and legal protection. To be at someone's disposal is indeed one of the original meanings of the verb abandon.[12]

An example from Yiddish literature reveals the parallel between abandonment as vulnerable exposure and the hefker term. David Bergelson's short story "Droyb" ("Down and out") first published in 1919, the peak year of pogrom violence, uses the term hefker in this way, to emphasize exposure. Bergelson writes, "Outside it turned cold, very cold, and dark, and the wind could penetrate everywhere"; literally, the "air was abandoned, abandoned to the wind" ("In droysn iz nor di luft geven shtark kil, tunkl, un hefker, hefker tsu vintn tsu").[13] The passage blurs the distinction between the forces of nature and the force of human violence.[14] Bergelson's language reveals that hefker and abandonment signify exposure to overwhelming force.

To be abandoned is to be vulnerable to the naked operation of power, whether by a sovereign state or by would-be temporary sovereigns during the Russian Civil War. A document produced during the ongoing violence of May 1919 in Elisavetgrad (present-day Kropyvnytskyi) gets to the heart of the matter: the relation between the sovereign and the bodies he temporarily rules. A certain P. Pavlov, naming himself as "commander of the front" (komanduiushchii frontom), seemingly from the Red Army, published the following statement in a newspaper (*Nasha zhizn'*) on May 19, 1919:

> Comrade workers and peasants:
> I have heard the voice of the peasants and your representatives and decided to terminate the destruction of the workers' life immediately. The city is coming under your power. I order all divisions subordinate to me to leave the city and appear at the train station with their troops. Representatives of the workers and peasants must carry out a decisive battle against banditry and provocation. I will punish at my own discretion all those who while disguised in grey overcoats—have violated discipline. From the moment of the publication of this order, power is transferred to the workers and peasants. The person and dwelling of the citizens are inviolable.[15]

The order is a primer in the rudimentary operation of sovereign power. There is no process for negotiating between the two categories of person that Pavlov names. He decides whose person and property are inviolable and who may be dealt with at his own discretion. He establishes his power by means of introducing a division between the two categories and naming himself as the one who categorizes others. For both Foucault and Agamben, dividing society is the quintessential operation of political power. The documentary and artistic literature to be discussed in subsequent chapters describes other temporary rulers who did not avail themselves of the niceties of Pavlov's rhetoric.

Necropolitics

The warlords, insurgent groups, and isolated individuals who took over towns and regions in the former Russian Empire were hardly in the business of "making live." Instead of caring for the populations under their control, they were intent on killing and forcibly removing property. Historian and theorist Achille Mbembe proposes "necropolitics" (the politics of death) as an alternative to biopolitics (the politics of life) as well as offering a critical perspective on Agamben's emphasis on Western Europe and the state. In addition to Nazi racism and the death camp, Mbembe points to colonialism, the slave trade, and the plantation. Mbembe argues for the importance of necropolitics found in late twentieth-century and early twenty-first-century wars (including, for example, Kosovo, the Gulf War, and wars in Africa), in which temporary forms of political power—"not necessarily state power"—are organized around "a fictionalized notion of the enemy" and the right to kill.[16] Instead of a single source of sovereignty, "a patchwork of overlapping and incomplete rights to rule emerges, inextricably superimposed and tangled, in which different de facto juridical instances are geographically interwoven and plural allegiances, asymmetrical suzerainties, and enclaves abound."[17] The various agents of violence, including state and nonstate armies, all "claim the right to kill."[18] The characteristics that Mbembe finds typical of what he calls "war machines"—namely, the fluid dispersion of power, permeable political boundaries, the temporary formation of authority, and rule by violence—are also characteristic of Civil War–era Russia and Ukraine when state and nonstate armies proliferated. In addition to the army of the Ukrainian People's Republic, the

Red Army, and the White Army, there were numerous peasant insurgent groups, warlords, and local militias, as chapters 5, 6, and 7 show.

The framework of necropolitics, as indicated by Mbembe, can shed light on the realm of violence in revolutionary Russia and Ukraine, in which local warlord violence played a significant role. Bill Rosenberg argues that deprivation, scarcity, humiliation, and loss were more important than ideology in the brutal violence of Russia's civil wars.[19] Serhy Yekelchyk's analysis of the civil war in Ukraine underscores the importance of violence, without using the term *necropolitics*. As he puts it, "The Ukrainian case helps problematize our notions of 'revolutionary,' 'counter-revolutionary,' and 'ethnic violence' by demonstrating a common culture of violence."[20] In a culture of violence, the opportunities for abandonment abound.

Abandonment also has implications for the 2022 war against Ukraine. Putin's October 2022 declaration of martial law in Donetsk and other illegally annexed regions subjects the population to summary arrest and execution, the seizure of property, forced resettlement, and, generally, the arbitrary exercise of power by the Russian army. Russia's war against Ukraine did not begin in 2022 but in 2014, with the annexation of Crimea; the Donetsk and Luhansk regional declarations of independence from Ukraine, orchestrated by Russia; and the subsequent military engagement on the part of the Ukrainian army against the Russian-backed separatists. In this earlier period as well, conditions of abandonment abounded. In his essay collection *In Isolation: Dispatches from Occupied Donbas*, Ukrainian journalist Stanislav Aseyev explicitly uses the term to indicate the economic degradation, rightlessness, vulnerability, and isolation of the population of occupied Donbas, exposed to the whims of numerous local militias, cut off from the rest of the world, and left behind by the Ukrainian government.[21] Aseyev was secretly arrested in the summer of 2017, on trumped-up charges of espionage and terrorism, and was tortured while in captivity (he was released in 2019). The final essay, written while in prison, uses the motif of dust, the virtual synonym for hefker and abandonment: "in the Donetsk People's Republic, the individual is nothing but dust."[22]

My primary focus is the experience and expression of being treated as dust, subject to another's arbitrary and overwhelming power. The Yiddish author Rokhl Faygenberg recounts that in 1919, non-Jews in Dubovo asked Ataman Kozakov what to do with the Jewish population of the town.

The answer was "you can do what you want with them."²³ The Yiddish poet Leyb Kvitko similarly wrote, "They use as they please."²⁴ In these instances, the parallel between hefker and abandonment as a biopolitical term emerges clearly. Poets enter where historians fear to tread, and the poets used the term hefker to describe the world in which there was no consequence for using others as you please. How it became possible to use a legal term to indicate lawlessness is the next question.

The Bible and Rabbinics

Hefker first appears in Jewish sources in the second-century rabbinic discussions on the acquisition and loss of property.²⁵ In this context, hefker means "ownerless, unclaimed," referring to an object that belongs to no one. There are four pathways to the hefker categorization. Property can become unclaimed or ownerless by declaration, as in the Passover ritual. An ownerless object is exempt from taxes and other regulations. When an owner gives up hope of recovering a lost object, or when the circumstances under which an object is found indicate renunciation (leaving it in a public place where anyone could find it), the object may be considered hefker, and another may claim it.²⁶ Objects and living things that could not have a (human) owner, including the seas, rivers, wilderness, and the objects and animals in them—are also hefker. Finally, the rabbinic court may exercise eminent domain by removing property from individuals and declaring it hefker (*hefker bet din hefker*). This could be a form of punishment, as retribution for wrongful behavior.²⁷ Some scholars see in this mechanism a means of "redistributing property in the interests of justice."²⁸ Others, in contrast, see a greater potential for disruption, even an "anarchic dimension," because the power of the rabbinic court to confiscate property reveals the potential for arbitrary disruptions of the livelihood of the community.²⁹

Hefker as a property term remains in current use in Jewish religious, ethical, legal, and political contexts. Some examples include queries regarding abandoned objects and whether they may be assumed to be ownerless, problems arising in relation to utensils not kosher for Passover, critiques of Israeli policies that render Palestinian orchards hefker, and in discussions of medical ethics, including, for example, whether embryonic stem cells may be considered hefker.³⁰

Hefker Persons

In religious Hebrew usage, a convergence developed between hefker as a term for ownerless property, the self-proclamation of freedom from Jewish commandments, and the name of the Greek philosopher Epicurus, considered by Jewish authorities to be the embodiment of unbelief and the nihilistic embrace of sensuous pleasure.[31] The term *hitpaker* התפקר means to become both licentious and heretical.[32] To make oneself hefker signals a conscious and deliberate abandonment of God and God's laws. The act of renunciation and disavowal was a two-way street. To be an *apikores*, or heretic, also meant that God had abandoned you. In Yiddish, the word hefker may similarly refer to lawless, dissolute, and licentious behavior. The Yiddish expression *hefker petrishke* means "free and easy"; *hefker-yung* can be translated as "lout" or "bully."[33]

Hefker appears in rabbinic literature in discussions about sexual behavior and promiscuity. Individuals could "make free with themselves" or, in other words, behave with abandon, as in the case of a woman offering herself in marriage to a man. In rabbinic literature when the term hefker is used in relation to human beings, the question of female sexuality is at the heart of the discussion.[34] The rabbis considered cases of sexual assault against freed slave women, for which there was no penalty, and, analogously, sexual assault against women who were still enslaved. Free men were not eager to marry former slaves, because as such, they resembled "ownerless property," and anyone could do what they liked to them. In another instance, the rabbis urged that a woman who was half slave and half free should be manumitted entirely so that others would not treat her as if she were hefker.[35] In this context, hefker describes a boundary condition defining the limit between those who enjoy protections over their bodily integrity and those who do not, those whose bodies are mere material for the pleasure others take from them. The boundary condition is key to the biopolitical notion of abandonment.

The legal ambiguity helped generate the moral ambiguity. Being positioned on the threshold between the right to protection and the lack of this right was understood to excite wayward desires. The person who ambiguates legal categories was presumed to behave in a hefker manner. The ambiguous legal status of the freed slave woman, against whom sexual assault could be carried out with impunity, became associated with morally reprehensible behavior and, thus, two forms of abandonment combined.

Rabbinic literature and later commentaries also include another dimension of hefker behavior that is the antipode to licentious abandonment: the devotional practice known as *hefker k'midbar* ("hefker like the wilderness or desert"). The rabbis observe that to receive the wisdom of the Torah, one must make oneself "ownerless as the wilderness" or "open to all."[36] The Torah was given to the Jews in the wilderness, in a place that was hefker, owned by no one, so that all could have access to it.[37] Many centuries later, prominent Hasidic figures added other dimensions to the meaning of hefker as self-abnegation. Menahem Mendl of Vitebsk (1730–1788), one of the most important mystical Hasidic authors, used the concept of "hefker as the wilderness" to prescribe the proper attitude toward receiving the Torah and also the proper way to approach a friend.[38]

The Russian Orthodox tradition canonized over thirty saints who practiced the form of kenosis known as "folly for Christ's sake": the deliberate cultivation of transgressive, "mad," behavior and the embrace of the lowliest forms of life on the street.[39] The concepts, terminology, and practices associated with kenotic hefker and Christian kenosis are well established in the milieu out of which Grinberg, David Hofshteyn, Kvitko, and other Yiddish writers arise. Confronting numerous sites of devastation and ruin in the aftermath of World War I and the Russian Civil War, they created secularized, poetic versions of the religious practice. To anticipate a point I will take up in subsequent chapters, Hofshteyn's poetics of self-effacement and Kvitko's descent into the body both reflect a poetics of "hefker like the wilderness," the abandonment of self.

Hefker Populations

Although hefker is not a biblical term, the motif of impunity appears prominently in biblical texts. Psalm 79 describes Jewish deaths left unaccounted for and unpunished. Jewish blood is shed "like water all around Jerusalem and there is no one to bury the dead." Jews have become objects of scorn and derision in the eyes of their neighbors. The psalmist calls on God to punish the wrongdoers and restore the Jews to his care.

The blurry boundary between law and lawlessness—and the violence thereby made possible—became especially important in the early years of the twentieth century in czarist Russia. The 1903 pogrom in Kishinev was a significant turning point. Simon Dubnow and Ahad Ha'am, the creator of cultural Zionism, used hefker to characterize Jewish life in czarist Russia: the life, property, and honor of Jews are "disowned" (hefker) and their blood "unaccounted for."[40] Frug's poem "Sand and Stars," which compares Jews to "sand, which is hefker, / which everyone tramples with their feet," likely influenced the 1903 statement. Bialik's "In the City of Slaughter," written in response to Kishinev, protests the impunity with which Jews were killed, without using the word *hefker*. In the pogrom's aftermath, two beheaded creatures can be found on a trash heap, "a Jew and his hound / The self-same ax struck both."[41] The "cry of the Jew's blood, mingled with his dog's, will not be heard, and the blood will be washed away and lost." There will be no record of the event: "All things will be as they ever were." A Jewish death counts no more than a dog's. God, nature, the czar, and the Jews themselves disregard these deaths.

In the same period, the Yiddish author I. L. Peretz published his poem "Don't Think" ("Meyn nisht," 1906). The first three stanzas begin with an admonition, detailing what a hefker world looks like. The fourth issues a prophetic statement promising the restoration of justice:

> Don't think that the world is a tavern—created
> So that you can punch and scratch your way
> To gorge yourself with food and drink...
> Don't think the world is a stock-exchange
> For the strong to trade in the weak and the tired
> Buying the shame of young girls...
> Don't think the world has been abandoned [hefker]
> To wolves and foxes, robbery and deceit...
> The world is not a tavern, not a stock-exchange, not abandoned!
> Everything will be measured and weighed!
> No tear or drop of blood will be forgotten,
> No eye has been closed, no spark extinguished in vain!
>
> Tears will grow into rivers, rivers will become seas.
> A flood will spread, and from the sparks, thunder.
> Oh, don't think there is no Justice and no Judge![42]

Unlike Bialik, Peretz focuses on not pogroms but, instead, institutions characteristic of the modern world, above all, capitalism. The hefker world of predatory capitalism resembles the Hobbesian state of nature in which humans are like wolves to other humans, and Jews and non-Jews are both perpetrators and victims. Peretz, however, promises that order will be restored. The language of the last stanza and the use of Hebrew-origin words for *justice* and *judge* project a vision of repair.

World War I and the Russian Civil War put this vision to the test. Shimon Zev Eisenberg (Ayzenberg) (1886–1950) was a Jew from the Lithuanian town of Girkalnis. Like thousands of other Jews forcibly removed from the Pale of Settlement during World War I, he was deported to Russia. He made his way to South Africa and, in 1935, published a book with the remarkable title *War Dust: Memoirs of a Lithuanian Refugee, 1915–1917* (*Milkhome-shtoyb: Zikhroynes fun a litvishn polet, 1915–1917*).[43] The "dust" in the title refers to Jews. Eisenberg was not a literary author or rabbinic authority; his use of the term hefker in the memoir reveals the way in which ordinary Jews understood the catastrophe of the war. The Germans who took control of the town, Eisenberg writes, treated Christian women as mere goods to be exploited and plundered livestock and property, removing what they could "for the Fatherland." His terminology is significant. Eisenberg sums up the situation simply by saying, "For them, everything was up for grabs" (Alts iz geven bay zey hefker).[44] It is also important that the rule of misrule applied to Jews and non-Jews. Eisenberg uses the term hefker with heightened intensity in his description of the situation of Jews during the war, not only regarding the German army but also universally, in relation to every population, group, and authority they encountered, including Lithuanian peasants, Cossacks, and the Russian Imperial Army. Rumors of Jewish collaboration with Germans, a fabricated story of a Lithuanian priest's death at the hands of Jews (in Kuz, a shtetl near Shavli), and the effect of the mass deportation of Jews conducted by the Russian army lead Eisenberg to conclude several times in his memoir that "Jews were hefker in everyone's eyes."[45]

Jews were "defenseless," the lowest of the low, everyone's victim. Deprived of their property, driven out of their homes, and universally accused of crimes, they had lost whatever claims to personhood they had previously enjoyed. This is not a question of civil or political rights but something far more elemental. In a war zone, accused by all sides of betrayal, Jews lost the ability to claim recognition as human beings. Indeed, the title of Eisenberg's memoir is helpful here. Jews became "war dust," vulnerable and exposed to everyone and anyone. The Russian Jewish author Andrei Sobol' similarly uses dust to emphasize Jews' lack of belonging in Imperial Russia and Europe in his 1919 novel *Dust* (*Pyl'*). Jews were like dust that floats about without a stable home.[46] In 2018, Ukrainian author Aseyev also called on the same motif. As these instances show, the language of the Passover declaration about being counted as null and as the dust of the earth resonates for Jews and non-Jews throughout the twentieth and twenty-first centuries.

In 1919, the Yiddish press used the term *hefker* to characterize the condition of Jews, and sometimes, non-Jews, living in the former Russian Empire (Ukraine, Russia, Poland, Romania, Hungary, and Lithuania). The New York *Yidishes togblat* reported on May 14, 1919, that cities were practically hefker. For self-styled Cossacks, everything was "as if hefker" ("up for grabs"): whether you were a Jew or merely a so-called bourgeois, if you met a Cossack on the street, everything of yours became his. The new Bolshevik order, which imposed a regime of privileges based on determinations of who was to be included among productive laborers, also rendered both people and animals hefker, according to the *Yidishes togblat* from June 22, 1919. The reporter quipped, "A horse or a cow without an identification card is hefker, like a person without a passport (forgive the comparison)." In this context, hefker means "rightless." Another article stated, "We are hefker like the dirt outside" ("Mir zaynen hefker vi di blote in droysn"). The October 19, 1919, *Morgn zhurnal*, also a New York paper, included lines of poetry to the effect that the murder and rape of Jews were taking place "as if in an abandoned [hefker] forest." An article in the *Forverts* (*Forward*) proclaimed that Jewish blood and lives in Ukraine, Poland, and Hungary had become hefker. *Dos naye lebn* (New life), a London newspaper, protested the ease and impunity with which Jews were exterminated and, furthermore, suggested that if Jewish lives were hefker in one place, they were equally so everywhere. For the Yiddish press, the term hefker meant that Jewish property, bodies, and lives were disposable. In this context, hefker and biopolitical abandonment maximally overlap.

Protesting the impunity with which Jewish blood was shed was codified in the phrase *abandoned blood* (*dam hefker*), which achieved wide currency in response to the Holocaust. The Soviet Yiddish poet Peretz Markish, who in the 1920s joyously named himself "unclaimed" (*hefker*), as

I discuss shortly, later used the same word in angry reproach to describe the "abandoned blood" *hefker-blut* of Jewish victims of the Nazi genocide.⁴⁷ "Abandoned blood"—used as an accusation—persisted beyond the Holocaust. During the AIDS epidemic Ethiopian Jews protesting the rejection of their blood by Israeli blood banks used the same language to register their outrage and proclaim their belonging in the larger Jewish community.⁴⁸

Jewish legal sources expanded the notion of unclaimed property, the original definition, adding lawless behavior and, significantly, categories of persons—perpetrators who could not be punished because of the uncertain legal status of their victims. Hefker creates a dangerous lacuna in the law. The institution of hefker reveals a human world with porous boundaries between the divine and the human, humans and objects, and humans and other humans. The term points toward a vulnerability to instability, precariousness, and unpredictability. Gil Eyal emphasizes this dimension when he writes that hefker is a term that designates something or someplace "outside sovereign rule, where sovereignty is disputed, and where no laws hold" and that is the "constant shadow always adjoining law."⁴⁹

Unlike abandonment in Agamben's theory, the Jewish legal term does not depend on biopower or biopolitics. It overlaps with Agamben's abandonment but is a broader and looser concept. Noam Leshem's 2017 article "Spaces of Abandonment" explains why.⁵⁰ Leshem, a geographer, argues that hefker as a concept "can appear beyond the strict confines of the sovereign relation, shifting attention to a myriad of mundane appearances."⁵¹ Because Jewish legal practice invoked hefker in a variety of everyday circumstances, not at the level of a state apparatus or national catastrophe, the concept illuminates the material and bodily dimensions of abandonment in ways that other notions tend to obscure. Leshem traces the specific case in 2008 of a Palestinian who had illegally entered Israel and was severely injured in an accident, subsequently prematurely discharged from the hospital, and abandoned by the police at a highway, where he died a few days later. Leshem's point about abandonment beyond sovereign decisions, and the material and somatic impact of abandonment on mundane life, has broad significance for the literary artists and pogrom investigators whose work I analyze in subsequent chapters. Molodowsky's poem about a tuberculosis sanatorium, discussed later in this chapter, is a case in point.

Modernist Departures

In Yiddish, hefker carries an array of meanings, including "anarchy," "arbitrariness," "chaos," "injustice," "neglect," "freedom," "wantonness," and "debauchery."[52] In the first part of the twentieth century, modernist Yiddish writers adopted it to proclaim their freedom from religious and aesthetic norms. To name oneself "hefker" marked a radical departure from the past and the refusal of limits and boundaries. Yet at the same time, Yiddish writers also used hefker in the negative sense of abandonment, dispossession, and disavowal—to name the condition in which Jews found themselves during World War I and the Russian Civil War.[53]

In 1923, critic Hirsh Bloshteyn wrote that the Yiddish poetry of his day possessed a "turbulent hefker temperament."[54] Modernist Yiddish authors of the late 1910s and early 1920s used hefker as a fundamental tenet of their aesthetic, declaring themselves hefker in the sense of wild and free, free to move across languages, cultural spaces, free to abandon the burdens of obligation to the past and the community, and thus free from poetic conventions and standards of taste.[55]

Markish's "Don't Know If I'm at Home" articulates the hefker aesthetic:

> Don't know if I'm at home,
> Or if I'm afar—
> I'm running! ...
> My shirt's unbuttoned,
> There are no reins on me,
> I'm nobody's, I'm unclaimed,
> Without a beginning, without an end ...
> My body is foam,
> And it reeks of wind;
> My name is: Now ...
> If I throw out my hands,
> They'd give the world a smack from one end to the other.[56]

The Yiddish original for "unclaimed" is *hefker* (*Kh'bin keynem's nit, kh'bin hefker*). The poet recognizes no "claims" against him, no demands from the past or present, no limitations demarking what he may or may not do or say. He is utterly free; his body is like foam and does not weigh him down. Even gravity makes an exception for him. But it is nonetheless a body with appetites (his eyes would "guzzle down the world"). Scholars generally agree about the central importance of the term hefker in this poem, as an assertion of freedom and power.[57] Even though the speaker in "Don't Know if I'm at Home" appears ethereal, Markish's interwar poetry embraces chaos, woundedness, and pain.[58]

"A keyword of Yiddish expressionism," hefker layers joy with alienation, freedom, and abandonment.[59] Max Erik, a Yiddish critic of the 1920s, wrote that Yiddish expressionism articulated chaos and ugliness in "fleshy, knobby" language, full of bumps and lumps.[60] Hebrew-origin words served this purpose well, and the term hefker itself a prime exemplar of this kind of disruptive, uneven language.[61]

In his work for the Berlin art journal *Milgroym*, Bergelson plays on hefker's double meaning, reveling in the wild freedom of new poetic forms and lamenting the abandonment of Jews subject to unbridled violence in Ukraine, forsaken by other human beings and God. In a programmatic essay titled "The Present Upheaval," published in the first issue of *Milgroym*, Bergelson proclaims there is "no longer any law, limit, and order." The new collective poetry is as hefker (free and wild) as the old individualistic approach is obsolete and hefker (abandoned).[62] In contrast, in the short story "The Beginning of December 1919" ("Onheyb kislev TaRAT"), published in the same issue, the Jewish world is a "God-forsaken" (hefker) world: "From the large Jewish shopkeeper's quarter right across the entire area around this locality an acrid old world lingers, a God-forsaken world, exposed to the chill of winter, to the wind that might gust down from the north, and to the trouble that had yet to erupt and sweep down from very far away."[63] In this landscape there is no thrill of freedom but rather the miserable isolation and pain of life and death in no-man's-land, where acts of violence can be perpetuated with impunity.

A darker, more precarious abandonment comes to the fore in interwar Yiddish writing generally.[64] As literary scholar Efrat Gal-Ed puts it, for many Jewish intellectuals and writers, the history of anti-Jewish violence in the first part of the twentieth century, and the subsequent "experience of being hefker destroyed all confidence in the possibility of belonging." The experience of being hefker meant the persistent sense of "being excluded from any system of law and abandoned to arbitrary power."[65] The unpublished, handwritten 1925 issue of Itsik Manger's journal *Limited Words* (*Getseylte verter*) ironically inserts the term hefker in the name of the journal's publication house; the title page states that the journal is published by the "Yiddish is homeless Press."[66]

Uri Tsvi Grinberg is an instructive example of the ways that Yiddish modernism in its expressionist mode articulates the sensory experience of hefker as abandonment, assaulting the reader with its violence.[67] The language, themes, and explicit aesthetic statements in Grinberg's writing in the early 1920s connect warfare (he was a soldier on the Serbian front in the First World War), political collapse, abandonment, and an intensified emphasis on flesh and wounds.[68] In Warsaw, Grinberg launched what amounted to a one-man journal, *Albatross* (*Albatros*).[69]

The prose and poetry published in *Albatross* are important for understanding the biopolitical and aesthetic significance of hefker in the wake of the collapse of the Russian empire. In the September 1922 issue, Grinberg dedicates the contents of *Albatross* to the generation who fought in the war and now wanders across Europe, "convulsed" in pain. Not belonging anywhere is a dimension of the hefker condition; Grinberg's language explicitly refers to the "homeless artists of Yiddish extraterritoriality."[70]

Albatross responded to the world of pain, a new order of suffering. The opening of Grinberg's "World Upside Down" ("Velt barg arop") imagines poetry in terms of flesh and blood. His book is a body without pages or binding; it is a "gospel of shame," a product of his "veins and skeleton." Enfleshment, however, is not merely the consequence of exposure to violence, as a set of tropes that emphasize the body and the wound, it is also a way of transforming violence into a new poetic idiom.[71] Poetry should express "the cry of blood," Grinberg writes.[72] Poetry that oozes and bleeds responds to the terror inflicted by the spectacle of mutilated bodies. Grinberg translates the wound into a mouth that speaks poetry. In "Uri Tsvi before the Cross," the poet refers to his lips as "red wounds in the darkness."[73]

"In the Kingdom of the Cross" ("In malkes fun tseylem"), published in the final 1923 issue of *Albatross*, paints a hopeless picture of the future of Jews in Europe, using the term *hefker*. The entire Jewish community has become timid; "wives and children" lament their fate and

> there is this fear of becoming abandoned [*af hefker*]
> As if you were a stone in the world, but the body is no stone.
> The body is blood and flesh and bone, that feels
> The stab of the knife.[74]

Stones do not feel their abandonment, but humans do, because they are made of flesh.[75] Feeling one's flesh, or better, feeling oneself as nothing more than flesh—is a consequence of abandonment, a point I explore in greater detail in chapter 4, devoted to Leyb Kvitko.

In Grinberg's interwar poetry the aesthetic, existential, and political ramifications of abandonment build on each other. Hefker means more than a poetic style or a rejection of aesthetic and religious pieties. It signifies a world utterly lacking in order, reason, and norms, a world in which Jewish life is flesh in pain—a parallel to the undifferentiation of mere life in Agamben's writings. For Grinberg migration to Palestine was the only political solution. The Soviet Yiddish writers who are the main protagonists of this study made other choices.

Molodowsky's Alternative Hefker Poetics

Kadya Molodowsky (1894–1975), born in present-day Belarus, was the author of poetry, stories for children, plays, novels, a literary autobiography, and nonfiction prose and the cofounder of the Yiddish journal *Svive*. Molodowsky lived in Poland until 1935, when she immigrated to the United States.[76] She was part of the Kyiv circle that also included Kvitko, Hofshteyn, Bergelson, and Der Nister, and a selection of her work appeared in Bergelson's journal *Eygns* (Our own) in 1920. In the interwar period Molodowsky published two volumes of poetry, *Khezhbndike nekht* (1927) and *Dzshike gas* (1936). Whereas critics in her own time tended to dismiss her work as overly focused on her own experience, more recent discussions have celebrated her attention to women's lives, particularly in her series called "Women's Poems" (Froyen-lider), as well as her profound engagement with the broad historical issues of the twentieth century.[77]

Molodowsky did not write about pogroms explicitly, but her experimental poetry imagines and interrogates conditions of abandonment occurring within and beyond the Jewish life world, using the key term hefker.[78] "Otvotsk" is about a tuberculosis sanatorium, and "Chako," a prison ship. Both reference real places and events: before World War II, Otwock, a small town just outside Warsaw, was the site of health resorts and sanitoria, where the Jewish bourgeoisie from Warsaw spent their summers and where Jewish tuberculosis patients from all over the

Russian empire came for a cure.[79] Molodowsky, whose mother died of tuberculosis, spent a few months in Otwock in 1923. Her poem "Otvosk," consisting of eight stanzas, was first published in an anthology in 1923 and later republished in *Nights of Khezhbn* (*Kheshvendike nekht*) in 1927. The poem emphasizes the precarious condition of the tuberculosis patients.

The poet depicts what it is like to be left behind, forsaken, and shunned. Molodowsky uses the language of Jewish family law to name this condition:

> Villas, abandoned like wives, forsaken by people and unoccupied.
> Fences are low, because there is no one to
> Steal things at night.
> Narrow pathways—stiffened fingers in the park,
> And the trees, gravestones of someone's spent heart.
> No footsteps. No voices.[80]

The unusual combination of "villas" and "abandoned wives" (*viles agunes*) in the opening phrase immediately draws attention. The elaborately decorated wooden buildings at Otwock were indeed referred to as "villas." The Hebrew word *agune* refers to an "abandoned wife"—that is, a woman who is still legally married to a man, even though he is absent and may be dead or, if alive, refuses to grant her a divorce. An agune is consigned to abandonment without the freedom to enjoy it, because she is subject to the arbitrary will of others. The space of Otwock resembles the condition of abandoned wives.

Later in the poem Molodowsky describes the behavior of new arrivals using the term *hefkerdik*, which means carefree, reckless:

> The young come, striding
> Carefree [*hefkerdik*] in the green, bearded city,
> Disappear there, and are lost.[81]

By the end of the stanza, the new arrivals, thin and bony, are no longer in a green city but, rather, one that is "consecrated to death." The thematic association between illness, social abandonment, and the suspension of norms builds across the different episodes of the poem sequence. The living have little interest in those sentenced to death. The first words of the poem about villas like abandoned wives anticipate what will follow, the double meaning of abandonment.

The opening stanza seems contradictory. The poet says that the villas are abandoned and there are no people, voices, or footsteps, but we hear coughing. Instead of deliberate personal expression, the poet emphasizes involuntary bodily sounds:

> No footsteps. No voices.
> Kho-kho-kho—a cough drifts down from an open window.
> Someone is dying there.
> Here my heart is a guest.
> My frightened blood races quickly.
> Am I here?
> Here, here, here, beats my heart.

Instead of voice, the language of the poem uses sound mirroring to stress and prolong the noise of coughing throughout the first stanza, alternating (in the Yiddish) between *kho* (the sound of the cough) and *h-*. Both sounds repeat in the words and phrases *hilKHt* ("drifts" or "echoes"), *hust* (cough), *a handler git hilkhik* ("a vendor's shout echoes"), and *hant* (a hand). The sounds play out the echoing that the poem's narrative describes.

A similar effect is achieved in lines 11–12, in which the repetition of the vowel *a* in a series of one-syllable words imitate the sound of the beating heart (*do, do, do klapt mayn harts*). The 1923 version is even more experimental in its citation of vital signs:

> My frightened blood races quickly,
> 37.5°, 37.3°
> Am I here?[82]

The use of numbers, the temperature readings (which indicate a slight fever), charts the speaker's progress from person to patient, the bearer of biometric data. In stanza 3, the speaker notes the way patients weigh their flesh in pounds and ounces, as if they were calves about to be slaughtered. The poet represents the measures taken in the provision of care, the tracking of temperature and weight, to show the loss of the patient's autonomy. The literary record of this transformation, especially the use of medical transcription, is part of a larger trend in poetry of the time, the introduction of "nonpoetic" language, imagery, and here, vital signs. The opening lines of the poem, with its ban on voices and footsteps, indicates the loss of the possibility of poetry in such a place as Otwock. The poem itself refuses this, by changing what poetry can be.

The sound pattern of coughing, established in the first stanza, continues in the second:

> We are sick here—a multitude of locusts (*heysherikn*)
> Fallen suddenly upon the whiteness
> Of the wintry wood.
> With mouths open in putrid breathing,
> We draw out a word like hoarse (*kheyzerike*) fiddles.[83]

The series—*heysherikn* (locusts) and hoarse (*kheyzerike*)—creates a beautiful aural and visual pun (the image of the dry insect bodies) on the raspy qualities of voices suffering from tuberculosis. The speaker repeats that she and the other patients are "wrapped up in shawls" (*in tikher ayngehilt; ayngehilt in tukh*). Reading the line for sound shows that the speaker is enveloped in the *kh* sound, the noise a body makes when it coughs, as in the "kho-kho-kho" of stanza 1, repeated here in *tiKHer* and *tuKH*. Poetry reasserts itself even here in the sanatorium. Molodowsky has created, to borrow Osip Mandelshtam's language, a beautiful and "strange, locust-like phonetics."[84]

In a world of disowned people, the poet has a hard time claiming herself:

> I am here, too, solitary,
> Sick, wrapped in a shawl,
> And I step slowly in the snow among the trees,
> And no one knows
> That I am still myself.[85]

These lines respond to the first stanza, in which there are no footsteps or voices. In a place lacking voice and step, and short of breath, poetry is unlikely, but the poet reclaims the possibility. The first line of the passage cited here reads in the original: "Bin ikh do oykh . . . a eyne."[86] Yiddish, like English, adds an *n* (*nun*) to the indefinite article when it appears before a vowel, so that the phrase "a eyne" would properly be "an eyne." Elsewhere in the poem Molodowsky follows the rule, rendering *a* as *an* before a vowel. Both the 1923 and the 1927 versions of the poem contain the apparent error.[87] The persistence of this usage suggests that it is a deliberate effort to create the impression of impeded speech, reflecting the physiology of illness and, at the same time, by breaking the flow in the production of sound, insisting on a pause between *a* and *eyne*, insisting on separateness and distinction. An alternative translation of the first line reads: "I am here too, a only one." Hofshteyn and Kvitko's poetry, as I show in the following chapters, also use sound to evoke bodily experience and to articulate an alternative subjectivity even amid abandonment.

Molodowsky's "Tshako" ("Chako") published in the Warsaw Yiddish literary journal *Literarishe bleter* and in her volume of poetry *Dzshike gas* provides an important example of *hefker* abandonment outside the boundaries of the sovereign state. The poem describes the fate of an internment ship, *El Chaco*, that set sail from Argentina but was not permitted to land.[88] Its passengers were deportees, strikers, and political rebels, as Molodowsky says. Nature turns out to be more hospitable than human society:

> The ship sails against wind and sky,
> iron waves wreathe it in prison bars,
> cannon snouts hunt the ship down
> on the furthest, widest ocean.
>
> The ship sails against wind and sky,
> all the wild waters welcome it to their common lot, abandonment.
> Howling, unruly waves carry it away,
> the moon with a mother's pale face floating nearby.[89]

Rabbinic law categorizes the ocean and everything in it as naturally occurring ownerless entities. The prison ship *Chako* is like the sea, not because it is a part of nature, but because, as the poet says, cannons and chains prevent the vessel from landing anywhere. The lawlessness of the sea and the lawlessness of the law overlap in this poem as well as in Marlene Nourbese-Philip's *Zong!*, a collection of poems about the murder of slaves thrown into the ocean and the insurance claim that followed (see the introduction). The welcome that the sea offers the prison ship may be nothing more than an invitation to death by drowning. Human violence exposes the passengers to dangers of the wild oceans.[90] Molodowsky invokes the history of hefker's meanings to characterize the abandonment of non-Jews.

This chapter has traced the use of hefker—broader than abandonment in Agamben—as a legal term designating unclaimed property, as well as behavior freed from limit or restraint, characterized by licentiousness and promiscuity. Hefker also reveals a paradoxical gap within the law, because it indicates a category of persons who could be treated lawlessly. To say that a life is not hefker is to offer a lament and a protest about the value of human life that has precipitously sunk to null. To be categorized as hefker politically and socially corresponds to Agamben's state of exception, the segment of the population that may be abused or killed with impunity. Whereas Grinberg uses hefker to designate the specific condition of Jews in the interwar period, Molodowsky, in contrast, uses the tuberculosis sanitorium and the prison ship to generalize abandonment beyond Jews and beyond the decisions of a sovereign state. Hefker also served as the key term of Yiddish modernist manifestos proclaiming freedom from old rules and old forms as well as celebrating the body and its pleasures.

I have provided the basic array of meanings associated with hefker; however, the poets and prose authors discussed in subsequent chapters create their own poetic worlds in which hefker is unique. David Hofshteyn's freest moments are not like Markish's, and his most despairing are not like Grinberg's. Kvitko's poetry is deeply corporeal, but he does not assault the reader in the same way that Grinberg does. For this reason, the next few chapters do not begin with pogrom poetry. I begin, instead, with Hofshteyn's early works in chapter 2 and Kvitko's in chapters 3 and 4 to trace how hefker evolves in each poet's corpus. Hofshteyn both revels in sensory experience and practices poetic self-limitation, another dimension of hefker, in order to record the suffering of others.

2

David Hofshteyn Listening

In his debut volume, *On the Road* (*Bay vegns*), published in 1919, David Hofshteyn goes to meet the world in joy. He professes his ignorance of weights and measures ("Ikh veys keyn vog, ikh veys keyn tsol") that would interfere with his experience.[1] Discarding these already-given instruments allows the streams of light reflected from the surfaces of things, like "mother of pearl," to play on his eyelashes. Crystalline structures, tentative, quivering, barely discernible—let alone recognizable—bring him sensuous delight. Hofshteyn encounters the phenomena of the world and his experience in an utterly new way, attending to every variation, and derives pleasure in so doing. As he writes in the same poem, "For every beam of light / My heart / Has prepared a nest of joy."[2] This is not to say that he avoids the "disquiet" (*umru*) that resounds in the literary milieu of the time or the conditions of abandonment and violence that dominated its historical reality. As one of his contemporary critics put it, Hofshteyn "feels the unease of the times and hears the cry of chaos."[3] The dark lining of hefker freedom makes itself felt even when mass public violence does not appear in the text.

This chapter examines Hofshteyn's poetic orientation in the world, his sensory experience of joy and pleasure, and his encounter with the catastrophe of 1919 through the lens of the hefker concept in its multiple ramifications and across a series of works published in 1919 and the early 1920s. Hofshteyn, one of the greatest twentieth-century poets in any language, has not received the critical attention he deserves, and even the few scholars who discuss his work have not treated it holistically.[4] I trace hefker as a modernist aesthetic and as a political and ethical category in his debut volume, his 1922 pogrom lament *Troyer* (*Sorrow*), and the virtually unknown "Bayomim ha'hem" ("In Those Days") a Hebrew prose poem from 1925. I begin with *Bay vegn* and Hofshteyn's exploration of hefker as freedom, the freedom of the open road and the pleasure of the sensory encounter with the world, especially through sound. The second part of the chapter turns to the Hebrew prose poem, which in reflecting the poet's experience of the violence in Kyiv in 1919 shatters the relationship with the surrounding environment. My analysis of *Sorrow* focuses on the ethical dimension of Hofshteyn's hefker poetics. In the pogrom lament, violence creates the condition of abandonment, but the poet's kenotic self-effacement and heightened attention to those around him allows him to discern the traces left by suffering. In both *On the Road* and *Sorrow*, the poet serves as an intermediary, not creating but, rather, receiving and transcribing both the sounds of the world and the messages left by others subjected to violent death.

Hofshteyn in the World

Hofshteyn (1889–1952) had both a traditional Jewish education in Korostyshev (Korostyshiv), where he was born, and a secular education in Kyiv, where he lived beginning in 1907. He had a brief stint at the St. Petersburg Psychoneurological Institute but studied primarily at an institute of commerce in Kyiv while also attending lectures on literature at Kyiv University.[5] Hofshteyn's broad knowledge of European and Russian poetry, as well as his awareness of the rudiments of the science of the brain are evident in the handbook on literature he coauthored in 1927. Hofshteyn started writing poetry in Hebrew, Ukrainian, and Russian; his first Yiddish poems were published in 1917 before being collected in *Bay vegn*. A member of the Kyiv group, he played a crucial role in the formation of the Kyiv Kultur-Lige (Culture League), an organization that promoted the arts in Yiddish. In his 1919 essay "Belles-lettres and the Social Order," Bergelson praised Hofshteyn for his lyricism, pointing out the subtle musical structure of his poetry, in contrast to Peretz Markish, whom Bergelson accused of "shouting."[6] Chana Kronfeld characterizes Hofshteyn's work as "low-key, lyrical, introverted modernism."[7] Like Grinberg, Manger, Leyb Kvitko, Bergelson, and many other Yiddish, Hebrew, and Russian writers, Hofshteyn lived in Berlin in the 1920s. He moved to Palestine in 1924, where he published poetry and prose, but unlike Grinberg, he did not stay long, returning to Russia in 1926. The reasons had to do in part with the hardship of life in Palestine. In an article published in 1926 in the Polish Yiddish newspaper *Dos naye lebn* (New life), Hofshteyn said that agricultural labor in Palestine was "no idyll."[8] The circumstances of his personal life in Russia also played a role. His two sons from his first marriage had lost their mother, and Hofshteyn was the sole surviving parent. His support for Hebrew made him the target of the new Yiddish orthodoxy of the Soviet Jewish literary establishment.[9] In the early 1920s, Hofshteyn was an editor at the first Soviet Yiddish poetry journal, *Shtrom* (Current).

On the Road (*Bay vegn*) begins in stillness and solitude and ends with storminess and change. It has six sections: "On the road," "Fields," "The Caucasus," "Dawns," "Streets," and "Among scattered stones" ("Tsvishn valger-shteyner"). It includes a few autobiographical notes: Hoftshteyn characterizes his youth as a "sheaf of quivering years"; he writes about his father's house, the experience of eating an apple, his service in the czar's army in Armenia (with a nod to Pushkin), the pleasure he takes in his wife's body, and his five-month-old twins. In the final poem, "We Grow from Stones" ("Mir shtamen fun felzn"), the poet proclaims freedom from the yoke of stagnation, and the brotherhood and sisterhood he celebrates is with the seas, winds, and distance.

The poem "On Distant Roads" defines open spaces as the source of Hofshteyn's creativity. The journey of four stanzas begins on "distant roads" and unfamiliar spaces and lands back in the poet's own garden. The term *hefker* plays a significant role in the poetic credo:

At roads distant and fleeting,
where wheels, all unseeing,
with wanton winds blowing,
are grinding the dust, the dust in its roaming—
There on untended fields I gathered my sowing.[10]
Bay vegn bay vayte,
vu reder vu blinde
far vintn farshayte
alts moln un moln di heymloze shtoybn—
dort hob ikh af felder fun hefker mayn zeyung gekloybn.

The original Yiddish for "untended" is *hefker*. The elements of wandering, homelessness, and dust—key motifs in the literature of political abandonment—appear in this poem as well. In this context, however, they suggest joy and expansiveness. To name oneself *hefker* poetically is to proclaim emancipation from the past, from established norms, and from the community and, thus, to make oneself open and available to the world and to a new sensory experience of the world. The poet roams everywhere as unclaimed as the dust and the wind. The "unseeing wheels" may refer to the wheels of fate, indicating that this freedom is not absolute; the speaker is subject to larger forces. Hofshteyn will return to the wheels of fate in a darker key in his pogrom lament *Sorrow*. The seeds he has sown grow everywhere in these wild, uncultivated places. Creating poetry resembles the act of gathering what the poet finds.

The new poetry of "wanton winds" does not, however, destroy the past, or separate the speaker from it, as the second and third stanzas make clear. The "seeds" are moistened with "grandfather's inheritance" and an "old, shrunken, dusty wineskin." Setting out on the road, the speaker carries all these things with him; *vogl*, "wandering," rhymes with *logl*, "wineskin." The third stanza introduces emotion. "Secret fear" and "loneliness" accompanied the act of sowing seeds in "completely strange, unfamiliar homes." The repetition of the sound "geHEYMEN" in *pokhed-geheymen*, "secret fear," and *heymen*, "home," intensifies the sense of hidden anxiety; the unfamiliar home and secret fear are virtually synonymous. The sound play synthesizes the experience of being at home, being away, and being homeless so that each is lined and brightened by both freedom and hidden anxiety, revealing the rich semantic field and undecidability that is the core of the term *hefker*.

The final stanza both returns to the beginning and marks a new departure. Instead of describing what the poet used to do and where he used to go, this stanza takes place in the present (*itst*, "now"). Instead of describing nature, the poet swears an oath. The poet stands now in his own garden bed, "sown with suffering," and swears to the birds, wind, and hail that he will no longer gather or thresh what he has sown. The Bible provides a gloss on this line. Leviticus 23:22 commands Israel not to "reap all the way to the edges of your field or gather the gleanings of your harvest" and to leave this as food for the poor and the stranger.[11]

The final lines of the poem thus reframe the poet's self-description. Instead of stating that he "gathered" what he sowed (*gekloybn*), as in the first stanza, he says that he "bore," or "carried it" (*dertrogn*); to bear something, as in English, can also mean to suffer it. A contraction of his own poetic creativity permits something to be left over, a blank space that allows some potential for others' expression; the word he sends out to the world may come back to him with a new meaning, in an unrecognizable form. His own "sowing" is also not his own. This aesthetic statement, signaling his attentiveness to another will reappear more forcefully in *Troyer*.

The oath that the speaker swears is significant, since it departs from the largely narrative and descriptive statements that otherwise characterize the poem: "I swear to you today, birds, you wind, you hail" ("Kh'bashver aykh haynt, foyglen, aykh vintn, aykh hoglen"). The incantatory repetition in its rhythm conjures forces beyond human control. The paradoxical oath points to the contradictions of hefker, the flexible, Mobius strip between law and lawlessness. Swearing to the winds resembles writing a promise on water, since there is nothing that can guarantee its fulfillment. There's no one to say you broke your oath and now must face the consequences. Utter wildness cannot be the object of a promise or agreement.

This is a poem about new departures lined by the past and arrivals that stay true to the open road, winds, birds, and the vicissitudes of the weather. The rhyme scheme of the final stanza hoglen/shlogn/dertrogn/vogl (hail, thresh/carry/wander) returns to the rhyme scheme of the second stanza logl/vogl (wineskin/wander). The use of rhyme, repletion, and especially the importance of liquid *ls* as in *vogl* (wandering) add dynamism, and the use of sounds that bleed into each other: *zeyung, vogl, vegn* suggest movement beyond limits, fitting for a poem about wandering. A stanza is a stopping point, a station, and the poem is about being on the road, thus each part of the poem represents a temporary stop on a longer journey, pauses and brief messages from the road that are part of a conversation that can't be transcribed just now. Even though the poem ends with the poet's return to the familiar space of his own "garden plots," the road as passageway and opening to the broader world persists, in both imagery and sound play.

In his 1922 article "The Present Upheaval," David Bergelson includes Hofshteyn in the new generation of poets worthy of praise, because their poetry was free, wild, unbound, chaotic, utterly joyous, and new and "lacking law, limit, and order"—in a word, hefker, the term Bergelson uses to signify all these qualities. The moment of upheaval is nothing less than a wedding with the whole world to which everyone is invited, and the wedding celebrates a union of flesh with flesh. The wedding is an "ecstatic dance," and the poems are made of opened veins, guts, and nerves. The rhetoric echoes Uri Tsvi Grinberg's *Albatross*, the most important statement of Yiddish expressionism of the time.

A distinction should be made, however, between expressionist hefker and Hofshteyn's play with a similar aesthetic. Hofshteyn's early poetry explores the new sensory relation to the phenomena of the surrounding world, and hefker signifies an openness to this experience. Openness and objectivism are the key terms of Yiddish critic Nokhem Oyslender's analysis of Hofshteyn's debut volume. Hofshteyn's "encounter with himself takes place in an atmosphere of broad openness," writes Oyslender.[12] Unlike Grinberg's or Markish's imagery, however, openness does not take the form of transgressive corporeality of open bodily orifices; Hofshteyn's openness more resembles Walt Whitman's poetic sequence "Song of the Open Road," in which the "efflux of the soul is happiness," which "pervades the open air."

Hofshteyn's encounter with himself in his debut volume is an encounter with the objective phenomena of his own experience in open space, on the road, and the fields—hence the significance of landscape in his work, not as a source of conventional, poeticized beauty, but as a laboratory for experimentation. Open space also signifies the possibility of freedom from the matrix of already-given categories and relationships and thus provides an enhanced capacity to interact with the world of objects and other people in a new way.[13] Hofshteyn's poetic practice thus resembles the work of phenomenology, which suspends, brackets, and reduces commonsense beliefs and presuppositions about a given experience.[14] Hofshteyn finds his voice in dialogue with the surrounding world of nature, objects, and people by means of his heightened attentiveness to its look, feel, and sound. He plays one sense against another so that the qualities associated with looking, touching, and hearing blend into one another, and looking and hearing resemble touching. "How Sadly Sweet It Is to Be a Person," his poetic portrait of his five-month-old twins, in which "lips, hands, and feet" take in the world, embodies this perspective.[15]

In his 1927 literary handbook, Hofshteyn rejects the view that poetry is merely entertainment. Poetry is instead an "act" and an "emotional and imagistic method of life knowledge," in which the bodily sensorium plays a central role.[16] Hofshteyn explains that different kinds of images depend on the "centers of the brain" which they stimulate. This physiological emphasis on the brain's role in perception reflects the science of the time. Hofshteyn describes the various images as sight, sound, touch, smell, taste, and "dynamic images," which provide the impression of movement. Sight-images indicate colors, forms, and the orientation of objects in space. Lyric poets express their individual relation to the world, bringing their audience into this experience through an indirect process that works on the senses.[17] The enhanced role of sense perception in consciousness, the reduced importance of vision alone, and the heightened importance of sensation for both the poet and the audience reflect the larger artistic and intellectual milieu in which Hofshteyn worked.

Sound

According to Hofshteyn, sound is the most important sense since it distinguishes poetry from ordinary speech. "Sound creates a special emotional relationship to itself" in poetry.[18] Hofshteyn cites his own Yiddish translation of Pushkin's poem "Autumn" to make his point. The poet's soul is besieged by lyric agitation and quivers and vibrates in its effort to express itself. The poet hears the sound-sense that obtained in language before words took on abstract meaning and evokes the primordial sound in the poetic work, thus recovering lost "sound-matter."[19] The notion that poets have a primeval ear was not unique to Hofshteyn. Alexander Blok's well-known 1921 "On the Calling of the Poet" makes a similar point. The poet discovers sounds in their "native, elemental existence," bringing them into harmony and giving them form, and then brings "this harmony into the external world." Blok suggests a correspondence between the elemental forces driving the poet and the elemental forces driving the universe. Roiling "waves of sound, like the waves of ether" are found in the very depths of the human being, inaccessible to civilized society.[20] The poet's task is to throw off the coverings of civilization and reveal these depths. Whereas Hofshteyn focuses on the history of language, granting to the poet access to its earliest origins, and Blok concentrates more on the human psyche and spirit, both argue that poets are defined by their work of listening to sounds. Hofshteyn's poetry explicitly tells his readers that he is listening ("ikh her zikh tsu").[21]

Hofshteyn reminds us that hearing and sight are senses that belong to the body and have to do with the flesh. Freedom from poetic cliché and already-given frameworks of meaning—one aspect of hefker poetics—makes possible a novel physical encounter with the external world. In the joyous poem "I Have Come to You, My World, Fresh and New" ("Ikh bin, mayn velt, afsnay tsu dir gekumen"), published in *Bay vegn*, Hofshteyn writes:

> Today I rang again
> the great bell at the transparent door,
> with new joy my quivering ear
> accompanied
> its pure ringing.[22]

The third line instructs readers in the physiology of hearing: the sound waves strike the inner structure of the ear and its vibration, communicated to the brain, results in the perception of sound. Hearing sound means being touched by it physically. The synesthesia of the image transfers the activity of one sense organ to another. Normally the mouth, tongue, or lips would "accompany" the ringing bell, producing some sort of sound, but in this verse, it is the ear. Hofshteyn's image suggests that hearing a melody involves first covibrating with it as an act of the body.

In the Yiddish, the second and fourth lines of the stanza, the sound of the bell and the action of the ear—are perfectly parallel:

> Afsnay hob ikh haynt ongeklungen
> in groysn glok baym durkzikhtign toyer,
> mit nayer freyd hob nokhgezungen
> dem loyter-klang mayn tsiteriger oyer...

The second and fourth lines rhyme the words for "door" and "ear" (*toyer/oyer*). Ears and doors are both openings between an interior and an exterior. The assonance of *groysn/loyter, baym/mayn*, and *durkhzikhtign/tsiteriger* create a vocal mirroring that underscores the relation between the poet and what he hears. He hears the sound because he can make it. He goes out to meet the sound. Receptivity, or attunement, and the production of poetry are linked, and linked through the fleshy receptacle of the body and its interaction with the fleshy world. The motif of "quivering," which Hofshteyn also uses in several other poems to describe himself ("the sheaf of quivering years" and the "quivering light" of his life) emphasizes the state of attentive listening. Quivering is an unsteady pulsation that both receives and produces movement; in this context, it suggests a process of listening *with* sound as distinct from listening *to* it. The emphasis is less on the poet as willing and intentional creative subject and more on the image of the poet as medium through whom the world makes itself heard.[23]

In Hofshteyn's poetry, fleshiness is a part of every sense, including sight. His images, whether imbued with sunshine or darkness, point to the intimate relation between bodies and the surrounding world. The third stanza of "In the long expanse of gloomy night," another poem in the debut volume, provides an example:

> A barefoot bunch of children
> spring forth
> from house to house,
> and cold puddles watch
> how dark feet avoid them.
> Es shpringt zikh durkh
> fun hoyz tsu hoyz
> a borves bintl kinder,
> un kalte kalizshes zikh kukn um
> vi fislakh tunkele zey maydn oys.[24]

Hofshteyn animates the inanimate world by attributing a sense of sight to the puddles. Instead of saying the puddles reflect the bare feet of the children as they skip over them, he sees how puddles might see what is happening around them, or, in this case, above them, in an instance of what could be called visual attunement. Furthermore, he transfers the qualities of the children's feet, which are cold, to the puddles and vice versa, rendering the bare feet as dark, the quality that make it possible for the puddles to reflect the feet. This is an example of a tactile image, even though it is not about avoiding being touched—the feet avoid the puddles. The image makes readers feel the cold of the children's bare feet and see them, from below, from the puddle's perspective.

In "A Whole Day" ("A gantsn tog"), which serves as a preface to the entire poem cycle, the speaker describes himself paradoxically as under the dominion of the road ("in reshus fun vegn"). Whereas this poem has been read as the expression of "virtual boundlessness" and the "complete immersion in open space," this condition also has a darker side, the potential for exposure and vulnerability.[25] The poet is betwixt and between the possibility and impossibility of passage, between the road and "roadlessness" ("tvishn veg un onveg"), on the narrow line between the two. He maps the external geography of passage and its opposite, the legibility of a domesticated space and its illegibility, the lack of roads, onto his body, transforming the boundary to the realm of his senses. His eyelashes, mediating between his eyes and the sunshine, demarcate a porous and pulsating boundary between his body and the surrounding world:

> Between the road and no road there is only a narrow line,
> Between my eyes and the sunshine, only my young eyelashes.
> What on earth
> could be more beautiful?[26]

Hofshteyn inhabits the boundary between wildness and domesticity, self and world, with a sense of gratitude, experiencing the threshold between the two as sensory beauty.

The Threshold to Nowhere

In another poem in the same collection, the boundary space takes on a different coloration. This untitled poem marks a departure from the mood that otherwise dominates *On the Road*. I have touched on one of its images, the reflection of bare feet in puddles. The poem was dedicated to Bergelson, and it is therefore helpful to consider his 1913 novel, *The End of Everything*, as a reference. The mournful heroine, Mirl Hurvits, takes long, meandering walks outside the shtetl with the lame student Lipkis. The two "wander in silence over the vast encircling fields" surrounded by a frozen world of wintery expanses. It seems to Mirl that everyone and everything has disappeared, and yet, no one protests, the world keeps silent.

Hofshteyn transforms the mood of Bergelson's novel into a set of interlocking images that suggest a similarly bleak landscape. The first line sets the scene in terms of both the image and its acoustic qualities: "In the long expanse of gloomy night" (in langn doyern fun nakht fun triber). The preponderance of unstressed syllables elongates the line. One gray day passes into another without any distinction between them. A door opens to release cows to pasture and houses release children to play. Mouths open to release coughs and joyous voices, but the wind snatches the sounds away. In a poem cycle that is full of joyous sound, the silence here—not merely the absence, but the destruction of sound—is all the more striking.

In the middle of the "dark, naked fields," there is a ditch (*grobn*), another concave space that resembles the opening of doors, houses, and mouths. Hofshteyn describes this ditch or trench as "a hefker-shvel":

> On the dark naked fields,
> there, as before, winds ride,
> there, as before, crows wander,
> there in the middle a ditch lies
> a threshold to nowhere in the desolate distance.
> Af tunklen naket fun di felder
> dort, vi amol, itst vintn raytn,
> dort, vi amol, itst voglen robn,
> dort in a mitn ligt a grobn
> a hefker-shvel in hefker-vaytn...[27]

The term hefker appears twice in the ending of the poem, in the line I have translated as "a threshold to nowhere in the desolate distance." The doors, houses, and mouths are all emptied of their contents, but nothing is transmitted thereby; the passage to the surrounding world is fruitless. The doors, houses, and mouths resemble the empty ditch, with its strong association of a grave waiting for a corpse. No seed has been sown in this wild place, and there is no echoing sound but, again, silence. In this poem, the empty space beyond human habitation offers no doorway to novelty and freedom. This border is a no-man's-land between the human world and what lies beyond it, not only in terms of space, cultivated and wild land, but also in terms of time, the world of the living and the world of the dead. There is a pun of sorts in the last line, as if the term *hefker-shvel* were its motto: the line is indeed the border between ordered, meaningful language and the blank white page. The poem takes us to the very brink of the known world and lets itself be swallowed by what remains beyond it. The poem teeters on the brink of the impossibility of writing poetry, the loss of the ability to make a mark.

"In a land split by scattered stones" (Af erdn oyfgerirte tsvishn valger-shteyner) places the poet in a landscape "churned up" by wild, overwhelming forces, hanging by a thread in the face of disaster:

> In a land split by scattered stones,
> under howling storms and raging blizzards,
> who am I, what am I,
> the one who carries his life's light quietly quivering?
> Af erdn oyfgerirte tsvishn valger-shteyner,
> in beyze onflien fun shnaydikn geviter,
> vos bin ikh, vos badayt ikh, eyner,
> vos trogt zayn lebns-likht mit shtilen tsiter?[28]

The landscape and the speaker who moves across it are strikingly at odds: on the one side, the chaos of earthquakes and storms, and the other, the quiet, sensitive light of the poet's life. The next stanza shifts to the sea, where the rudder and mast of the poet's ship provide no security. Psalm 114, in which God makes the "mountains skip like rams" and forces the sea to flee, is likely one of the intertexts for this poem. The final stanza turns from the geography of disaster to something resembling prayer:

> I am ready at any moment to entrust
> the quivering flame of my life
> to the master of destruction and creation,
> the lord of the earth and seas . . .

Hofshteyn's poem entrusts his life to the "master of destruction and creation" (dem har fun khurbn un boyen). The use of the term *khurbn* is significant, since in contrast to other, more neutral terms, this word refers to Jewish national disaster, at first to the destruction of the Two Temples and subsequently to war and pogroms, politico-historical events. Hofshteyn declares his readiness to entrust his life to God, who rules over history as well as nature. This trust contrasts significantly with the image of stones and stoniness in the work of Leyb Kvitko, to whom this poem is dedicated. For Kvitko, stones signify the unpredictable, intractable forces of the external world, as I show in the next chapter.

"Justice" ("Gerekhtikeyt"), one of the concluding poems of the volume, gives voice to both the joy and the sorrow of the Russian Revolution. In this work, in contrast to the landscape poetry, openness includes an element of the public and publicity, especially since the poet emphasizes others' voices:

> I hear them with a quivering heart
> the thousand breaths exhaling joy,
> with suffering stilled I feel
> the mute quivering pain . . .
> mit hartsn-tsiter her ikh zey
> di toyznt-otemdike freydgeshrayen,
> mit gliver-leyd dershpir ikh zey,
> di shtume tsapldike veyen.[29]

The restraint that quiets and condenses his own suffering allows others' emotion to resonate more powerfully. Yiddish critic Shmuel Charney identifies the qualities of quieting and condensing (as in the neologism above, *gliver-leyd* [stilled suffering]) as the very essence of Hofshteyn's poetry.[30] The internal rhyme of *gliver-leyd* with *dershpir ikh zey* (I feel them) suggests an identity between the speaker's own stilled suffering and the pain of others; the quality of condensing and constraining is the instrument by which the other's suffering is sensed, especially important because the voice of suffering is muted (*shtume*).

Deafening Violence

The question of sound, hearing, and the muting of sound that is central to the debut volume also plays a key role in Hofshteyn's Hebrew prose poem, titled "In Those Days: Fragments from My Recollections of the Civil War in Russia," written and published when the author was in Palestine but referring to his experience of Kyiv.[31] Kyiv changed governments more than ten times during the civil war. Denikin's Volunteer Army carried out pogroms in October and August 1919. Hofshteyn's memoiristic "fragments" are the most explicit account of his inner and outer life in war-torn Kyiv.[32] They have not been discussed in the critical literature. I begin with the second part, in which the poet articulates his own personal terror. Hofshteyn is in a city besieged from "outside and inside," where fires are burning, even whole neighborhoods. Hofshteyn is guarding a building; his shift is for three hours, and he is grateful for the structure the schedule gives him, as a defense against the "terrifying form" that the next moment could bring. The inhabitants of the building, including Jews and non-Jews, take shelter in the basement, and Hofshteyn notes that in the past people used to open the door for those who rang the bell for their neighbors. He wants to know what "they," the attackers, shooting at the city, are thinking. A noise from the apartment next door produces a new thought: his experience in Kyiv resembles what happened when he was a soldier in the czarist army in the Caucasus. He served in the years 1912–13, and several poems in *On the Road* are set there, including one in which he suggests a kinship between the generations of suffering among the Armenian people and himself.[33] Hofshteyn describes how at night in the military camp in the Caucasus, he heard the door and the ceiling move about and felt as if he had been hurled back in time to the *toyhu-vavoyhu*, the "welter and waste" of the period before creation, and the sounds he heard were the "elements of Genesis talking among themselves." The world is being torn apart and the forms of human life and culture that had been developed have suddenly and inexplicably been unmade.

The first part of the memoir is utterly unlike anything else Hofshteyn wrote. It is an allegorical reworking of the Jericho story, written in markedly biblical language, with phrases and words taken from the books of Joshua and Jeremiah. The unnamed "big city" in the story is identifiable as Kyiv, because of its mixed terrain of hills and flat areas; Kyiv was organized culturally and spatially along a vertical axis. Jews lived in the lower region. In Hofshteyn's piece, a "giant, wild, and cruel creature" assaults the city with deafening noise. The creature, or monster, is not named; it is possible that Hofshteyn had in mind some variant of the Golem. The windows of the buildings are figured as eardrums. At first the city resists, but the "cruel creature" forces it to listen "and the city suffers from listening," tortured by the unbearably loud sound, until it falls to the ground, "howling from its wounds."[34] It is important to consider what Kyiv meant to Hofshteyn at this time. In his poem "Shtot" ("City"), first published in 1919 but written earlier, Hofshteyn did not employ the motifs of shock and mechanization that diminish the self, typically associated with modernist representations of the overwhelming experience of urban space. Instead, the city offers the poet comfort, community, and a vital connection to the larger world. A line from the poem gives the sense of the whole: "I arrived in your harbor on the ship of my loneliness" (Af shif fun mayn elent bin ikh in dayn hafn gekumen).[35] The city that provided shelter, a world of others with whom he breathes, and a world of other sights, surfaces, and sounds (the whistling of trains, the ringing of bells)—into which he could insert the "small change" of his own poetry—has been dealt a death blow. The city as soundscape has gone quiet. I note in passing Hofshteyn's image of Kyiv under attack resonates with Shklovsky's portrait of St. Petersburg in 1918 as "a city that had gone deaf."

Whereas in *Bay vegn* the poet celebrates the pleasure given by the simple act of hearing, in this work, the same act results in pain. The city surrenders to the creature, which only responds with its inchoate noise, "Boo-boo-buk." As in the Jericho story, and in an inversion of Genesis, the destruction of the city lasts six days and nights. Avant-garde poets and prose authors had experimented with the devolution of speech into sound, and as I discuss earlier, Hofshteyn also wrote about the poet's capacity to discern the primordial relation between sound and sense in present-day language. In this piece, the very thing that poets love—the medium of their artistry—is a weapon that inflicts terrible pain. The end of the piece returns to the motif of deafness: there is no point in challenging or questioning what is happening, because there is no one to ask, and human artifacts and the natural world are no longer available as interlocutors. "The tree is impermeable," Hofshteyn writes.

The creative interchange between the poet and the surrounding world has been cut off. The poetic vision of the chaos of primordial time and the poet's life experience merge. In conditions of utter abandonment, the condition of poetry, the possibility of listening diminishes to a null point. Creating art is part of the remaking of the world. It is a projection of liveliness into the "impermeable" unresponsiveness of the people and things. In Hofshteyn's work, the projection takes the form of a dialogue, and in the Hebrew prose work, the dialogue has been cut off. Poetry has been called into question. Something has been tipped in the delicate balance between mournfulness and joy so palpable in Hofshteyn's debut volume. Hofshteyn has come right up to the edge of the abyss. He had done so before, in his language about the "hefker threshold" in his debut volume. In the central poem of his pogrom lament *Sorrow*, the speaker kneels at the very edge of the "abyss" and addresses it directly.

Grieving

In the poem cycle *Sorrow* Hofshteyn returns to the motif of poetry as listening and "gathering" that he had used earlier. Gathering, but in a different sense, was also a motif of Hofshteyn's daily life in Kyiv. According to his wife Feyge Hofshteyn, the poet obsessively collected old, rusty objects that he found discarded on the street—typewriters, clocks, and lamps—and would spend hours attempting to repair them.[36] Abandoned objects held an irresistible attraction for him. The gesture from daily life and the poetic gesture echo one another. In *Sorrow* (*Troyer*) the poet gathers scraps of messages left by others. Discerning them requires an intense attunement to what otherwise would go unnoticed, debris that has grown ancient from neglect.

As in his previous volume, the same restraint, the withholding of the full force of the poet's emotions is essential to the quality of attunement. The epigraph reads, "I don't demand / I only ask." Hofshteyn's language is not one of mutilated flesh but an expression of grief in his uniquely restrained voice, lamenting the pain, injury, and bloodshed that other also poets responded to but in a different key.

Published by the Kyiv Kultur-Lige in 1922, *Sorrow* consists of eleven poems; the cover page and drawings are by Marc Chagall.[37] Hofshteyn's and Chagall's project was developed while they were both working at a colony for homeless Jewish children at Malakhovka.[38] It is dedicated to those "cut off before their time," and the proceeds from the sale of the book were dedicated to the orphanage. Seth Wolitz sees a chiasmic pattern of alternating order and chaos in the work, and Jordan Finkin convincingly shows the importance of consolation as its conclusion. My analysis focuses on the hefker dimension of the poem cycle, the wild, chaotic, and yet self-effacing qualities of the poet's grief that create an opening to others' suffering.

Sorrow is a journey through the broken time and space of pogrom violence. The place-names of major killing sites punctuate the cosmic landscape of the "abyss" (*opgrunt*). There is no reference to his own experience of pogroms in Kyiv, unlike the Hebrew work discussed earlier, and similarly, no documentary impulse to state that the poet was there where violence took place. Time has lost its ordering. The week goes by without Sabbaths or Sundays, indicating the destruction of the Jewish as well as the Christian calendar. God is no longer the source of the times and seasons. The Zodiac wheel occupies this role, and it produces time that is only ruinous and destructive. As the Zodiac wheel turns, its signs "glint like knives, like skewers."[39] The free and joyous wandering that is the leitmotif of *On the Road* is gone, because the poet cannot determine his motion through space and time. The turn of the Zodiac wheel takes him where it will; he is compelled to wander, float, and fall. The loss of ordered time, however, also contains a potential for openness to the past and future. Distinct epochs merge into one another, including the time of the poet's grandfathers, the future of the children at the orphanage, the biblical time of Job, and Hofshteyn's time in Kyiv, as well as Ukraine's past as "a place of refuge," its present history of violence, and its unknown future.

The landscape of violence encompasses abandoned fields, ruined shtetls, and houses without roofs or walls. "Boundless power" (ongrenetsdiker shlite) has been unleashed in the entire space, filled with the arbitrary, limitless, and lawless will of violence. "Bandits' steps" have left traces of destruction everywhere; every speck of space is "shadowed by your shame / Ukraine."⁴⁰ Hofshteyn does not use the term hefker to characterize the pogrom landscape, as other authors do; for example, Bergelson in "The Beginning of December, 1919" describes the abandoned space of a railway line where a Jew's frozen corpse lies unattended. The sense of abandonment in *Sorrow* nonetheless comes across clearly. To be subjected to lawlessness means exposure to limitless power. Ukraine—the former place of refuge (*miklet-plats*)—has become a zone of abandonment.⁴¹ The earlier condition guaranteed safety and protection against enemies; the second allows enemies to act with impunity.

The sixth poem, "Falling" ("In faln")—the longest, at 132 lines and fifteen stanzas—literally and figuratively constitutes the center of the work.⁴² The meaning of hefker as a poetic quality, existential condition, and consequence of violence emerges from this central poem. The first four stanzas unfold in the abstract realm of some "cold and silent wasteland," where the abyss is found, a place removed from normal time and space. Its dimensions are cosmic and mythical, but Hofshteyn's voice does not ascend to the peaks of oratory or prophecy. He remains quiet. The first line of the poem graphically pictures the action of falling: the phrase "a wanderer" runs vertically down the page. The falling stress ("a VALger") emphasizes downward motion. The falling poet nearly tumbles into the black maw of the abyss. In "The long expanse of gloomy night," discussed earlier, the threshold to nowhere was far away, removed from the here and now, but in this poem, in contrast, forces beyond Hofshteyn's control transport him to the *hefker-shvel*, the threshold of desolation and abandonment.

The fourth stanza introduces the theme of poetry with the motif of a sound that falling makes, an echo that resounds somewhere. Perhaps the echo of falling will reach the poet, even though it makes no sound:

A deaf echo,
far away
for you here,
remaining
kneeling
with outstretched arms—
what can it mean?
An opklang a toyber,
a vayter...
Far dir do,

far shteyen
far knien
mit hent oysgeshpreyte—
vos kon er bataytn?

The use of anaphora in the three lines that begin with "far" (far dir do / far shteyen / far knien) and the near rhyme in vayter,' shteyn, oysgeshPREYte, and bataytn acoustically repeat the echo that has come from afar. Decoding (*bataytn*) the meaning of the echo is tantamount to decoding the meaning of the poem.

Kneeling at the edge of the pit, the poet asks a question:

What are you still in a position to do?
The most beautiful,
the purest,
the greatest of pains, of sorrows
you can still receive
a slight string of verses
rhymed and
compressed—
a slight string of verses on a crumpled page
drifting about some place over there
in giant baskets of years![43]

Earlier in the poem, falling, standing, and kneeling referred to physical positions, which the poet was compelled to assume. In contrast, asking the question about the course of action left open to him provides some measure of choice.

The poet is still in a position to listen or "receive" someone else's words, rectifying the compulsory passivity of his earlier condition. In the context of force and violence, receiving blurs the distinction between activity and passivity. It is passivity that is also a form of action.[44] The powerlessness of the poet's own position, his immobility, and the silencing of his own voice make it possible for him to "receive" the verse that has been lost for years. Hofshteyn deliberately avoids making a claim on or emphasizing the immediacy of his own experience, as in the poem with which this chapter begins.[45] The creative act is akin to a form of intensified listening, which can only take place because the poet is quiet. The first stanza explicitly asks for silence. The fourth line, "Quiet! . . ." (Un sha! . . .) both contains the admonition to silence and puts it into practice; a row of ellipses appears between the fourth and fifth line of the stanza. The poet ceases speaking. The assonance created between "Un sha!" ("Quiet") in this stanza, "Ikh kni do" ("I kneel here"), and "Far dir do" ("For you here") underscore the poet's quiet self-abnegation and his ability to detect the nearly inaudible reverberations of suffering. Facing the extreme, at the border of the abyss, a response is still possible. When there is nothing to do and no place to do it in, the only thing to do and the only way to do it is to silence oneself to discern the barely audible echo of another's cry.

The emphasis on the act of reception is clearer in the original Yiddish:

Vos bistu in shtand nokh
dos shenste,
dos reynste,
dos greste—
fun veyen, fun leydn
nokh kentstu
bakumen
a shnirele shures.[46]

Modifying Wolitz's translation to reflect the Yiddish more closely:

What are you still in a position to do?
the finest,
the purest,
the greatest
of pains, of sorrows
you still can
receive
a slight string of verses

The alternating lines of three and six syllables reach their culmination in the seventh line, which consists solely of the word *receive* (*bakumen*), thereby emphasizing its importance. The symmetries of the first eight lines of this stanza in Yiddish are worth noting, the amphibrachs underscore the poet's upright position as a human being even while kneeling. The enjambment of the line carries the poem forward to a surprising resolution, because what the poet says we all can still receive at the edge of the abyss is not some cosmic growl or human cry of pain, but instead a "slight string of verses" that has been drifting and floating about for years. Catastrophe makes ancient that which happened just a minute ago and transforms the immediacy of voice—one's own or another's—into a barely decipherable written text.

Utterly still, the poet hears the echo of pain, detecting its distant sounds. The poet "receives" the scrap of paper on which some lines of verse have been written by someone else, serving as a conduit of something that originated elsewhere and at some other time, that has been drifting about, as if carried in baskets held aloft through the passage of time. What he receives is so faint and insignificant that it is hardly noticeable, nothing more than a "shnirele shures," a slight or thin string of verses. His silence makes it possible for him to discern a barely noticeable trace left by someone else. Writing poetry is akin to receiving and rewriting the words authored by others, suggesting an image of the poet as an archivist, or the poet as one who gathers testimony.[47] Indeed, the entirety of the poem "Falling" may be imagined as a compilation of the messages left on the scraps of paper. The poet and the poem fall to the ground after wandering and drifting in time and space. Hofshteyn represents his own pain and his own language as someone else's. His poetry consists of the remnants left by others. Hofshteyn's hefker poetics resist all claims of ownership and stable boundaries.

A Poetic Conversation

The stanza about listening and transcribing the words of others is itself part of a larger poetic conversation. Hofshteyn is responding to another poem by a second poet, and a third poet, in turn, responds to him. The first poet in the series, whom Hofshteyn echoes, is Osher Shvartsman, and the third, who echoes Hofshteyn, is Arn Kushnirov. Shvartsman, born in 1890 and killed in 1919 while serving in the Red Army, was Hofshteyn's cousin and much revered by the members of the Kyiv group. Kushnirov was also a member of the same circle.

Shvartsman's poem "In the Realm of Tribulation" ("In tribn mentshnland"), written in 1919, a few months before he died, poses a question about the poet's role in the face in of overwhelming suffering:

> In the realm of tribulation
> where people stumble under burdens
> what can I say?

> What can I offer
> those who soothe their pain
> with ashes?
> In tribn mentshn land,
> Far dem, vos falt shoyn unter last fun plogn,
> Vos kon ikh zogn?

The poem questions the meaning and value of language in conditions of oppression and suffering. How can the poet respond to others' pain, what answer can he give to those bent by affliction? The words for "burdens" and "pain" (*plogn, leydn*) rhyme with the words for "say" and "offer" (*zogn, redn*), underscoring the question of the relation between suffering and responding. Following in the footsteps of Bialik's prophet in "In the City of Slaughter," the speaker in Shvartsman's poem withdraws from the land of affliction and leaves for the desert, the sackcloth that he wears and the silence he keeps both a form of self-mortification and a way of honoring the suffering of others. He vows not to return until he hears the "word of salvation."[48]

The third interlocutor in the poetic conversation is Arn Kushnirov, who dedicated his poem "Azkore" ("Memorial") to Hofshteyn. It was published in the first issue of the Moscow Yiddish literary journal *Shtrom*, on whose editorial board Hofshteyn served; the journal's title came from a line of poetry by Shvartsman.[49] "Memorial" paints a bleak picture of pogrom abandonment and violence. There is no one to hear the poet's cry, no one to help in the face of ongoing killing. In the following stanza, the inhabitants of a house have fled, leaving their home to the winds. Kushnirov listens together with Hofshteyn, trying to discern what there is to be heard:

> Murderous winds struggle and wrestle
> with the faithful bolt on the door.
> And on the slight string of sound
> I will hang my ear.
> Vintn-rokhtsim, ranglet zikh, ranglet
> mit getrayen rigl af toyer.
> Un ikh vel af shnirl fun klangen
> afheyngen mayn oyer.[50]

The sound of the "bolt" (*rigl*) and the sound of the wind's action, wrestling with and pulling at the bolt (*ranglet zikh*) echo one another. Kushnirov renames the sounds of the winds as the "slight string of sound" (*shnirele klangen*). He knows there is nothing to be heard, save Rachel crying for her children, as the next stanza tells us.

Shvartsman asks what he can say; Hofshteyn asks what he can do, "What are you still in a position to do?" (*Vos bistu in shtand nokh?*). By including "you" (*bistu*) he extends the challenge to readers of his work. The answer is not the production of more speech; Hofshteyn, unlike Shvartsman, is not searching for the right thing to say but, rather, the right thing to do, transcribing the scraps of others' verses. Poetry is not merely something you say but also something you do, and the doing calls into being an ethical relation to another.

From Sound to Sight

In contrast to Kushnirov, whose reference to Rachel is unsurprising, Hofshteyn's next move, thematically and stylistically, is shocking. Hofshteyn modifies the "slight string of verse" changing "verse" to blood: a "slight string of blood drops." Narrative description of the poet's memory replaces the rhetorical question about what there is to be done. Recalling his experience as a child, the poet writes, "There could often be seen" on the rust-brown, filthy stones another string or strand, not consisting of lines of verse (*a shnirele shures*) as in the previous stanza, but this time, "blood drops bright and pure" ("a shnirele blut-tropns hele un reyne").[51] The source of this blood is unimportant, the poet tells us. It didn't matter who "lost" it. The catastrophic events of 1919 strangely echo ordinary, daily life events from the past, and the revelation of their kinship with violence is disturbing. 1919 stirs up time, pushing fragments of the poet's consciousness that might otherwise be suppressed to the forefront. The poet draws together the spatially, temporally, and graphically remote scene at the abyss (line 12) and the shtetl courtyard (line 45) using parallelism, sound mirroring, and rhyme. Line 12 reads, "Ikh SHTEY do fun OYBN," and line 45 reads, "In SHTEYnere HOYFN."

The poet's journey through time and space takes an abrupt turn in stanzas 10–12, set in the snows of Siberia. A hunter pursues a white fox, killing it, and the fox leaves behind a string of bloody drops on the snow. Blood drops, lines of poetry, and the fox's fate come together here and run through the work as a whole. The fox's pure drops of blood visually echo the earlier occurrence of blood in the scene in the filthy courtyard and the drop of blood spilled from "a child's innocent being," which nothing could outweigh, found earlier, in the second poem of the work, "Ukraine."

The ninth stanza compares drops of blood and lines of poetry, using the term hefker:

> And if
> you should have the fortune,
> if your song could be as wild [*hefker*] and pure
> as the bloody drops
> on the far snows of Siberia. . . .
> that were scattered at the last minute
> A fox cub from the north, a pup from the snows.[52]
> Un oyber
> es vet dikh baglikn,
> un zayn vet dayn lid azoy hefker un zoyber,
> vi blutike trofns
> af shneyen fun vaytn Siberyen . . .
> es hot zey bavizn tsezayen
> in letste minutn
> a fiksl fun tsofn a hintl fun shneyen . . .[53]

The stanza is an incomplete hypothesis: the first part ("and if") is not resolved (the consequence, "then") until a later stanza. Readers must wait for the answer. The use of monosyllables and internal rhyme makes the third line "if your song could be as wild and pure" stand out from the rest in pacing and tone, giving it the air of solemn proclamation. The parallelism of *hefker* ("wild") and *zoyber* challenges conventional language. I have translated *zoyber* as "pure," but it ordinarily means "neat, tidy." Hefker unruliness and wildness is at odds with the orderliness of zoyber. The semantic association between hefker and purity also demands attention. Hefker is wild, beyond the boundaries, transgressive, an attribute of a thing or person that upsets categories, and thus the antithesis of purity.

The problem becomes more difficult in light of the graphics that accompany the previous stanza about the filthy courtyard. Chagall accompanied the passage about the courtyard's "blood drops bright and pure" with an image of animals copulating, an outhouse and a half-naked woman upside down alongside it, suggesting that the "bright pure drops" in the filthy courtyard are the blood drops of a menstruating woman.[54] In Jewish law, the menstruating woman, ritually unclean, cannot have sexual relations with her husband. Describing these blood drops in the same way as the fox's and the child's, as "bright and pure," thus pushes readers beyond what is conventional and accepted. Hefker as the desideratum for poetry also describes the fox's spilled blood and the blood of the innocent child; it is wayward, boundary-defying, and yet also innocent.

A consideration of other hefker moments in the poem is helpful. The hunter's act of violence alludes to the murder of Jews; the hunter kills the fox with impunity; the "boundless power" unleashed in Ukraine, the "bandit's steps," and the beatings and killings of Jews are acts of violence for which there is no penalty, carried out in a state of reckless abandonment and, thus, hefker in the senses that I have developed earlier. In the fourteenth stanza, the poet describes his own task as a "seeker, dreamer, and wanderer." He "grasps" and "gathers" the fox's bloody drops from the snow, one by one, transforming the strand of blood into a strand of poetry. As in the earlier stanza, in which the poet detects an echo, here the poet describes his own creativity as attunement to another's pain. Sight and touch replace the sense of sound. The poet sees and grasps, but in so doing, Hofshteyn emphasizes the palpable, tactile qualities of vision, and not its abstract capacities for conceptual mastery. The gesture of gathering, as in Hofshteyn's earlier poem "On the Road," corresponds to the creation of poetry. In the previous work, the poet brought together his own "sowing," his own words that he had scattered across untended fields. Here, in contrast, the poet gathers the blood left behind by others, including the drops he saw in filthy courtyards as a child, the child's blood, and the fox's, uniting them—"in your own heart / it was all the same, whoever had lost them."

As others have pointed out, the little white fox is associated with the Jewish victim.[55] Wolitz describes the shooting of the fox as an allegory of the pogroms, and both he and Finkin cite Ezekiel 13:14 and Lamentations 5:18, in which "foxes walk upon the desolate mountains of Zion." The fox, however, is not necessarily a figure of innocence. In Nehemiah, the fox can destroy a stone wall. In Peretz's poem, discussed in chapter 1, foxes are predators who capture their prey through trickery. The world abandoned to wolves and foxes is a hefker world. The biblical allusions and other dimensions of the poem's language, including the use of the term hefker, suggest a wider interpretation of the fox's significance beyond Jewish victimhood. Hofshteyn, like the fox, is also a denizen of ruined, desolate places, as I have shown.

In the ninth, untitled, poem in the *Troyer* cycle, he finds himself in a place that used to house "hundreds of hearths" but now has "no roofs, no walls," and only "thresholds" and "doors" through which he is pulled and pushed. The "autumnal doors" are "draped in pure transparency." In the poem "Falling," Hofshteyn uses the qualities of brightness, cleanness, and purity to describe both drops of blood and poetry. In the last stanza of the unnamed poem, purity, light, and poetry emanate from pillaged buildings:

> What good to me is pure transparency,
> that also pours through ravaged fissures,
> and through which my very bitter
> prayers for the dead (for now only mine) will be borne by the wind...⁵⁶

The light streaming through the rubble of ruined buildings corresponds to poetry and prayer. The poet's prayers escape through the openings of the ruins. In the original Yiddish, the rhyme scheme creates an association between "pure transparency" (*di loyterkayt di klore*) and the poet's "bitter prayers" (*bitere azkores*).⁵⁷ The violence of pogroms leaves cracks and fissures, but they are not merely ruins; even here, there is an opening to something beyond destruction. There is a striking contrast between this image of openness and Markish's heap of open, oozing mouths.

The traces left by pain, injury, and violence may be rendered as poetry. This is the essence of the solace and comfort the poem offers, and the conclusion of the hypothesis raised in the ninth stanza. If the poem and the poet could be as hefker and pure as the blood left in the courtyard and on the snow, it could provide comfort. If a human gaze could gather the bloody drops, "Then would this not be comfort?" (*Den iz dos keyn treyst nit?*). Hofshteyn creates a pseudo-etymological sound association between the word for poem (*lid*) and the word for suffering (*laydn*). The sound change between *i* and *ay* normally occurs in Yiddish declensions and conjugations. It is as if there were a grammatical relationship between the two terms, as if the plural of suffering were poetry.

The drawing and graphics that accompany the poem emphasize other dimensions of its meaning. The hunting scene is especially significant (see fig. 2.1). The contours of the hunter's body are difficult to read, particularly in light of Chagall's use of upside-down and floating figures in other work. In this image, it is not clear whether the hunter is upside down or lying on the ground. The outline of the gun is sharp and clear, but the stippling on

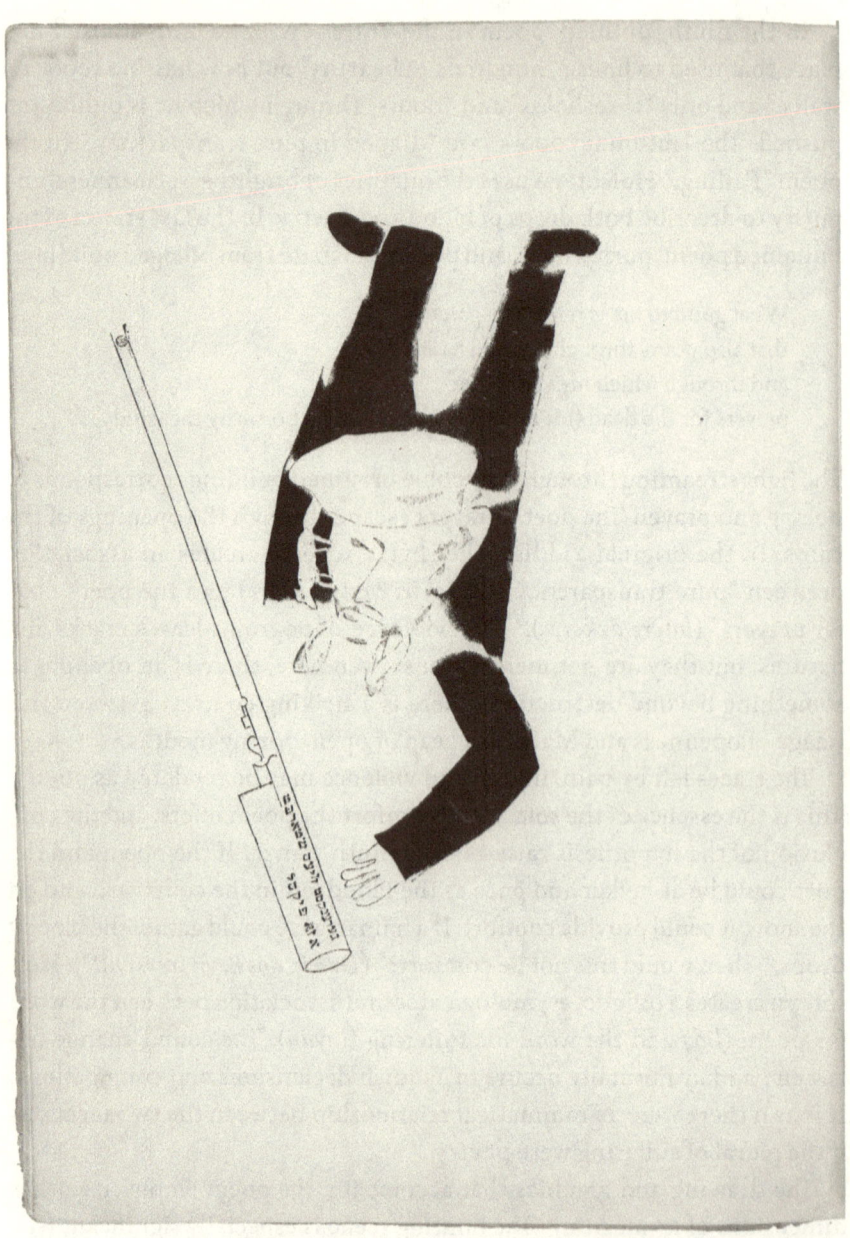

Fig. 2.1. *The Hunter and the Fox* by Marc Chagall, from Hofshteyn, *Troyer*. The words on the gun: "Do you remember how the fox dies?" © 2023 Artists Rights Society (ARS), New York / ADAGP, Paris.

what appears to be the mustaches or beard on the hunter's face are less easy to make out. A miniature figure of the fox climbs up the disproportionately large hunter's face. The seemingly one-armed hunter reaches for his gun with his left hand going for the trigger, not the typical position. The lines created by the gun and the hunter's legs and bent arm suggest the spokes of a wheel, the very same Zodiac wheel whose turning compels the poet's journey. The outline of the hunter figure puts the entire image in motion, turning it round.[58] When inverted, the hunter's mustaches turn into the ears of a human figure with a tiny head and huge fox. This figure is standing right side up, his right hand about to grab the gun, and the little fox crawls up its side, peering into a reflection of its own face. Chagall draws out the larger themes of Hofshteyn's sorrow, both the emotion and the poetic work *Sorrow*: the intimacy and interrelatedness of the killers and those they killed. What Chagall's image and Hofshteyn's words suggest is that the Jewish tragedy of the pogroms was a Ukrainian tragedy; the destruction of Jewish lives was thus an act of self-destruction. The second poem in the cycle, titled "Ukraine," and dedicated to the Ukrainian poet Yakov Savchenko, underscores the importance of the twin catastrophes. Hofshteyn "still feels love" for Ukraine. His lament is not only for Jews; it is also for Ukraine.

In the pogrom lament, the creative act depends on the maximum constriction of the poet's own voice, his poetic will, and the maximum extension of his capacity to hear, receive, see, and, impossibly, touch the pain of others. Hoftshteyn's representation of his poetic practice resembles the devotional activity of "hefker like the wilderness," the deliberate attempt to empty oneself of oneself to receive Torah, discussed in chapter 1. Noting the significance of the giving of the Torah to Moses in the wilderness, the rabbis observe that in order to receive its wisdom, one must make oneself "ownerless as the wilderness," or "open to all." Indeed, the poet describes his confinement to the wilderness, or wasteland (*vistenish*).

Hofshteyn's designation in the critical literature as a Soviet Yiddish poet tends to obscure his exploration of Jewish religious concepts, even in work that predates the formation of officially regulated Soviet literary culture. I argue that one such concept is a source for the lament and the message of comfort in Hofshteyn's pogrom cycle. The practice of self-abnegation as a religious act reappears in the secular act of poetry's creation. Hofshteyn establishes an ethical relation to the readers of the text and the inhabitants of Ukraine, both Jewish and not. The poet can speak of the abandonment of the Jews, because he has poetically expressed the condition of "hefker like the wilderness." Finkin points out that the dedication of all proceeds from Hofshteyn's and Chagall's *Sorrow* to the orphanage at Malakhovka adds a significant ethical dimension to the work. I add that the kenotic qualities of Hofshteyn's poetic voice lend yet another relational dimension to his pogrom lament. The ability to make oneself "open to all" is necessary for the poetry of consolation that Hofshteyn seeks to offer. It is in this sense that he speaks of hefker poetry.

In the poem cycle *On the Road*, the broad expanse of space allows for openness to the objective phenomena of the poet's experience, in both pain and delight. Scholars have described Hofshteyn's modernism in terms of his use of free verse, poetry of open spaces, and his use of a montage of images and scenes. The shift from lyric interiority to the externalization of the "encounter with the self" is another distinguishing feature of his work. In the pogrom lament, the abyss replaces the open road, and the poet's openness permits him to discern the barest trace of others' pain. Kneeling at the edge of the abyss, in a realm beyond recognizable space and time, and removed from the raw immediacy of violence, the poet turned archivist gathers the scraps of paper inscribed with another's "slight string of verse." The entire lament may be understood as the string of verse that the poet managed to discern while kneeling at the abyss. The words that he collects floating in the "baskets of years" may have come from speakers who are already dead. The turns of the poem, the slight string of verse, the string of blood drops, and the larger poetic conversation respond to the turns of the Zodiac wheel, offering poetry as a counterforce to its implacable might. Poetry, the smallest, frailest thing is the greatest comfort. The counter to the violence of untrammeled power is only hefker poetry: free, wild, denuded of self, and maximally open to others.

In contrast, Leyb Kvitko, the subject of the next two chapters, describes the grotesque violence of 1919 far more explicitly than Hofshteyn. Acutely attuned to the phenomena of violence, Kvitko, however, in contrast to Hofshteyn, places more emphasis on his own experience, his own pain, and his disorientation in time and space. He insists on the importance of having been in Uman during the 1919 pogroms. Hefker is a keyword of his early poetry, prior to his pogrom volume—but here too a distinction may be drawn. For Kvitko, unlike Hofshteyn, hefker indicates a kind of existential homelessness, not the joy of the open road.

3

Leyb Kvitko's Poetry of Abandonment

Leyb Kvitko (1890–1952) was one of the most well-known authors of the USSR. His poems for children, written in Yiddish and widely translated into Russian, Belorussian, and Ukrainian, celebrated the happy childhood made possible by the new Soviet society.[1] In the period of the Russian Revolution and Civil War, in contrast, Kvitko created a different kind of poetry, dark and chaotic, in response to his own impulses and the chaos of his time. "Darkness is in me," Kvitko wrote.[2] I read Kvitko as a poet of abandonment, tracing the hefker poetics of his three early works: his debut volume *Steps* (*Trit*) and his revolutionary poem "In a Red Storm" ("In roytn shturem"), both published in 1919, and his pogrom cycle, titled *1919*, published in 1923.[3] For Kvitko, hefker is an existential condition, theme, and stylistic point of departure. Hefker—a multivalent term having to do with an entire realm of human life that is unclaimed, abandoned, and wild—is particularly well suited to Kvitko's life, his time, and his poetry.

At the risk of artificially separating what was a single process of poetic evolution, the discussion that follows breaks down into three phases. In *Steps*, Kvitko is consigned to abandonment. Stuck in a peculiar space of isolation, and attending to its contours and rhythms, he creates poetry. In *1919*, the pogrom cycle, abandonment is no longer only personal and idiosyncratic; it emerges in the outer world as a presence in the landscape, in the form of mass public violence. Kvtiko the poet knew this landscape in advance; he was ready for it. Stripped of all ways of knowing the world save for his basic senses and already attuned to what was monstrous and frightening, Kvitko the poet listens to violence and transforms it into the sounds of his poems. In the pogrom cycle, abandonment makes itself felt in a particularly embodied form of sound. Finally, the pain of abandonment, openness, and exposure that permeate *Steps* suggest a pathway toward forgiveness, the problem of the last poem of *1919*.

A brief recapitulation of the broader question of violence will help set the stage for what follows. The use of physical force to inflict bodily injury, the most conventional definition of violence, is not my emphasis here, because it is not the approach used by Kvitko or the other authors examined in this study. In Kvitko's poems, violence corresponds to an all-encompassing disorientation: the breakdown of the categories by which experience is understood, the collapse of the social community and the world of physical objects and nature, and the continuity and predictability of time and space. This breakdown intensifies the strange physicality of sound. As I showed in the previous chapter, sound in Hofshteyn's first volume is a source of physical pleasure. In Kvitko's debut volume, in contrast, sound is uncanny, catastrophic, and painful.

First Steps

Kvitko's hefker status is broader than political and social abandonment. It is an already-given condition, prior to specific historical events; it is existential and ontological. Being alive, having been created means having been wounded and abandoned. The melancholy restlessness that ensues makes him particularly attuned to the state of the world. Kvitko's writing from the early 1920s generally imagines a half-life, a realm, in which there is no community, no world, no continuity in time, and instead of recognizable human beings, strange, interstitial creatures, supernatural and monstrous. In *Steps* the poet is a denizen of the world of chaos; he feels his way through the darkness and the void, claiming the freedom to create wild poetry. Whereas Hofshteyn encounters darkness and the void in response to the specific events of war and pogroms, Kvitko lives in this realm as a matter of course.

Most of the poems in *Steps* are focused on the poet himself, isolated from the wider community and more in tune with the ghosts and monsters of the past than with other human beings in the present. Kvitko lives and breathes melancholy in a particularly vivid and visceral way. Biographical information can shed light on the reasons. He was born in the shtetl of Holoskovo, not far from Odesa but far from the railroad and, as he described it, full of crippled beggars.[4] Kvitko's parents and most of his siblings died of tuberculosis when he was very young. Kvitko lived the life of an abandoned child as well as using the persona of the abandoned child in his literary work.[5] His grandmother raised him, and Kvitko started working at the age of ten; his itinerant labor included house-painting, processing animal skins, and working at a slaughterhouse.[6] In the preface to his pogrom cycle, Kvitko writes about the "concrete yet fragile fear of the child." This language well captures his experience of childhood. Kvitko later published an autobiographical novel, *Two Friends: Lyam and Petrik* (*Tsvey khaverim: Lyam un Petrik*), in 1930 that describes the brutal conditions of his early years. His debut poems amplify its fantastic and grotesque features. It is as if from a very early age his ear and voice were in training for the revolutionary epoch, preparing his unique receptivity and attunement to the grotesque dimensions of its mass public violence.

Folklore—that is, the oral traditions, stories, beliefs, and rituals he encountered during his itinerant childhood—and specifically Ukrainian folktales, which he translated into Yiddish, as well as the influence of the Yiddish author Der Nister (Pinkhes Kahanovitsh, 1884–1950), who reinvented the Yiddish magical tale, are the other components of what I am calling Kvitko's "training." In his autobiographical *Two Friends*, a magician hypnotizes a child, compelling him to remain immobile. In one of his poems from *1919*, Kvitko depicts a pogromist as a magician who stuffs a Jew into his hip flask, leaving his family vulnerable to attack. In the final section of his first published collection of poems, dedicated to "demons," a cat and a dog play with a peacock tail and a child's skull. A castle made of human bones appears, decorated with human heads and steps formed from human hearts. The folkloric elements important for Kvitko's poetry of violence include children left on their own and adopted by spirits and animals; the looming presence of malicious forces and supernatural beings who harm more than help; the dizzying pace of metamorphosis as animals, people, and objects transform into one another; and the proximity of life and death. Kvitko's experimental and surreal poetry embraces the fragmentation of personal identity and the unpredictability of change, features that also appear prominently in folktales. Even his description of his own poems lends them a strange, magical animation. Complaining to the editor of the New York Yiddish journal *The Future* about work that remained sitting in the editorial office unpublished, Kvitko wrote, "They [the poems] want to breathe in the world with open eyes full of sorrow and belief—the sinners!"[7]

The broader artistic and intellectual milieu is also significant for the development of Kvitko's poetic voice. In manifestos published in the early part of the twentieth century, Russian avant-garde poets created a parallel between the disaggregation of the parts of the body in the new visual art and the switch from semantics to sound in "trans-sense" (*zaum*) poetry. Dadaist sound and dance poetry provide other examples of the new focus on the body's role in the production of artistic language.[8] Mayakovsky, who was well known to Yiddish poets and who was aware of Jewish poetry in Hebrew and Yiddish, explored a new relation between his own disaggregated body, things, and the urban landscape, projecting his physical self onto the surrounding world.[9] He plays the flute with his own backbone in his famous 1915 poem, "Backbone Flute" (*Fleita-pozvonochnik*). Kvitko also uses his body as a sounding board, and describes his internal organs as separate beings, as I show.

Kvitko taught himself to read and began writing poetry at the age of twelve (he participated in a handwritten journal in his native shtetl). He made his way to Kyiv, where he became acquainted with other Yiddish writers. Bergelson learned about him, encouraged him to write, and even arranged lessons for him and included Kvitko's poetry in his journal *Eygns* (Our own) in 1920; the journal was published under the Kultur-Lige imprint. Bergelson included Kvitko in a select list of younger poets who collectively rejected the aesthetic norms of the past and embraced the chaos of "the present upheaval."[10]

Kvitko worked as a book distributor for the Kyiv Kultur-Lige, the organization created in 1918 to build Jewish culture. He and Kadya Molodowsky worked in the same children's home. Bergelson also arranged for Kvitko's departure from Ukraine to Berlin in 1921; Kvitko joined the general exodus of Yiddish writers from the Soviet Union. In 1923, he worked at the Hamburg harbor unloading animal hides from South America, as he recounts in his novel, *Riogrander fel* (Riogrande hides). Having joined the German communist party and worried that the Germans would arrest him as a communist, Kvitko returned to the Soviet Union in 1925. He became the managing editor of the Kharkiv Yiddish literary journal *Di royte velt* (The red world).[11] His scathing attacks on a leading member of the Yiddish literary establishment, Moyshe Litvakov, the editor of *Der emes*, led to his dismissal from this post. He began working at a tractor factory, wrote a novel about it and increasingly turned to literature for children. His reincarnation as a writer for children made his redemption as a Soviet author possible. His earlier persona as a child shows, however, that there was continuity even in this change.

In all his autobiographical statements, published and unpublished, Kvitko stressed the precariousness of his existence: "Not spending your days where you spend your nights. Inside—dread (*umru*), and outside—dreadful clouds, hard rains."[12] Unlike his wealthy patron Bergelson, whom he resented, Kvitko emphasized that his was the school of hard knocks. The "rod of cut-off ox penises, the rod of ice-cold days and lonely nights in the absolutely strange, dead-drunk city of Nikolaev, or hungry philosophical Kherson" taught him well.[13] Kvitko worked for a time as an apprentice to a man who neutered oxen. Aside from the physical suffering, a constant state of anxiety and fearfulness come across vividly in this brief autobiographical statement. Homelessness, wandering, hunger, cold, exposure, and threats to his safety are the leitmotifs of his early years.

The ever-present possibility of death looms large, the "thin, thin edge" between life and death, as Kvitko says in one of his poems. In *Two Friends: Lyam and Petrik*, Kvitko describes himself as a boy carrying the skins of freshly slaughtered cows from the slaughterhouse to the tannery where he worked. The heavy skins draped over his back drag his body down to the earth, and he is covered in the blood that still drips from them.[14] At night, he dreams that all the animals whose skins he has hung on the tannery racks come back to life and escape, and he with them.

Abandonment in terms of both the hefker concept and Agamben's political theory has to do with vulnerability.[15] To be abandoned is to be thrust onto the border between social, communal life and its rights and recognition, on the one side, and on the other, the realm of mere life, fleshly existence. Kvitko's grotesque self-portrait of his childhood self, covered in the skins of just-killed animals, reveals this boundary. The loss of a sense of bodily and psychic integrity that Bergelson identified as a key characteristic of the new poetry was no mere artistic device for Kvitko; he represents it as part of his lived experience. This episode reveals the ways in which abandonment, neglect, and disavowal take place in daily life, not as part of the exceptional circumstances of mass public violence. Abandonment is the loss of the ability to make the claim, you can't do this to me, I'm the same as you, a member of this community, a child dependent on your care. As objectionable as Kvitko's neglect was, however, Kvitko the artist transforms the child's proximity to slaughtered cattle into a pathway for escape and fantastical freedom. The intimate link between humans and other animals will be a central motif in his pogrom poetry.

Abandoned by the World

In his debut volume *Steps*, Kvitko carries "a great deaf anxiety" in his heart ("Angst"). In "Silence" ("A shvaygns"), he dances with his partner, silence, hearing its rhythms as no one else does. In the poem "Too Late" ("Farshpetikt"), an abandoned room is filled with the traces of violence. A pair of women's shoes suggests a story:

> Two shoes are on the carpet
> One lies sprawled, its tip girlishly tilted up
> The shoe flap stretched open.
> The second shoe caresses it.
> The high heels flash and blaze and blaze.
> The second stands upright, dumb with anger.[16]

The episode of violence indicated by the shoes is embedded in a broader history: the carpet woven from "the many stories of many people's sorrows." Ordinary domestic objects bear witness to events that are otherwise ignored. Kvitko will return to this device with even greater intensity in his pogrom poetry. Kvitko's "first steps" and his pogrom volume share the atmospherics and mood created by vulnerability, exposure, and isolation.

Attunement and mood indicate the way subjects find themselves in the world, as a precondition to experience, and not only in response to a stimulus. The focus on the internal emotional state was a new point of departure for Yiddish poetry of this time, as I discussed previously regarding the New York Introspectivists. Kvitko's poetic attention to his own mood is important both in his debut volume and in his pogrom cycle as well. Focus on one's own emotional state need not indicate isolation. Literary scholar Eric Santner explains, "Mood in general is a sort of *virtual archive* in which are inscribed the traces of an originary—and at some level traumatic—opening or attunement to otherness" without deliberately setting about to do so.[17] What "we are delivered over" to demands attention from us.[18] Kvitko was "delivered over" to abandonment; it speaks to him, and he answers. It is the source of the restlessness and disquiet that dog his every move. Abandonment is his point of departure, shaping his characteristic form of attunement, the way he listens to the world, dancing to its silence. The steps of the dance are his poetry. Receptivity to the abandonment that is the heart of the world allows for the emergence of a unique poetic voice, and form of knowledge, more sensory than visual, more intuitive than cognitive.

In an essay first published in the New York journal *Di tsukunft* (*The Future*) in 1922, the critic Shmuel Charney heralded Kvitko's debut volume for its innovative language and deliberate incoherence. That which was dark, chaotic, and mute in Kvitko's poetry reflected in an utterly new way the chaos of Kvitko's historical reality. He went so far as to pun on the Yiddish word for "chaos" and Kvitko's name.[19] Other critics of the time focused on the embodied, corporeal qualities of the poetry. In his handbook on poetry, David Hofshteyn used Kvitko's poetry as an example of "tactile" imagery, and Dobrushin remarked on his "strangely developed sense of touch." Kvitko felt his way toward his physiological images.[20] There is a parallel between his use of the haptic and its expression in Russian avant-garde work.[21]

Reading Kvitko gave his contemporary Peretz Markish the overpowering impression of abandonment in the classical rabbinic sense of hefker. In "Masks" ("Maskes"), published in 1921, Markish created a prose poem about Kvitko that reaches its climax in the following miniature narrative: "Someone took Kvitko, a child, on a ship, and sailed with him to the heart of the sea, threw him onto its foamy bosom, and said: 'Go wherever you want.'"[22] The sea and its contents define the quintessential unclaimed, hefker space. In Jewish law and in Molodowsky's "Chako," as I have shown, to be left at sea is the distillation of the experience of abandonment. The key to Kvitko's poetic persona, according to Markish, is precisely this intensified sense of having been utterly discarded without hope of recovery.

The opening poem of *Steps*, "Memory" ("Gedekhnish"), expresses the poet's primordial condition of abandonment:

You go to meet the day that curses you
like a yoke around your neck,
your bare neck.
You carry your head exposed to the desolate rain,
The baking sun.

Pain!
The one for whose sake
you were destined to be abandoned,
[Der, far vemen bist farshprokhn
zayn af hefker]
the one for whom you pray,
you, naked child, with other children,
he himself is blind.
He is blind.

And I?
In welter and waste,
like my countless ancestors
That's how my memory will pass.
And if from this slinking time
Should mornings blossoming with dew arise
For people and beasts—
Tell them I'm gone
Off to welter and waste.[23]

The last stanza in Yiddish:
Un ikh?...
...in toyhu-vavoyhu
vi mayne ontsolike oves,
vet mayn gedekhnish fargeyn azoy.
Un oyb fun der shlaykhnder tsayt
veln oyfgeyn bliende morgns mit toy
far bashefenish un layt—
zoln zey visn, az ikh bin avek
in toyhu-vavoyhu.[24]

The first stanza describes a habitual, everyday life of exposure to the elements, rain, cold, and the baking sun; the day itself is hostile. The tactile language compels readers to feel the sensations of hot, cold, and wet. The address to the informal second person "you" (*du*) suggests that this misery is a repeated and common experience; by saying "you" he suggests that this is what happens to everybody. The second stanza, with its cry of pain, offers a history of the present suffering. A new figure is introduced, "the one, that one" (*der*), the mysterious figure who sealed the fate of the poet. At some time in the past, the child was sacrificed to this unknown but powerful figure, given over to neglect (*af hefker*) for his sake. Here is the attunement to otherness, the paradoxically relational quality of hefker abandonment, discussed earlier. I am alone because of you. The sound associations between *hefker*, *blinder* (blind), and *kinder* (children) amplify the sense of vulnerability and dependence. The "you" of the first stanza is identified as a naked child in the company of other naked children. To be abandoned and neglected is to be like a blind child. The suffering caused by neglect and abandonment is not the result of a moment in history or the conditions of sovereign power exercised by a state. The hefker condition is already part of the poet's world even before he was born. It is something he inherits, displacing and fragmenting who he is.

The early loss of the poet's father may offer some explanation. Kvitko's father frequently disappeared from home, dying of tuberculosis when Kvitko was a young child. Kvitko was neglected by his father even before his father's death. Another Yiddish expression for the phrase "to be abandoned" (*lozn af hefker*) is to be left to God's will (*af Gots barot*). The description of the weakness and fragility of the father figure suggests that Kvitko has in mind a particular notion of God. The addressee of the poem was sacrificed—"fated to be abandoned"—for his sake, and yet this figure is also vulnerable and exposed, "blind," like the children.

The third and final stanza of "Memory" invokes the condition of the universe before creation: "welter and waste." The stanza opens and closes with this phrase. "Toyhu-vavoyhu," a term originating in the Hebrew Bible, refers to the primordial chaos and void that precedes the creation of the earth in Genesis. In Yiddish, it also signifies varying degrees of disorder, anarchy, unrest, including pogroms, and thus the phrase overlaps with hefker, the boundary between law and lawlessness, the Mobius strip on which law and lawlessness line each other. In Kvitko's poem "Memory," "formlessness and void," or, "welter and waste," can be understood both as the primordial condition before creation and as the condition of the world after the fall and, especially, in its present abandoned state. It is a continuity and not a unique occurrence, as in Hofshteyn's description of war and pogroms. Whether abandoned by his father, God the father, other human beings, or the chaos of revolutionary Russia and Ukraine, Kvitko finds himself in a condition of abandonment that corresponds to the experience of welter and waste, chaos, the indeterminate state. While "welter and waste" logically precedes the creation of the world, in this poem as in others, it is always adjacent to the created world; the poet slips off to this other realm in the present unredeemed time. Should redemption come, Kvitko would reject it. The poem creates a relationship between the pronouns that begin each stanza: *you*, *that one*, and *I*. There is a love triangle at work here, and in the last stanza, the poet breaks it off.

In 1919, the same year that Kvitko published *Steps*, he also published his great ode to the Russian Revolution, "In a Red Storm" ("In roytn shturem") in the Kyiv literary journal *Dawn* (*Baginen*).[25] Celebrated as the first revolutionary poem to appear in Yiddish literature, the work bears the imprint of both Alexander Blok's *The Twelve*, with its march rhythms and street language, and the Ukrainian Pavlo Tychyna's *Instead of Octaves and Sonnets*, in which the violence and fury of the revolution replaces poetry.[26] Blok has twelve sections in his work, Tychyna twelve, and Kvtiko thirteen. Both Kvitko's and Tychyna's poems begin with an address to the speaker's mother; both conjure the image of a world grown "moldy." Unlike the isolation and darkness of *Steps*, in this work, Kvitko leaves his room and joins the youthful army of revolutionaries, implacably opposed to the old world. Unlike "Memory," in which the poet turns his back on new beginnings, in this work, Kvitko embraces the political "morning" of the new revolutionary era, full of sorrow and joy. He steels himself against the desperate calls of the older generation; he torments himself, using his characteristically visceral imagery: he "roasts his rage on his flesh." The line "the thousands of transformations I live," especially, the use of the Hebrew-origin term *gilgulim*, reincarnations, a process that takes place after death, absorb the triumph of 1917, pointing to the uncertainty of the revolution and the toll it exacts from even its staunchest proponents.

The keyword hefker indicates both Kvitko's inner experience and the cataclysmic political events of the time:

> A fearsome world
> with glazed eyes
> stubbornly lurks
> lies in wait against us

lies wildly against us
like a wild beast outstretched.

ligt a shrekendiker droysn
mit fargleyzte oygn:
ligt hartnekik kegn unz
ligt af hefker kegn unz
vi a khaye oysgetsoygn.[27]

The surrounding environment is implacably hostile. The quality of abandonment, hefker, translated above as "wildly," is richer than I can convey. The revolutionary struggle unfolds in a space of untrammeled violence. The world, unbound from any restraint, waits, like a wild animal, supine, yet tensed. The community that the poet joins, the "we" of "In a Red Storm," becomes more and more tentative, ultimately fading entirely. The last line of the long narrative poem (not quoted) consists of a single word, "we" (*mir*), framed by ellipses, underscoring the fragility of the new community created by the revolution.

Uman, 1919, and *1919*

In Uman in 1919 there was no community. The city, located 130 miles south of Kyiv, had approximately sixty-five thousand inhabitants, out of whom thirty-five to forty thousand were Jews.[28] The Ukrainian Directory held power in Uman until a brief period in March 1919, when Soviet forces took over, left, and then regained power, imposing harsh taxation and requisitions on local inhabitants. The Extraordinary Committee arrested and shot a popular Ukrainian Left Socialist revolutionary, S. Shtogrin, which incited the local peasantry against Bolshevik rule and against Jews, thought to be Bolsheviks. Various insurgent groups, under the leadership of Makar Klimenko, succeeded in driving the Soviets out. Power changed hands many times in Uman and the Uman region in 1919. Atamans from the Ukrainian National Army, and those opposed to it, including Nikol'skii, Zelenyi, Tiutiunnik, and the anarchist Makhno, all briefly held the reins.[29] As Kvitko put it, "Why cry out, that I still don't know / Who commands the city today?"[30] Individual lower-level leaders switched allegiances several times, which also meant joining and then abandoning the Volunteer Army. There were at least three pogroms in Uman. During the May pogrom, the Jewish population was subject to humiliation, extortion, robbery, the destruction of property, torture, rape, and murder. Jews were compelled to strip naked and dance before being shot. The subsequent Soviet reconquest of Uman was also accompanied by the robbery and murder of Jews. The May pogrom had approximately 160 victims. Christians offered their Jewish neighbors protection by lending them icons to display, but local non-Jewish inhabitants also participated in anti-Jewish violence. Reports from the time state that the "entire population of Uman" was at the mercy of armed military units.[31]

In the preface to his poem cycle *1919*, published in Berlin in 1923, Kvitko expressed his concern that because the work came out in "pogrom season," it could be wrongly interpreted:

> It would be a mistake and would cause pain if my book—moments on the thin, thin edge between living and dying—if the book were understood as poetry, verse about pogroms.
>
> Just as the horrible fear that children experience is delicate, concrete, and pure, so was the pain, cowardice, sunshine, and bloodshed of 1919—
>
> The moments too were physically real.
>
> As the air of grief and love in the rays of sun above were different for us there, infinitely different—so too were home, wives, children, common sense, and the will of 1919.
>
> So too were the moments different.[32]

Kvitko's concern about the reception of his book reflects his desire to distinguish it from other works published in "pogrom season" and to mark his difference from Bialik's prophetic national voice and Peretz Markish's expressionist *Di kupe*. What makes the work distinct is the focus on the poet's own emotional and physical experience of surviving violence. Kvitko's contemporary critics recognized the difference between his pogrom cycle and other work that came out in the same period. Kvtiko had avoided memorializing and documenting, because he wrote about his own experience not with dates and names but through the sensations of his body.[33] For the Yiddish essayist and political activist Nokhem Shtif, writing for the New York *Tsukunft* (*The Future*), the importance of Leyb Kvitko's pogrom book *1919* went beyond poetry. It was a new vision of the Jewish people. According to Shtif, Kvitko had overturned the traditional Jewish poetic motifs of lament and penitential prayers. He proclaimed the importance of his own "young and blossoming life," and he wanted to live his life free from the burden of national enmity.[34]

The desire to live is paramount, and I return to this poetic and biographical trait in subsequent chapters. Shtif was familiar with the raw material out of which Kvitko had created his poems, having produced his own work on the pogroms in Ukraine based on testimony and reports compiled by Jewish relief agencies. Readers could decide for themselves what to make of Kvtiko's physiological approach; his visceral, bloody pogrom poem "Mayne oygn" ("My Eyes") was published in the New York journal in 1922.

The title of Kvitko's poem cycle is significant because it draws attention to the specific qualities of a moment in time, 1919. Kvitko reiterates several times that he was in Uman in 1919. The preface articulates an important statement about the relation of poetry to violence. The prospect of violent death disaggregated the flow of time, leaving in its place the accumulation of "moments" (*reges*). These moments had a substance, weight, and feel different from all others. Kvitko re-creates these moments for his readers in the form of poems. Their harshness, hissing, rustling sound patterns, discontinuous rhythms, and startling imagery produce effects and emotions in the reader that resemble the disorientation of violence.

For both Kvitko and other poets, the experience of being abandoned to violence becomes the poetry of abandonment and, thus, hefker in multiple senses of the term: hefker poetry for a hefker world. The theme of attunement, listening to the condition you find yourself in, central to Kvitko's first volume, is important here as well. The poem cycle *1919* takes the same emotions and tropes from the intensely personal realm of *Trit* and expands their meaning to the Jewish community. Describing his poetry in a 1922 letter Kvitko said that it reflected his own unfinished state, his lack of refinement, his "unhealed wounds," his bitterness, and "disquiet" (*umru*).[35] His sense of his own personal abandonment and the pain of the Jewish people's abandonment reflect and intensify one other. Kvitko's outer world and his inner world were parallel. The term hefker thus describes the all-encompassing psychical, physiological, and kinesthetic experience of the year 1919 and the book of poetry titled *1919*. In no other poet but Kvitko is the dreadful synchrony so perfect.

Loss of Common Sense

Attending to the phenomena of experience as brute facts without historicizing, narrativizing, or providing any other framework of meaning was part of the new aesthetic of the time and the new shattered reality of the time. Violence in Kvitko's poetry and his world means the imposition of a certain kind of experience, shrinking or expanding time and space, drastically changing interactions with others, and undermining the ability to make sense of the world.[36] Severe illness provides a parallel. Irina Sandomirskaia discusses the case of a meningitis patient who lost her sight and hearing and later wrote about the "self-defamiliarization" it caused, the transformation of the ordinary world into a terrifying monstrosity that required a new form of attentiveness, a "phenomenological suspension of judgment" in order to develop an alternative way of interacting with the objects around her and thus minimize the danger they presented, namely, by touch.[37] Kvitko also resorts to touch, as his critics remarked. In the pogrom cycle, Kvitko charts how mass public violence distorts the continuities of daily life, the feel of home, the organization of time and space, and the expectations of what the next moment will bring. His preface about the different quality of discrete moments and the changed nature of common sense reveals something akin to a phenomenological approach to the strange new world of violence. The poets of his time left behind preexisting categories, images, and forms of expression to defamiliarize the encounter with everyday reality. Poets and indeed, anyone who faces catastrophic illness and violence have no choice. Something and someone outside their control restructures reality for them, deforming the basic categories of their experience.[38]

Kvitko's poem "How Many Hours in a Day?" ("Vifl shoen in a tog?") describes fear as the disruption of time:

> How many hours in a day?
> Minutes in an hour?
> The moment flashes by
> A carriage of fear. I am the driver.
>
> Quicker—faster—swifter—rip,
> I chase terror, it chases me,
> Thousands of fears, thousands of me.
> Moments burst, shatter to pieces.
> I am stuck on one.
> Stuck.[39]

Fischel Schneersohn, a psychologist who worked with child pogrom survivors, noted that for adults, the anticipation of violence was in some ways worse than its onset, and that waiting for a pogrom's eruption caused some people to lose their reason.[40] In these opening stanzas of Kvitko's poem, readers gain some awareness of that experience. Time loses its sequential ordering as each moment splinters into manifold fears. The distinction between active and passive roles is lost, as are the boundaries that demarcate the individuality of the poet, who divides and multiplies. Nonsense syllables replace everyday speech, and the rational question with which the poem begins ("how many hours in a day?"), and indeed all the interrogative pronouns listed in the poem—how many, where, and what—fail to order experience.

The mass violence in Uman in 1919 shattered ordinary assumptions about the continuity of any single human life. In "From not being to not being" ("Fun nit-zayn tsu nit-zayn"), Kvitko states explicitly that human life is nothing more than the momentary flicker between two oceans of nonexistence. The consequence is the loss of the ability to make simple, basic distinctions: "what is hard and what is soft / where a person and where his smell," as the poet writes in "How many hours in a day?"

"Look, I'm blinking" ("Kuk, ikh pintl mit di oygn") inverts the commonplace that "seeing is believing." The poet asserts that his blinking eyes are proof that he is alive:

"Look, I'm blinking, see?"
My neighbor says I'm dead,
They murdered me, he says.
Should I believe a Christian?
They set lizards against me—with green, horned eyes.
I tore the quilts from the bed at night
Measured them a hundred times
A hundred times sealed off the windows and doors.

I wrapped my head tightly in towels.
I spent the whole night listening.
The lizards scrabbled
Outside along the walls
With their green piercing eyes.

My neighbor scares me so, saying I'm dead,
They murdered me.
Should I believe a Christian?
"Look, I'm blinking, see?"[41]

Kuk, ikh pintl mit di oygn—a?—
mayn shokhn zogt, az ikh bin toyt,
az m'hot mikh derharget—
zol ikh gloybn im—a krist?—
Shrotsim mit grine oygn-shtekher reytst men on af mir.
Kh'hob baynakht fun betgevant
ale tsikhn opgetsoygn,
hundert mol gemostn zey,
hundert mol farshtopt di fenster, tir.

Kh'hob shtark mit hantikher farprest mayn kop.
D'gantse nakht zikh ayngehert.—
... hobn shrotsim gesharevet
in droysn bay di vent—
mit grine shtekher-oygn—shrotsim.

Shrekt azoy mayn shokhn mikh, az ikh bin toyt,
az m'hot mikh derharget.—
zol ikh gloybn im—a krist?—
Kuk, ikh pintl mit di oygn—a?

The poem opens in a prosaic narrative style, using reported speech and interjections. The speaker is perhaps the victim of mistaken identity; his neighbor says he's been murdered, and the poet has trouble convincing him otherwise. Blinking his eyes doesn't do the trick. The Yiddish words for "believe" (*gloybn*) and "eyes" (*oygn*) rhyme. Belief that comes from the evidence of the eyes is subject to doubt. The distortion of ordinary, everyday logic and common sense (the reference to *seykhl* in the preface) extends in two directions: the neighbor sees the poet blinking and doesn't believe that he, the poet, is alive; the poet, in turn, wonders whether he should believe the neighbor's report that he, the poet, is dead. How can this be? Surely the poet knows he's alive, and surely, the neighbor can see the poet blinking. Later the poet addresses his readers, asking whether he should believe his neighbor. Readers are thus invited into the alternative universe in which common sense no longer has value. In this realm the clear distinction between life and death is gone. This is the new common sense created by mass violence.

The fourth line shifts from realistic narrative to fantasy and the grotesque: the poet recounts the night when his house was besieged by lizards with green eyes. This is the longest line in the poem, the syllables multiply, as do the lizards: "Shrotsim mit grine oygn-shtekher reytst men on af mir/ They set lizards against me—with green, horned eyes." The word he uses, *shrotsim* (singular, *sherets*) occurs in Leviticus, in the category of animals that may not be eaten: "All winged swarming things that go upon all fours are a detestable thing unto you" (Leviticus 11:20). What's forbidden in Leviticus becomes fashionable in Weimar Berlin, where Kvitko wrote this poem. His friend David Bergelson's Kafka-inspired story about a hunger artist is set in a restaurant decorated with green plastic crocodiles. While Heinrich Heine uses a pleasant image of lizards sunning themselves in *The City of Lucca*, the closest source for Kvitko's lizards may be Poe, who described lizards on the walls in his poem "Coliseum." Where emperors used to step now glides "lit by the wan light of the hornéd moon, / The swift and silent lizard of the stones!"[42] In Kvitko's poem, the neighbor turned murderer, the lizard-human is a creature of the pogrom.[43]

There is a striking parallel between the image of the poet's house, sealed with quilts in the first stanza and the image of the poet's head wrapped tightly in towels, in the second.[44] The physical strain multiplies across the poet's senses: the strain of listening hard all night long, the physical pressure against the poet's temples, and the physical pressure against windows of his house. The structure of the line suggests this sense of pressure, of being locked in. It opens and closes with similar sounds: "Kh'ob shtark mit hantikher farprest mayn kop" ("I squeezed my head hard with hand towels"). The words *kh'ob* and *kop* open and close the line and echo each other, pressing together what falls between them.

Listening to Violence

Kvitko announces the all-important act of listening to violence early in the 1919 cycle. "Midnight's Heavy Yoke" ("Halb nakht zitst a shverer yokh"), a seemingly straightforward narrative poem, tells the story of a family's unsuccessful flight from an attack, including snippets of conversation about where to hide and what paths to take. The turn comes in the penultimate stanza. A child witnesses the death of his father, tries to wake him, kisses him, and then does something unexpected. The child "lays his ear on his father's bloody wound," and listens.[45] The poem departs from its realistic narration to place poetry and the poetic act center stage. The child listening is Kvitko listening. Blok had also placed his ear to the ground in his poem of 1907, "I Put My Ear to the Ground" ("Ia ukho prilozhil k zemle"). He heard the gloomy rumblings of new forces.[46] Hofshteyn, as I show in chapter 2, listens by contracting and quieting his own voice. Kvitko, in contrast, combines touch, sight, and sound in all-embracing synesthesia of violence, picturing the act of listening as a fleshy, bloody act.

In May 1919, Betty Kvitko was pregnant. She recounts in her memoirs that even though she was shot at on the street, her husband was more nervous and fearful about the pogroms than she was.[47] In addition to their own immediate survival, uncertainty about the long-term effect of the violence on the unborn child tormented her husband. The experience of the pregnant woman might leave its traces on the next generation. In "I Don't Want to Complain" ("Vilt zikh nit klogn"), Kvitko expresses his anxiety that the baby would become a fearful, disconsolate child. After the birth, the couple feared that the sound of the newborn's cries would attract the attention of pogromists, and they muffled the noise with pillows, creating new risks for the infant.[48] One mother, according to a pogrom report written shortly after the violence, suffocated her baby in this way. Kvitko and Betty's daughter was born in 1920, without complications.

For those hiding in Uman in May 1919, making noise could be dangerous. The sounds that could be heard on the street during episodes of mass violence drew the attention of Jewish investigators. Although the most typical first sign of a pogrom was the sound of glass shattering—as the poet Molodowsky, among others, attests—in Uman, there were other sounds.[49] According to the testimony of survivors, in addition to the noise of shooting, the bells of the city's churches rang "all day."[50] Whether they rang to announce, muffle, or celebrate what was happening on the streets was not specified. In the *1919* cycle the ringing bells, a familiar sound, occasions dread. Kvitko interprets it as the sound of triumph. The poet doesn't know why, as he puts it, the "church bells rejoice."[51] Sound is one of the expressive poetic devices that Kvitko uses in a radically new way in the poem cycle *1919*.

I have already noted the importance listening as a strategy of survival in the context of pogrom violence and the new prominence of sound in Yiddish modernist and Russian avant-garde poetry of the time. To approach Kvitko's aural archive requires a fuller discussion. A sound pattern works as a signifier only in the network of meaning and sound that a particular poem or set of poems establish. Readers sense the significance of sound not only in the case of onomatopoeia but also when sounds express emotion and, furthermore, when sound expresses the overall mood, atmosphere, or "shtimung" of the poem as a whole.[52] Poe's "The Raven," as Harshav puts it, "activates the onomatopoeia in 'rustling' in the line 'And the silken, sad, uncertain rustling of each purple curtain.'"[53] Critics in Kvitko's time compared him to Poe, and Oyslender remarked that Kvitko's expression of fear in the pogrom cycle made him closer to Poe than Bialik, suggesting that Kvitko's poetry was more gothic than national.[54] Poe's "Raven" and other work were well known in Hebrew and Yiddish literary circles, and he was credited with creating "musicality in poetry."[55]

The "clamor-filled shell" of Kvitko's language leaps from the page.[56] "Look, I'm Blinking," discussed previously, makes a startling transition from realistic narrative to the grotesque. Sound mirroring unites the two parts, the conversation with the neighbor (*shokn*) and the night terror created by the lizards (*shrotsim*). The key *sh* sound occurs in "neighbor," SHokhn; "lizards," SHrotsim; "horned eyes," oygn-SHtekher; "scrabbled," geSHarevet; "scares," SHrekt; and "strong," SHtark. Using the same sounds in all three stanzas of the poem creates an association between "lizards," "neighbors," and fear. The rustling sound *sh* is the noise lizards would make if they were scrabbling along walls in dry underbrush. Yiddish has another term for "lizard," derived from Slavic, *yashtsherke*, which does not provide the initial consonants Kvitko clearly preferred. This aural image is the product of terror, set in motion by the pogrom. In the preface to 1919, Kvitko warned his readers that he had not written poems about pogroms but, instead, moments on the edge between life and death. The hissing sounds of fear and revulsion, the use of aural images, the epistemological confusion about who is alive and who is dead, and the rejection of common sense compel readers to enter the disorientation that violence creates, to experience a "moment" on the edge.

"Confused Sidewalks" ("Farmishte trotuarin"), the first poem of 1919, conveys the atmosphere of dread in the "shadow city," rendered in sound patterns of *ooo-aaa* (as in the title word for street, "trotuar") and the consonant cluster *sh*. Sound has material, bodily force in the world the poem describes, in contrast to its dying inhabitants, compared to "green teeth in a watery saw" and "rustling reeds." Day and night are inverted: the city's youth "glow in the dark" and "are extinguished by day." The sound imagery of the poem tells the story of the community's death, their return to an inanimate condition, stated in the final couplet: "We are shrinking, / Disappearing" (Mir vaksn tsurik, / Mir geyen eyn).

The fourth stanza raises a question about the pain inflicted by sound:

> Does rustling bite?
> Are a chat and a wink
> Forboding? Painfully wounding?
>
> Zaynen take shorkhn eserig?
> Un di shmuesn un di vunken
> Take khoshedik? Take vundik vey?[57]

The poet develops the association between the sh of the Yiddish word for "rustling" (*shorkhn*) and pain (*vey*) by using them together in nearly every line. The *sh* sound appears in the title word *farmishte* (confused) and every stanza; it is especially significant in phrases thematically linked to the destruction and loss of life, including: "vi liskelakh fun otsheret" ("like the husks of reeds"), "shotn-shtot" ("shadow city"), "meshuge-meturef" (used to refer to mad dogs), "sharfn" (here, "blades of grass that wither"), and "lesht oys" ("extinguish"). The final stanza reunites the *ooo-aaa* of the gloomy evening and the terrorized streets, the *sh* sound of fear, and the *ey* sound of pain in the word *disappearing* (*geyen eyn*).

The penultimate stanza reunites the *sh* and the *ey* sound of pain:

> Mouths grimacing in fear
> Curse—
> Hurling abuse in stony fragments
> Pieces of gall
> Onto the streets and intersections
> Of the waiting city.
> Meyler, fun shrek farkrimter,
> Sheltn zikh—
> Varfn shtiker shteynerdige kloles,
> Shtiker gal
> Af gas, af rog,
> Af vartndiker shtot.[58]

The poet transforms sound into particulate matter, something that resembles stones. Thus, uttering curses is like throwing stones that land everywhere on what Kvitko, in another poem in the *1919* cycle calls the "naked flesh" of the city ("dos nakete layb"). The g sound of *gall* reappears in the words for street and intersection (*gas, rog*) creating an aural and visual image corresponding to the meaning of the lines. The stony curses cause the city pain (the *ey* sound of *stony*).[59] The entire poem resonates with sound that painfully wounds.

Kvitko transforms the sound of pain into sound pain, the infliction of pain by means of sound in another poem from the *1919* cycle, "Death, That Panhandler." The first stanza, translated for meaning, reads:

> Death, that panhandler,
> Is poking around again,
> Out in the open.
> It's right here, meting out murder,
> With brass cymbals, curses,
> And the beat of the drum.[60]

The march rhythm sustains the sound play, suggesting an army of death. As in "Confused Sidewalks" the cluster *sh*—the rustling sound that can wound—takes center stage, appearing in *shnoret* (begging), *mise-meshune* (violent death), and *meshene* (copper); the Hebrew-origin term for violent, terrible death, *mise-meshune*, replacing the more standard Germanic word for death, *toyt*. The opening lines of the poem read:

> Zi shnoret shoyn vider,
> Di mise-meshune (She's come begging again / Violent-death).[61]

Using the alternative, marked phrase *mise-meshune* accomplishes several things at once. The term takes up the entire six-syllable line, invading the space of the poem. Picturing death as an aggressive beggar also calls to mind the exorbitant demands for money and goods that were the typical opening salvos of pogrom violence. The aural pattern *mise-meshune* creates with its rustling *s* and *sh* sounds carries through the entire poem. A translation aimed at imitating the sounds of these verses reads:

> She shoves in for coins sweeter,
> The Medea-machine
> In open tracts
> Oh comes she whining for coins
> With machines tapping
> Calling, crawling with pikes.

Medea famously killed her children, chopped them up, cooked them, and served them to their father. The bizarre images I have used in this rendering are consistent with Kvitko's embrace of grotesquerie: in other works in the cycle, snakes appear from children's eyes, and the dead return from their graves to besiege the poet. Grotesque death was a fact of pogrom violence.

Kvitko draws attention to his own poetic device of wounding sound by addressing the children in the house threatened by the figure of marauding death:

> Didn't I say:
> "Children, play,
> Don't listen?"
>
> Only now, aquiver,
> They pull away
> Their tender ears,
> Pierced through and bloodied,
> Inflamed by the embers.
>
> Didn't I say:
> "Children, don't listen,
> I know what the drumbeats mean?"[62]

As a poet in 1919 Uman, Kvitko has foreknowledge of the realm of sound pain; he hears what others cannot hear and knows the meaning of what he hears. The poet realizes his trope of aural violence in the image of sound that stabs and burns the children's delicate ears.

In the poem "Biz toyb tsu vern" ("Until I'm Deaf"), the poet says that he's expanded his hearing to the point of deafness and sharpened his sight until blindness, weighing and measuring every rustle and squeal. These two words in Yiddish as in English are onomatopoetic: rustle/*shorkh* and "squeak" or "peep"/*pips*. Sound normally has no weight, but Kvitko gives it fleshy palpability by weighing and measuring it. The relevant stanzas are:

> I measured every rustle,
> weighed every squeak,
> absorbed them whole
> into my wounded heart
> my burning flesh.
> opgemostn yedn shorkh,

opgevoygn yedn pips,
un zey opgeben gants
tsu mayn vundig-vey gemit
tsu may brenendign layb.⁶³

The words for weighing, measuring, and giving are related acoustically; they have the same first two syllables (*opgemostn, opgevoygn, opgeben*). In David Hofshteyn's debut volume, weighing and measuring impede the poet's encounter with the phenomena of nature. Here, in contrast, weighing and measuring are a way of attending more closely to the phenomena of violence. Taking the sounds into himself and giving himself over to them bring together active and passive processes. Kvitko takes the sounds into his own pain, his "vundig-vey gemit" ("painfully wounded spirit"), or even mien or face (*gemit* primarily means "mood") and into his inflamed body, to keep and shelter them. In his poem of the revolution, Kvitko's own troubles were the vehicle by which he tormented his body; in this poem, in contrast, in a maternal, relational image, he welcomes others' suffering into his body. In this sense *1919* represents a poetically imagined bodily repository of others' pain.

Kvitko's receptivity to the abandonment that is the heart of the world allows him to articulate a sensory, emotional form of knowledge. In the pogrom volume *1919*, he explicitly refers to his own attunement. "Death, that panhandler" ("Zi shnoret shoyn vider") one of the opening poems of *1919*, asks rhetorically whether the poet knew in advance that:

In a minute
houses would be torn down
turned to hulking stones,
big and heavy,
homeless (af hefker)?
Vi vert es fun hayzer
in eyner a rege—
tsevalgerte shteyner,
groyse un shvere,
af hefker?—

In this poem, the term hefker, in contrast to its use in "Memory," describes not only Kvitko the child but also the entire community, abandoned to violence, and the built environment, reduced to "hulking stones."

In a letter to Shmuel Charney from 1922, Kvitko uses the language of stones to characterize his sense of time. He lives "among stone suddenlys" ("tsvishn shteynere plutsemkaytn") and doesn't know what the next moment will bring. This marvelous neologism doesn't render the stone stoney, as in Victor Shklovsky's famous dictum about the purpose of art, but rather makes the brutal, intractable, and capricious precarity of Kvitko's existence vividly present. How did he know that houses would be demolished and become nothing but stone? Rejecting the promise of redemption (in the poem "Memory"), the poet nonetheless senses what others do not. He already had experienced the wildness of living among stones. He had had a memory of the future.

The restless melancholy, isolation, and dread so palpably present in Kvitko's first volume of poetry—and indeed, in his own life experience as he represented it—made the poet supremely attuned to the multifold and far-ranging ramifications of pogrom violence. Who else but "night's bridegroom," as he called himself in *Trit*, the one who was fated to be abandoned, could write poetry that embodied in its wild, untamed (hefker) form, the inner experience of the shattering of the external world? Kvitko makes palpable the experiential consequences of the hefker condition of abandonment.

The final poem in *1919*, and the longest work in the cycle, poses a question in its title, "Forgiveness?" ("Mekhile?"). The poem is a study in transformation in imagery, rhythm, language, and emotion. It opens with the attic room, the place that promises shelter from violence. The speaker asks unspecified "loved ones" why they have brought him to this place: "why have my loved ones brought me here?" The first six stanzas, contained in the attic room, expand on the speaker's confusion as to why he has been singled out; all he is and all he has is poetry. He isn't worth the trouble of special treatment. The next eight stanzas rehearse the history of violence, describing the "hatred" that seethes in the poet as the result of the unforeseen eruption of violence in a formerly peaceful world of towns and villages. In the middle of this section, an apparition appears that commands the poet to forgive his enemies. The third section of the poem removes the poet from his familiar surroundings to a strange, cosmic configuration of time and space, "mountains, valleys and years." The trip resembles the forced journey undertaken by the speaker in Hofshteyn's pogrom lament *Sorrow*. The final and longest stanza of the poem contains a lengthy address, set off in quotations, that commands the poet to forgive. The last line of the poem reads: "Who can forgive like you?"

Sabine Koller shows how the poem "Forgiveness?" recapitulates the pogrom cycle. The use of the personal pronoun *du* (you), she points out, extends the injunction to forgive beyond the poet to the reading audience. Building on her approach, I explore a broader recapitulation, namely, the relation between Kvitko's debut volume and this work, as well as the sound play that draws the other poems in the cycle to into its conclusion. In the opening stanza, the poet is locked into the attic, but not alone, because he is accompanied:

> by emptiness and neglect
> and the opposite, the trace of footsteps.
> mit der pustkeyt, mit farloztkeyt
> un farkert dem shpur fun trit.[64]

Indeed, a dusty attic room preserves "the trace of footsteps." Someone else has been in the attic. The word *trit*, however, is also the title of Kvitko's debut volume. A broader set of possibilities emerges. The trace of *Trit* (*Steps*) corresponds to the condition of neglect and abandonment to which the poet was fated in the poem "Memory." The trace of the earlier volume could also refer to the poet's ancestors (*oves*), who made their first appearance in "Memory" and reappear in "Forgiveness?" In the earlier poem, the speaker rejects the promise of new, blossoming mornings, preferring to remain: "In welter and waste, / like my countless ancestors."[65] In this poem, in contrast, the "ancestors" no longer belong to the realm of primeval chaos. They are associated instead with order, new beginnings, and the quality of stillness. The poet refers to them collectively as a "still" or "quiet figure": "dos shtil geshtalt, / dos shtil geshalt fun mayne oves." The ancestral figure appears three times in the poem: first, in response to the poet's growing sense of hatred as he sits in the attic; second, during his journey through time and spaces, in conjunction with the biblical image of spring of water; and finally, as the narrator of a long section of the poem that describes Ukrainian history. On each occasion, it tells the poet to forgive; the poem ends with its injunction.

In "Forgiveness?" as in the pogrom cycle generally, sound assumes a palpable emotional force. English words that most closely resemble the Yiddish make the pattern more prominent. The liquid sounds of the "still gestalt" lulls and calms *sine* (the Hebrew-origin word for "hatred"). The figure implores the poet to recall that each "murderer" was once a child and is also a parent who "laughs" (*lakht*) and smiles (*shmeykhLt*) at his child. The *l* sounds extend throughout the speech, culminating in the repeated injunction to forgive, punctuated by the same *l* sound: "zay moykhL, zay moykhL" ("forgive, forgive"). At the end of the poem, readers discover why the poet is stuck in the attic room. His task is to contemplate forgiveness. Forgiveness could mitigate the loneliness and pain of abandonment. Kvitko the poet has a uniquely trained ear for the sound of violence; it turns out, however, that he also is acutely attuned to what softens its tremendous destabilizing force. Yet the ultimate poem of *1919*, for both the book of verse and the year is left without resolution. The resentment and rage that Kvitko describes in "Forgiveness?" is not so readily overcome. The ghostly figure of Kvitko's ancestors implore and command him to forgive, but he leaves the matter undecided, posing it as an unanswered question. Kvitko, unlike Hofshteyn, is not a poet of quiet tones and restrained emotion, and what resounds more loudly in *1919* than the lull of forgiveness is the stoniness of pain.

4

Enfleshment

In his Yiddish poem "A freylekhs" ("A Merry Dance"), Bialik addresses his readers with ferocious bitterness.[1] The poem, first appearing in 1913, was republished in a 1922 Berlin volume in a section titled "National Poems." It also contained a Yiddish version of "In the City of Slaughter," written in response to the Kishinev pogrom of 1903. Both poems had fresh significance for the Jewish audience in the aftermath of the Russian Civil War. In "A Merry Dance," the world has been emptied of families, social relations, and moral precepts. The emotional and material support for human life is gone. There are no fathers, mothers, relatives, or friends, just as there is no bread, meat, or fish. The divine attributes of justice, judgment, and mercy are nowhere to be found. The final stanza captures the new condition of utter abandonment with a single word: "Hefker, hefker, all is hefker, / just like our blood is hefker."[2] In the world of chaos, human life is merely life without meaning or value. The state of the world as a whole and the specific condition of the Jews reflect each other. Lives are destroyed with impunity. What replaces the ordered social community with its distinctions and boundaries is a mass body that has no choice but to dance:

> Everyone locked into
> one great firm ring
> beards and curls, shoes, and socks
> old and young
> entangled together.[3]

For the post-1945 reader, this image is eerily prescient, suggesting the accumulation of human hair and shoes dreadfully familiar from Holocaust photography. For the 1922 reader, there was also a familiar note. Marauding armies invading the Ukrainian countryside in 1919 compelled Jews to strip and dance before them in a form of ritual humiliation.[4] Bialik hints at a connection between the hefker condition—that is, abandonment as a form and consequence of violence—and the emergence of nonindividuated, entangled bodies and lives. A world without social relations, moral order, and the foodstuffs necessary to support the life of the body becomes a world of entangled, undifferentiated flesh.

Thus far, I have concentrated on the way that violence undermines the human capacity to make sense of the world. This chapter turns to another dimension of abandonment and violence. For Bialik, Kvitko, and other authors, the political and social abandonment of the Jews, their exposure to overwhelming power, leaves them exposed in another sense. The corporeal and intracorporeal dimensions of their lives and human life generally are laid bare. Images of naked, wounded flesh dominate pogrom literature. Peretz Markish's *The Heap* (*Di kupe*), published in 1922, paints a picture of a new altar to God, made of the rotting, oozing bodies of Jewish victims. The orifice of the mouth dominates the work: the multiple mouths of the heap issue ooze, and the heavens, wind, and earth lick it.[5] Instead of words, flesh; instead of nurture, death. Lamed Shapiro's pogrom stories describe human flesh that is carved and bitten into. Uri Tsvi Grinberg's poetry speaks through the wound of his mouth. Isaac Babel's *Red Cavalry* stories have been both celebrated and excoriated for their portraits of human beings as flesh. Because Kvitko's corporeal poetry is distinctive and because so little has been written about his pogrom cycle *1919*, the chapter continues the focus on this poet in dialogue with other authors. What makes Kvitko's voice distinct is that he puts himself into the world of undifferentiated flesh. His reference is always his own experience.

I use the term *enfleshment* to signify the transformation of socially recognizable human beings possessed of distinct identities into a mass body.[6] In the work discussed in this chapter, enfleshment appears as heightened sexuality and an intensified focus on bodily organs, the transformation of individuals into animalistic creatures, and the loss of a distinction between death and life. In terms of the larger theoretical argument I have been pursuing, the separation between mere biological life and ordered political life no longer holds. Kvitko's pogrom cycle shows how the entire surrounding milieu of Uman, including the streets, buildings, and the very air itself, has been transformed into physiological material. Life becomes separated from the individuals who live it. There is strangely too much and too little vitality, so that inanimate objects become animated, and the dead refuse to stay dead.[7] Yet at the same time, his poetry also reveals the possibility of an expanded, relational self even during ongoing abandonment.

The chapter begins with the image of the cityscape as flesh in Kvitko's *1919*, drawing attention to the way that hefker signifies exposure. I distinguish Kvitko's use of the theme of the undead from its more common occurrence as a feature of Gothic literature. The vulnerability of exposure (hefker abandonment) and the embrace of licentiousness (another meaning of hefker) come together in Kvitko's poem about the life of dogs, especially in comparison to a similar work by his friend and colleague Der Nister. Unlike his fellow Yiddish author Lamed Shapiro, whose hero embraces a Nietzschean will to power, Kvitko dispossesses his own body, an instance of kenotic hefker. Finally, a new image of the poet emerges, spoken by and speaking with the entire milieu of wounded bodies, things, and animals. Poetry's strange language and the emphasis on sound over sense enact this new reconfiguration of relationships.[8] The capacity of the imagination, one of the most important but least studied aspects of Elaine Scarry's *The Body in Pain*, sheds light on this new set of possibilities. The chapter includes graphic descriptions of violence, and the reader is warned.

Cityscape as Flesh

The year 1919 was a time of deprivation, requisition, and shortages of every kind of product. Historian Elias Cherikover characterizes the civil war period as one of starvation for manufactured goods.[9] What is unobtainable becomes the object of intensified interest.[10] Viktor Shklovsky's description of the first siege of Petersburg, in the period from 1919 to 1920, emphasizes the continual preoccupation with flesh. Shklovsky writes, "The hungry spoke with the hungry about hunger."[11] In the original Russian, the verb "spoke" and the adjectives and nouns having to do with hunger all start with the same sound (*golodnye, govorili, golod*). Only one sound can be heard in this phrase, the hunger sound—underscoring the phenomenon of hunger as a force separate from human beings. Hunger became an external part of the surrounding environment: "We were immersed in hunger like fish in water."

Kvitko similarly describes Uman as overwhelmed by pain; its houses and streets are suffering flesh and blood. The "air outside is bloody."[12] To be subject to violence is to be *immersed* in it, as Shklovsky writes about being immersed in hunger. An abandoned house becomes naked flesh in in Kvitko's "We Wander" ("Mir voglen"): "Now the house is abandoned [*hefker*] / Stripped bare, its skin flayed."[13] The comparison of the house to a tortured body suggests a conceptual shift in what it means to inhabit a house, a town. Physical nakedness is part of a larger vulnerability caused by the violence of abandonment: the loss of rights, the loss of the right to own property, to have an address, to dispose of one's own body. Violence exposes the life of an entire city, a geography and a social space, a set of social and economic relations, and a network of interactions between groups, individuals, and cultural spheres as nothing more than mere vulnerable flesh.

Fleshy excess manifests itself in the open, wounded body, heightened sensation, and the loss of sensation, the deadening and alienation of the body. The body part in pain is felt in ways that draw attention to its separateness from the overall smooth and hence unnoticed flow of the body as a whole. Bergelson's short story "The Hole Through Which Life Slips" ("Der lokh, durkh velkhn eyner hot farloyrn") is an example. Bergelson was in Kyiv during its rapid changes of power, bombardment, and pogroms, and the story takes place during this time. The protagonist feels a profound separation from his body, which wants to go outside, even though he doesn't, and he finally agrees, in the same way that an adult gives in to the demands of a capricious child.[14] The phenomenologist Samuel Todes describes pain in terms that are recognizable from even this brief excerpt. The unmet need or injury in a part of the body leads to its objectification and "disappears from the felt schema of my active body."[15] Enfleshment thus can take the form of separation from the body, and its responses to its own stimuli and those from the outside world. The conditions of confinement, waiting, and the environment of menace are common to cities subject to bombardment and the mob violence of pogroms.

In Kvitko's "In mayn invelt, in mayn oysvelt" ("In my inner world, in the outer world"), the poet's body loses its capacity to sense the outer world. Poetic parallelism has been made into physical suffering when a "muted deafening" and a "deaf fog" have taken hold in both the inner and outer realm. The Yiddish for "deaf fog" (*toyber nepl*) accentuates the sense of immobility and silence with sound mirroring. The poet's eyes, ears, limbs, blood, his gait, and his house are all "stuffed up." The final stanza, with its play on *deaf* and *death* in both the original Yiddish and my translation, aurally heightens the loss of feeling, the repetition of sounds reflecting the loss of a distinction between the inner and outer world:

> Deafening death strides about,
> coloring and painting everything with a deaf deadness,
> a bloody deafening
> in my inside world, in my outside world.[16]

The abstractions of death and deafness become qualities with material form that coat the surfaces of things. The neologisms *toybenish* and *toytenish* make this clearer in the Yiddish original. The deafening that makes the narrator mute in the first stanza has become "bloody" and "deadening" in the last stanza. Kvitko's poetic body, the center and source of his synesthesia, absorbs the city into itself so that it becomes full of deafening pain.

Things

In the strange world created by violence, in which there is both too much and not enough life, too few material supports to sustain flesh, and yet too much flesh, inanimate things come to life. Physiology becomes separated from distinct living organisms and spreads throughout the entire surrounding world. In spaces of confinement and fear, the relations between people and things change dramatically. In the poem "In shtub farhakter" ("In a Locked-Up House"), household possessions, thrust aside and left behind, shrink as they wait in the house. Kvitko repeatedly uses the motif of decreasing physical size to suggest death, as this and other poems show. The objects in the locked-up house are lined with shadows, the shadows of children. The "shadow children" are both the result of abandonment and the offspring, so to speak, of the objects that used to be handled by people. People in conditions of confinement and fear turn into shadows of themselves.[17]

The poem displaces the terror of abandonment from people to the objects they own. The flowerpots drag themselves across the floor, the tops of the plants drooping. Stuck in the abandoned house, the things that people used to use wait for signs of life, a glimmer of light at the window, but they stop believing that there is such a thing as sunshine. It is significant that the crisis of belief, the radical doubt, takes place in things, and not people. The crisis is a phenomenon created by violence.

By the end of the poem, human forms are conjured out of the gloom: the narrator's old sisters, spinsters, "silent and mute," who plait something, a shroud, perhaps, out of the window hangings. A single aural image unites people and things into an atmosphere thick with dread: the sound mirroring that takes place among the various elements of the poem: "moth-mouths" (*milbn-maylekhlakh*), dread (*more-shkoyredike*), and "tired old maids" (*meydlekh mid farzesene*). The use of trochees and dactyls, with their downward rhythm, extends the sense of longing and waiting. These combinations echo the starting consonant and use internal mirroring as well: *mil-/mayl-*; *moy-shkoy-*; *meyd/mid*. There is little movement or change in the locked-up house or the locked-up rhymes. The "moth-mouths" are the specks of sunlight on the dusty surfaces of buildings visible to those confined in the locked-up house. In the very last line, for the first time, the poet uses the first-person plural *we*. The uncertainty experienced by the household objects as to whether there is such a thing as sunshine permeates the entire poem, bringing the reader into its uncanny dread. Readers cannot know whether the use of *we* indicates a living human presence in the abandoned house, whether the narrator giving voice to the things and shadows left by people or whether the poet is revealing for the first time that there are indeed people hiding in the house. The last two lines build on the uncertainty by extending it into the future. "We wait / we will wait until the end." What they will finally see, what they will have waited for is left open.

The Undead

First-person testimonies, found in the archives of Jewish aid organizations, provide numerous accounts of home invasions, the transformation of a place of shelter into a space of terror. In "Guests Poking around Downstairs" ("Untn shnorn um di gest"), Kvitko adds a twist to the tale. The uninvited guests in this poem are not marauding soldiers or hostile neighbors, but instead, their reanimated dead victims. The first three stanzas describe the speaker's feelings about hiding. It's good to be concealed in the attic, because:

> Downstairs guests poke around,
> each bearing a wreath of death,
> each wreath the color of pained eyes.
> They're looking to torment me.
> I'm in the attic,
> In the wreckage.[18]

Repetition and pleonasm dominate the poem's opening. The second stanza twice repeats the phrase "It's good to hide among the rafters-crossbeams (*bantines-dronges*)," as if the long, drawn-out dactylic phrase would offer some additional shield against the invaders. The speaker's insistence that everything is fine sounds increasingly shrill. The repetition of words and phrases at the beginning of each line, far from offering reassurance, suggests instead hopeless confinement. The line affirming how good things are also concludes the poem, by which time it becomes obvious that everything the speaker has been trying to keep out is in fact already within.

The third stanza marks a turning point as the speaker recognizes his mother among the dead. Whereas before the uninvited guests were separate from the speaker, "there" (*dort*), not with him in the attic, the mother suddenly turns up "here" (*do*). The safe distance has been breached. Questions replace statements as the poet attempts to determine how she died and how she managed to return to her house. The mother and son engage in a direct conflict when she implores him to come down from the attic (stanza 5). He refuses, preferring to stay in the attic, holding on to the rafters, where "it's good."

Kvitko uses a neologism to describe the sight of the reanimated mother:

> Which murder
> Left its death-mark on my mother's face?
> Ver hot mayn mamen oysgemest dos ponim?
> Velkher toyt?[19]

The original poses uses two interrogative pronouns—*who* in the first line and *which* in the second, drawing out and repeating the same question of how the mother died. What I have translated as "left its death-mark" corresponds to the verb *oysmesn*, which Kvitko invented for this poem. Death is the active force in the poem, marking or stamping its image on the faces of its victims, who became emblems of its power.

Kvitko uses puns to reanimate parts of bodies independently from human consciousness. The son wants his mother to take her dreadful eyes away because he doesn't want to fall into their hands ("Gey, bayt zikh op mit di oygn! / Kh'vil tsu zey in hent nit!"). The mother's face has turned into a monster with eyes and hands that can take hold of him. Bialik also serves a point of departure for "Guests." "In the City of the Slaughter" includes a scene in the attic, full of the ghosts of the dead: "Multitudinous eyes will look upon thee / From the somber silence."[20] Kvitko's "Guests" responds to this passage, intensifying the emotion of dread by taking the position of a participant in the scene and introducing the dead mother's demand. Kvitko's poetry about mass public violence is always also about himself.

The mother beckons her son to "come down" to her, join her downstairs and rejoin her lower body; the play between the womb and tomb adds to the uncanny dread. The dead mother speaks without a voice from a skull wrapped in a headscarf made of reeds, and her skeletal hands reach out to the poet as if to seize him. The added detail that the mother has come from the "women's mass grave"—or, in the original, a *shvester-grub*, literally, a "sister-grave"—builds on the sense of fear. The single figure of violent death in "Death, That Panhandler" (discussed in chapter 3) has multiplied into a swarm.

The mother has returned home, bringing her "neighbors" from the grave; here, as in "Look, I'm Blinking," discussed in chapter 3, the word *neighbor* is associated with terror. Kvitko creates a sound pattern of rustling consonants that orchestrate fear: the words for "stones" (*af di SHteyner*), "women's mass grave" (*SHvester-grub*), and "female neighbors" (*SHkheynes*) all contain the *sh* sound, as in the key term of the preface *violent* or *unnatural death, mise-meSHune*. In "Guests" Kvitko introjects the breakdown of order of pogroms as the loss of differentiation between the dreadful mother's body and her child.

Kvitko's biography sheds light on the figure of the mother in the poem. Tuberculosis, which killed nearly his entire family, shaped his mother's interactions with him, as his novel *Two Friends: Lyam and Petrik* (1933) reveals. The child hero Lyam loses his older sister and brother to tuberculosis; his wandering father returns home only to die there. His mother, increasingly deaf and depressed, spends hours sitting on the floor, her head between her knees. She would beckon to Lyam, her remaining son, lift his shirt, feel his belly, and tap his ribs, searching for symptoms of the disease. These inspections created "a sense of desolate horror" (*viste shrek*) in the little boy, who would run outside to get as far away as possible.[21] The novel suggests that the only physical contact between mother and child were the tuberculosis examinations, which, from the child's perspective, consigned him to death in advance. The feeling of dread in association with the mother's touch appears consistently in both *1919* and the novel. Kvitko's family history and the universal play between womb and tomb generate layers of uncanny terror of "Guests." Violence is unpredictable, utterly strange, and, yet also, dreadfully familiar.

Some of these images and motifs, associated with the Gothic, appear in literary work written before and after 1919 and in other languages besides Yiddish. Gothic motifs are usually understood to reflect anxiety about change as well as the converse, threats to modern progress. Typically, the skeleton in the attic, the leitmotif of Gothic works, shows how historical violence has been disavowed.[22] In contrast, the work I explore is less haunted by the past and more overwhelmed by violence in the present.

Dog Life: Kvitko and Der Nister

The Hebrew and Yiddish terminology of abandonment recognizes the relation between the disavowal of a possession (declaring it *hefker*) and the disavowal of behavioral norms (*hefkeyres*). In English, as well, one can abandon property and act with abandonment, or licentiousness. Kvitko's "They're Pushing Me" ("Zey shtupn mikh") suggests that those who have been made hefker should embrace hefkeyres (shameless, licentious behavior). The image of the dog captures both meanings:

> They're pushing, shoving me here, fucking me up.
> Day and night squared off against me—
> I crawl here with my brothers and sisters,
> We've been chased here.
>
> We're not at all ashamed.
> Disgrace? Where?
> We're falling like dogs here.
> In the middle of the day.
> Like young hermits
> In deep silence

We regard
The dog day.
Like market hags
We bite and tear,
Bark and curse
And fall down—
Shame? Where?
In this dog world?[23]

Who or what drives the poet with his brothers and sisters to this spot is rich with ambiguity. The list could include: their oppressors, the pogromists, or their own emotions and drives. The repetition and dactylic meter of the opening phrases ("zey shtupn mikh, shtupn mikh, shtupn ahintsu") heighten the driving motion.

Shtupn, which occurs three times in the first line, means to push or shove as well as to have sexual intercourse with. Pursued by unnamed forces, the poet and his brothers and sisters fall to the ground and shamelessly imitate the behavior of dogs. Their "fall" is both physical and moral. In the second stanza, the use of the Hebrew-origin word for "disgrace" (*di kharpe*) is significant; the more ordinary term for being disgraced or ashamed occurs later in the poem (*shemen zikh*, to be ashamed). The term means "genitals" in the plural (*di kharpes*); in Yiddish, genitals are referred to as the most shameful place. The "disgrace" is the resemblance to dogs. In the pogrom context, the more typical reference to animals would be language about the bestial cruelty of the perpetrators. This poem in contrast emphasizes a canine transformation among victims. The exchange of qualities among perpetrators and victims, Christians and Jews, calls their differences into question.

The image of the Jew as a dog has a long history in Christian and Jewish literature and culture.[24] In the Talmud, the dog "is wild in the ways that humans are, in its appetites for meat and for sex."[25] The link between Jews and dogs in Christian sources is part of the ritual murder accusation.[26] In *The Merchant of Venice*, Shylock sarcastically affirms the dog-like position into which Antonio and the other merchants of Venice thrust him with their kicks and curses. Shylock "betters the lesson" by mocking Antonio in turn.[27] Kvitko's summons to his fellow Jews to fall to the ground resembles Shylock's gesture. Bialik's "In the City of the Slaughter" juxtaposes the image of a decapitated Jew and a dog: both have no value.[28]

The next stanza, however, imagines another kind of existence, beyond the distorted space and dog time of pogroms, in some other realm of sea, sun, and "eternity."

> Will I bring my hatred—
> of something,
> someone,
> Here, to eternity, in the sun and at the sea?—
> .... My heart is still a child!—
> It would accept a toy,
> a ray of sunshine would blind it,
> a mother's smile would heal the wound,
> How did I come by hatred [*sine*]?
> My heart is still a child.
> A child.

This stanza, about the poet's heart of a child, is located at the center of the five stanzas of "They're Pushing Me." The ellipses, the pause in the stream of utterance, slows the wild, reckless pacing of the poem's opening and departs from the chaos and anger of the previous lines. The unnamed place where the narrator was chased in the first stanza undergoes a dramatic change in this, the third stanza. "Here" refers to an alternative setting, a place of sun, sea, innocence, and eternity. The shameless nakedness of dog life fades as another persona, Kvitko the child, comes to the foreground.[29] The speaker struggles to retain something of his noncanine existence, declaring twice that he is a child, and indeed, the stanza ends dramatically with the single words a child (*a kind*). The stanza stages a reprieve from the driving force of the dog day.

In the midst of dog life, Kvitko imagines another possibility, a glimmer of hope: release from his own emotions. "They" of "they're pushing me" refers not only to his pursuers but also his own feelings. The narrator is both the dog and the dogcatchers, split between the two. His hatred and enmity would trap him, and he doesn't know whether he wants to be trapped or freed from them. The poem ends, however, with the same driving rhythm with which it began. The poet remembers his dogcatchers as his heart changes back into a ravening wild animal. The reprieve was only momentary, but it was there, nonetheless.

There are direct parallels between Der Nister's "The Dog" ("Dos hintl") and Kvitko's "They're Pushing Me." The two authors belonged to the same Kyiv circle in the years before they both left Russia for Berlin. More than one critic at the time drew a connection between the two, especially when it came to their use of folklore and the grotesque.[30] In Hamburg, Der Nister dealt with materials used in the processing of animal skins, the leitmotif of "The Dog."[31] The story was published in a volume of other "tales in verse" just a few years before Kvitko's book *1919* appeared.[32] A dog is so tormented by a flea that he bites off his own skin and sells it to another dog, who makes the skin into a drum. The skinless dog runs off, his raw flesh, with its meaty, bloody wounds exposed, and a gang of butcher dogs start licking him and then nibbling at him; they "start pushing and shoving" to get closer to the skinless dog, and finally consume him entirely.[33] Der Nister's stories rarely refer to concrete historical settings or events. He cloaked his meanings in other forms: "The horrors of wars and pogroms generated scenes of sadism and cannibalism, disguised by Der Nister as animal tales."[34] The skin is the outermost barrier protecting the animal, including the human animal, from the surrounding environment. The human being subject to violence is nothing more than naked flesh, the dog, a step lower than the human, and the dog stripped of his skin, one step more, but both are on the same continuum of enfleshment.

Lamed Shapiro's Nietzschean Alternative

The Yiddish author most famous for shocking pogrom images of wounded flesh is Lamed Shapiro (1878–1948). Shapiro's stories "White Challah," "The Kiss," and "The Cross" depict the human body in acts of intimate violence: rape, mutilation, and cannibalism. Shapiro did not witness the pogroms of 1905, the inspiration for these stories; he had already left eastern Europe with his mother, arriving in New York in 1906.[35] "The Cross" was published in New York in 1909 in Yiddish; a Russian translation appeared in the Moscow Russian Jewish journal *Evreiskii mir* (Jewish world) in 1918. Compared to David Bergelson for his mastery of atmosphere, Shapiro's stories garnered considerable critical attention and have been called a turning point in the Yiddish representation of violence.[36]

A young Jewish man, a member of a revolutionary circle, makes plans to sacrifice himself for the cause, when a pogrom erupts in his town. The pogromists invade the apartment where he lives with his mother, beat him and tie him up, and then rape his mother. Sexual violence was a significant dimension of the pogroms. Rape and the spectacle of rape were part of the campaign of terror against the Jewish population.[37] In Shapiro's story, the pogromists carve a cross into the hero's forehead, to "save his kike soul from hell."[38] He kills his mother to end her suffering and then finds the woman he is in love with, Mina, whom he rapes and kills. After committing this act of revenge, he leaves his native town for the United States. Readers learn this story from the lips of the unnamed protagonist, who tells it to his companion as they tramp around the American prairie by train.

Like Kvitko, whose poem "My Eyes" was published after "The Cross," Shapiro was responding to Bialik's "In the City of the Slaughter." Kvitko orders his eyes to fall out; similarly, as Shapiro's hero watches his mother's rape, he wishes for the same thing. Shapiro, like Kvitko, shows the human body transformed into mere flesh, but with a different emphasis.[39] Some critics have argued that Shapiro was encouraging Jews to see themselves in a new way, as people who would have to learn to wield the energy of pogromists if they were going to survive.[40] The author was experimenting with Nietzschean will to power. All of human "suffering and feeling is nothing in comparison with blind, insane, mocking power."[41] Both the pogromists and their Jewish victims are nothing more than vehicles for brute power, and the chaos and violence of the pogrom is the expression of an already existing but suppressed dimension of human existence. This interpretation helps to explain why, despite the gore and blood, "The Cross" remains surprisingly abstract, especially in comparison with Kvitko's focus on his own experience of pogrom terror. Shapiro's hero, a Jewish Nietzschean superman, embraces violence. Whereas other literary responses to the civil war pogroms call for revenge, Kvitko's poetic persona rejects the will to power, performing instead poetic acts of self-implication and self-dispossession.

Desire and Violence: Poetic Self-Implication

"Who Could Have Known?" ("Ver hot es gekont visn?") was published in the pogrom cycle *1919*. In a poem about sexual violence, readers might expect fleshy imagery resembling "My Eyes" or "They're Pushing Me." Instead, the poem takes us through a series of unrelated spaces, times, and protagonists, including heaven, hell, dining rooms, and Africa; the compressed instant of the present and the memory of the recent past; and "young toughs," Jews, a first-person speaker, a woman he knows, Gitl, her "uncle," and her child. Conversational questions, narrative description, and an extended use of reported speech create the impression of a larger world, resembling the effect of a realist novel.

The poem opens by invoking Genesis 1, "there was evening, there was morning," to establish a contrast between the time before and the sudden inception of violence:

> Who could have known
> what'd happen?
> Last night, heaven
> showed off
> with Ursa Major's violet majesty.
>
> Then a pure, clear morning rose.
> At distant wells
> The dawn's buckets, full and empty
> Clanged joyously.
> All eyes were still bare of spectacles.
> And the ladders at their places.
> Who could have known
> what'd happen?[42]

Devoid of human actors and human action, the adjectives for purity, distance, and emptiness suggest an abstract landscape. In Yiddish, the sounds of these words reflect one another (*loyter*, *vayte*, and *leydike*). But the beautiful scene is also disturbing: the eyes without glasses are separate from the people who own them, and they can't see. People without ladders can't escape from windows. The conversational, low-register refrain bookends the first two stanzas, providing a stark contrast with its biblical imagery. The menacing refrain anticipates the sudden acceleration of action in the compression of the second line ("vos'et zayn").

The third stanza describes the invasion of a home:

> In only an instant
> Everything was erased and in its place:
> In dining rooms—beds
> For the groom's side and the bride's.

And the young toughs
In heat, hurled themselves down
Brimstone smoked,
Pitch seethed red.

Nothing could be more distinct than the heavenly evening and the stillness and purity of dawn's first light and the frenzy and hellfire of the scene in the house. The attackers transform the house into hell. The assonance in the words "roykhert" and "royt" ("smoked" and "red") fill up the space with a hellish color, blotting out the majestic violet of the opening stanza. In a poem without a fixed rhyme scheme, the color change provides a counterpart in visual rhyme. The sardonic reference to the forced wedding of the "groom" and the "bride" point to rape without explicitly naming it. In the Yiddish, the word I have translated as "beds" (*gelegers*) appears twice, and it forms a weak rhyme with *rege* ("moment"). In the preface to *1919*, Kvitko says that the *reges* of the pogrom were different from all others. This is one of the differences: the instantaneous (*in eyner nor a rege*) proliferation of "beds" (gelegers). Violence suddenly replaced everything that had been in its place.

The final and longest stanza shifts significantly. A first-person speaker and new protagonists appear (a woman named Gitl), and the speaker reveals his attraction to her:

There with my relations
I soon recognize that doll, the beauty Gitl.
How often would I wait, inflamed,
For her to bring me her round breasts?
How she would cry and smile!
"Listen!"
"I'll only come with my uncle."

The pogromists are "in heat," inflamed by lust and their own power, but the poet too was often "inflamed" by Gitl's beautiful breasts. The demand he makes, while far from rape, nonetheless compels her to cry in protest and fear. The question about who could have known what would happen, the title of the poem, is not merely rhetorical. It expresses shock in response to unforeseen violence, and yet an uneasy familiarity contaminates the speaker's surprise because he used to feel overwhelming desire for Gitl. The poet places himself at the scene of sexual violence, implicating himself.

In contrast to the opening, devoid of human action, the ending of "Who Could Have Known?" is novelistic in its description of domestic spaces and ordinary events lined with menace. In response to the speaker's request that she visit him, Gitl says:

> I'll come in only with my uncle.
> My little boy is sitting on a chair,
> riding it, pretending!
> "Where are you riding, bastard?"
> Uncle asks.
> Upset, so upset,
> twisting and turning,
> "To Africa!
> They're fighting
> The black slaves and the whites!"
> We're waiting, yes, yes,
> We're waiting for them . . .
> already on our way . . .
> and turn away again,
> pained and tormented.
> He stomps his feet, stamps them
> As the chair scrapes and squeaks.[43]

Gitl's narration quotes the voices of her uncle and her child, whom the uncle frightens. The child on the chair pretends that he is going to Africa. Africa was a destination of Jewish migration in the late nineteenth and early twentieth centuries. Images of African exotica were part of Berlin visual culture in the 1920s, and Africa also appears in Grinberg's journal *Albatross*. For the Yiddish-speaking community, the events of the Boer war were well known, as were African rebellions against the colonial powers throughout the period of World War I.[44] Russian authors, including Gumilev and others, wrote both prose and poetry about Africa. Gumilev's 1921 "Lost Tram" traverses the Nile, the Neva, and the Seine; there is no food at the grocer's and instead of beets, bleeding heads are sold.[45] Kvitko is making a similar comparison between pogrom space in Ukraine and the image of Africa as a place of violence.

The poem concludes with the sound of the child playing: "And the chair scrapes and squeaks" ("Un dos benkl ripet-skripet"). These words refer to repeated action in the past, the child's playing, but also return to the present, to the rape that is taking place in dining room, on furniture turned into beds. The innocence of the childlike rhythm of the closing lines belies what its sound both masks and reveals. The chair squeaks when a child plays horsey on it, but it also squeaks when two bodies are moving on it. The noise speaks of a violence that the poem otherwise does not narrate. The poem has traveled far from the opening scene of heavenly majesty and the bell-like clanging of buckets at a distant well. The final move of the poem, the emphasis on the sound the bench makes is a sounding board for another's pain. Here, however, the poet's shame and guilt, in contrast to the professed shamelessness of "They're Pushing Me," resound as well.

Self-Dispossession

Campaigns of terror work not merely by killing but, additionally, by the spectacular display of murdered victims. Grotesque violence characterized the May 1919 Uman pogrom. Beheaded and mutilated corpses, with lopped off ears, breasts, noses, and sexual organs, were left in heaps on the streets, according to eyewitness accounts.[46] One woman reported that her husband, who was removed from his home by unidentified soldiers, was later found dead, his "face shredded." Staged scenes of violence reported from eyewitness accounts also included a corpse at a dining table, a living infant nursing at his dead mother's breast, and a dead body propped up for use as target practice. Victims were transformed into emblems of their murderers' power, marking out the realm of necropolitics, where there is no government and no provision for life but instead rule by means of the right to kill.

In "My Eyes" ("Mayne oygn"), Kvitko describes the experience of seeing the aftermath of murder and the urge to avoid the burden of describing what he has witnessed. Archival accounts of pogroms confirm that survivors saw pigs and dogs "gnawing at" the remains of family members.[47] The poet sees the pig slurping up "bloody puddles in the courtyard" and wants to punish his eyes for what they have seen:

> My eyes
> Cold lumps,
> And hot,
> Fall out!

> Haven't you seen everything?
> Winked at secrets?
> Widened madly in astonishment
> When the pig guzzled
> Red puddles in the courtyard?
> Why do you remain?
> Lumps of carrion
> Fall out!⁴⁸

The speaker issues a set of questions and commands at parts of his body as if they were separate from himself. The harsh *zh* sounds in the words of Slavic origin for "guzzle" (*gezshlyaket*), "puddles" (*kalizshkes*), and repeated in the particle *zhe* (which I omitted in the translation) stand out from the rest of the stanza, drawing attention to the scene. The second stanza informs the reader why the speaker wants his eyes to fall out—because of the abomination of what they have seen. The transformation of human beings into food for pigs, mere flesh, also transforms parts of the poet's body into dead flesh. In Bialik's "In the City of the Slaughter," the speaker excoriates the fathers and husbands who saw their daughters and wives raped but did nothing. Bialik writes, "They saw it all / They did not stir or move: / They did not pluck their eyes out."⁴⁹ As if responding to this accusation, the speaker in Kvitko's poem would blind himself.

He doesn't stop there, however. He would also dispose of his heart, which seems to him alien and useless, as the next stanza indicates:

> I could ask you,
> Heart of mine,
> Are you mine then?
> Aren't you an empty pump,
> The work of vandals
> Soon to flee
> Into the thickest part of my flesh?⁵⁰

The language I have rendered as "empty pump / The work of vandals" is especially striking in the original Yiddish as *nishtik nigzl*, because of the strong sound mirroring, both consonance and assonance. The Hebrew-origin term *nigzl* means to be a victim of robbery or one deprived of rights; in colloquial Yiddish, it means to be utterly ruined, the lowest of the low, useless, a nothing. The term also appears in a series of expressions indicating the condition of loss and impoverishment, both mentally and materially.[51] A clear parallel with the hefker condition emerges. The poet is uncertain as to whether his heart is his, because it is the victim of a robbery, hence my language "an empty pump / The work of vandals." From his carrion flesh eyes to his empty pump of a heart, the poet dismembers his body, disavowing his relationship to his own organs.

His heart, no longer his own, seeks escape and a place of refuge in his body, fleeing to "the thickest part" of the poet's "flesh" ("Inem grebstn ort mayn laybs") and into the darkness of his buttocks ("Inem tunkl / Grob-fleysh tunkl"). The poet turns aside from his own heart, which begs him to hide it. The heart's hiding spot, the buttocks, the place of filth, changes in the last stanza. The poet denies acknowledgment of his heart, now "draped in white cobwebs," as if it were in an old attic or abandoned dwelling, a place of hiding, and a significant space in other poems in the 1919 cycle. Again, the poet asks whether his heart is truly his. In "My Eyes," internal physiology and the external environment merge into a single enfleshed space. The entire Jewish population has been abandoned, and they and their possessions have been declared up for grabs by the invading armies and pogromists. Then they are victims without recourse; they lose all status and all claims to dispose of their belongings and themselves. Kvitko condenses the experience of the marauded city into the dimensions of his own body, plucking out his eyes, and rejecting his vandalized heart. Kvitko poetically renounces ownership of his body, and although he does not use the term, the concept of hefker, disowned property, comes into play. Kvitko symbolically makes his own flesh hefker. He disavows himself.

One permutation of the hefker concept is the religious notion of self-renunciation, making oneself "hefker like the wilderness." Poetry and philosophy adapt concepts from religion even in a secularized environment.[52] In Hofshteyn's poetic cycle *Sorrow*, the narrator quiets his own voice to maximally discern the pain of others. Kvitko's "My Eyes" performs a similar gesture but in his own characteristically enfleshed style. It is worth recalling the Yiddish critic and poet Yekhezkil Dobrushin's description of Kvitko's imagery. Dobrushin writes that Kvitko, who arrives at his images "almost by palpating them with his hands," transforms "pieces of his experience into embodied, carved materiality [*gashmies*]."[53]

In a 1922 letter, Kvitko writes to the Yiddish literary critic Shmuel Charney that while some people are upset with him, "Dostoevsky is not upset with me, and things with Prince Myshkin are very good [un mit Knyaz Mishkin iz mir zeyer gut]."[54] Prince Myshkin is the hero of Dostoevsky's 1869 novel *The Idiot*; Dostoevsky called him his "Prince Christ," but Prince Myshkin fails to save the heroine from murder. Prince Myshkin leaves the novel as he enters it, in a moribund, catatonic condition, an "idiot." Prince Myshkin, like his creator, experienced ecstatic aura before his attacks of epilepsy. He would feel a sense of union with the "highest synthesis of existence" (Dostoevsky's language), before falling to the ground and, thus, approximating the lowest form of existence. Kvitko feels affinity with Prince Myshkin because of his simplicity and his highs and lows.

Another figure with whom Kvitko feels some connection also in relation to highs and lows is the real-life Rabbi Nakhman of Bratslav, associated with Uman. One of the poems in *Trit* begins with a quotation from Rabbi Nakhman about the necessity of correcting and rectifying the imagination. The principle and practice of spiritual self-abasement, descent into the realm of appetite and materiality for the sake of spiritual ascent was central to Nakhman.[55] The references to Nakhman and Prince Myshkin indicate that holy foolishness and kenoticism were on Kvitko's mind during the period when he composed *1919*. What these various traditions share is the relation between the trajectory of descent, into the flesh, into the body's lower regions, into folly—for the sake of spiritual ascent. The upward movement, the promise of transcendence, however, is missing from Kvitko. What replaces it is a lateral movement, a form of poetic expression that can hear and speak another's pain.

Poetic Remaking

Violence wounds bodies, animates things, and reduces people to biological matter. Yet from within this environment of enmity and loss, Kvitko imagines an alternative, relational expansiveness toward things and other people. "Geshet" ("It Happens"), in the second half of the *1919* cycle, begins with a dialogue between an unknown *I* and *you*. The dialogue also includes objects and animals, but the poet places himself at the center of the strange ensemble of voices and noises:

> It happens:
> Buds of joy and pain flutter,
> I get a whiff of hearts, freshly exposed.
> It becomes clear to me:
> There's not a bit of difference,
> Who and what speaks through my mouth:
> A person
> a squeaky chairback,
> or a foolish goat.
>
> You there, whom I love and hate,
> I'm asking you, I'm begging:
> Feel it!
> You speak through my mouth, after all
> to yourself
> even with your echoing well-voice.
>
> I speak through your mouth
> to myself
> even with the whistle of my whip!⁵⁶

Poetry creates a relation even among enemies inflicting pain on one another. These stanzas articulate voices that are not human and not animate; they include the piece of furniture, the well, and the "foolish goat." It makes no difference who or what speaks through the poet, according to the fourth and fifth line of the first stanza. The noise from a chair, a goat, and a terrified human being sound the same in a world in collapse.

The formal features of the first stanza suggest something more. Here it is necessary to look at the original Yiddish:

> Ver un vos se redt fun mir aroys:
> Who and what speaks through me:
> Mentsh,
> A person
> Tsi skripnde parentsh,
> Or a squeaky chairback
> Tsi narishevate tsig.
> Or a foolish goat.⁵⁷

The abrupt shift from eight-, six-, and seven-syllable lines (longer in the Yiddish than the English) to the one-syllable "mentsh" (person) draws attention to this single word. Kvitko rhymes "person" (*mentsh*) and "chairback" or "railing" (*parentsh*, accented on the second syllable) drawing attention to some relation between the two.[58] The chairback in Kvitko's poem could refer to an episode of violence when a chair was used to inflict injury or defend against it. In another poem from *1919*, "Kinder-vigelakh tsehakt" ("Broken Cradles"), children are hanged on gallows made from cradles. The narrator recognizes a piece of his own cradle around the neck of a child, who stares at him; the term is the same, *parentsh*, here meaning, "railing." Pieces of furniture assume a terrible new significance during the peculiar circumstances of confinement, waiting, and attack.

Elaine Scarry's discussion of pain and its mitigation clarifies the relation between the "chairback" and the person. For Scarry, objects of human manufacture are projections "of aliveness" into the world. The made object reciprocates the live body and contains a material record of the sentience out of which it derives its power to act on the body and perception. A carpenter fashions a chair to relieve the tiredness of his companion; the chair, in turn shapes the human body. Even before this, the material out of which the chair is made changes the process of the manufacture since what can be imagined and what can be manufactured may differ dramatically. Every act of "making up," whether it be a poem, a chair, or a town, expands the world by introducing a new configuration of imagined and material reality; war and torture diminish the world by reducing the potential of the manufactured object to one purpose: the weapon that diminishes human aliveness. Acts of imagination help make the world; the deliberate introduction of pain unmakes it.[59]

The opening rhyme and repetition of "Broken Cradles" reiterate the process of unmaking and making, especially in the rhyme "tsehakt / gemakht" (chopped up / made): "Kinder-vigelakh tsehakt, / Tlielakh gemakht" (Children's cradles chopped up / Made into gallows).[60] The rhyme that links the image of the person (mentsh) with a squeaky chairback in the poem "It Happens" reflects the making, unmaking, and remaking the world. Some unnamed act sets the chair in motion, it makes noise, which the poet describes, and in so doing takes a step toward the remaking of the world. Poetry can express the sense of complete collapse, and yet the poem itself, no matter what subject matter it imports, may re-create a moment of belief in the connections among people, objects, and animals and the possibility of their strange, shared language, another word for which is poetry. The possibility of poetry even in conditions of abandonment is the smallest thing, as Hofshteyn says in his pogrom lament, that is also the greatest thing, a token of comfort.

The poet's voice, a vehicle for others, encompasses nonhuman and inanimate others and those whom he hates, who injure him, and whom he would also injure: those who speak with whips. Who is speaking cannot be determined; *I* and *you* (the second person singular *du*) are confused. The blending of positions, people, and things is distinct, however, from Bialik's mass body or Peretz Markish's altar of broken bodies, because here there is a voice that articulates suffering and explicitly addresses *you*. Kvitko as a poet is a sounding board—a device that broadcasts sound more loudly and serves as a way of listening to another, allowing oneself to resound with the utterances and noises others make. He offers an image of the poet as vibroscope, a technological device used to detect sound and the term Helen Keller used to describe how she received the sounds, noises, and voices of the outside world.[61]

This chapter has drawn attention to the significance of hefker as exposure in Kvitko's depiction of naked, undifferentiated flesh, the creature of violence. The cityscape, the body politic, is a body in pain. The explosive terror experienced during ongoing violence reflects the more ordinary fears that Kvitko experienced during childhood. Both Kvitko and Der Nister imagine human beings in terms of dog life, a naked shameless state of uncontrolled appetites, another dimension of hefker. Enfleshment, however, does not necessarily create more vivid bodily states; it can also lead to the loss of sensation, diminishment, and miniaturization. Yet even in conditions of absolute compulsion, Kvitko's poetry also depicts a form of kenosis, an act of self-dispossession that permits the expression of others' voices and that which is beneath voice, sound.

Kvitko does not document facts about the mass public violence of 1919. Instead, he lends the voice of his own experience to his pogrom poetry, inflecting its alternative "moments" with moments from his childhood. Yiddish prose author Itsik Kipnis's *Months and Days*, in contrast, provides a realistic geography of the author's native town and specifies the names of real-life individuals, both perpetrators and victims, involved in the pogrom that took place in 1919. Notwithstanding the stylistic differences between his prose and Kvitko's poetry, similar motifs emerge. Kipnis depicts the uncanny transformation that took place among his Jewish and non-Jewish neighbors that made them unrecognizable, stamped by death. He too calls attention to the loss of the calendar. In *Months and Days*, his novel about the 1919 Slovechno pogrom, the months of his life unfold in the ordinary way, punctuated by days that destroyed time.

PART II — DOCUMENTATION

5

Chronicling a Hefker World
Itsik Kipnis's *Months and Days*

Two thousand days passed since then—two thousand days and two thousand nights.

Days like polished brass disks shining in the sun; and nights, like sated deer stock-still for hours. Or maybe the opposite: days, like foreheads bruised and broken; and nights, like cups of oleum tipped onto animal skins, poisonous sulfuric acid that flows, burns, and brings death.

In any case, the first thousand days and nights were like that.

And before then, it was summer. Summer with blossoming days like poppies in June. I had just been married.[1]

This passage opens Itsik Kipnis's 1926 Yiddish novel, *Months and Days: A Chronicle* (*Khadoshim un teg: A khronik*). Kipnis uses a unit of time that does not appear in any calendar: "a thousand days." The first thousand days were suspended between utter stillness and violent injury. Their undetermined quality only adds to the horror; the experience of this time was nightmarish, painful, and, ultimately as lethal as the acid that "brings death." The choice of poisons is not accidental. Kipnis had worked as a tanner, and sulfuric acid was used in the processing of animal hides. The substance that is an instrument of manufacture appears here a metaphor for a peculiar temporality. Before the bizarre, unrecognizable time, it was summer, a familiar, pleasant season, made even pleasanter by the fact of the author's recent marriage. As the passage suggests, the novel "chronicles" violence and desire and by intertwining two incommensurable stories: the author's honeymoon, and the 1919 pogrom in Slovechno (Slovechne, at the time, Volhynia province), around 120 miles northwest of Kyiv. Kipnis's mother-in-law and two of her children were killed in the Slovechno pogrom; his first wife, pregnant in July 1919, later died of typhus, after giving birth to their daughter. This fact is not part of the novel; Kipnis published another work in 1926 that recounts these events.[2] In *Months and Days*, he gives the names of Jewish victims and non-Jewish perpetrators, lamenting the first and calling for revenge against the second, and yet, in a postscript to the novel, he comments on the "strangeness" of seeing orphaned children, including both victims of pogrom violence and its retribution, eating together at feeding stations. "It was a bit strange for the grown-ups to contemplate this. Indeed, even very strange."[3]

Itsik Kipnis was born in Slovechno (Slovechne) in 1896.[4] He worked as a leather tanner until the Leather Workers Union sent him to Kyiv to study in 1920. He became acquainted with the leading Yiddish authors in Kyiv, especially the group called Vidervuks (New growth), whose mentor was David Hofshteyn. His work began to appear in print in 1922, in the Moscow journal *Shtrom* and elsewhere; his slender volume of poetry *Oksn* (Oxen) was published in the same year under the Vidervuks imprint. *Months and Days* was the first work for which Kipnis received significant critical attention, earning praise for its simplicity and accessibility. Kipnis, like Kvitko, later became widely known as a children's author in Yiddish and Russian translation.[5] Kipnis returned to the pogrom in Slovechno in subsequent work, including *Untervegns* (On the road), in which desire and violence are also linked.[6]

In the preface to the 1926 edition the literary critic Isaac Nusinov called Kipnis's novel a "rare testament [*eydes*] to the tragedy of 1919."[7] The term *eydes* refers to both the witness and the witness's testimony. Kipnis's novel-chronicle recounts events that he directly witnessed and participated in and thus his fictionalized testimony offers a window into the experience and conceptualization of pogrom violence not readily available from other published sources in his time.[8] As I have shown, Hofshteyn and Kvitko imagine the role of the poet as transcribing and serving as a sounding board for others' messages, voices, and inchoate sounds. Kipnis's narrative also encompasses others' utterances. In contrast to the poets, Kipnis introduces documentary elements into his narrative and, furthermore, describes scenes of care, as in the postscript of the strange sight of feeding stations serving Jews and non-Jews.

Both the Yiddish-speaking and the Russian-speaking worlds of the 1920s were preoccupied by a drive to document events.[9] The central event, of course, was the Russian Revolution. Avant-garde Russian literary and visual artists promoted an activist approach to the arts known as "factography" or the "art of fact." Anyone with a camera or a pen could provide snapshots of the present on the way to the future, whether the facts being reported were positive or negative, and the negative included acts of destruction. Critics of his time considered Shklovsky's memoir, discussed in chapter 6, an instance of the new factographic trend. The same term was not used in reference to Kipnis, but the origin story of his novel has to do with the documentary drive of the time.

The documentation of communal catastrophe was a key feature of the new Jewish secular historiographical self-consciousness of the late nineteenth and early twentieth centuries.[10] Shimon An-sky's ethnographic expeditions in the Pale of Settlement before World War I and his subsequent accounts of the deportation and devastation of Jewish communities during the war are prominent examples.[11] Artistic literature also played an important role in documentation. Commissioned by Shimon Dubnow and others to document the 1903 Kishinev pogrom, Bialik instead wrote a stunning poem of lament and accusation—against Jewish passivity in the face of violence.[12] Dubnow saw "no substantive difference between the tasks of a chronicler and those of a poet."[13] Clearly Dubnow's sense of the insignificant difference between artistic literature and documentation does not overlap with prevailing notions of the present.

The civil war–era pogroms generated a new impetus to record and preserve what had taken place. Jewish relief agencies considered artistic literature an important dimension of the documentation of the civil war pogroms and instructed relief workers to collect poetry, prose, and proverbs, along with other data. On September 16, 1921, the Information and Statistical Division of the Jewish Public Committee for Assisting Pogrom Victims (*Evobshchestkom*) considered a proposal from David Hofshteyn to employ literary artists to document the pogroms in Ukraine.[14] He suggested that Jewish authors return to their native shtetls to gather information about the pogroms "in the form of a chronicle, which should contain the factual side of the pogroms" and also added that "the chronicles could be composed in the form of diaries or memoirs." Other members of the executive committee doubted the feasibility of the proposal, however; in writing *Months and Days*, especially in the choice of the subtitle "a chronicle," it is reasonable to assume that Kipnis, Hofshteyn's protégé, was fulfilling his mentor's request. Indeed, Kipnis's phrase "brass disks shining in the sun" (*tatsn antkegn der zun*) is poetic homage to Hofshteyn's *Sorrow*. Hofshteyn describes the blinding glare of day as "the sun dances with a thousand burning disks."[15] Including Kipnis's 1926 novel in this part of my study, dedicated to documentation, reflects the conceptual map of his time, when artistic literature and factual reporting overlapped.

I am not arguing that there is no distinction between documents created for the express purpose of recording events and works of fiction. A work of fiction that uses a first-person narrative, a seemingly unadorned, uninterpreted statement of facts, including place-names and dates may create a documentary effect, but may nonetheless be distinguished from legal documents and survivor testimonies.[16] Documents available from the central state archive of Ukraine, YIVO, and other sources makes it possible to compare eyewitness testimonies and Kipnis's fictionalized version of eyewitness testimony. I discuss this in greater detail in chapter 7, noting here in brief that the narratives collected by aid organizations reveal very little emotion. Kipnis's novel, in contrast, expresses an array of emotions, including rage, love, delight, bewilderment, resentment, and frustration. What the comparisons also reveal, aside from some variations between the accounts, is Kipnis's unique artistry and, especially, his emphasis on the singular strangeness of the experience of life and death in Slovechno in 1919. My discussion highlights the ways in which Kipnis makes the strangeness of both violence and care even stranger.

Kipnis uses the keyword hefker at a crucial turning point in the narrative. Describing the onset of violence, he writes, "Now we were like animals, which at nightfall would become utterly abandoned and helpless" (*Itst zaynen mir geglikhn tsu bashefenishn, vos inovnt vern zey ingantsn hefker un hilfloz*).[17] In chapter 1, I discuss the importance of this statement in relation to notions of the role of pastoral care in biopolitical theory. This chapter focuses on other aspects of hefker, central to *Months and Days* as a whole, before and after the pogrom began. Hefker permeates the "poisonous nights," the time of violence, but also the "blossoming days" of the protagonist's honeymoon. In the hefker world of abandonment, offering care to the injured is thus even more significant and unusual. Unlike Kvitko's existential condition of abandonment, and distinct from the kenotic qualities of Hofshteyn's hefker poetics in *Sorrow*, Kipnis shows how violence pushes the transgressive potential of ordinary life beyond all limits.

After a discussion of the novel's reception, I provide an anatomy of the July pogrom in Slovechno, relying on *Months and Days* and testimonies from 1919, giving particular attention to the role of neighbors. The largest section of the chapter examines the hefker theme as the catalyst for the strange, off-kilter world of love, violence, and care in the novel, tracing the transformations to which Kipnis and his Jewish and non-Jewish neighbors were subject. The disorientation created by violence pulls against the documentary strategies of the novel.

Kipnis and Sholem Aleichem

Critics reviewing *Months and Days* in the 1920s commented on two aspects of the novel: the naive style and the role of the love story. Most considered the honeymoon problematic. In a review for *Literarishe bleter* in 1927 Isaac Bashevis Singer found the "artless" tone of the love story out of place in a chronicle of a pogrom.[18] I note that deliberately structuring a literary work to include that which is out of place may be a hefker strategy. Shmuel Charney wrote that Kipnis, like other beginning authors, had attempted to do too many things in one work, thereby undermining its unity. Nonetheless, even though the results were not completely successful, the task that Kipnis had set himself was worthwhile: depicting the "shtetl, the distant revolution, and the pogroms" from the perspective of a couple in love.[19] In his preface to the 1926 edition, which I have already cited, Nusinov, unlike other critics, praised the combination of love story and pogrom narrative. *Months and Days* was a "rare witness to the tragedy of 1919," because of the "enormous contrast between Ayzik and Buzi's consciousness and the pitilessness of their precarious path along the edge of destruction."[20]

David Bergelson's review emphasized Kipnis's dependence on Sholem Aleichem. Kipnis had taken a page from Sholem Aleichem's book and had transformed Sholem Aleichem's fictitious shtetl of Kasrilevke from the 1890s into Slovechno in 1919. It was as if Motl Peysi, the cantor's son, had traveled not to America but to Kipnis's native shtetl. The language of the love story between Ayzik and Buzi came straight out of Sholem Aleichem's "Song of Songs." The greatest flaw of the novel was the reliance on language, ideology, and tone that belonged more to the late nineteenth century than the era of World War I and the Russian Revolution. Sharply disagreeing with Nusinov, Bergelson found that the perspective of the hero in love as the focal point of the narrative was wrong, especially since the novel passed itself off as a document about a pogrom. Bergelson attacked Kipnis's myopia about historical catastrophe. A young man got married with the idea of taking as much pleasure as possible from his married life even though it was the time of pogroms; the same thing could have happened at the time of the destruction of the Second Temple. Bergelson's criticism inadvertently reveals traces of the traditional Jewish historiography in his implicit comparison between events recounted in the Bible and 1919. Nonetheless, Kipnis was very talented, and the chapter "Wednesday, Thursday, and Friday"—the "days" of the title—portrayed the pogrom in "rare colors."[21]

Kipnis's contemporary critics all commented on the merits of depicting a pogrom from the perspective of a young man in love. They may have been looking through the wrong end of the telescope, however. It wasn't the love story that determined the pogrom story but the other way around. The epigraph (cited at the beginning of this chapter) begins with the poisonous days and nights of sulfuric acid and then turns back to what came before, blossoming summer. As I will show, the pogrom story, the story of hefker abandonment, colored and contaminated the love story and everything else that came earlier chronologically.

Neighbors

An explanation of the Slovechno pogrom will help set the stage for the discussion of *Months and Days*. Unlike other pogroms, instigated by warlords, the anti-Jewish violence in Slovechno was primarily the work of neighbors. Jan Gross and other scholars have written about neighborly, or intimate violence, in relation to the Holocaust, but this topic has received less attention regarding the pogroms of the Russian Civil War.[22] Gross's emphasis on the "situational dynamics" of episodes of violence provides a point of departure for understanding the neighborly violence that took place in Slovechno.

From Kipnis's perspective in *Months and Days*, the Russian Revolution of 1917, and the subsequent regime change in Kyiv had little meaning except for the violence these events unleashed. He asks, "Who doesn't know that in Russia it's been a year since the great revolution? Of course we know.

But no revolution occurred in the places where we lived."[23] The reports in the Kyiv District Committee Archive and Kipnis's novel both describe common economic conditions shared by Jews and non-Jews in Slovechno. Slovechno is about twenty miles from Ovruch; there were approximately 1,475 inhabitants in Slovechno in 1919, out of which 905 were Jews. As Isaac Goldberg, age twenty-three, put it in his testimony about the events in Slovechno, "The Jews worked just like the peasants; they walked bent over, and were tattered and oppressed."[24] Not all Jews matched this description, as the local businesses were largely owned by Jews. The town included a mill, several tanneries, a slaughterhouse, a church, a zemstvo hospital, an elementary school, and two Jewish cemeteries.[25] Kipnis's mother-in-law, whose husband was in the United States, provided for herself and her children by selling crockery to peasants in the neighboring villages, including Behun (Begun). Jews from Slovechno and peasants from the surrounding area knew one another. In Slovechno proper, Jews and non-Jews lived in close proximity, except for in the center of the town, where there was a greater concentration of Jewish families.

Jews and non-Jews, according to the sources, lived together peacefully. Peasants brought Jews potatoes, flour, honey, a calf, and Jews provided processed animal hides, coats, and boots.[26] Kipnis's father, a tanner, had Jewish and non-Jewish customers; during the pogrom in 1919, Kipnis reports, one of his non-Jewish customers was anxious that his hide would be taken during the looting. The damage inflicted by pogroms had economic consequences for non-Jews as well as Jews. Before the violence of July 1919, to use Kipnis's words, there was every indication that Jews and non-Jews "would live well together until the Messiah came."[27]

They did not do so, however. One source of tension stemmed directly from economic hardships imposed by the new Soviet government's requisitions of manufactured goods; Jews and non-Jews were on both sides of this tussle for goods. Kipnis blames the eruption of violence in his native shtetl on his neighbor Marko Lukhtan, the chief of police, and an individual named Kosenko, in addition to peasants from the town and the surrounding region. Unlike other contemporary accounts, he does not mention the indifference of the executive committee of the communist party in Slovechno, emphasizing instead the importance of these two individuals. The names Lukhtan and Kosenko with the variant Kosinko appear in both the archival documents and *Months and Days*.[28] Kipnis describes Lukhtan, a veteran of World War I, in derogatory language as a "liar, a gypsy, and a beggar."²⁹ According to the eyewitness account of Itsko-Mordakovich Pashkovskii, who worked in the forest in the area surrounding Slovechno, "Lukhtan" was a nickname; Marko's real last name was "Detskii."³⁰ A sixty-year-old shoemaker who lived on the outskirts of the town said that at first he thought his family would be spared the looting and violence because of their poverty. Their neighbor Lukhtan, however, chased them out of their house with a revolver. Hiding with other Jews in a house in the town center, he remained alive by pretending to be dead, as did other survivors.³¹

Relations between the Kipnis and Lukhtan families were uneasy at best. Lukhtan, according to Kipnis, used to look the other way when Jewish children took cherries from his trees. When Marko returned from military service one Friday night; the door of Kipnis's parents' house was open, and the sunset was visible through the trees in the Lukhtan garden. This is one of the few images of neighborly harmony in the entire text. The non-Jewish cherry trees provide the backdrop for the onset of the Jewish Sabbath. To herald Marko's arrival, Kipnis's youngest sibling ran to tell Marko's wife that he had come back from the war. He brought candy for all the children, including the Jewish ones. But Kipnis's mother did not accept the gift. As if to compensate for her refusal, she gave Marko some freshly baked cookies with cinnamon, a Sabbath treat.

According to first-person accounts in the Kyiv District Committee Archive, Kosenko was a young man of the age of nineteen or twenty. He was literate and worked for a time as a clerk for the Food Board; in the period before July 1919, he had no definite occupation but then joined the local police and, together with the police chief, began an anti-Jewish agitation campaign in nearby villages and settlements. The main points of the speeches were that Jews were going to seize churches and transform them into synagogues and force peasants to register marriage, births, and divorces with rabbis. Jews were hoarding manufactured goods—particularly salt—to fleece peasants.³² Kosenko's activities were not limited to speeches; more than one eyewitness account describes him attacking Jews with an ax.³³ *Months and Days* adds to the picture.

Another significant voice of anti-Jewish agitation belonged to the local priest. After the initial attacks against Jews, a meeting was held in the town center, at which the local rabbi and priest spoke. Kipnis writes that the rabbi was "covered in blood," but other accounts show that the rabbi's attack took place after the meeting. According to Pashkovskii, the priest said the Jews were beaten because they "were guilty since time immemorial and would never repent," alluding to the crucifixion, and even though he concluded his speech by noting that the Gospels do not permit even the guilty to be killed, at least two contemporary Jewish accounts say that his words stirred up the crowd. In *Months and Days*, Kipnis omits these details and remarks that the priest was more restrained than he would have been because he was aware that the church no longer held power.[34] Significantly, he characterizes the event using the term *strange*. It was a "strange gathering, not festive and not ordinary."

Rumors about the possibility of violence prompted Jews to seek assurance and protection from Lukhtan, as chief of police. Goldberg's testimony suggests that Lukhtan had made a prior arrangement with a group of "bandits" to storm the town on his signal. Pashkovskii also testified that he heard the cry "Begin!" (*Nachinai!*) around 2:30 in the morning on July 15, 1919.[35] What these accounts show is that in the case of Slovechno, the manipulation of emotions and careful planning played a key role in neighborly violence. Violence did not erupt spontaneously.

The chapter Bergelson liked especially, "Wednesday, Thursday, Friday," describes the beginning of the pogrom. Ayzik and his wife go to sleep in their clothes. The sound of shooting wakes him, and the couple flee through the garden. The next day they learn that one Jew was severely beaten and another killed and that shops and houses were ransacked. Kipnis remarks with special irony, "Each family celebrated the holiday their own way."[36] The killing and destruction continued for two more days. Kipnis writes, "All our streets were crisscrossed with filaments of dread."[37] One eyewitness reported sixty-eight killed and forty-five wounded in Slovechno; other reports give slightly different numbers: "more than sixty" killed and more than one hundred wounded.[38]

Kipnis accuses his non-Jewish neighbors of carrying out violence. He poses the rhetorical question "And you, goyim, my faithful neighbors, did you at least wash the blood from your scythes and your knives?"[39] However, not all the interactions among Jewish and non-Jewish neighbors before and during the pogrom were violent. Pashkovskii says that a fellow worker, a non-Jew, warned him that he had heard rumors of impending anti-Jewish violence from the peasants in the area. The archival record provides examples in which members of the same non-Jewish family treated

Jews differently. Even though Kosenko perpetuated violence against Jews, his mother attempted to intervene and care for Jewish victims. Khana Avrom-Berova Gozman, age forty-five, testified that her children were severely wounded during the pogrom. A peasant sheltered and fed them, and Kosenko's mother washed the children's wounds and warned Gozman and her family to flee as quickly as possible.[40] *Months and Days* also provides an example of neighborly care between Jews and non-Jews as well as the failure of Jewish neighbors to take care of each other.

Kipnis's description of the behavior of his non-Jewish neighbors suggests that they had undergone some sort of metamorphosis. They were familiar but had mysteriously changed: "heymishe goyim, nor zey zaynen megulgl gevorn." As I discuss earlier, among the reasons for the change was the fact that the neighbors had listened to Kosenko's provocative speeches. In works of Yiddish literature with which Kipnis was familiar, "megulgl gevorn" refers to transmigration. Sholem Aleichem's "The Penknife" offers an example. In the story, the child-hero wonders why a nonobservant Jew doesn't suffer punishment from God for his failure to observe the commandments. The boy's teacher explains this strange Jew is a "transmigrated soul [*megulgl gevorn*] and might later appear as a wolf, a cow, a horse, or even a duck."[41] Even though Sholem Aleichem's use of transmigration is comic and Kipnis's is frightening, both passages show that the term has to do with a state of unexpected change, a boundary condition, where the definition of being human becomes uncertain, and the line separating humans from other animals grows unclear. At moments of historical rupture, human beings appear not in their usual guise, in the clothing of civilization, but as strange creatures, stripped of social recognition but not free from their own and others' desires. According to Kipnis, in addition to attacking and killing Jews, non-Jewish neighbors looted Jewish goods and prevented Jews from fleeing Slovechno.

Hefker in the Everyday World

Kipnis's description of the shtetl's Jewish community presents a picture of an ordered world of family life, holidays, and work. In his subsequent novel *Untervegns*, set in the aftermath of the 1919 pogrom, he writes, "It happened to be a Friday in the shtetl. Slovechno did not get very far away from itself. As long as it was Friday, it was Shabes; the two things came together."[42] Even before the violent events of July 1919, the "days" of the title *Months and Days*, something else pushes against the image of pious, orderly life. The first month of the hero's marriage was a time of heightened, fleshly sensuousness, excessive desire on the verge of transgression. Kipnis emphasizes the hefker wantonness of Ayzik's relationship to Buzi. Ayzik and Buzi are ecstatic, "beside themselves," in a constant state of intensified and contagious pleasure. Kipnis indicates their condition by describing the room the newly married couple shared:

> I had just gotten married and lived in our room, a room for a newly wedded couple. Why not? After all, we were a married couple, she and I.
> Anyone who entered our room would be overwhelmed by the tipsy fragrance of early spring. It would make you drunk, if you inhaled it with an open heart, your blood would tingle all the way down to your little finger.... Every speck of air was bound up with us both.... Every hands breath of space was not hers and not mine separately—but bound up with the both of us ... with our shameful, polished wooden beds; the homey curtains on the windows; the enameled blue water jug with big handles.... We were in everything and everything was in us [ellipses added].[43]

Everything Ayzik and Buzi touch and all the objects that surround them are permeated with their passion. They behave with abandon and are a source of licentiousness for other people and, strangely, things. They are at the center of the metonymic chain that links their desire to the space of their room, the curtains on the windows, the enameled jug, the "shameful" beds, and anyone who enters their room. The poetics of pleasure rely on deferral and metonymic transfer to heighten the erotic effect.[44] The boundary between self and other and human beings and objects is erased as objects take on human corporeal features and the qualities of human pleasure. In Yiddish, as in English, the word for *handle* corresponds to a part of the body: in English, "hands," in Yiddish, "ears" (*oyer*). The fact that Ayzik was subject to censure from other shtetl inhabitants for his failure to go to the synagogue to pray on the Sabbath—preferring to stay home with Buzi—adds to the transgression of the love scene.

The love scene in *Months and Days* relies on the artistic device of metonymy, which can create other literary effects as well. Alan Mintz argues that the dominant trope of Bialik's "In the City of Slaughter" is metonymy, which he characterizes as "annoying," because the thing itself, violence, is "deflected," leaving readers access only to its "residuum, its atmosphere, its paraphernalia."[45] Kvitko's *1919* similarly uses metonymy, and the transfer of qualities from people to things, as I showed in chapter 4. The poem "In shtub farhakter" ("In a locked-up house") shifts the terror of abandonment from people to objects they own. Household possessions, thrust aside and left behind, lined with the shadows of children, shrink as they wait in the locked-up house. In other poems in the same cycle, ordinary objects, including chairs and cradles, become instruments of violence, and inanimate objects speak and in other ways respond to violence with human emotions. In both Kvikto's and Kipnis's work, emotions solidify, infusing the surrounding world with their specific qualities; Kipnis describes fear that is so thick that it could be touched. The volatile emotions of abandonment, whether having to do with pleasure or pain, escape the boundaries of a single individual and permeate the surrounding world of people and objects.

The kind of transgressive sexuality that Kipnis evokes in the love scene is a far cry from the use of sex as an instrument of power and tool of violence. In the first case, subjects define their own pleasure, and the awareness that it may violate others' sense of what is proper adds to the pleasure. In the second case, pleasure is taken from subjects and their bodies without their consent. Kipnis includes the latter in his account of the actions of Ataman Oleksander Kozyr-Zyrko in the neighboring shtetl of Ovruch. Kozyr-Zyrko terrorized the Jews of Ovruch from December 1918 through January 1919. Petliura had dispatched him to the town to restore order, but he created a whole new realm of chaos instead. This was typical of his behavior generally; he had previously been in trouble with the Ukrainian government for his arbitrary and violent actions, but his treatment of Jews was far more extreme.[46] Kipnis describes him as a "big, tall, black-haired beauty, a hero." Before leaving Ovruch, he summoned a delegation of town worthies to the train station, where he forced them to sing "songs of Zion," dance, and slap each other on the cheeks while he watched; then his men opened fire on the Jews with rifles and handguns.[47] The archival account differs slightly. Kozyr-Zyrko and his men lie in bed and compel the Jews to sing, and when the Jews can't remember the words, they are whipped. One of the Kozyr-Zyrko's men laughs so hard that the bed breaks under him.[48] The "king for a day" creates a scenario for himself in which the strange element of ritual humiliation is a prelude to the act of killing. In both, there is a sexual charge in the creation and viewing of a spectacle of dancing Jewish bodies compelled to strike each other. This is heightened in the version in which Kozyr-Zyrko and his men watch the Jews in an intimate setting, from their beds. Every violation of the hefker person is a reinscription of the power to make the distinction between those who are protected and those who are not. Kozyr-Zyrko comported himself in the manner of an outlaw, enacting his position on the boundary between the realms of law and nonlaw.

Kipnis's focus on his hero's profession as a tanner emphasizes the blurring of distinctions. His extensive description of the tannery's workings reveals a fascination with all kinds of boundary states. These conditions are part of hefker territory, the line of demarcation separating order from disorder that also undermines it. The tanneries mark the western, eastern, and northern borders of the town, beyond which lay peasant dwellings and arable land, and to the north, the Slovechna River. The tanneries were located within the space defined by culture but at its margins because of the stink and the filth they produced.[49] Ayzik makes his living by working on a boundary object, the skins of animals that are alive and dead at the same time, still alive in the sense that they can decay and thus spoil. The tanning process kills them again.

In the opening passage of *Months and Days,* Kipnis refers to "nights, like cups of oleum tipped onto animal skins," that is, the sulfuric acid used in the "pickling" of animal hides so that they are more readily infused with tannic acid. His descriptions of the tanning process emphasize the strange aliveness of the animal hides and the factories that transform them into usable leather. His father's courtyard presents a "lively" scene, and his father feels the skins as if they were alive. When the skins imbibed sufficient quantities of the tanning chemicals, his father would say "they are full," in other words, sated. Bark used for the tannic acid it contains was left in various stages of drying. Hides hang on racks and workers hovered around them, turning them over and smoothing them out. A rhythmic banging and squeaking coming from a shed indicated the work of pulverizing bark. The rising and falling of the well crane moved the water used in the steaming process. Kipnis writes that the water seems to be frightened of the sudden sunlight it encountered. The skins were worked with chemicals and knives, scythes, and planes that are used to remove imperfections. The various substances used in tanning, including oleum, dung, salts, and oak bark also penetrated the skins of tannery workers, who, Kipnis notes, had separate hours in the bathhouse. Leather tanning is a boundary process that takes place on the border between the town and the countryside, the skin and the rest of the body, and across the border separating humans from other animals. Most importantly, Kipnis's depiction of the manufacture of leather focuses on the "excessive vitality" that brims over the edge of ordered life, blurring the boundaries between what is alive and what is dead.[50] A continuity can be noted between Kvitko, Der Nister, and Kipnis. As discussed in previous chapters, both Kvitko and Der Nister worked with animal hides, and Kvitko's autobiographical novel includes a scene of the child hero carrying bloody cowhides from the slaughterhouse to the tannery. It is not merely the common biographical fact that is important. The literary images of animal skin and skinlessness that they create evoke a hefker realm of uncanny boundary states between life and death, culture and nature, human and nonhuman animals, violence and nurture.

Abandoned Creatures

The world of work, the realm of desire, and the deathworld of violence reveal the human being as animal body, subject to and not master of larger forces. I have previously noted the significance of the animal theme in Der Nister's work and Kvitko's pogrom poem "They're Pushing Me." Kipnis was also fascinated by this theme, as his earlier work shows. Reviewing his first published book, *Oxen*, the Yiddish critic Shmuel Gordon observed that Kipnis was particularly attracted to "zoological playfulness" (Gordon's term), the ease and childlike joy that animals take from their existence.[51] In one of the poems in *Oxen*, the poet exchanges glances "in partnership" with a dog. Another poem describes a beggar girl and her lice, the dust and dirt of the street, and the golden leaves that form a crown around the poet's head.[52] The title poem addresses the oxen as "brothers" and ends with an image of their dead, intertwined limbs, horns, and pelts, their "eyes protruding / in vacant joy." A "skinner" and a few dogs follow behind.[53]

Kipnis's prose poem "Gnod" ("Grace"), published in 1922 in the Moscow Yiddish journal *Shtrom*, contains seven "miniatures"; the fifth is titled "Hefker." Other sections include "Croaking Frogs" and "Prayer," which addresses the "God of thieves" and lovingly depicts a dog waiting for food. "Hefker" paints an ostensibly peaceful scene of children playing in a garden, but

a boy, a young boy, lies under a fence.
A holy smile rests on his young face.
Off to the side his hat and mouth and some paper money.
Left to heaven and abandoned [*tsu hefker*]—
He wasn't expecting anything and it happened so quickly
What do I know?
He's dead.[54]

The disaggregation of the boy's facial features is a hallmark of the modernist style frequently used by David Bergelson. The mouth "off to one side" also suggests the kind of grotesque violence typical of pogrom killings, but the question of what led to the boy's death is left unanswered. The metonymy of violence that Bialik and other authors use is at work in this poem as well. The children who were playing guard the boy, but the speaker does not know whether they watch over his "abandoned hat" (*hefker-hitl*) or the "holy smile that shines on his young face."[55] Hefker in the same position in line as *heylik* suggests a parallel between the space of abandonment and the space of the sacred.

In *Months and Days* the pogrom transforms Jews into animals that may be disposed of. To quote the key passage from the novel one more time, Kipnis writes, "Then we were like animals which at nightfall would be utterly abandoned and helpless" (*Itst zaynen mir geglikhn tsu bashefenishn, vos in ovnt vern zey ingantsn hefker un hilfloz*).[56] Indeed, one of the testimonies about the pogrom in Slovechno reports that after the violence had stopped, abandoned Jewish livestock that had been released from their enclosures wandered freely throughout the town. Abandoned creatures, including humans and other animals, were part of the pogrom landscape.

Note first the term *creatures* (*bashefishn*)—that is, not merely animals but creatures who have suffered a particular fate, having been pushed outside domesticated life and the care that comes with it. Their master has left them up for grabs (hefker) and thus subject to anyone's whim. To be "abandoned by" an owner, authorities, or the government opens the door to the condition of being "abandoned to" whatever forces, urges, or whims those in power hold. Abandonment, whether simply neglect, or the heightened abandonment to sheer power without legal protection transforms human beings into something other than socially recognizable human beings.[57] Even though the human beings who inhabit creaturely roles appear to resemble livestock and wild animals, the shifts they have undergone are not the product of nature. They are the product of specific historical and political circumstances of the hefker condition: exposure to the violence of unlimited power, at the boundary between law and nonlaw.

The Strangeness of Pogrom Violence

The pogrom section of *Months and Days*, regardless of Bergelson's criticism, is not narrated from the perspective of a young man in love or any single overarching narrative perspective, thus adding to the reader's disorientation and the overall sense of a world suddenly thrust out of joint. The story of the pogrom rests instead on a series of miniatures narrated by other characters. Each vignette builds on the strange, grotesque nature of pogrom violence; like Kvitko, Kipnis uses the term *mise-meshune*, "unnatural death."[58]

An unnamed Jew describes the murder of one Yekhiel Dorfman, who had at first hidden in the garden of one of the small synagogues but then decided to go home and sat down at the head of his table. The "bandits" killed him there at his place at the head of the table, "and perhaps he is still sitting there."[59] It is not merely that Dorfman was killed. Far removed from the ordinary rituals of life and death in the everyday world, the dead body was transformed into a prop of a spectacle intended to terrify those who came across it. In this as in other instances, Kipnis uses a real name: Yekhiel Leybovich Dorfman, age seventy, appears on the list of victims of the Slovechno pogrom compiled by the Information Division of Kyiv District Committee to Aid Victims of Pogroms.[60]

In another vignette in *Months and Days*, a woman describes the slaughter at Motl Ratner's. This was a house that many Jews mistakenly believed would be a haven, because of Ratner's prominence in the town. Kipnis blurs the lines between the woman's narration and his own wording, omitting quotation marks, and using language that emphasizes the significance of the killing as a process of enfleshment: "a woman said that a lot of meat [*fleysh*] was killed tonight in the shtetl." Kosenko ordered Jews to flee threw the window and beheaded them as they ran, and a man and his son-in-law "ran down the street like chickens without their heads," a physiological impossibility. At the scene of slaughter, the former house of refuge, "shoulders, hands, feet were mixed together in one 'bloody lump.'"[61] The slaughter scene presented a picture of the remains of individuals, undifferentiated and reassembled into a mass body. This picture in some ways resembles Peretz Markish's image of a blasphemous "heap" of corpses, and comparisons can be made to Kvitko's waking nightmare of a swarm of uninvited, undead women calling him down from his hiding place in the attic. Kipnis is emphasizing the nature of "strange death" as not merely making proper burial impossible, but what is more, undermining the basic distinction between one person and another, a fundamental assumption of social life. A basic feature of hefker abandonment, found in both Bialik and Agamben, is the effect of undifferentiation. Using the real-life names of victims is a way of remembering that they were individual persons.

The pogrom began on a Tuesday, as Kipnis notes, the seventeenth of Tamuz, when the walls of Jerusalem were breached, one of the events leading to the sacking of the Second Temple. The seventeenth of Tamuz is a minor fast day in the Jewish calendar. "Tuesday" is one of the days of terror that the title of the work *Khadoshim un teg* indicates.[62] Kipnis, according to his own self-description in *Months and Days* was not a particularly observant Jew; nonetheless, he evokes the traditional Jewish historiographical mentality that sees ongoing reality in light of biblical history. Kipnis adds the utterly unique days of the pogrom in Slovechno in July 1919 to the recurring cycle of ritual observance of Jewish national catastrophe, but his own framing of the impossible calendar of pogrom time pulls against this more traditional view. As is the case in Hofshteyn's and Kvitko's poems, in *Months and Days*, violence upsets the normal ordering of time.

On the same evening that Ayzik and his wife go to sleep in their clothes, he recalls a nightmare from childhood:

> Once, however, when I was a child (I must have been five when it happened) I dreamed that there was a pogrom in our town: it was winter, the shopkeepers had built themselves white inner doors, and their wives, masked and with revolvers in their hands, stood on the other side of those doors. They knew how to shoot. It was in the middle of the marketplace, in winter. The place was full of frozen, bloody clods, so full that you couldn't get through. The lumps, smeared over with snot, consisted of frozen blood. It looked as if a big pogrom had taken place. I wandered around alone the whole night and couldn't escape the labyrinth of bloody lumps.[63]

This description of the aftermath of slaughter comes before the description of what happened at Motl Ratner's house, the vignette that I described above. It is as if the carnage happens twice; the reader is twice confronted with the same image. Kipnis presents the events of July 1919 as the real-life fulfillment of a childhood nightmare from the past, dislodging it from the stable calendar of Jewish historiography and any larger framework of ordered meaning. The literary device of the nightmare heightens the strangeness of the real-life event.

In the context of the concern with dates and anniversaries that Kipnis develops in *Months and Days*, a startling question appears in the penultimate chapter: "Does anyone know what day it is?"[64] It is as if the reading audience is also asked the question; the "anyone" could be anyone reading the novel. No addressee is specified. No speaker is identified as the source of the question; there are no quotation marks or any other punctuation that delimit who the speaker is. The simplicity of the question belies the profound disorientation that created it in the first place as well as the disorientation it causes. The loss of an ordered sense of time is a consequence of life in conditions of abandonment, lived without calendars. Kipnis repeats that pogrom time was not like Purim or the intermediate days of any known Jewish holiday, again, not because he was a pious young man, but to highlight that the pogrom disrupted the structure of time. The term *sheteh hefker* denotes a "no-man's-land"; pogrom time can be understood similarly as "no-man's-time," a dimension of time that deranges all other temporal ordering. This is a recurring theme of the poetry and prose written in response to pogrom violence. As Kvitko wrote in his preface to *1919*, pogroms changed every aspect of experience; "the moments were different" (azoy zaynen oykh di reges andersh).[65]

To quote Kipnis, "Tuesday was a day, and we, it seemed were human beings."[66] The affirmation of the day of the week and the affirmation of the unspecified community that constitutes the *we* of the statement reveal how closely the organization of social identities and the organization of time are linked. The line also reveals the speaker's realization that neither humanity nor the predictability of the calendar can be taken for granted. The statement suggests radical doubt that either of these things is the case. The pogrom has destroyed the possibility of assuming that just because I am alive right now, I will continue to be alive tomorrow or in the next instant.

Later in the novel, the narrator expresses his inability to distinguish the living from the dead; he can't believe that those who have been "tortured are really dead and those who are speaking are still alive." The span of human life has been drastically foreshortened, and an hour is the same as a hundred years: "On whom does the mark of the scythe lie? Look and find out. Because now one hour by night or one gibe by day can do what a hundred round years cannot erase or rinse off. Just look at our living together with the dead."[67] The phrase "look and find out" (*kuk un derken*), while reminiscent of the Talmudic "come and see," signifies the opposite: "come and see" generally introduces an interpretation offered by a scholar, but here, in contrast, there is no clarification, what we are invited to contemplate boggles the imagination. Deciphering and interpreting the marks left by the scythe on the bodies of the dead and possibly the living is a reading practice for which there is no rabbinic commentary. An hour of pogrom time leaves incalculable harm on the bodies and psyches of victims. Transforming the inchoate mark of the scythe into an element of a textual narrative is a step toward restoring humanity to those abandoned in a world of death.

The Strangeness of Neighborly Care

Providing care, as in the postscript at the feeding station offers a form of intervention. When the world is made strange through violence, the restoration of neighborly relations through acts of care also appears strange. In Kipnis's novel, the offering of food, described in the postscript and elsewhere in the text, is treated as an inexplicable act. Under the conditions of abandonment, the simplest gesture of care confounds expectations. The surprise and strangeness appear all the more starkly especially when the protagonists of the novel, Ayzik and Buzi, fail to provide care for their Jewish neighbor.

Ayzik and his wife encounter the widow of Dovid Freynk, the furrier, as she wanders through the streets singing a dirge for her husband, killed in the neighboring village of Behun together with his mother and younger brother. This is another instance in which Kipnis uses a real-life name. In *Months and Days*, Freynk is Yeshue or Joshua's son; Yeshue is a furrier. In the Kyiv District Committee list of Jewish victims for Ovruch and Slovechno in 1919, the same individual is listed in Russian as "David Evseevich Freink," age twenty-eight, occupation, tailor.[68]

Kipnis remarks that Freynk's widow was not singing but "muttering like a golem" (*zi premplt nor azoy vi a golem*).[69] Seven stanzas of the dirge she sings appear in the text, beginning with the line, "Of course, you all know Dovid" ("Avade kent ir ale Dovidn"); the singer goes on to describe her husband's beauty, her love for him, and how she begged her husband's killers to kill her too.[70] She wants to follow him in death but doesn't know what to do with their child. The sudden appearance of this woman maddened in grief terrifies Ayzik and especially Buzi. His "blood runs cold," and he worries that the widow will recognize him and demand his help. Kipnis's description of the widow amount to a portrait of uncanny undeadness, including wandering, muttering, the repetition of the same words, and the comparison to a golem, which can mean simply that she seemed like a fool, someone without intellect, but also refers to the legendary creature made of clay animated by day and dead by night.

Ayzik and Buzi react to the sight and sound of the widow without empathy. Their response is instead fear. Ayzik wants to speak to her but fails to do so; he turns away to take his wife home. The widow resembles an "ownerless creature," abandoned by her fellow Jews. Kipnis's account does not provide any further information about her; there is no larger contextualizing discussion. The very lack of information accentuates the sudden unsettling appearance of the wandering widow, adding to the strangeness of the scene and the stark refusal of her neighbors, including Jewish neighbors, to help her. Her accusation against her husband's murderers is thus also an accusation against Jewish and non-Jewish bystanders, about whom she says, "Of course *you* all know Dovid Freynk" [emphasis added]. In citing this line and the rest of the dirge, Kipnis allows the widow's, Dobe Freynk's voice to address readers, as if her lament and accusation were also directed against them.

The reports of eyewitnesses and pogrom investigators reveal that in the aftermath of pogroms, it was not unusual to see individuals who had apparently lost their reason wandering about the town. Isaac Goldberg's testimony about the pogrom in Slovechno is an example. He had trouble recognizing a young woman he knew, because she seemed to have gone mad; she looked "crazed."[71] This instance, and the episode in Kipnis's *Months and Days* were fairly typical; indeed, one physician wrote of the "traumatic pandemic" that had befallen the Jewish population generally. Given the prevalence of the problem, the account in Kipnis's novel stands out even more, not because it was unique, but because his account of the widow Freynk intensifies the uncanny effect.

Ayzik's failure to offer care stands out against other episodes in the novel. During one of the nights of the pogrom Ayzik, his extended family, and other Jews seek shelter in a close-by village, where his father knew someone, and their wagon is allowed into this man's courtyard for a time. An old woman, not Jewish, appears from one of the houses. Unlike other instances in which Kipnis provides names, in this one, the woman remains nameless. Her appearance is strange, although Kipnis does not use the term. She is half naked, wearing only "a canvas shirt and two aprons, one in front and one in back—this is her dress." She cries and laments that she was fated to see the day when such things should go on as taking other people's property, referring to the looting of Jewish homes, and wonders whether World War I played a role: "did the damn war so corrupt the people?" (*hot es di farsholtene milkhome azoy tselozn dos folk?*). The old woman goes on to say that the Jews are also guilty because they "hid" salt. Even animals are given salt, and the old woman hints that Jews treated their non-Jewish neighbors more poorly than animals in denying them salt.

Salt was a flash point in the neighborly violence in Slovechno. Kipnis's account of prepogrom interethnic interaction stresses this point. Instead of dishes and bowls, his mother-in-law started to take salt to the neighboring villages, because "for salt you can get everything." "Everything was upside down at the market," Kipnis goes on to say. Peasants would exchange a wagonload of wood for "a bit of salt," which was frequently adulterated with chalk, flour, saccharine, paint, or dye.[72] The old woman points out that even animals receive salt and goes on to say that the people are angry because the Jews withheld it. Then she brings out baked potatoes for the child-refugees in the courtyard.

The miniature of the strange old woman could have ended differently. She cries, accuses her own people, accuses Jews, and justifies the people's anger against Jews. This sequence could have become the prelude to more violence. The outcome, however, confounds expectations. Instead of a final statement or action of anger, the woman feeds the Jewish children. The woman herself and her action are strange in the sense of breaking with expectations that violence leads to more violence. The old woman, who accused her own people of corruption, blamed the war and the Jews but still gave Jewish children her own food, is strange to begin with because of her costume and her behavior adds to the strangeness because she interrupts the continuum of violence and neglect that pervades the narrative.

Providing food in and of itself does not necessarily restore ordinary social relations because the way it is given can be yet another expression of power. The restoration of social recognition depends on some evidence of an acknowledgment of the common humanity and vulnerability of the provider and those she feeds. In this episode, the old woman's strangeness, expressed in her emotional display and her nakedness, show evidence of mutual susceptibility and vulnerability.

For most of his text Kipnis expresses his own desire for revenge; he wonders at one point, for example, when Jews will go out and murder "shikses," and it is highly likely that his dream of revenge also included other forms of violence against non-Jewish women. Non-Jewish children (whom he describes with the derogatory term *shkotsim*) are, as he says, treading on the bodies of his dead.[73] The novel's postscript includes a few episodes of retributive violence. Kipnis reports that nine local non-Jews plus three others were taken by wagon to Ovruch, where they were killed. Chinese soldiers were given alcohol to drink and told to shoot the men, and they complied. A significant number of Chinese nationals took part in the civil war. In addition to internationalists, who joined the Bolshevik cause, unemployed Chinese migrant workers received salaries from the Bolsheviks if they fought in the Red Army.[74] The 1930 Russian translation of the novel omits these details, in all likelihood because of the extremely negative portrait of the ethnic Chinese, for whom, the narrator says, shooting these men meant nothing.[75] Marko Lukhtan, Kipnis's neighbor, managed to hide at first but was later discovered. He was taken outside the town limits and shot in broad daylight, together with his brother and brother-in-law; their bodies were brought back in a wagon. Unlike other episodes in *Months and Days*, Kipnis does not name who did the shooting. The number of murdered victims in Slovechno that I gave earlier does not include non-Jews.

I return to the postscript: "Marko had murdered Jews and Jews murdered Marko. And the orphaned children came running with their bowls to the kitchen. They didn't think about anything. They only lifted their eyes and mouths to their food. For the grownups it was a strange sight to see, a very strange sight."[76] The strangeness of the scene requires explanation. During episodes of violence, time, space, and human beings lost their ordinary qualities. The animal body of the human emerges more clearly. The distinction between life and death vanished, as the living struggled to stay alive by hiding among the dead and pretending to be dead.

The perpetrator/victim distinction was erased, revealing the common vulnerability of human beings on both sides of the conflict. This most basic fact of common social existence, having been utterly undermined during the pogrom, now appears peculiar, unrecognizable, because overwhelming mass violence has made it so. What is strange in the scene is the same thing that is strange about the bizarre old woman in the courtyard: when unthinkable neighborly violence is taking place, neighborly care is also unthinkable, "strange." When violence unmakes the world, the simplest steps toward remaking it appear to be completely foreign and unfamiliar. Kipnis, unlike Kvitko, does not raise the question of forgiveness in *Months and Days*. The closest he gets is this moment of reflection on seeing Jewish and non-Jewish children eating together. Characterizing the scene as strange is not an expression of forgiveness, only surprise.

Documentary Indeterminacy

Kpinis's emphasis on the uniqueness of pogrom time has implications for the status of his novel as a "witness" text, to go back to Nusinov's term. The breakdown of ordered time would seem to challenge the veracity of Kipnis's account. To put it differently, if he didn't know what day it was, how can we be so sure that refugees sheltered in Avrom-Ber's house, or, to give another example, how can we believe that Motl Ratner's house (another householder the text explicitly names) was the place where many Jews were killed? Documentary accounts collected by pogrom investigators also name these specific individuals as householders in Slovechno, but the typical reader of a literary work like Kipnis's would not have the opportunity to verify facts in this way.

As if anticipating that there might be doubt in his credibility, Kipnis addresses his readers directly. Ownerless, abandoned creatures are not conventionally reliable witnesses. To overcome the gap and rebuild the social recognition that has been lost, Kipnis addresses readers directly with simple, concrete questions. Slovechno had served as a place of refuge for Jewish inhabitants of Ovruch fleeing pogrom violence. The pogrom in Ovruch, which lasted approximately two weeks, was the first major outbreak of anti-Jewish violence in Ukraine in 1919. Kipnis writes, "'How,' you ask, 'did forty people manage to sleep at the house of Avrom-Ber, the ladies' tailor?'"[77] The answer begins with another question, a challenge to the reader: "Perhaps you've never been a refugee?"[78] Then follows a description of people sleeping under tables, on tables, between sewing machines, along slop buckets, on beds, and under the beds. The question vocalized by the narrator in the name of the reader is also a question turned back at the reader. It addresses readers' possible skepticism that Avrom-Ber's house could shelter so many people. It demands that readers believe Kipnis's testimony. The experience of the listener or reader approaching the witness text filters the reception of the testimony; one can be more or less likely to accept the narrator's credibility.

No matter how much corroborating evidence there is, witnesses' testimony does not become truth unless and until their listeners believe them. Every statement witnesses make is thus preceded by an unspoken imperative: "Believe me." The witness's relationship to the events being testified to, her faithfulness to her memory of the events—the conditions that support the truthfulness of the testimony—do not matter without the satisfaction of this third condition of the listener's belief in the witness. The testimony has to be incomplete, open, and imperfect in order to allow space for the other's affirmation or denial.[79] The witness text is performative in the sense that it performs or creates the relationship. Rebuilding the relationships among a community of destroyed individuals is one of the most important effects of the narrator's repeated address to the reader.

Buzi, the narrator's wife, asks, "Is it so easy to slit a person's throat with a knife? Like a sheep or an ox?"[80] As I mentioned in the beginning of the chapter, critics in Kipnis's time remarked on the naive qualities of his narrative, seeing a link between Kipnis's style and Sholem Aleichem's.[81] Buzi's seemingly naive question compels readers to imagine the gestures and movements necessary to perform acts of violence and, even, a rehearsal of these movements and, hence, a certain kind of complicity in violence or, at least, a contemplation of what that complicity might look like. Kipnis's apparently simple style thus draws readers more immediately into violence as an experience.

In *Months and Days*, hefker life is found inside the framework of daily life and emerges all the more starkly during conditions of extreme and intimate violence, when human beings are thrust out of the structures and ordering of their lives, including time, space, and the recognition of common exposure to the power of others. Kipnis's narrative straddles the border between fact and fiction. His text uses the devices of documentation, and its impetus can be traced back to the documentary drive promoted by Jewish aid organizations, for which chronicles and memoirs were sources of information. Nonetheless, Kipnis's novel—in its emotionality, its call for revenge, and its emphasis on the strangeness of pogrom death—is distinct from the kind of eyewitness testimony collected by Jewish aid organizations, the subject of chapter 7. Kipnis uses the literary resources of indeterminacy, shifting perspective, multiple time frames, and a changing emotional and stylistic register to explore the boundary where dates and names lose their specificity and meaning. His reliance on certain documentary strategies does not mean that his text is exhaustive, complete, or impartial. As was typical for accounts of the time, Kipnis is reticent about rape. He strongly hints that his young sister-in-law was raped without providing details.[82] The biblical cadences and violent imagery of the opening passage, as I have already discussed, work to destabilize the testimonial dimension of the text. The various threads of witnessing and testimony, on the one side, and estrangement and lyric nightmare, on the other, pull against each other in *Months and Days*. The ambiguities and tension among them create the unique texture of the novel/chronicle.

The next chapter turns to a text that also treads water between genres, drawing on features of the memoir, document, deposition, and accusation. The range of the sights, sounds, and voices it encompasses expands to include the entirety of the former Russian empire. While not focused on antinomies between Jews and non-Jews, the author reveals parallels between anti-Jewish violence in Ukraine and other forms of mass public violence elsewhere in revolutionary Russia. Abandonment as a form of violence is a central theme of Victor Shklovsky's *Sentimental Journey*.

6

Victor Shklovsky's Archive of Abandonment

Victor Shklovsky is best known for his theory of defamiliarization, or estrangement (*ostranenie*).¹ The purpose of art is to make the world strange. Habit dulls perception, "eating away at things, clothes, furniture, our wives, and our fear of war."² Art can stimulate perception by means of techniques that make things strange, impeding mere recognition. In so doing, art could help restore human capacities to sense the world.

During World War I, Shklovsky served in the czar's army as an instructor in an armored car division. He actively participated in the February Revolution, and the provisional government sent him to the southwestern front as a war commissar; he served in the same capacity in northern Iran. In Petrograd in 1918, he took part in preparations to overthrow the Bolsheviks, and escaped arrest by fleeing to Kyiv. He made a return journey to Petrograd only to flee again, this time through Finland to Berlin. Shklovsky ended up supporting the Bolshevik cause and fought with the Red Army. Wherever he went, he wrote. He named his two-part memoir of this time *Sentimental Journey: Memoirs, 1917–1922* (*Sentimental'noe puteshestvie: Vospominaniia, 1917–1922*) after Laurence Sterne's *A Sentimental Journey through France and Italy* (1768). Shklovsky's memoir was first published in 1923; republication in 2006 and 2019 attest to renewed interest in the twenty-first century.³

Although the literature on Shklovsky has largely focused on his theoretical contribution, scholars have recently turned to the historical and social environment that gave rise to his ideas. Recent scholarship sees in

Shklovsky "more than art as device."[4] and some, including the author of this study, have situated him in a Jewish context.[5] The appendices to his *Theory of Prose* include discussions of the Babylonian Talmud; in *Sentimental Journey*, Shklovsky calls himself a "half Jew" and says that he would gladly leave Russia and settle in the east because of anti-semitism. Shklovsky and his contemporary literary theorists were not cut off from politics and history, as has been argued previously; they were, on the contrary, engaged with World War I, the Russian Revolution, and its immediate political conflicts, as Shklovsky's life history and memoirs demonstrate.[6] Putting Shklovsky in the context of Yiddish work on pogroms shows that he, like other Jewish authors, understood that abandonment was a primary form of violence.

Kvitko is focused on Uman and Kipnis on Slovechno; for Shklovsky, the space of abandonment is the entire disintegrating Russian empire, transformed into a no-man's-land. I examine Shklovsky's use of "abandonment" in *Sentimental Journey* in light of the hefker concept in other sources. Shklovsky discusses the abandonment of specific populations and their recreation as undifferentiated flesh. He contemplates a notion of human violence as a force field that can be animated or suppressed, dependent on contingencies.[7] He deploys his own technique of estrangement to make the violence that had become shockingly ordinary in the revolutionary period unfamiliar and disorienting. This was not estrangement from the world, a turning away, but rather "estrangement for the world," a return to it.[8]

In *Sentimental Journey*, the technique of estrangement also draws attention to acts of care, which, in the off-kilter world of abandonment, appear unusual and even bizarre. The Yiddish authors discussed previously also emphasized the strangeness of violence and care. Kipnis remarked on how strange it was to see victimized Jewish and Ukrainian children eating together. A new form of violence had entered the world and a new response was required. Shklovsky and the Yiddish authors were thinking along similar lines.

After an overview of *Sentimental Journey*, I examine the relation between attention, failures of attention, estrangement, and abandonment. I discuss the reception of *Sentimental Journey* in the context of the "literature of fact" and then turn to abandonment in the text. Shklovsky's descriptions of the revolutionary destruction of law and the collapse of the entire political and social order show how former human beings made each other mere flesh to be disposed of. I trace the concept of "ownerlessness" in his description of anti-Jewish and other forms of ethnic violence. Shklovsky's distress over the destruction of machinery, both the machinery of human life and that of technology can be compared to Elaine Scarry's discussion of material culture as a projection of human life. Shklovsky devotes considerable attention to pogroms not directed against Jews, and my analysis reveals important parallels between his accounts and the Yiddish works discussed earlier. I focus on the story Shklovsky tells about his intervention in a pogrom in northern Iran, and the story he does not tell about the May 1919 pogrom in Elisavetgrad (Kropyvnytskyi), where his grandmother lived.

A summary of the two parts of *Sentimental Journey* sets the stage for the analysis that follows. "Revolution and the Front" begins with the carnivalesque joy of the revolutionary crowd, but at the end of "Writing Desk," Shklovsky says that his life is in fragments. The first section of part 1 provides a narrative of the initial period of the February Revolution in Petrograd, describing the growing restlessness of the army and the city generally. Shklovsky explains his trip to Russia's southern and western border (the Austrian front) as a war commissar as "living proof of the Russian democracy's intention to stay in the war."[9] He travels to Kyiv; west and south to Stanislav, Czernowitz, and Nadworna; and journeys back and forth across the Carpathian Mountains. He stumbles into battle and receives a severe injury in the stomach. The first section of "Revolution and the Front" ends with an appeal to his readers to remember the blood of his comrades shed in the "cornfields of Galicia."

The second section begins with the Kornilov mutiny against Kerensky's provisional government. Shklovsky leaves St. Petersburg and travels to Mogilev (Mohyliv-Podil's'kyi), where two telegrams arrive at once, one from Kornilov proclaiming his supreme authority and the other from Kerensky proclaiming Kornilov a rebel. Shklovsky goes south to Jassy and then to Lipkany, where he decides to find another post.

The third, final, and most extraordinary section of "Revolution and the Front" describes Shklovsky's new position as a war commissar in Persia. Shklovsky characterizes the Russian adventure in Persia as "stupid Imperialism."[10] It is here that he is moved to declare that "nowhere was the lining of war, its predatory essence, so clear as in the crevices of Persia."[11] Violence "lay bare" what otherwise would be concealed. He dwells on what takes place in these cracks and crevices: the pogroms carried out by Turks and others against Christian groups, and the violence carried out by the

Russian army against the local population generally. Shklovsky details his own efforts to stop a pogrom in the market at Urmia, the city in northwestern Iran where he was posted.

Part 2 of *Sentimental Journey* opens with a statement of regret. Shklovsky is sorry he attempted to direct events. He compares himself to a falling stone, moved by external forces he cannot control. Borrowing from Spinoza, he can only "light a lantern" to illuminate his downward trajectory. Shklovsky works as a commissar charged with the protection of antiquities and becomes involved in preparing an armored car division for the defense of the Constituent Assembly. Grigory Semenov, one of the witnesses for the prosecution at the 1922 trial of the Socialist Revolutionaries, delegates someone to see Shklovsky about this task. The Cheka interrogates him and he leaves St. Petersburg for Moscow and then Saratov, where he spends his time in "a maze of hideouts," including an insane asylum.[12] He retraces his steps, returning to Moscow and from Moscow to Ukraine. He is in Kyiv when Hetman Skoropadskyi falls and Petliura enters the city and takes part in sabotaging vehicles used by Petliura's forces. He makes an important statement about what could have been: "There was more than one occasion when the civil war in Russia could have been stopped."[13] The condition contrary to fact, called on by more than one author in this study, pushes against the inevitability of violence. After his return from Ukraine, Shklovsky's life in St. Petersburg is marked by cold, hunger, and the writing of several important critical works. Serving in the Red Army in 1920, he tries to fix a bomb while smoking a cigarette, and it blows up in his hands. He stays with his grandmother in Elisavetgrad (a significant pogrom site) after being released from the hospital. "Writing Desk" ends with an homage to the "strange" (*stranen*) Dr. Shedd, who saved thousands of lives after Russian forces left Persia.[14]

Violence, Knowledge, and Estrangement

In his introduction to Veena Das's *Life and Words*, the philosopher Stanley Cavell writes, "Social convulsion lays bare the question of a society's will and right to exist, to name and honor itself." To know a society, Cavell goes on to say, is to "know its capacity to inflict harm on itself."[15] Violence makes knowledge available that otherwise would remain obscure; violence lays bare the mechanisms on which society functions. Cavell's formulation would appear to owe a debt to Shklovsky. Although Das writes about India in the late 1960s and Shklovsky, Russia in the revolutionary period, both provide descriptions of daily life amid and in the aftermath of large-scale public violence. Shklovsky's travels through the Russian empire show him what happens when every habit, custom, rule, and type of behavior; every economic and material mechanism, including railways, factories, and machines; every structure both physical and figurative is violently torn apart. Or, as Shklovsky puts it succinctly, using a word for which there is no English equivalent, there was no *byt*, no "regular life," only "fragments" of what had once been.[16] Shklovsky lays bare the device not merely aesthetically but also in a broader sense, because what he chronicles in *Sentimental Journey* is nothing less than the stripping away of social forms and the subsequent exposure of life in the condition of abandonment.

He shows how ordinary people were exposed to the whims of the arbitrary power of the crowd and self-styled temporary rulers; he traces the consequences of this exposure throughout the social space, detailing the strange and fantastic look, feel, taste, and smell of the new revolutionary world. The term *strange* (*stranno, strannoe*) occurs numerous times throughout Shklovsky's text, sometimes paired with *terrible* (*strashno*).[17] He characterizes the Russian Revolution, for example, as "terrible and fantastic" (*strashnaia i prichudlivaia*).[18] The daily life of the time is "strange."[19] The strangeness is overwhelming; Shklovsky writes, "I can't put together all the strange things I have seen in Russia."[20] In Russian, as in English, *strange* is a building block of the term *estrangement*, as Shklovsky himself pointed out.[21]

The intensification of experience was characteristic of life in revolutionary Russia. This historical moment resembled a work of art, which according to Shklovsky, makes strange and lays bare the underlying mechanisms of its own operation. "Everything was as bare and open," Shklovsky writes, "as an open face watch."[22] The revolution suspended the routinization of habit, because the revolution destroyed all the conditions on which habit depended. Shklovsky says so explicitly in a passage he attributes to Boris Eikhenbaum: "The main distinction between revolutionary and ordinary life is that now everything is felt. Life has become art."[23]

Life became art not because someone's aesthetic intention had recreated it beautifully but because nothing remained of previous forms of life. Violence made everything unrecognizable, strange, and therefore more intensely perceived, "felt," and sensed. The problem was that the overwhelming force of human habit made the new conditions acceptable. People became habituated to naked violence and stopped seeing its consequences, no longer acknowledging what they were doing to each other. It is not only habit that destroys our fear of war, to go back to "Art as Device." War destroys the fear of war; the new habitus of war became easy to get used to. Shklovsky demands that his readers see its grotesque horror. Galin Tihanov has shown the significance of World War I for the development of Shklovsky's early ideas. Art was complicit in lowering humanity's sensitivity to pain.[24] This chapter shows how Shklovsky raises his readers' sensitivity to pain, compelling attention to it, by making violence strange.[25] As Boym puts it, "In describing pillage, slaughter, pogroms, and the daily cruelty that he witnessed at the front, Shklovsky redirects his estrangement" from art to life.[26] The all-pervasive sense of strangeness in *Sentimental Journey* is a response to violence.

The concept of hefker, the state of being "up for grabs," goes to the heart of Shklovsky's understanding of violence. The people and things that fill the pages of *Sentimental Journey* share the common feature of abandoned ownerlessness. Shklovsky finds abandonment in the actions of the Russian army and other armed groups, in the designation of ethnic and religious groups as enemies, including Jews, Kurds, and others, and in the collapse of norms and law in the aftermath of the October Revolution, evident in the behavior of ordinary people in the capital cities. The result in these cases was similar: those who were abandoned became subject to arbitrary power, which usually took the form of direct assault. What mitigates abandonment is care, attentiveness to suffering and death. Attentiveness to others' suffering takes several forms; one of the most important was simply counting the dead, a task that in fact was not so simple, as Shklovsky and the next chapter show. He characterizes this form of care as "strange." He discovers a new awareness of his own ethical obligation in the face of suffering as well as an ethical relation to his readers. The failure of attention that *Sentimental Journey* tracks is not a deficit of sensation but, rather, a lack of moral attention to others. Shklovsky demands from his readers and himself an engaged attentiveness to the suffering of abandonment.

Factography, Witnessing, and the Emotions

Shklovsky's contemporary readers emphasized the documentary qualities of his book as its most important innovation. In the 1920s, proponents of the "literature of fact" argued that novels and poetry should be replaced by nonfiction genres, including memoirs, travelogues, accounts of courtroom proceedings, "sketches" (*ocherki*), any form of "human document," and history. Devoid of plot, characters, emotion, and psychology, this type of writing was focused on facts. To put it in Shklovskian terms, the fact was the device out of which the new art was to be made. For the Russian factographers, new conditions created by the revolution demanded a new form of narrative art. Whether the facts being reported were positive or negative, reporting them meant attentiveness to what was changing in the new revolutionary society and, thus, charting how the dynamism of the present showed the way to the future. In this way, the new literature of fact was part of art's chief task, the construction of life. Shklovsky's *Sentimental Journey* was a case in point. Shklovsky's active work as a Socialist Revolutionary in opposition to the Bolsheviks did not diminish the factographers' appreciation of the innovation of his memoirs, and neither did his attention to the chaos of the new world created by the revolution. "The ideological correctness of a particular perspective" didn't matter.[27] Nikolai Chuzhak, one of the main factographers of the time, had this to say about Shklovsky's affect in *Sentimental Journey*: "He sniffs at the entire world like a puppy that has opened its eyes for the first time."[28] To a certain extent, Chuzhak's image is strangely appropriate; Shklovsky "sniffs at" the strange creatures created by the revolution in all of their fleshly existence. This is a form of engaged attentiveness to the sheer novelty of the phenomena that Shklovsky as observer encounters. Yet, at crucial moments in the text, Shklovsky leaves puppyhood and factography behind. One such moment occurs at the end of "Revolution and the Front," when Shklovsky asks his readers to remember the dead. There are others, as I show.

The writing in "Writing Desk" reflects the orientation toward the sketch. The entire narrative consists of brief vignettes and interjections and embedded accounts from others. In comparison even to "Revolution and the Front," the descriptions are truncated, the paragraphs shortened. Indeed, most are no more than a sentence. Logical and psychological connections between various statements are lacking.[29] There is no ascending and descending narrative arc in "Writing Desk" but, rather, bits and pieces, like the fragments of shrapnel that come out of his body. Shklovsky writes, "Only our clothing, not the body, joins together the disparate moments of life."[30] This is not a joyous release from the stultifying conventions of the past; Shklovsky the writer continues to craft truncated segments of prose, but Shklovsky the person would prefer the moments to dilate into more sustained, larger sections. In *Third Factory*, another autobiographical work from the 1920s, he declares his love for "long strips of life." The fragmentation of life and art reflect each other in *Sentimental Journey*, as they did in Hofshteyn's pogrom cycle and Kipnis's *Months and Days*. The only thing that kept Victor Shklovsky Victor Shklovsky was his writing desk, he tells us, meaning both the object and the text it helped him produce.

The argument has been made that Shklovsky's motivation in writing *Sentimental Journey* was strategic and political. Shklovsky sought to regain, if not favor with the Bolsheviks, then at least the ability to live and work in Russia in the aftermath of the June 1922 trial of the Socialist Revolutionaries, the party to which he belonged. The death sentences of the defendants were reduced to life imprisonment. Scholars have argued that the sentiment in *Sentimental Journey* is Shklovsky's way of making a plea for himself and the victims of the February and October Revolutions.[31] Shklovsky's autobiographical text was, for all intents and purposes, a document that he presented to the court in his own defense.

The deposition, however, is also an accusation against others guilty of betrayal and violence: "I drowned no one, I stomped no one to death and I made peace with no one due to hunger."[32] Shklovsky declares himself innocent of perpetuating the kind of extraordinary violence that he encounters everywhere in the former Russian and beyond its borders. Eric Santner characterizes witnessing as the act of transforming material and emotional deposits—wounds to the psyche into depositions, acts of giving evidence. *Sentimental Journey* is a "deposition" in this sense. It is an accusation, directed against those in power, which in the era of "local power and local terror," as Shklovsky says, includes a certain portion of his readers.[33] Shklovsky attempts to take responsibility for some aspects of the abandonment he sees, not only by documenting it but also by directly intervening. Chuzhak's "puppy" does not merely "sniff" at what others ignore; he actively tries to mitigate suffering.

Abandonment

Shklovsky details an entire catalog of abandoned machines, animals, and human lives. Sometimes he explicitly uses the Russian term *broshennyi* (abandoned); related terms also appear. Shortly after the February Revolution, St. Petersburg was "jammed with automobiles abandoned to the whim of fate" and patrols began to "pick up the automobiles that were running aimlessly about the city."[34] The White Army "mobilized high school students" and then cast them aside; their parents searched for these "abandoned" children left alone on boats on the Dnieper.[35] The Russian army in northern Iran "abandoned to the whim of fate" the detachment of Assyrians it had created as a "special militia," and their lot became terrible.[36] There was insufficient forage for the army's horses, which were driven into the steppe and died slowly; Shklovsky notes that he simply "rode past" them without attending to them. An "abandoned" Kurdish child lay before a soldier who couldn't decide whether to kill him and therefore would start and stop the process without noticing the terrible suffering he was inflicting.

The actions of the Russian army in Iran and the actions of various non-state armed bands and individuals in other parts of the former Russian empire reveal certain parallels. Fleeing Moscow, Shklovsky travels by train to L'gov in the Kursk region, continues in a southerly direction, and then, together with many other passengers, disembarks, planning to complete his journey to Ukraine on foot. A soldier stops him and a "small Jew in an unusually long overcoat," directing them away from the railway station toward a field. They are both ordered to undress, and the soldier takes whatever he wants. The soldier displays no affect during his search; it is conducted in a matter-of-fact style, which Shklovsky's description emphasizes: "It's as if he's in a store." The lack of emotion is comparable to the scene in Isaac Babel's "Berestechko" in *Red Cavalry*. An old man tries to escape from the Cossacks, who believe he is guilty of espionage, and intend to shoot him. The man tries to get away; however, a soldier takes hold of him, and the Jew calms down. The soldier then goes ahead and slits his throat carefully, so as not to splatter himself. There is no particular venom in Babel's scene or in Shklovsky's. In both cases, the victims do not protest, and the perpetrators do not take the trouble to demean or dehumanize them because they are already disenfranchised. There is a new reality on the ground in which outrage plays no role, and Shklovsky's deadpan tone exaggerates it to make his point.[37] Shklovsky and the "Jew" have already lost their ability to claim ownership of their own things and themselves. Even though Shklovsky does not use the term, for the soldier Shklovsky and his companion are hefker. Readers never learn what happens to the "Jew"; in all likelihood, the same soldiers who disposed of his things also disposed of him.

In "Writing Desk," the second part of *Sentimental Journey*, Shklovsky uses the term *up for grabs* explicitly. The term, as Shklovsky explains, is from criminal argot. He had been tinkering with a bomb while smoking a cigarette, and it exploded in his hands (an apogee of inattentiveness). Hospitalized in Kherson, Shklovsky found himself next to a one-legged "local communist" named Gorban'. A fellow Socialist Revolutionary, Gorban' had been in prison in czarist times and had fought against both the Greeks and the Germans who occupied Kherson.

According to Shklovsky, Gorban' had been active in Nikolaev. Nikolaev, around forty-three miles from Kherson, was the scene of a three-day pogrom in May 1919, during which approximately one hundred Jews were killed. Women and girls were raped, and Jewish shops were pilfered.[38] It is from Gorban' that Shklovsky learns the term *na sharap*, "up for grabs," an invitation to make off with whatever could be found, parallel to the Jewish term *hefker*, with regard to both "unclaimed property" and persons who could be abused with impunity.[39] Gorban' tells Shklovsky how in Nikolaev he and his men "used to seize railway stations and declare them 'up for grabs.'"[40] Anyone could take whatever he wanted, and even though the pickings could be slim, according to Gorban', it was "fun" (*interesno*). They "massacred trains full of refugees," meaning mainly Jewish refugees, killing everyone, but spared the life of a Jewish woman weighing 350 pounds because she was a "rarity." The type of railway pogrom that Shklovsky's fellow patient Gorban' describes, using the term *up for grabs*, was prevalent in Kherson province during August and September 1919. Jews were thrown out of the windows of moving trains.[41] Whether Shklovsky was using a real name for the figure of Gorban' and who he was remain unclear.[42]

Mob Rule

In the immediate aftermath of the revolution, there were bullets in the air like clouds in the sky. Local violence carried out by specific groups and individuals was as inevitable as the weather. "The blood of the revolution," Shklovsky writes, "entered daily life." *A Sentimental Journey* chronicles what happens when arbitrary power extends its reach to ordinary people. In Petrograd, a boy is shot for stealing a pair of boots; his body is put in a cab together with a drunken soldier, and the cab is ordered to go to the hospital morgue. The difference between live bodies and dead bodies frays in a time when ad hoc summary execution, or "mob rule" (*samosud*) became the norm.[43] The question was not whether victims would die but by what means, and Shklovsky details various horrific methods of torture and death. Shklovsky talks to a soldier about samosud, who says "it's when a dead man talks." When Shklovsky asks what this means, the answer is "a man who's shortly going to be dead talks."[44] Shklovsky's interlocutor speaks as if not he but some external force were going to kill the victim. In the strange world of revolutionary violence, death is the only actor; everyone else is merely a vector through which death moves. Kipnis's insistence that it was impossible to tell the difference between the living and the dead, and Kvitko's personification of death as an aggressive panhandler make a similar point about the world of pogrom violence. The mob rule of revolution and the warlord rule of pogroms invert the order of things. Necropolitics, politics oriented toward death, is the common factor between the two.

Shklovsky's journey through the former Russian empire involves death at every turn. Shklovsky, however, is unlike other victims, because he comes back from the dead. He survives the kind of stomach injury that is usually fatal; he remains alive after a bomb explodes in his hands. He is not condemned to death in 1922. Ironically, the false passport he carries lists the person on it as already dead. Shklovsky imagines the humorous conversation he might have with the authorities on this very point. He returns to St. Petersburg disguised as a German POW in "a naked throng" of POWs, making the journey with them in a railroad car full of coffins, marked "Return Coffins." Shklovsky himself is one of the undead on the same continuum as the death-stamped skeletons that swarm Kvitko's apartment.

Enfleshment

In chapter 4, I discuss enfleshment as a product of specific forms of violence. Bialik and Kvitko depict a loss of individuation and the emergence of an entangled, intracorporeal form of human life. I introduced Shklovsky's description of hunger during the blockade of St. Petersburg in 1919 and continue my discussion of the fleshly consequences of the revolution here. Kvitko relies on the grotesque and Shklovsky's style is deadpan, but the similarity between them is nonetheless clear: violence and social collapse bring forward dimensions of human life that ordinary existence otherwise obscures. Estrangement for the world requires attending more closely to these other aspects of existence.

After the revolution, food supplies were catastrophically diminished. When the simple business of sustaining bodily life became nearly impossible, the fleshiness of the body became even more noticeable.[45] There was a paradoxical excess of fleshiness at a time when there was too little to maintain it, thus too much flesh and too little flesh coexisted in the same space. Shklovsky describes the brain as a fleshy organ with needs of its own, as if it were a separate organism.[46] The dead bodies of humans and animals could be seen everywhere. The language favored by the Bolsheviks resembled extinct forms of life, "dead, but not yet decayed monsters."[47] Dead, but not yet decayed humans were also in evidence; corpses were left in empty apartments, because it was impossible to bury them. People used cocoa butter to fry food and later learned to make chocolate; as food supplies diminished, they wondered which greens they foraged for were better to eat and devised a way of making soup from oats. This work required considerable effort and ingenuity, which was pointless, however. All the time people spent on feeding their phantom flesh was wasted because it was merely a distraction from dying. Shklovsky compares the laborious methods for producing foodstuffs in St. Petersburg to the efforts of beggars in Iran to find slight hollows in the walls of Urmia because they believed additional warmth could be found in the tiny bit of shelter the hollows provided.

A continuity can be observed across the poets, prose authors, investigators, and memoirists who wrote about the experience of violence. In the face of overwhelming destruction, the suspension of rule, economic collapse, and material deprivation, the distinctions characteristic of social class, gender, and indeed, the boundary between humans and other animals faded away. The loss of these categories is a landmark of the hefker condition. People urinated and defecated on the streets, in courtyards, because the toilets in their apartments were frozen. Emphasizing the loss of distinction among humans and between other animals and humans, Shklovsky sarcastically writes that he was too inattentive to provide a comprehensive account of dog life in Petersburg, and thus, he confined his description to beggar dogs. As I discussed in chapter 4, Kvitko uses the image of dog life to capture the experience of pogromed Jews. In the poem "They're Pushing Me," he suggests with bitter irony that Jews should indulge their animal urges, since they were treated as if they were dogs. Both authors turn to the motif of dog life to describe the common conditions of pogroms and the immediate postrevolutionary world.

Shklovsky's portrait of fleshly life is tied to mechanical repetition. The image of dying children in Hayderabad, which occurs near the end of "Revolution and the Front," emphasizes this point:

> Children about five years old wandered all around the camps with nothing but a black rag for a shirt. Their eyes festered and swarmed with flies.
> Hunched over, with the mechanical gesture of a tired animal, they picked through the garbage looking for something edible.[48]

The mechanized behavior of the starving inhabitants of Petrograd (who pointlessly repeated the same processes to obtain nutrition) and the starving inhabitants of Hayderabad stems from different causes. In the latter case the rapacious action of the Russian army is the most significant factor. Regardless of the differences, Shklovsky's account places shows both groups to be victims of war.

He emphasizes a failure of attention in both cases. It is worth dwelling on this point, because it connects Shklovsky's theory of art with the ethical appeal he makes in *Sentimental Journey*. Henri Bergson's view of comedy, one of the building blocks of Shklovsky's aesthetics, is also relevant. Mere recognition, or as Bergson puts it in his essay on laughter, merely reading the labels of things diminishes experience. The unchanging, automatic response of the body resembles a machine, and this similarity is the essence of the comic.[49] We perceive the comic in proportion to our sense of something mechanical that has imposed itself over life: "the attitudes, gestures, and movements of the body are laughable in exact proportion as that body reminds us of a mere machine."[50] The children of Hyderabad and the starving inhabitants of Petersburg were not comic, of course. The automatic gestures of the former and the obsessive pursuits of the latter, show, however, that they were no longer fully alive. The starving inhabitants of Petersburg were distracted from their deaths by incessantly fussing over what was not nourishment. Mechanical repetition and distraction both fall on the same spectrum of inattention to life. Shklovsky excoriates himself and his fellow soldiers in the Russian army for their indifference to others' suffering; the habit of war had made them accustomed to beggars. He thus reveals two forms of mechanization, in both the starving children's "mechanical gestures" and their indifferent spectators.

Bodies and Machines

In depicting the proximity of humans to things and other animals, and detailing their excessive and inadequate flesh, the disaggregation of bodies, the mechanical repetition of their movements, and other expressions of undead life, both the Yiddish authors discussed in previous chapters and Shklovsky similarly demonstrate the consequences of abandonment and violence. The focus on machines in *Sentimental Journey* requires a separate discussion, however. Elaine Scarry's *The Body in Pain: The Making and Unmaking of the World* is helpful, not only in relation to the mechanized body but also regarding Shklovsky's broader understanding of violence. Shklovsky, like Scarry, is concerned with bodies in pain, his own and others.[51] Reading Shklovsky in light of Scarry helps explain the connection between Shklovsky's account of the destruction of machinery in "Writing Desk" and the plundering of the bazaar in Urmia, in the "Persia" section of "Revolution and the Front."

Scarry argues that the purposeful infliction of pain in torture and the mitigation of pain depend on acts of imagination. Pain itself works to separate the torture victim from the world; people suffering from injury or illness often cannot express their pain except in figurative language that imagine instruments inflicting pain. The example Scarry gives of relieving pain is a carpenter who fashions a chair for his pregnant wife. The design and manufacture of the chair project sentience into the world. The chair alleviates the burden of carrying weight. In addition, the manufacture of the object creates and enhances the relation between the maker and the person for whom the object is intended. There is also the reciprocal activity of the object and the person. Scarry, like Shklovsky, sees a reciprocal relation between the objects we make and how they remake us. "The basic work of creation is to bring about this very projection of aliveness" into the external world, Scarry writes.[52] Torture, in contrast, reduces the victim's world to the confines of the tortured body and transforms all the objects in it into instruments of pain, unmaking the world; the "artifact is deconstructed to produce pain."⁵³ Kvitko's poem about infant cradles made into gallows comes to mind.

Artifacts are not merely inert things. Making objects, poems, towns, or furniture depends first on making them up. Laying bare the device of social and technical mechanisms takes us back a step from the made object to the processes that go into its construction and from there back to its making up, its projected status. The pain that Shklovsky expresses over the destruction of things in the context of his comments on the destruction of human life reflects his awareness that the destruction of objects also destroys acts of human imagination, craftsmanship, and the projection of the human into the world. Both pain and imagination are forms of sentience and "conditions of intentionality." Torture and war lend the "aura of material reality" to whatever power claims victory. The artfulness of invention remakes the world that has been destroyed, replacing the spectral world of pain and dead bodies with new forms of life. Shklovsky explicitly creates an equivalence between saving life and saving machinery in the conclusion to "Writing Desk." He ends the book in the name of Dr. Shedd, who saved children in Persia, another doctor who saved the lives of prisoners in Kherson, and "the nameless driver who asked me to save his lathes."⁵⁴ A lathe rotates a wooden or metal object against various instruments that cut or shape it. Shklovsky creates a parallel between the lives of children and the lives of lathes, so to speak, not because he devalues the former, but because he sees the latter as a means for human creativity that sustains and remakes the world.

Shklovsky devotes considerable attention to the abandonment and destruction of machinery in revolutionary Russia. In "Writing Desk," Shklovsky laments the ignorance of Russian mechanics, who confused the oil and gas lines on Gnome rotary engines. This is comparable to the inability to distinguish cows from horses, he explains. The wrong oil was used in tank cars, and it congealed in the cold of Petersburg. Shklovsky decries these mistakes in emotional terms; he doesn't know whether the French mechanics called in to repair the Gnome engines "fainted or started to cry."⁵⁵ The episode of the tank cars was one of many: "You had to listen to stories like this every day. If I could just relate the things that happened to automobiles alone!"⁵⁶ This expression of dismay about objects does not mean that Shklovsky had no emotions about human beings. Since the machine is an extension of the human, the destruction of the machine is also human destruction.

Shklovsky's interest in the relation between the body and the artifact reaches a grotesque peak in his account of how he blew himself up. Describing Russia's massive self-inflicted harm, he follows suit in his own life by smoking while attempting to repair a bomb. The group of soldiers Shklovsky was involved with at this time lacked the substance used to prime the main explosive material in a bomb. Shklovsky, distracted by thinking about literary criticism, smoked a cigarette as he tinkered with the substitute primer the men devised. Inattentiveness, the same problem that prevents the soldiers departing Iran from responding to the starving children in Hayderabad, leads to disaster: the bomb explodes in Shklovsky's hands. His blood is splattered on the grass; he keeps shrieking even after the bomb stops; his "arms and clothes were all in shreds and holes"; and his body shakes. Shklovsky writes, "The flesh on my bones was quivering."[57] The doctors can't remove all the shrapnel from his body. What happens instead is:

> the fragments came out by themselves.
> I'd be walking along and something would sting. Something would scrape against my underwear. I'd stop and take a look and there'd be a small, white fragment showing from the wound, sticking out.
> I'd pull it out and the wound would heal right away.[58]

The bomb stopped exploding, but his body keeps on exploding: fresh wounds open and extrude shrapnel, then close. Shklovsky's continually exploding body also realizes his metaphor of the fragmentation of life in postrevolutionary Russia and his assertion that the "clothing, not the body, join together the disparate parts of life." The explosion and Shklovsky's injury echo the opening of "Writing Desk," which describes St. Petersburg in 1918 as a time and space in which an explosion had occurred that blew everything up.

Hidden Linkages: Shklovsky as Jew

Gorban', the figure who introduced Shklovsky to the term *up for grabs*, plays a starring role in the revelation of the author's family history. The accidental meeting between Shklovsky and Gorban' echoes a scene from Tolstoy, the author Shklovsky famously associated with the technique of estrangement.[59] In the third volume of *War and Peace*, Andrei Bolkonsky, wounded in the stomach, ends up in the same field hospital as Anatole Kuragin, who had seduced Natasha Rostova. Kuragin has had his leg cut off, and he is "shown his amputated leg stained with clotted blood and with the boot still on."[60] Andrei asks himself what the connection (*sviaz'*) is between the man with the amputated leg and his, Andrei's, childhood and life.[61] He recognizes his rival and feels compassion for him. In *Sentimental Journey*, Shklovsky recounts that Gorban' was severely wounded in one leg, and it apparently had been cut off "with penknives." This is one of the moments in the text that the author addresses readers directly: "If you don't like this description, don't make war."[62]

Shklovsky is playing with Tolstoy's well-known characterization of his novels as "hidden labyrinths of linkages." There is a parallel between the two pairs Bolkonsky/Kuragin and Shklovsky/Gorban'. After describing what happened in Nikolaev and Kherson, Shklovsky informs his readers that he and others from the dressing station were put on a train to Elisavetgrad and placed in a Jewish hospital there. It is at this point that the narrative changes: "Now I must explain my genealogy," says Shklovsky.[63] The Shklovsky family came from Uman and "were massacred in the Uman massacre"; the surviving members of the family went to Elisavetgrad.[64] Uman was the site of a peasant uprising in the eighteenth century. Ivan Gonta, who commanded the garrison, surrendered the city, and tens of thousands of Poles and Jews were killed. In the twentieth century, Uman and Elisavetgrad, both in Kherson province, were also well-known and significant killing sites in 1919, as I discuss in chapters 3 and 4, in connection with Leyb Kvitko's poem cycle *1919*. Elisavetgrad was subjected to an "extraordinary number of pogroms."[65] Archival sources, including reports from representatives of the Kyiv Public Committee to Aid Victims of Pogroms, attest that in May 1919, Grigoriev forces, joined by local criminals released from jail, killed two thousand Jews in the city.[66]

Shklovsky reports that two different groups of marauders entered his grandmother's apartment. When she hid her hand with her wedding band; the "officer" said they didn't take wedding rings, but the Cossacks said they did, and they took it from her. That the author of *Sentimental Journey* does not depict the terror his grandmother must have felt at this moment, or any other details of the encounter, does not mean that there was no terror or that he did not understand it. The marauding armies that terrorized

Elisavetgrad did more than remove wedding bands; they also removed limbs and committed numerous rapes.[67]

Shklovsky's grandmother died of pneumonia "in the ruins of the city." He notes that the letter she wrote him a few days before her death reaches him via a circuitous journey from Ukraine to Denmark to Finland, more plot "retardation" and delay. She had translated excerpts from her Yiddish-language memoirs to Russian for him and included them in her letter. Her memoirs, Shklovsky says, begin with her parents' stories of Gonta and end with Makhno.[68] Makhno, the leader of an anarchist peasant movement that fought against the Red Army, the Volunteer Army, and Petliura's forces, publicly stated his opposition to pogroms; however, dozens of armed insurrectionist groups associated with his name participated in anti-Jewish violence throughout the region. In Elisavetgrad, where Shklovsky's grandmother lived, marauding bands consisting of locals from the region called themselves "Makhnovists" (*makhnovtsy*).[69] Grandmother Shklovsky occupies the same position in the Gorban'/Victor Shklovsky pair as Natasha Rostova in the Kuragin/Bolkonsky pair. As Shklovsky says, art is the deformation of material. He is "deforming," that is, changing, Tolstoy's material but using the same plot structure.

In pointing out that his grandmother's memoirs start with Gonta in the eighteenth century and end with Makhno in the twentieth, Shklovsky expands the "disparate moments" of life, held together only by clothing, into a longer strip of time. Shklovsky's temporal framing, and indeed, the entire section of *Sentimental Journey* that discusses anti-Jewish violence in the Kherson region, thus departs significantly from factographic temporality. Chuzhak, whom I discuss in the opening of this chapter, emphasized the importance of the synchronic snapshot. The genre favored most of all by the factographers, the *ocherk*, or sketch, was committed to presentism.[70] Hence it is significant that one of the few places in *Sentimental Journey* that departs from the quick pacing and presentism that Shklovsky found characteristic of the new genre of his time is his discussion of his family background and their tragic history.

Persian Pogroms

Shklovsky does not, however, dwell on anti-Jewish violence in *Sentimental Journey*; indeed, the term *pogrom* appears largely in relation to other ethnic and religious groups in Persia (Iran), including Christians, Armenians, Tatars, and Kurds, "none of whom," Shklovsky adds, had gotten along "since time immemorial."[71] His characterization of the tail end of World War I in what he calls the "East," which I cite earlier, bears repeating: "nowhere was the lining of war, its predatory essence, so clear as in the crevices of Persia."[72] It was in the crevices of the city walls that Shklovsky saw Kurdish beggars attempting to find extra warmth.

In a letter from 1917 to Maxim Gorky, Shklovsky describes the conditions of life and death in Persia in a few brief lines: "I live in Urmia. I've seen Persia destroyed and people dying of hunger on the street. Right in front of us. I've seen pogroms and suffered the Golgotha of impotence. My cup will soon be full. I feel terrible here. We trample on people as if they were grass."[73] Recall Frug's poem "Sand and Stars": Jews had become like "sand, which is hefker, / which everyone tramples with their feet." Shklovsky does not use the same term, but the parallel is clear. Both authors are describing populations subjected to the impunity of abandonment.

A few words of historical contextualization are helpful.[74] Shklovsky uses the term *Aissor* (*Aisor*) to refer to Aramaic-speaking Christians in northwestern Iran, Azerbaijan, and Turkey; scholars today refer to these groups as Syriacs or Assyrians. Syriacs, or Assyrians, include Nestorians, considered heretics by the Christian church, because they do not believe in the dual nature of Christ. They believe their patriarch to be descended from Simon, the brother of Christ, and every patriarch is referred to as "Mar Simon." The massacres carried out against the Assyrians are distinct from the Armenian genocide, although they took place in its immediate aftermath. Urmia, the city where Shklovsky was posted, had around ten thousand Assyrians at the time. In January 1915, Russian forces left Urmia, returning in May, and then leaving again in July. In the intervals, Turkish and Kurdish forces slaughtered Assyrians in the city; several thousand sheltered in the foreign compounds located in the city, especially the American compound. Russian policies toward the Kurdish population were extremely harsh, leading to famine; Shklovsky refers frequently to Kurdish beggars in Urmia, as I discuss. The 1917 revolution led to the definitive withdrawal of Russian forces. Angered by exchange rates, Russian soldiers razed the bazaars of Urmia, and Shklovsky describes his own efforts to stop the plunder. In 1918, the Assyrian patriarch was killed at what was supposed to be a peace summit with the Kurds. The entire Assyrian population decided to leave the region and flee to the British in Iraq. Shklovsky describes this event, which amounted to a death march, and, in particular, Dr. Shedd's rescue work.

Peter Holquist compares Russian imperial policy with regard to the civilian population in the Caucasus and Persia to parallel policies conducted in Austrian Galicia during World War I and finds that whereas antisemitism led the Russian army to deport thousands of Jews, there was no consistent or ideologically motivated or nationalistic campaign against ethnic groups in Iran.[75] Russian policy was internally contradictory, and the violence the Russian army carried out against various ethnic groups stemmed from its long-held assumption that it came first and civilians second.[76] Holquist quotes the telling language of the chief of staff for the Caucasus, General Ianushkevich, who said that a mortality rate of 10 percent in the civilian population was "normal."[77] Holquist's point is that Ianushkevich did not distinguish ethnic groups in his decimation quota, but Shklovsky, in contrast, cannot accept the norm and recoils from it, attempting to estrange the habit of war that allowed the general to reach this conclusion in the first place. He sees the normal 10 percent mortality rate in children mechanically pecking at garbage heaps. He discerns greater continuities between the Russian army's violence in the Caucasus in 1917, in the aftermath of the Armenian genocide, and public violence generally in revolutionary Russia, including anti-Jewish violence along Russia's southwestern border. Shklovsky says, "I saw the incinerated villages and houses reduced to pulp, but I wasn't prepared for the sight of the Persian ruins."[78] He agrees with Holquist on the matter of antisemitism in the Russian army more generally and muses that if not for personal ties and his library, he would remain in the East, because there was no antisemitism there.

To return to Shklovsky's language, the predatory essence of war is that everyone and everything not already belonging to the army is "up for grabs." Whoever was not part of the army was material for its own use; individual life was granted no recognition other than what could be extracted from it. Shklovsky emphasizes the point by saying the soldiers "had a good attitude toward each other—they weren't like wolves with each other."[79] The implication is that toward nonsoldiers, they were like wolves. *Homo homini lupus*, "man to man is an arrant wolf," occurs in the dedication to Thomas Hobbes's *The Citizen* (De cive), published in the seventeenth century. In *Homo Sacer*, Agamben argues that Hobbes's state of nature is perpetually available on the threshold of political life.

The Russian army in Persia revealed the threshold and their own wolfishness by regarding the local populations as mere material to be plundered, killed, or raped. Shklovsky's language heightens the monstrous transformations in both those who perpetuated the violence and those who were its victims; both were the creatures of war. He saw corpses on the road, people who had been killed "like dogs by someone wanting to test his rifle."[80] The Kurdish beggars in Hayderabad had nothing left to wear except "strange" felt capes, worn in such a way as to resemble "the imploring stumps of a man with no arms."[81] The children pecking through trash heaps had already lost their human appearance, resembling instead "tired animals." "We looked at these beggars calmly," Shklovsky writes, "the way we looked at a wall, the way we looked at all of Persia."[82] Women tried to avoid being raped by Russian soldiers by destroying their human appearance. Shklovsky reports how. They smeared excrement over their torsos, necks, and faces, but the soldiers wiped it off and raped them anyway.[83] Rape was used as an instrument of genocide during the Ottoman massacre of Armenians and during the pogroms of the Russian Civil War. Women everywhere had fallen out of the realm of human care.

This sort of carelessness took various forms. Under the rubric of what he characterizes as "some strange stories," Shklovsky recounts how some prisoners from the stockade approached him. It turns out that anybody in the Russian army could arrest anyone from any of the local populations, and once arrested, men remained in prison, not questioned for months. They were forgotten, "out of a general lack of concern for people."[84] Lack of concern, carelessness toward other people, and not taking care and the inverse, taking care, are all labeled "strange" by Shklovsky.

A similar indifference characterized the local Russian leadership's attitude toward the pogroms in the marketplace in Urmia. Shklovsky describes one of them, provoked in part by what the Russian soldiers saw as unfair exchange rates; however, there was no real reason for this episode of looting and violence any more than any other episode. The pogroms "were constant."[85] Since no one else in the military command would take action, Shklovsky entered the bazaar alone. The scene he describes is the stuff of nightmare: "and there was a constant cry—ow, ow, ow, as in a bathhouse. A blind, dull rage swept over me. I picked up a board and with a shout ran down the dark tunnel hitting all comers. . . . Men were rummaging in the insides of the dark stalls, jerking out long strips of material like intestines.... The dust raised by the vandals made you want to cough and spit up your innards [ellipsis added]."[86] The metaphor of the body, particularly, the insides of the body, dominates the description of the pogrom. Its sound is reminiscent of the bathhouse, where naked bodies congregate; the bazaar as a whole is a mass body, full of numerous internal caverns and spaces. The looters rifle through the hidden interiors, ripping out the bazaar's intestines, their behavior resembling the actions of predatory animals, an example of more wolfishness. Shklovsky's description indicates the state of nature on the periphery of the Russian empire and on the threshold of ordered life.

It is important to understand the significance of the image of the marketplace as a vast body. The cloth that looks like intestines, pottery, shoes, and other leather goods, the stalls themselves, the doors hanging from their hinges, no less than Gnome engines, automobiles, and construction cranes that are part of the landscape of revolutionary Russia are also projections of human sentience into the world. Moreover, in an immediate way, these objects are embodiments of and sources for human life, inventiveness, and ingenuity. The material objects that are for sale at the market emerge out of the bodily labor of the people who make them. In addition, the marketplace itself, not only its physical structure of tunnels, stalls, and doors but also the system of exchange, is also an artifact of human inventiveness and, importantly, human sociability. The marketplace where goods are manufactured, bought, and sold sustains and is a projection of human bodies and the social body writ large. The bazaar both resembles and is an extension of human bodies. The market vendors, Shklovsky notes, fear that defending themselves would cause the marauding soldiers to extend their pogrom to the rest of the city's inhabitants. The plundering and destruction of the market thus amount to the destruction of human bodies and the larger social body, both "up for grabs" (hefker).

Earlier, I discuss the apparent lack of emotion in Shklovsky's *Sentimental Journey*. He uses a flat, laconic, "factographic" style to describe events that we might expect would provoke some emotion. These include his reception of Gorban's narrative, the description of his grandmother's experience of the pogrom in Elisavetgrad, for example, and the episode in which a soldier in Ukraine calmly and deliberately robs him and an unnamed "Jew." The narrative of the pogrom at the market in Urmia, in contrast, is full of emotion. The victims are crazed. Shklovsky writes that the Persian vendors "ululated in high-pitched, maddened voices and gouged their faces." The perpetrators are crazed, and Shklovsky, who wants to stop the pogrom, is no less so: "I drove a mob as crazed and blind as I was myself."[87] He catches a looter who has managed to steal two left boots and a few currents and remarks how strange it is and how wild-eyed the looter was. The looters and Shklovsky himself are driven by some force they cannot identify, excited by something beyond them unseen and unnamed. Driven beyond rationality, everyone wants a piece of the market's already ravaged and depleted body—even two left boots will do. The question of emotion should not be directed at the actual real-life person Shklovsky but rather framed in terms of the larger strategy of displacement and estrangement in the memoir generally. Shklovsky examines his own capacity to be caught up in a larger force field of rage, appetite, and aggression in which he becomes a stranger to himself.

The aftermath of this episode is one of the peaks of emotion in *Sentimental Journey* as a whole. Shklovsky is "ashamed": "the grief and shame of the dust of the pogroms lay on my soul."[88] Dust is a product of violence, linked with the body's fleshiness, the dust that makes you want to vomit up your innards, and in addition, the emotion of shame and regret. Dust is a remnant of the built environment that sustained life and is now destroyed. It is a concrete sediment of the abandonment to which the vendors in the market and the entire surrounding population have been consigned, and which Shklovsky cannot alleviate. Dust is significantly also linked to the Jewish notion of hefker, "up for grabs." The Passover holiday begins with a ritual statement abandoning ownership of leavened foods. Leavened products remaining after the cleaning of the house are declared to be "counted as null and *hefker* even as the dust of the earth."[89] I am not arguing the Passover declaration was on Shklovsky's mind when he wrote about the grief and shame of the pogrom's dust. I am pointing to a parallel between hefker in Jewish sources and Shklovsky's understanding of the violence of abandonment.

Temporal Ruptures and Repetitions

Shklovsky's intervention at the bazaar reminds him of a nightmare he used to have, being chased down long, low, narrow corridors with doors everywhere; during the pogrom he remembered and relived the nightmare.[90] The public real-life repetition of a private individual nightmare augments the strangeness of the experience. The Yiddish author Itsik Kipnis also adds to the strangeness of the 1919 Slovechno pogrom by recalling a childhood nightmare of a similar event. Even though Shklovsky was a participant in the events he recounts, nonetheless the pogrom appears enigmatic and uncanny because it resembles his nightmare. People he does not know and a setting that he has never encountered appear familiar in a distorted, dreadful way.

In his theoretical work, Shklovsky includes chronological displacement as a literary technique that prolongs perception. He uses this device in *Sentimental Journey*. A participant in ongoing events, he stages the temporality of the aftermath in the very opening of "Writing Desk," the second part of *Sentimental Journey*. St. Petersburg in 1918 resembled

> a city that had gone deaf.
> Like after an explosion, when everything ended, when everything's been blown up.[91]

The violence set in motion by the events of 1917 had the extraordinary capacity to create a postapocalyptic chronotope even as events kept on unfolding. An unspecified and all-encompassing "everything" was over and nothing remained. The profound sense of living on after the end of everything thrusts events of the present into the remote past. As I note in chapter 2, Hofshteyn renders recent catastrophe ancient in his pogrom lament *Sorrow*. Like Hofshteyn, who depicts Kyiv as a city that had lost its hearing, Shklovsky compares St. Petersburg to a city that had gone deaf. Here it is not routinization or stale art that suspends the human capacity to sense the world but violence.

Geographic displacement and temporal displacement parallel one another. In Transcaucasia, just beyond the boundary of Russia, the army's geographic location is a no-man's-land (another dimension of the term hefker) created by the end of World War I and the February and October Revolutions. Shklovsky emphasizes this point using an image from science fiction. The telegraph machine spits out "gibberish . . . like white macaroni." Then it breaks off like the telegram to the moon in H. G. Wells's novel *The First Men in the Moon*. Abandoned to his lunar landscape, Shklovsky is the "commissar of a nonexistent government."[92]

In *Sentimental Journey* generally, Shklovsky stresses the strangeness of life after the end, when everything was over, to use his language. He can't make sense of all the strange things he saw and experienced. The mob justice in St. Petersburg, the robbery at gunpoint in Ukraine that was like a shopping expedition, his own body's response to the bomb that exploded in his hands, the bizarre appearance of the Kurdish beggars, and the pogrom at the bazaar in Urmia are strange in a special sense, beyond the fact that Shklovsky uses this term to describe them. His elliptical style, aphoristic narration, the deliberate omission of context, and choice of language make it difficult to grasp what is taking place, thereby heightening the strange impression created by the text generally. The disconnected episodes and vignettes are the stuff of nightmare, not history. This is no mere aesthetic device, however. The violence that has overtaken Russia makes bloodshed and the loss of human life very nearly normal, and Shklovsky wants his reading audience to engage with the abandoned creatures that lie in its wake rather than stepping over them blindly. The distortions of time, space, and common sense in Kvitko's poetry; Hofshteyn's call to attend to barely discernible traces of pain; and Kipnis's seemingly naive address to his readers show the same purpose.

The Strangeness of Care

In the off-kilter realm of abandonment, the attempt to mitigate suffering is also strange. When the Russian Imperial Army started to withdraw from Persia, the Assyrians whom they had used as a "special militia" were abandoned, and Shklovsky, quoting Dr. Shedd, says that more than forty thousand were "massacred." The fleeing Assyrian troops abandoned their children along the way, but Dr. Shedd rescued thirty-five hundred of them. Again, Shklovsky uses his narrative art to exaggerate Dr. Shedd's strangeness. He omits certain key details and emphasizes others. Dr. Shedd (William Ambrose Shedd, 1865–1918) used a surrey to get around Urmia. This was a four-wheeled, horse-driven cart with a fringed canopy on top. To Shklovsky, the former instructor of an armored car division and connoisseur of automobiles, the surrey was an outmoded relic. Twenty years before in the United States, Shklovsky remarks, they were probably ordinary, thus implying how strange it was to see Dr. Shedd driving his surrey in northern Persia in 1917. At a meeting between Russian army officials and Persian mullahs in 1917, Dr. Shedd appears, wearing his black frock coat, his gray hair fluffed out. Shklovsky writes in biblical language, "He stood among us like a black pillar."[93] Dr. Shedd tells the assembled officials that he found the corpse of a six-year-old boy along the wall of the bazaar. He then compares Dr. Shedd to Robinson Crusoe: if Defoe's hero, "wearing his shaggy pelts," had appeared on a London street, "it would have been strange," and Dr. Shedd, counting corpses when no one else did, was also "strange" in the same way.[94]

Dr. Shedd, however, was not nearly as odd a figure as Shklovsky makes him out to be. He was in fact a native of the place, born in Urmia, the son of an American missionary to the Nestorian Church. Although he lived in in America for a limited time, including his student years at Princeton, Shedd spent most of his life in Persia and spoke more than one of the languages of the ethnic groups who lived in the Urmia region. He died of cholera in 1918, having left the area together with the fleeing Assyrian Christians.[95] Dr. Shedd was not a stranger to northern Persia, not out of place; what was strange was the care he extended to those whom others had abandoned.

Dr. Shedd counts the dead one by one rather than consigning them to an abstract percentage. Bringing the attention of others to a single dead boy thus brings back something human into the larger picture of violent abandonment that dominates Shklovsky's depiction of Persia. Where the predatory essence of war is plain for everyone to see, when local populations suffer a 10 percent mortality rate, noticing a single dead six-year-old, and sheltering, feeding, and rescuing thousands of others, seems oddly out of place. When separate human beings have been grotesquely transformed into mere killable flesh, extending care to them as individuals also appears strange.

The end of "Writing Desk" intersplices the discrete events of the two parts of *Sentimental Journey*. Shklovsky gives a purely formal explanation, to the effect that the ending of a two-part book should link elements from both parts. The thematic and emotional connection, however, is more important. The strange creatures created by the violence of revolutionary life in Petersburg and Moscow and the pogroms in Ukraine and the Caucasus resemble each other. Shklovsky's description of his personal relations with Assyrian Christians explicitly uses the motif of Jewishness. The local Assyrian Christian population considered Shklovsky favorably for his role in attempting to stop the pogrom in the marketplace and other measures he took to try to limit violence and plunder. He recounts that a "delegation of Aissors [Assyrian Christians]" brought him sugar and said, "Our people and your people will once again live together side by side. True, we once destroyed Solomon's temple, but later we raised it up again."[96] Shklovsky undercuts his interlocutors' claim by defining himself as "not all Jew" and the Assyrians as Aramaic-speaking Semites. Shklovsky's protestations, however, mask an important set of convergences. In the mist of what is almost a chronicle of the daily news, Shklovsky's text refers to events from before the beginning of the common era. Presentism and puppyhood are suspended. He remarks on the "sense of uninterrupted tradition" characteristic of the peoples in the region. In the second part of *Sentimental Journey*, as I previously discuss, a similar sense of a long history, knitted together by parallels and repeating patterns, also appears. Shklovsky's grandmother's Yiddish-language memoirs begin with the seventeenth-century Gonta and end with Makhno in the twentieth century. In both instances, what David Roskies calls the "analogical" mode of thinking prevails. Shklovsky chronicles the appearance and significance of the wholistic, coherent historical view, even though he stands outside it; he is not "all Jew" and his life is "in pieces." To put it in terms of the metaphor of consciousness as a film projector, in emphasizing 1919 Shklovsky is pulling together disparate geographies, illuminating their common features, and "paying no heed to ethnographic boundaries."[97]

Shklovsky the ethnographer of violence and abandonment is himself an inhabitant of the strange realm these forces created in the aftermath of the February and October Revolutions. He is a falling stone, subject to overwhelming external forces; he experiences the fleshiness of his existence both in his desperate hunger for sugar and in the continual extrusion of shrapnel from his injured body; he imagines himself as the victim of torture, who cravenly seeks warmth from the torturer's hand; he is a disenfranchised Jew, whose belongings and person are up for grabs. He is both melancholy and hyperactive. Shklovsky's and others' fleshy, fragmented lives penetrate each other, and he wants these bits and pieces to enter the lives of his readers. For example, after he describes a particularly drawn out and painful method of killing, he accosts the reader by asking, "What, am I supposed to keep this locked up in my own soul?"

This chapter has explored the relation between the violence of revolutionary Russia and the subsequent appearance of a strange new form of life in the realm of abandonment. The conditions created by the revolution exacerbated the always available potential for abandonment in any social order and accelerated the pull toward the threshold of law and nonlaw. To find oneself at this threshold is to enter a state of abandonment, stripped of social recognition. Shklovsky makes the sense of abandonment, the feeling of life as "up for grabs," as palpable on the streets of Moscow and St. Petersburg as it is at the railway stations in Kherson and the marketplace in Urmia. What Shklovsky chronicles by describing the destruction of people and property is thus also the destruction of a particular way of being human in the world.

The byproduct of destruction is the creation of a strange new world at right angles to the old world, in which violence became the norm. Shklovsky uses his own discovery, the device of estrangement, to heighten the strangeness of the creatures he encounters. He addresses readers directly to exhort them to see their world with the lens he provides and thereby respond to it differently, to engage in moral attention. The forms of social interaction that obtained before constituted a kind of technology, a design for living, as important as engines, cars, and plumbing. The specific configurations of art, social life, technology, and material culture that Shklovsky describes as shattered, "blown up" were not empty, neutral forms and hence the shortcoming of seeing Shklovsky as a mere "formalist." These modes of embodied human life were full of sentiment and sensation, intention, creativity, and care. The hope he derives at the end of "Writing Desk" is that after the end of everything, people will remain who care about human life and the forms of its expression. He projects himself as one such person.

Shklovsky's depiction of Dr. Shedd's strange appearance and behavior, caring about individuals and counting the dead, reveals the upside-down world of revolutionary Russia. In the context of overwhelming violence and utter abandonment, as the Russian army left Persia, counting the dead made no sense, thus, it was strange and out of place. What Shklovsky shows, however, is that it is a way of attending to the other, restoring the tiniest flicker of personhood to a mass of dead bodies. Pogrom investigators also tried to count and account for the dead, and in the next chapter, I describe their goals and the limits of their success.

7
Counting

In "Day Grows Darker," one of the poems in *1919*, Leyb Kvitko depicts the aftermath of a pogrom:

> . . . An unlucky survivor
> will count the dead.
> He will write my dead name
> with all the others
> in tiny letters on a long list.
> Oh, let him not forget
> to record my age
> on that long list![1]

Representing himself as one of the dead, the poet posthumously pleads with some future documentarian, the "unlucky survivor" who counts the victims and writes their names "on a long list." Why the survivor is unlucky is left unspoken. The speaker's "dead name," inscribed in miniscule letters, will be preserved; however, it will not convey how young he was, how full of love, and full of "the will to live," which was as "strong and mad" as his last day. The list fails to chronicle the "young, blossoming life" attached to the dead name, recording only the fact of death. The inscription does not consider the poet's emotions: his joy in his own youth and life, his sorrow and protest against its violent abbreviation, and his desperate desire to augment the record of his death with his poem.

Kvitko's poem and the lists he describes were both responses to the violence and abandonment of the civil war. Poems and lists of the dead were left behind in the aftermath of one of the bloodiest and most chaotic periods in Russian and eastern European history and can be found intermingled in the archive of violence, the vast trove of documents compiled by aid workers in the early 1920s.

Kvitko poetically registers the real-life phenomenon of investigation and documentation that took place after the pogroms. Investigators traveled to killing sites, interviewed refugees in Kyiv and other cities, gathering information, and compiling what were indeed tragically long lists of the dead, noting their names, ages, and occupations. The documents created by various aid organizations include multiple handwritten and typed lists of names. The Kyiv Public Committee to Aid Victims of Pogroms, for example, published a regular bulletin with a section titled "List" ("Tsetl"). Sometimes information was lacking, and individuals remained nameless; in these cases, they were noted only by occupation or family relation, "her daughter, her son."[2] The Kyiv Public Committee and other organizations, both local and international, some organized during the First World War, working with the independent Ukrainian government and the newly established Soviet government, stepped into the breach of abandonment, neglect, and disavowal that had prevailed during the civil war. They sent workers to collect data and provide assistance. The activity of the aid organizations was also short-lived, however. By 1924, they had been disbanded. The vast records they compiled went into Soviet-controlled repositories in Kyiv and elsewhere and remained closed until the 1990s. Elias Cherikover, who created the Editorial Board attached to the Jewish Public Committee, took what he could first to Berlin and then New York, where it became the basis for the YIVO archive. He wrote several pogrom histories based on the materials he had amassed. Others did the same, including Sergei Gusev-Orenburgskii, whose *Crimson Book* was published in Harbin in 1922.

The aid workers, both women and men, were not professional historians or ethnographers. They were journalists, attorneys, medical professionals, social scientists, and individuals without any professional training. They were not archivists, but guided by instructions and protocols, they filtered what they heard, saw, and read through specific paradigms. These determined what information was worth preserving and how the larger pogrom narrative was to be structured. When I began to read first-person testimonies about the pogroms, I was struck by how cut-and-dried they were: first this happened and then that—the "bandits" broke in, demanded goods and money, started shooting, such and such a family member was injured or killed. I wondered where the expression of emotion was. It is commonplace in the early twenty-first century to expect public expressions of emotion in response to catastrophic events, but things were different a century ago.[3] Reading the instructions to aid workers showed that there was little talk about emotions because the guidelines for gathering information about a given pogrom generally did not include questions about the victim's inner experience as individuals who had undergone catastrophic events. This does not mean, of course, that the investigators and their informants did not have emotions. There was certainly an awareness of the consequences, both emotional and psychological, of the experience of violence.

The guidelines omitted other things as well. The interaction between relief workers and informants was not recorded. Non-Jewish deaths were not recorded.[4] Although in some respects the methodologies used by the Jewish Public Committee to Aid Victims of Pogroms (Evobshchestkom) go back to Simon Dubnow's instructions to Bialik in his investigation of the 1903 Kishinev pogrom and An-sky's pre–World War I ethnographic expeditions, the aims of the civil war–era work had one important difference.[5] The aid organizations' immediate, short-term aim was providing relief and also legal evidence to be used in Soviet trials of pogrom perpetuators, and other court cases, including the trial of Shlomo Schwartzbard, who assassinated Symon Petliura in Paris in 1924 and was acquitted by a French jury in 1926.[6] The long-term goal of the written forms and questionnaires was the production of scientific evidence that would show the continued vitality of the Jewish population despite losses that had been suffered.

This chapter focuses on the aid workers' understanding of their own mission. The documents created by Evobshchestkom and its sister organizations reveal a deep rift. The instructions from the center reveal the desire to see progress and recovery. I trace the responses to these instructions by examining various reports, completed questionnaires, telegrams and other correspondence sent from the field to the center. There is abundant evidence of the attempt to comply with the instructions to provide factual accounts—thus the centripetal pull of the documents and yet, at the same time, specific, local, highly emotional accounts pulled away from the guidelines and protocols, the centrifugal force also evident in the material. The ungovernable emotions of shock, outrage, grief, and despair expressed by pogrom investigators coexisted with counting and classifying, the tools of governmentality, that they relied on in their reports. I explore the threshold between chaos and control, drawing primarily from documents produced by Evobshchestkom.

Biopolitics

I have used Achille Mbembe's concept of "necropolitics" to characterize the specific nature of violence during the period 1919–22. Necropolitics is rule by killing, and in the former Russian empire in this period, numerous actors ruled by killing. Jews were particular targets. The nonstate actors in Ukraine and elsewhere during the civil war were not interested in preserving or caring for the life of the population, either Jewish or non-Jewish, hence the appropriateness of the term *necropolitics*. The Jewish aid organizations sought to remove the Jewish population from the space of necropolitics and abandonment and place them instead in the realm of life. Instead of "letting die," agencies such as Evobshchestkom wanted to make the Jewish population live. "Making live" means the provision of care, the care for life, of the body and the population, enhancing the population's biological capacities with the goal of producing and maintaining a suitable labor force. This goal was particularly important, since the so-called nonproductive traditional Jewish occupations left Jews vulnerable to losing rights that the new Soviet government offered.[7] Poised between the damage done in the immediate past and the threat from the immediate future, the relief agencies that are the subject of this chapter sought to enhance the biopower of the Jewish population. The absence of emotion—avoiding the picture of pogromed Jews as objects of pity—served this goal. Jewish relief agencies used the instruments of modern biopolitics to promote a positive image of Jewish life.[8]

The focus on the Jewish population and the Jewish body reflects modern biopolitics in their positive dimension, as a form of care and a means of overcoming the chaos and abandonment of the civil war. The same tools could and were used for the opposite purpose. Indeed, as Peter Holquist has shown, the Russian military in both the late imperial and the Soviet periods used the tools of statistics as an instrument of violence to "extract" elements of the population considered undesirable.[9] In contrast, the efforts of relief organizations to count and classify were aimed at redressing harm. Evobshchestkom was trying to show its Soviet audience that the Jewish population could be healed, that it was vital, that it could serve in the new Soviet labor force, and that it was creative even in the midst of chaos. This aim is evidenced in the support for Yiddish cultural organizations, including the Kyiv Kultur-Lige and other ways that the relief agencies promoted the arts and culture. The foci—the Jewish body, the Jewish population, and the Jewish town, even in its pogromed state—and the emphasis on statistics, including statistics of their own relief work, reflect the larger agenda. Evobshchestkom's self-reflective statements about its own role add another dimension: Jews could restore the Jewish national body, which could then function successfully in the new Soviet society.[10]

The precise instructions, the protocols, forms, questionnaires, telegrams, receipts, lists, and reports generated a framework of nested hierarchies, in short, a bureaucracy. The request for information created a flow of authority from a center to a periphery, a set of resources and a way of distributing them and a way of checking up on the effect of the distribution.[11] In so doing, the combined efforts of these various agencies created something resembling a world and a social order. Their work was an attempt at mitigating the effects of the hefker condition, to move from abandonment to care. Gathering information through written media was the chief instrument for doing so.[12]

The aid organizations sought to reduce chaos, and yet, chaos crept into everything they did. Aid workers were exposed to violence, and some lost their lives, including two members of the Joint Distribution Committee; members of the Russian Red Cross were detained, beaten up, and killed in Kyiv in 1919.[13] The organizations had a brief life and the archive they created had a nomadic existence. Something more fundamental, however, also brought uncertainty into the very center of their documentary work. This was not a matter of an opposition between Jewish and non-Jewish forms of documentation and narrativization, since the authors of all the various types of narrative were Jewish, and Jewish social science played a crucial role in the development of modern Jewish identity.[14]

The instructions to pogrom investigators repeatedly stressed the importance of precision, completeness, corroboration of data, and the consciousness and reliability of informants and yet also acknowledged the difficulty of meeting these criteria. Striving for complete, verifiable information and at the same time acknowledging that it could be fragmentary and unreliable, the authors of the documents speak to the difficulty and, in some ways, impossibility of their mission. The gap between what a life was and what the registration of a death could say, suggested by Kvitko's poem, also emerges in the documents created by the aid organizations. A certain degree of chaos and contradiction made their way into the very mechanisms and procedures designed to mitigate the effects of chaos. The hefker threshold that David Hofshteyn described in his poetry made its way into the archive.

Structure

Evobshchestkom, the Jewish Public Committee to Aid Victims of Pogroms, was founded in Moscow in the summer of 1920. It was a legally recognized entity that could pursue lawsuits, negotiate contracts and receive money from donations from individuals and groups abroad, among other sources. The presidium of the Jewish Public Committee met regularly to consider financial matters, the work of its deputies, relationships with other aid organizations, and requests from individuals.[15] The "All-Ukrainian" counterpart of the same committee was established in Kharkiv in the same year; the Kyiv Committee had been in operation from 1919. The various aid organizations typically had the following divisions: administrative, statistical/informational, financial, labor and employment, medical, judicial, a division devoted to children, and one on culture and "enlightenment." Additional subdivisions could include a photography and cinema unit, and within this commission, a smaller unit on artistic literature. Men and women over the age of eighteen could serve as deputies of Evobshchestkom. Authorized representatives traveled to locations in need of aid and were supposed to establish ties with local Soviet officials and Jewish communal organizations. "Persons with a thorough legal training" were deputized to investigate large-scale pogroms in certain locations, and their reports and witness statements supplemented the material that had already been gathered.[16] A schematic drawing of the typical structure of aid organizations can be found among the documents of the Photography and Cinema Division of the All-Ukrainian Committee to Aid Victims of Pogroms. The elegant drawing shows four spheres: the Moscow, Kharkiv, Odesa, and Kyiv regional committees orbiting a central planet.

The Jewish Public Committee included representatives from previously existing nongovernmental Jewish agencies, and groups, including socialist Jewish political parties, EKOPO (Jewish Committee to Aid Victims of the War), ORT (Organization for Skilled Labor), OZE (Organization to Promote Health among Jews), and the JDC (Jewish Joint Distribution Committee).[17] The rationale and vision of these Jewish aid commissions found their way into the postrevolutionary organizations, including the emphasis on statistics and documents.[18] On the eve of joining with Evobshchestkom, various Jewish public aid societies held a meeting to discuss their reorganization. World War I and the civil war had dealt a "profound blow to the entire Jewish national organism, physically, psychically, and economically."[19] Even though Jewish nationalism was not to be tolerated in the new Soviet society, a concern with the Jewish national body, damaged and injured but capable of healing, was on the agenda of the new Soviet-era public aid organizations. The focus on bodies and populations and not individual biographies was the modern, scientific way of working with communities, and it was the prevailing working principle of OZE, the Jewish health organization, as Marina Mogilner has shown. During World War I, OZE introduced the use of separate medical cards for each child enrolled in day care; in the aftermath of the Russian revolutions and the civil war, "OZE leadership urged their followers to collect statistics . . . as an important way of serving the national cause."[20]

Statistics

Statistics made it possible to paint a picture of the population as a whole; it was part of the battery of analytic tools that had seen a significant increase in use in the nineteenth century.[21] In the revolutionary period, the use of statistics was a way of building a new society on a scientific basis. In the immediate aftermath of the Russian Revolution, statistical studies showed progress toward what was called "the construction of life." The Russian experimental writer and proponent of "factography," Sergei Tretiakov, argued for the importance of a newly established Soviet statistical bureau in one of his many statements about the need for a new type of scientific, fact-based literary art.[22] In the first part of the twentieth century, Jacob Lestschinsky (1876–1966) was the key figure responsible for the turn to statistics as a tool for the advancement of Russian and East European Jewry.[23] Lestschinsky, who had studied in Switzerland, began his work on the statistics of the Jews before the First World War and continued after the second. His first published work, "The Statistics of a Town," the study of his native shtetl of Horodyshche, was published in Hebrew in 1903. In the early 1920s, he edited a journal on Jewish statistics, and he went on to head the statistics and economic section of YIVO. In the same period, he published book-length studies on Jewish statistics, immigration, and the Jewish economic situation. He also served as a special correspondent for the New York Yiddish newspaper *Forverts*, and his byline named him as a former member of the "famous Kyiv pogrom committee."[24] In his study of Horodyshche, Lestschinsky compared the town to the "cell" and the entire Jewish population to the "organism" and, arguing on the basis of the "biological law" that permits extrapolation from the cell to the organism, claimed that knowledge of the Jewish population as a whole could be gained by the study of individual places.[25] The purpose of the study of the Jewish economic and social condition was to rebuild the "Jewish organism," not to pathologize it. In his book on Jewish statistics published in 1922, Lestschinsky wrote that the purpose of statistics was to show the "life tendencies" that were latent in them and to indicate future trajectories. Note the emphasis on life. Lestschinsky was a proponent of biopolitics without using the term.

He explains that he finished writing the book in Kyiv in the summer of 1919; the assault on the city by Denikin's Volunteer Army gave rise to a pogrom in August, one of many. He also justifies the time frame of his material, limited to before World War I. The war, the breakup of empires, and the Russian Revolution had churned up the waves of "sea of life," and it had flooded its shores, making it impossible to count or measure them.[26] In an article published in the Yiddish *Forward*, "After the Pogroms," Lestschinsky listed one negative statistic after another: 40 percent of Jewish families had lost one or both parents. Jews generally did not show evidence of "nervous disease," but many had lived with pogroms for a period of up to three years, and this would influence their capacity for work.[27] The questions of the labor force and normalizing Jewish labor were of central importance to Lestschinsky and his contemporaries. Lestschinsky lost faith in positive outcomes for Jews in the new Bolshevik government, but the Jewish Public Committee did not. Regardless of the difference, Lestschinsky's methods, which incorporate modern biopolitics, remained central to Jewish aid work in this period.

Instructions

The instructions Evobshchestkom issued to its authorized deputies reveal the fundamental principle of counting and classifying as well other working assumptions, including what a pogrom was, its possible causes, what constituted reliable information, and who were considered reliable informants. The emphasis on statistics is unmistakable. A set of instructions from the "All-Ukrainian Jewish Public Committee" from early 1921 states that deputies had to be "reliable," both intellectually and morally; they had to show their "conscientiousness," dedication to the matter at hand and experience in statistical work. Experience in relief work was not among the qualifications. The chief task of the deputies was to provide a list of all the "pogromed places" in the region that had been assigned to them, which was to be sent to the committee for "verification" (in the document I examined, the word *information* here was crossed out and replaced by *verification*).[28] They had to characterize the social and political nature of the "counterrevolutionary elements" in their area. The success of the work, in its "statistical, scientific, and practical" aspects, depended on the energy and exactitude of the deputies and their complete fulfillment of all requests. Providing reports was central to the assignment of aid workers in the field. The same memo from the All-Ukrainian Jewish Public Committee noted the "shame" experienced at the center when requests for the completion of various questionnaires had not been satisfied. The memo went on to announce a new, more frequent regime of reporting that would be audited. The new forms would be made available as soon as they were printed.[29]

The various organizations posted announcements seeking information in the broadest terms possible. Cherikover's Editorial Committee posted an appeal that described the enormity of the Jewish catastrophe against the backdrop of ignorance about it: "The world doesn't know, and we ourselves know little." It was the duty of all Jews to come to the office (except for on the Sabbath) and describe everything so that their stories could be written down and the information preserved.[30] Other appeals asked survivors and witnesses to provide stories, photographs, accounts, personal correspondence, and clippings from newspaper articles. At a meeting held on March 15, 1921, the leadership of the Photography and Cinema Division of the Jewish Public Committee to Aid Victims of

Pogroms descried the lack of attention to the pogroms. Since the "bloody epoch of violence and pogroms directed against" the Jewish population had not been documented, and the available materials not collected or systematized, Evobshchestkom had no choice but to take on the task.[31] The organizing committees of the aid organizations claimed unique capacities and responsibilities in chronicling the catastrophe. Similar appeals had been issued only a few years earlier in response to Jewish suffering during World War I. The collection and systematic cataloging of the various materials that had been collected, the documentation of the events, even apart from the relief work, was a way of responding to the condition of abandonment across the continuum of violence of this period.

The various aid organizations relied on similar tools for the collection and preservation of information as well as for recording their own relief work. Before lists of the names of the dead could be completed, as in Kvitko's poem, many preliminary steps had to be taken. Separate forms were supposed to be completed for each murdered victim. Here as in other instances, the instructions veer between rigid demands and the acknowledgment that these demands were unrealistic. The form should be filled out in ink, but if there wasn't any, pencil would do. Three copies were necessary; two should be sent to the regional committee of Evobshchestkom. If the Russian and Yiddish names of the deceased did not correspond, another name had to be provided. If the name of the victim could not be found, then the name of the victim's relation could be used instead. The death date, using either the Russian or the Jewish calendar, had to be given. Where the killing took place should be indicated: in the victim's own apartment or someone else's, in a barn or shed, for example. The form also asked who was responsible for the death, and here the military unit, armed gang, and/or group was to be indicated as well as whether the local inhabitants were guilty. Two sources of information as to a particular individual's death were better than one.[32] At a meeting of the Statistical-Information Division of the Kyiv District Committee to Aid Victims of Pogroms, held in August 1921, Lev Iakovlevich Ioffe, the head of the division, stressed the importance of the double verification of information. Deaths were to be verified by consulting burial registers and noting where graves were located and by questioning those who buried the victim.[33]

What Is a Pogrom?

Before a form could be completed detailing the deaths of individual pogrom victims, investigators had to determine whether a pogrom had taken place. Just as separate forms were to be prepared for each murdered individual, separate forms were also necessary for each pogrom.[34] I. Ia. Khersonskii, an attorney who worked for the Statistical Division of the Kyiv Public Committee, traveled to Fastov (Fastiv) (the site of pogroms in August and September 1919) to assess the utility of pogrom questionnaires.[35] He stated in his report that the first problem was the lack of a precise definition of what a pogrom was. The question, which has received considerable attention from historians to this day, might appear surprising.[36] The term had been in use for several decades prior to 1919, and the signs of damage in Fastov were unmistakable. A report by Zinaida Litvakova, who had traveled to the area in 1920, stated that Fastov (Fastiv) was "almost completely destroyed."[37] Wasn't it obvious what a pogrom was? Impressionistic images of overwhelming destruction were inadequate, however. The statistical work of the Jewish aid organizations in 1921 required apples to be compared to apples. If deputies were going to count pogroms, they had to know how to count them: if the violence started, stopped, and then resumed, was it one or two pogroms? Ioffe answered that indications of a pogrom included both the "mass" scale of the destruction of life and property and the involvement of a crowd, whether organized or not.[38] The All-Ukrainian Jewish Public Committee provided a similar definition. Two criteria had to be met: the killing, rape, theft, and destruction of property had to have a "mass character," and an entire group, whether organized or not, had to carry out these acts of violence.[39] It is significant that there is no specific requirement that the victims were Jewish.

The questions that were to be asked of the "reliable witnesses" on the pogrom forms suggest a broad-ranging understanding of the violence, its causes, its main actors, the nature of the loss of life and property damage. The Jewish response to the violence, especially, self-defense, was a key question. If Jews defended themselves, what weapons did they use? Investigators had to determine whether the pogrom had an "organized character"; whether there was some "immediate cause"; which organizations and military units took part; was there a "sharply expressed anti-Jewish character" to the violence; the slogans used; the degree of participation from the non-Jewish population; the number of victims according to specific categories, including death, wounding, and rape; and whether there was a particular manifestation of "savagery" (burning, drowning, burying alive, and cutting off parts of the body). The number of orphaned children had to be noted. Other considerations in both questioning witnesses and writing reports included the names of the leaders, the social strata of those members of the local population who took part, and Jewish participation in armed gang violence and pogroms. There is no assumption that pogroms were necessarily marked by anti-Jewish impulses; the nature of the anti-Jewish dimensions of the pogrom had to be specified, and the possible involvement of Jews themselves in the violence was not discounted. Information pertaining to identifying the dead and determining the number killed had to be corroborated. Details acquired from local inhabitants as to who was killed or injured were to be checked against hospitalization and Jewish burial society records.

The instructions for writing reports on specific pogroms required nothing less than a comprehensive history of the multiethnic and multiconfessional life of the town under investigation. Lestschinsky's influence is evident in the focus on the town as the object of study. Regardless of the need to compare apples with apples, the demand for detailed information about interethnic relations for each locality suggests that the Jewish Public Committee considered local contingencies crucially important. Reports were to include material on the Jewish and non-Jewish population before and after World War I, the Russian Revolution, and the pogroms; the economic conditions, class composition, and social and cultural life of the Jewish community; the number of houses, stores, factories, and social and religious establishments in the locale before the first pogrom took place; the number of unemployed; Jewish and non-Jewish political parties and groups; the relations of Jews with non-Jews, including the peasantry, before the war, during the revolution, and all the succeeding governments in Ukraine; and the role of the Ukrainian intelligentsia in the changing relations between Jews and non-Jews. The socioeconomic makeup of the entire population was a factor in violence against Jews, as was the political landscape in the broader community. World War I and the Russian Revolution were of critical importance. The aid organizations clearly believed that incitement was necessary for violence to take place.

The working assumptions of Evobshchestkom in significant ways coincide with recent historiographical trends regarding pogroms and interethnic violence generally, especially the attention to the specifics of a given place. The pogrom questionnaires reveal an overriding interest in the situation on the ground, from below, from the perspective of ordinary people in their immediate daily life circumstances. Pogrom investigators were asked to document the activities of organized groups in the violence, as well as the participation of the local population, against the backdrop of their interactions before World War I and the Russian Revolution.

More than one report concluded that there was little in common between the pogroms of the czarist period and the civil war. This focus accords with current historiographical tendencies, which distinguish between czarist era and subsequent pogroms.[40] It was not only a matter of the limited time frame of the pogroms of the earlier period, usually confined to the Easter season, in contrast to the later period, when populations faced ongoing pogrom conditions. Other circumstances had changed as well. A report dated August 1919 drew a direct line between the conduct of the Russian Imperial Army during World War I and the Russian Revolution and the forms of violence used during pogroms. The war introduced requisitions; the revolution brought forced contributions of money and goods as well as the taking of hostages, "and as a result, the form of pogroms was enriched," this investigator concluded.[41] Several scholars have come to similar conclusions, characterizing World War I as the training ground for the anti-Jewish violence of the civil war period.[42] The 1919 pogromists took everything from their victims, leaving them in their underwear or completely naked. The same report goes on to say that whereas earlier pogromists could take advantage of the "acquiescence" of the authorities, in the 1919 period, the pogromists had become the authorities. They were the "sovereign masters" of the cities and towns they occupied and could do as they wished in conditions of complete "impunity."[43] Yiddish sources, as I have shown, use the term hefker to indicate impunity. For the warlords who reigned in 1919, sovereignty could mean the right to kill; the report quotes Ataman Kozyr-Zyrko, whom I discuss in chapter 5, stating this explicitly. For the political theorist Agamben, the right to kill is the backbone of sovereign power without distinction as to legitimacy. From their position on the ground, the investigators writing reports make the impact of exposure to such power particularly vivid and clear. Examining the conditions leading to abandonment and documenting its consequences reflect the other side of the coin, the provision of care.

Perfect Witnesses

To gather the necessary information, investigators had first to gather qualified informants. Questions were to be addressed to heads of households. Whether this was practical was doubtful, however. The testimonies of a twelve-year-old boy and an eight-year-old girl can be found among the first-person accounts of the July 1919 pogrom in Slovechno, for example. Investigators were instructed to provide their opinion of the degree of likelihood that the information they received was correct and, furthermore, what led them to this opinion in a separate report. As Elias Heifetz, the former head of the All-Ukrainian Relief Committee explained, the information bureau in Kyiv rejected information that seemed dubious.[44] Agents were supposed to ask questions following the order set in various protocols. In cases in which informants gave varying responses to specific questions, the most conservative answer was to be selected. For example, if some said thirty-five Jews were killed in a pogrom, but others said forty-one was the correct number, the investigator was to use the lower figure in the report. Pogrom investigators struggled to establish exact numbers.

The qualifications for informants resemble the qualifications for investigators. In conducting their research into a pogrom in a particular location, investigators were told to assemble individuals who could provide "more or less" exact information about the events. Even though the purpose of such assemblies was very different from that of pogrom perpetrators, who also had demanded that leading members of the community should gather in one place, it seems likely that this sort of request might have made surviving informants uneasy. The witnesses to be questioned had to have taken particular care to inform themselves about what had happened. If no such persons were available, investigators had to assess the "conscientiousness" and the extent to which potential informants met standards of "proper behavior" (*kul'turnost'*).

There is no discussion about how to approach pogrom survivors, even though one of the questions on the standard pogrom questionnaire asks what changes the pogrom brought to the "psyche" of the local population.[45] The form completed by an authorized local deputy in the town of

Litin responded to this question by reporting that "constant fear" of the non-Jewish population and the possible repetition of the violence led to a dulling of the consciousness and energy among Jews as well as "neurasthenia and psychoses."[46] A Yiddish-language report authored by a deputy of Evobshchestkom in the Ovruch region noted that "dread ruled the city" in which he was working long after the departure of the pogromists.[47] Statements by medical experts clearly show an awareness that those interviewed had suffered a significant blow to their "psychic equilibrium," to quote the language of a medical report written by a prominent member of the medical profession and the Jewish intellectual elite, Abram Moiseevich Bramson.[48] Bramson was one of the founders of OZE; served on the staff of Narkomzdrav (People's Commissariat of Health), established in 1918; and was a founding member of the first tuberculosis institute in Russia. Bramson proposed the establishment of psychiatric units to help address the mental health issues of pogrom survivors, especially women and girls who had been raped and subsequently saw the bodies of their relatives on the streets. Among the documents of the All-Ukrainian Jewish Public Committee is a report from the Medical Division, whose title alone is revealing: "On the Traumatic Pandemic among the Jewish Population of 1919."

In light of this information, the instructions reveal a surprising assumption: that individuals suffering from overwhelming psychic and physical injury would be able to demonstrate proper decorum, knowledge of the immediate circumstances surrounding the violence to which they had been subject, and the skill to narrate what they knew in the necessary way. Presumably, the desired decorum and behavior excluded emotional displays, shouting, incoherence, or any other evidence of the psychological disturbances that authorized deputies reported. Informants were tasked with providing a complete and perfect record of the damage done to them and their communities as if they had not suffered any damage or as if they had been damaged and healed on the spot. Investigators nonetheless recorded accounts in which informants explicitly stated that they could barely recall what happened to them. One such account has to do with the murder of forty Jews on the steamship *Baron Ginzburg*. The sole survivor of the episode, Khassia Karpirovskaia, testifies that "bandits" boarded the ship, bound from Kyiv; separated Jews and Christians; and threw Jews in the Dnieper River. Karpirovskaia, who managed to get to shore and was cared for by nuns and peasants, begins her story by saying that the entire event "remained in her memory only partly" and that she "saw, heard, and did everything as if in a lethargic sleep."[49] This account does not meet the evidentiary standards stated in the instructions to pogrom investigators, but the investigator in question, I. S. Braude, a member of the leadership group of the Kyiv Committee nonetheless includes it among his reports. It points to damage done to the psyche of a victim. The report indicates a point of fissure in the entire enterprise conducted by Evobshchestkom: the tension between the agenda of recovery and the evidence of lingering harm.

The gap between the desire for complete and verified information and the difficulty of providing it emerges clearly in the changing instructions dispatched to aid workers in the field. At one point, Evobshchestkom realized that its demands for precision, synthesis, and corroboration limited the information that deputies from the Odesa and Kharkiv region could send. A memo informed investigators that if they lacked verifiable material, they could substitute "stories of witnesses" and "descriptions of pogroms," as long as they "more or less" confirmed the information on the spot, in order to discard "unchecked rumors."[50] This and other instructions outlining the need for double checking and the verification of information show that the problem for the Jewish Public Committee was not an all-consuming desire for "primary, original, and untouched" sources.[51] They suffered not from "archive fever" but its opposite: original material was not to be trusted, but concessions had to be made nonetheless when it came to verification. On the one hand, the order was to evaluate the data immediately, on the spot; on the other hand, the phrase *more or less*, which is an admission that standards of reliability might not be met, was used. Rumor, which pogrom investigators were instructed to discard, was a part of the uncertainty and fear experienced by victims of pogroms. Kvitko contemplates the rumor that he was dead in "Look, I'm Blinking."

Ambivalence about the purpose and value of witness testimony was common at the time. The editors of document volumes about the Armenian genocide withheld names of witnesses to protect them but felt compelled nonetheless to affirm their upright character and standing.[52] The victims were less reliable than bystanders who did not belong to the targeted national group. The Jewish Public Committee obviously used members of the target group as a source of information but also included testimonies from others. In addition, as I will show, refugees from pogromed places could go on to serve as authorized representatives of aid organizations.

Aid workers were instructed to preserve the language of witnesses as they wrote down their testimony. Grammatical mistakes were not to be corrected. The testimonies were to be written down from the words of the informants, without corrections, read back to them, and signed. There is little, however, in the instructions that would have directed interviewers to ask their subjects about their overall experience and emotions. The goal of the interaction with survivors and witnesses was information gathering, according to questions that had been determined in advance. The records of some divisions of the aid organizations, however, reveal something of a different take on the fundamental approach that I have sketched out. The charge to the Photo Bureaus attached to the regional committees in Kharkiv, Odesa, Gomel', and Minsk included the responsibility of providing a "picture of the personal experience [*perezhivanie*]" of victims. They were to ask refugees and orphans about their "lives and experience" during the pogrom, before the revolution, and at the present time. Their stories and their photographs would be registered with archivists in a well-defined systematic order according to location and date.[53] The leadership also discussed the possibility of using cinema to depict the pogroms. They contemplated bringing together literary authors, visual artists, and actors for the purpose of creating films that would "capture the horrors" of the violence. The dramatic staging of the pogroms would provoke American audiences to make greater contributions to help victims and it would also have a beneficial effect on those who participated: they would be "put to shame." This idea was soundly rejected. "Capturing the horrors" would only serve the goals of a museum dedicated to the counterrevolution.[54] Shock and sensationalism were not appropriate. The number of films produced by this committee's work was extremely limited.[55] Even though "capturing the horrors" and providing accounts of individual experience were not part of Evobshchestkom's plan, the reports written by investigators reveal their struggle to describe what they saw directly or learned about from others. Emotions that statistics could not indicate surfaced in the reports, as I show shortly.

Other types of questionnaires and forms were also used to register requests for aid and track amounts dispersed. Written documents used for refugees in Kyiv seeking aid included questions about their profession; previous employment; whether they had previously received aid; where, when, and in what way they suffered from pogroms and the civil war; whether someone in the family died during a pogrom; how long they had been in

Kyiv; what sort of housing they lived in (the answers could include the quality of the apartment, for example, dark, light, or damp); whether they had relatives in America; whether they wanted to immigrate; and finally, what sort of assistance they sought. There were thirty-three questions in all. The respondents in the source I used were all women, and the answers entered in the forms were similar. They had come to Kyiv from Berdichev, Uman, and other locations and were unmarried; literate in Yiddish and Russian (and some in Ukrainian as well); they had previously been employed as teachers, seamstresses, and staff workers at orphanages; they had been robbed and had experienced the death of family members; and they were seeking underwear, shoes, and sweaters.[56] Reading these completed forms, aside from confirming the conclusion that the desire for data trumped the need for narrative accounts, also leads to the impression that there was one respect in which they were not complete. Rape was prevalent throughout the civil war pogroms, and yet there is no mention of it in these questionnaires, although it appears in pogrom forms.

The Culture Front

Culture created out of the chaos was also evidence of the Jewish capacity for regrowth. Museum exhibits could advance the agenda of the Jewish Public Committee. Discussions about an exhibit in Kharkiv that would show the work of the All-Ukrainian Jewish Committee demonstrate interest in showing the efficacy of Jewish relief efforts. The same memo I discuss earlier describes a plan to display both "pogrom chaos," using photographs of victims, perpetrators, and scenes of destruction, on the one side, and the work of the committee in giving aid to the Jewish population, on the other. For the latter, documents, including photographs of institutions that the committee had created, were to be collected, and images of children and children's homes were especially important. The focus of the exhibit was not the display of atrocity or capturing "pogrom horrors"; rather, it was on a narrative of progress, from harm to healing. The accent on children would show that Jews were a people with a future. The memo excoriated deputies for their failure to send adequate materials in time for the planned opening of the exhibit. What is remarkable here is the unshakable faith of the leadership that these materials existed and that the problem was only the negligence of the aid workers.

Interest in promoting art and culture reveals another dimension of the same agenda about potential, vitality, and creativity. A memo from the Information Division of the All-Ukrainian Jewish Public Committee about children's art makes this point clear. The art, music, and literature produced by the children in orphanages sponsored by the organization showed the "rare talent and superior intellectual and cultural level" of the children; collecting and systematizing the material would demonstrate the "positive results" of the work of the committee generally, and especially its cultural work.[57]

The relationship between the Kyiv Kultur-Lige (Culture League) and the Jewish Public Committee, although marked by disagreements and internal struggles, reveals the same goal.[58] The poetry discussed thus far in this study, including Hofshteyn and Kvitko's debut volumes, and the critical essays that responded to them were published by Kultur-Lige in 1919. The culturist ideals that went into the formation of Kultur-Lige did not evaporate in the aftermath of the pogroms; they intensified and underwent a shift. It was less a matter of bringing culture to the masses and more a matter of showing that the masses, albeit injured, demanded education and culture, and could produce the latter. A request written in Yiddish and dated January 11, 1921, from Kultur-Lige to the Kyiv Public Committee points out that Jewish towns had suffered the destruction of their libraries, which had contained valuable religious books and "interesting archival materials." It was especially important to organize children's libraries for the pogromed and homeless children living in orphanages, and to this end, Kultur-Lige was asking for a half a million rubles.[59] An internal report from the Kyiv Public Committee shows that Kultur-Lige was operating and budgeting for evening courses for adults and schools for children on a large scale.[60] A lengthy memo written by Zinaida Litvakova (whom I have not been able to identify further) concedes that the cultural work, including theatrical performances and education in and out of school, was taking place in devastated areas solely due to the efforts of Kultur-Lige, and not the Jewish sections of the communist party.[61]

The leadership of Evobshchestkom and its sister agencies believed that pogroms, vectors of contingency and unpredictability, could be counted and classified as could bodies and populations. The presidium of the All-Ukrainian Jewish Public Committee referred to pogroms in terms of "elemental forces"; one memo, for example, urging deputies to send materials in a timely fashion (a constant theme) asked for documents pertaining to "pogrom elemental forces" (*stikhiia*).[62] These forces, which produced chaos, could be controlled by thirty questions and answers. Scenes of primordial "welter and waste," to borrow the poets' language, could be organized into information. Individuals who had suffered nearly indescribable harm could be held accountable for a perfect account of the history and circumstances leading to the occasion of harm. The assumptions, or desires, underlining these expectations, while extraordinary, reveal the goal of the Jewish relief effort. In 1921, Jews had fallen into the gap—into the *hefker-shvel*, the chaos threshold—and the Jewish Public Committee was going to get them out. The statistics and verified information of harm done and aid given showed that Jews, regardless of what had befallen them, remained a vital population, capable of recovery, productive labor, and self-governance. Characterizing the instructions, memos, questionnaires, forms, receipts, lists, and reports only as a set of constraints on the possibility of what could be said about pogroms is too limited an approach. These instruments represent a methodology of care. Nonetheless, the reports of pogrom investigators also tell another story. Refugees and survivors who became investigators document their own inability to write reports. The reports gave voice to a sense of overwhelming loss and destruction. The centrifugal force that pulled the narrative away from recovery has a palpable presence in the investigators' struggle to reduce chaos to order by classifying pogroms according to instructions.

Pechora

Materials pertaining to the June 1919 Pechora (Pechera) pogrom provide an example. Located in southwestern Ukraine, Pechora had one church, two synagogues, a mill on the Bug River, and approximately one thousand Jews and five thousand non-Jews (including those in the surrounding villages). This information was included in the report written by one N. Lifshits, who was an authorized deputy from the Kyiv Public Committee and a refugee from Pechora, where he had worked in the local pharmacy. He appears in multiple roles in his own Pechora materials, as an informant and witness, and as a commentator and compiler of testimonies. His voice changes with each role, in the first case, highly emotional, in the second, more oriented toward the recitation of facts. Another document provided by the

Joint Distribution Committee (in Yiddish) gives different numbers about Pechora: the town itself had only around one thousand inhabitants, about half of whom were Jews.[63] The town, according to another report, was far from the railroad and was more rural than urban. The sources do not agree as to whether there were forms of political organization in Pechora.

The two groups responsible for the destruction, killing, and rape in Pechora were headed by Atamans Sokolovskii and Evgenii Liakhovich. The pharmacist turned pogrom investigator Lifshits reported that Liakhovich, a former officer in the czar's army, was a morphine addict. Petliura subsequently had him arrested, but he escaped and was later killed by one of his own staff members.[64] The local population was incited to participate in the violence by rumors that the Jews in Nemirov were using churches to house horses. Nemirov—another small shtetl, important in the history of Hasidism—and Pechora are approximately eleven miles apart, and Liakhovich at first assured the Jews of Pechora that he would protect them. After the money he had saved ran out (presumably spent in buying morphine), he organized his group that attacked Jews in Nemirov and Pechora. Approximately 130 Jews were killed in Pechora, according to the statistics of the Kyiv Public Committee.[65] Other sources give higher figures. Lifshits says he "saw 160 corpses" and the document from the American Joint Distribution Committee states that there were 200 dead.[66] The disparity in the numbers reveals the difficulties of the Jewish Public Committee's attempt to secure an accurate count of the dead. The disparity among eyewitnesses and investigators in the early 1920s may help explain why there is such a disparity in subsequent scholarly enumerations of pogrom deaths.

Lifshits's testimony and that of and others exceed the brief and go beyond numbers. Lifshits records his own emotional reaction to the sight of severed limbs. When he recognized the hand of a little girl who was a friend of his own daughter, he burst into tears and sobbed like a wounded animal, as he put it. Among the documents regarding the events in Pechora is the testimony of the son of the local priest, who wrote that not even the best writers could describe "a tenth of what happened."[67] A Yiddish-language report said that the horrors of the Inquisition could not compare with the pogrom in Pechora: only two Jews were killed by bullets; the rest were hacked into small pieces.[68] Another eyewitness, one V. Broytman, a member of the Pechora Committee to Aid Pogrom Victims, writes that "there is no fantasy that could imagine" and "no pen that could describe" what took place. The local orchestra played in the marketplace to drown out the screams. "Only the dozens of men and women who wander barefoot through the empty fields, driven out of their minds attest to the fact that there was once life here."[69] He means Jewish life. Broytman denies the possibility of rebuilding Jewish life in Pechora. His testimony depicts a landscape of utter devastation.

Lifshits also notes that "almost all" the Jewish girls and women were raped, many on the street. Pregnancy, venereal disease, mental illness, and suicide resulted from these rapes. It is likely that Lifshits's more detailed discussion of the consequences of rape had to do with his profession as a pharmacist because women may have been accustomed to telling him about their health problems, particularly seeking medical help for unwanted pregnancies. Broytman reported that thirty-six women were raped and needed "immediate abortions." The conclusion of Lifshits's testimony is far from certain about the future of Jews in Soviet Ukraine. The Jews of Pechora and all of Ukraine had paid for the "coming of the bright future" with their blood and the honor of their daughters.[70]

The local priest attempted to stop the pogrom in Pechora. Pogromists wounded his son as punishment.[71] It should be noted that the portrait of the clergy that emerges from the Pechora documents is exceptional and contrasts sharply with other depictions of the role of the clergy in anti-Jewish violence of this period.[72] The same testimony explains that since the pharmacy was owned by non-Jews, it remained unscathed until the last moment, when the attackers realized that Jews were hiding there. The pharmacist's family—that is, Lifshits and his daughter—survived because they were able to leave the building, hide in the church garden and ransom themselves. Lifshits himself did not include these details saying only that he survived "by a miracle."

Deputies were asked to note on their pogrom questionnaires local legends, lore, and proverbs that had emerged in the aftermath of violence. Lifshits's materials also include a "legend" that he heard from local peasants a month after the pogrom. He repeated it in Ukrainian in his Russian-language report. A woman noticed that the church was lit up at night as if it were a holiday. She entered the church and saw the mother of God crying. "Stop killing Jews," said the mother of God, "my son Jesus can't bear their groans." Then the church became dark.[73] Lifshits concluded that this story revealed the local peasantry's pangs of conscience for their role in anti-Jewish violence. Folklore about the intercession of the Virgin Mary was well established in Russian culture, and Dostoevsky includes an example in *The Brothers Karamazov*. What distinguishes this legend, however, is that Mary intercedes on behalf of Jews.

Among the lists, testimonies, and reports included in the Pechora materials is a Yiddish poem cycle written by Moses Carton (Moshe Karton). Carton was born in present-day Horodkivka in 1888 (his birthplace is approximately thirty miles from Pechora). He had no definite occupation and served in the Russian imperial army during World War I; his plans to leave the Russian empire were delayed by the Russian Revolution and Civil War. He had started writing poetry in Hebrew and Yiddish at an early age and, after a meeting with Bialik in 1917, began publishing.[74] The poem cycle titled "Ukraine, 1919" stresses "national feeling" (why must Jewish blood flow eternally?) and includes work dedicated to "Jewish daughters." The influence of Bialik is evident in his poetry; the depiction of the experience of survival is less prevalent. An exception may be seen in "My Child" ("Kind mayns"), which was published in the New York Yiddish journal *Di tsukunft* (*The Future*) in December 1922. The speaker tells his young child not to make a single sound as they hide in an abandoned field so that their enemies would not discover them. Kvitko and Hofshteyn, as I discuss in chapter 5, used the same motif in their poems about 1919.

Failing the Brief/Exceeding the Brief

In addition to the Pechora materials, other documents also show how pogrom investigators strayed from their brief. The communications sent by authorized deputies of relief agencies read like haikus of disaster. A relief deputy working in Elisavetgrad, where from thirteen hundred to three thousand Jews were killed in the May 1919 pogrom, wrote to Moshe Rafes, working at the People's Commissariat for Social Welfare in Kyiv, "You provided one million rubles in aid; three million would be inadequate."[75] Other telegrams from the same city read: "The colossal work of the local forces is inadequate" and "There are cases of typhus in the dormitories provided for the victims; hurry."[76]

Earlier I mention Lev Iakovlevich Ioffe, who had a terse exchange with an aid representative about the definition of a pogrom. Ioffe, the head of the

Statistical Division of the Kyiv Public Committee, also departed from his own brief and the forward-looking agenda of recovery. Additional information about Ioffe's background and his position after leaving his position as head of the Statistical Division provides the necessary introduction to this other dimension of his work. Having previously worked for ORT, in 1923 he asked to be released from his work for the Kyiv Public Committee, stating his need for frequent departures from Kyiv, without explaining what these trips were for. He went on to work for the Leningrad Jewish Religious Society, in charge of kosher meat and the ritual bath, and assumed an administrative position for a synagogue in 1928.[77]

In a report to Evobshchestkom, Ioffe argued for the need to create a card catalog of the pogroms and, in addition, a series of "monographs," each one of which would be dedicated to a typical pogrom site, based on information already collected and supplementing it by carrying out further research. The monographs would include "everything that could be said" about each individual place, for example, its initial history, and its "tragic past, if it had disappeared from the face of the earth."[78] Ioffe's language suggests that at least in this instance, he was less concerned with the future and more with the task of memory and a specific form of Jewish memory at that. He wanted to preserve a trace in narrative form of Jewish places that had been obliterated. His description of a series of books, one for each pogromed town, approximates the *yizker-bikher*, the traditional Jewish memorial book, understood by the community as a substitute for a grave marker and memorial service.[79] These memorial books proliferated after World War II, but they appeared well before World War I. A memorial book for Proskurov was published in 1924. Rokhl Faygenberg's *Record of a Dead Town* (Pinkes), dedicated to Dubovo, is a lightly fictionalized version of the town monograph that Ioffe calls for.

One of the difficult questions facing Evobshchestkom was immigration. If a sufficient number of Jews sought to leave, then the case for their future in Soviet Russia was significantly undermined. The language officials and aid workers used to discuss this issue reveals the high-stakes tension it caused. Itskhok Sudarsky, a member of the Central Committee of the Jewish Section of the Ukrainian Communist Party, reported that there were twelve thousand Jews on the Romanian border; their desire to leave approached "psychosis."[80] Able-bodied men who wanted to leave were characterized by some as "counterrevolutionary elements." Political propaganda would be necessary to change the minds of those who sought to leave the country.

A representative of the Kyiv Public Committee, H. Hokhgelernter, who together with another colleague mounted a separate investigation of the conditions of refugees living along the border, strongly disagreed with this approach. He characterized the emotions of the would-be émigrés in more sympathetic but similar terms, commenting on their "psychological attachment to the border." In his Yiddish-language report, he emphasized the inner experience and emotions of the refugees using the word *hefker*. Gelerntner said "the homeless [refugees], having been pushed out of their destroyed communities, made for the border through chaos [hefker] and despair."[81] Gelerntner is using hefker as a noun, parallel to *despair*, as if the conditions of chaos, dispossession, and abandonment were a zone or a space to be traveled. Gelerntner described the wretched conditions of the temporary living quarters: corpses were not removed, boiled water was not distributed, rooms were overcrowded, and infectious diseases were on the rise, since there was no separate housing for the sick. Indeed, the same conditions could be found in refugee housing in Kyiv. The desperate, nearly "psychotic" desire of the refugees to leave Russia undermines Evobshchestkom's narrative of the continued vitality and capacity of Jewish pogrom survivors to take part in the new socialist labor force.

Chaos in Numbers

The case of the Yiddish poet Moses Carton tells an important story about numbers and their potential unreliability. In the same "List" of the dead that I mentioned earlier, in the Kyiv Public Committee's *Bulletin*, under the entry for the dead in Pechora, the name Moshe Karton (age twenty) appears. This is an error. The author's preface to his book of poems, published in New York in 1926, informs readers that during the pogrom in Pechora he and his family were hidden by two peasants in a nearby village. The two men, Evangelical Christians, risked their lives to save Jews. Carton later made his way to New York. Whoever was responsible for reporting the names of the dead in the Pechora pogrom came to the mistaken conclusion that Carton had been killed, possibly because he was in hiding and thus appeared to be missing. This history adds a layer of interpretation to Kvitko's poem, "Look, I'm Blinking" (discussed in chapter 3). The speaker cannot convince his neighbor that regardless of the report of his death, he, the poet, is alive and blinks his eyes as a sign of life. The neighbor denies the evidence presented by the living poet before him. The poet transforms the false report into a moment of vertiginous horror, blurring the line between sanity and madness; he becomes terrified of the sound of lizards scrabbling over the garden wall. The false report of Moses Carton's death was likely not a unique case. The line between life and death, as he and others said of this period, was blurred to the point of illegibility. Poets work well with that which cannot be decided or settled definitively, in contrast, statisticians, whether at the Jewish Public Committee in 1921 or elsewhere, do not.

The problem of reliability reaches its peak in the anguished statement of a member of the medical division of the All-Ukrainian Committee to Aid Victims of Pogroms: "As far as an exact count of the dead is concerned, it must be said that murderers do not keep lists and the dead do not pursue lawsuits for their ruined lives."[82] The author of this statement was Mikhail Stepanovich Tarasenko (1879–?), a physician who worked in Belarus and Ukraine at this time; he later became a professor of public hygiene at Tomsk State University. His language resonates with Psalm 115: "The dead do not praise God." The most perfect sources of information, the murderers and their victims, would not and could not provide the numbers and evidence that the instructions to pogrom investigators required. The entire statistical enterprise thus suffers from a fundamental flaw, because the best witnesses were not available; "the dead do not pursue lawsuits." In response to Holocaust denial, the French philosopher Jean-François Lyotard formulated the concept of the *differend*, the case in which the wrong suffered by a party in a dispute cannot be expressed according to the demands of the other party.[83] In the case of Tarasenko's medical report, the required idiom, an exact count, is not a demand issued by an opponent, but those on the same side as the victims, the agencies that sought to help them. Tarasenko's despair over the necessary indeterminacy of the numerical count indicates the chaos threshold that is part and parcel of documentation and relief.

Instruments that produce the condition of abandonment may also aid in the regeneration of the lifeworld, including counting, classifying, and making distinctions between different segments of population. Despite their best efforts, however, the work of Evobshchestkom did not resolve the question of Jewish recovery, self-governance, and capacity for productive labor. The leadership of the committee and its sister organizations were clearly aware of the problem, as Tarasenko's report shows. The experience of chaos and abandonment (hefker) also made its way into the task of documentation. The case of the apparently dead but still living poet Moses Carton cannot be unique, and the story of how his name appears on a list of the dead even though he was still alive echoes the poet Leyb Kvitko's encounter with the premature report of his own death. The testimony of survivors of the Pechora pogrom reveals both neighborly brutality and instances of neighborly care. The Virgin's intercession on behalf of Jews, an example of "folklore and legend" that the Jewish Public Committee sought to preserve, departs from traditional folkloric tales of Mary's intercession on behalf of sinners. Regardless of Lestschinsky's denials that the Jewish population showed evidence of psychiatric disorders, medical experts argued the contrary: the Jewish population suffered a "traumatic pandemic." The head of the Kyiv Commission's Statistical Division turned away from the future and sought to preserve the past in a plan for what amounted to the traditional Jewish memorial book.

The Jewish Public Committee did not focus on the experience of individuals, but the individual voices of its own pogrom investigators provide a counternarrative to the story of recovery and vitality that its statistics sought to emphasize. Testimony has been called a chaos narrative because of its lack of connective tissue, and the bare-bones accounts I summarize in the opening of the chapter reveal this very quality; however, the reports of duly authorized pogrom investigators are also chaotic in their own way because they pull against the desire for order and structure implicit in the instructions they received. The examination of the documents left behind by Evobshchestkom show that the socialist future was shadowed by the unpredictable hefker space of ambiguity and abandonment.

8

Children

In the aftermath of the Russian Civil War, thousands of children were left without adults to care for them. The Russian term for those who ended up on the street was *bezprizorniki* (the unsupervised).[1] Jewish relief agencies created various institutions to house and educate orphaned and abandoned Jewish children, most of whom were victims of pogroms. The proceeds from Hofshteyn and Chagall's *Sorrow (Troyer)*, published in 1922, for example, were earmarked for a colony for homeless Jewish children at Malakhovka. The Russian-language Jewish writer Doyvber Levin (1904–1941), created a volume of children's testimonies in thinly veiled fictitious form, titled *Ten Wagons (Desiat' vagonov)*, first published in 1931. The book was based on his visits to a Jewish orphanage in Leningrad. Fischel Schneersohn (1887–1958) an ordained Hasidic rabbi, was also a novelist and a psychologist who took special interest in the influence of pogroms on young children. In his Yiddish-language study, *Catastrophic Times and Growing Generations*, published in Berlin in 1923, Schneersohn used the word *hefker* ("abandoned") to characterize the "great army of children" growing up without supervision, creating a "nest of degeneration."[2] He used the same word to describe the haphazard state of pedagogy and care when it came to pogromed children. Hefker, the key term of this study, here indicates the neglect, abandonment, and rightlessness in which these children found themselves—and their waywardness. Schneersohn's innovation in *Catastrophic Times* was his exploration of the children's capacity for storytelling as both a diagnostic tool and a therapeutic instrument. David Hofshteyn's pogrom cycle names poetry as the smallest, weakest thing and also the greatest comfort. From a different angle, but sharing a set of common concerns, Schneersohn, too, finds powerful potential in the creation of the simplest forms of literature.

In chapter 7, I discussed the lack of emotion in survivor testimonies. *Catastrophic Times* begins with this very question, only with a focus on children. Schneersohn argued that the children's apparent failure to respond to their own experience requires a deeper analysis and a methodology overlooked by clinicians, psychologists, and social scientists. This chapter examines Schneersohn's approach in the context of the broader question about children and care, and especially the role of storytelling in revealing the children's potential for creativity. I begin with the questionnaires used for children's institutions and children, then turn to Levin, and reserve the longest part of the discussion for the multifaceted and largely overlooked figure of Schneersohn. This chapter is not about great works of art by Yiddish poets. It is focused instead on the great work of care in which art plays a key role in repairing a hefker world.

Questionnaires for Institutions

The preliminary stage of providing care required a count of how many children in how many localities needed what kind of care and how many institutions were available for the task. The overall impression from documents compiled by various relief organizations is that the number of children needing care far exceeded the organizations' capacity to register their need. Statistics were drawn up that showed how many children were left without one or both parents, the age of these children, and where they were located. Belaia Tserkov', a district center located in Kyiv province and home to 20,000 Jews, was in a "state of permanent pogrom" in 1919, according to Nokhem Shtif.[3] A 1923 report about Belaia Tserkov' written by a certain I. M. Kovalsky, a representative of the American Joint Distribution Committee, shows that about 400 children were in institutions but 1,000 more needed care.[4] An undated document from the Statistical Division of Evobshchestkom stated that 707 children with one parent remaining ("half-orphans") in Belaia Tserkov' needed care. The greatest number of these children were between the ages of eight and twelve. This number included both local children and those who had come to Belaia Tserkov' from elsewhere. An additional 155 children were listed as complete orphans.[5] These numbers seem low in comparison to other reports, possibly because it was a single snapshot, and not a comprehensive overview. Zinaida Litvakova, whose work I discussed in the previous chapter, reported about general conditions in the region. She stated that there were 4,500 refugees in Belaia Tserkov' and that in this city as well as elsewhere most of the refugee population consisted of children. Most of them slept in improvised living quarters, where there were numerous cases of measles, scarlet fever, and other infectious diseases.[6]

To demonstrate and track the progress of care, the Kyiv Public Committee to Aid Victims of Pogroms created questionnaires for children's institutions. The forms were designed to provide basic information about overall conditions. They included the location and type of institution; the date of its founding and by what organization; questions about the physical plant, the overall state of sanitary conditions, and the number of rooms; questions about the staff; questions about the children, their ages, and whether and how many were victims of pogroms and counterrevolution; whether and how many children suffered from illnesses both physical and other kinds of debilities; what the illnesses were; whether the institution received aid from Evobshchestkom (Jewish Public Committee to Aid Victims of Pogroms) and how regularly; and finally, what supplies the institution needed.[7] The children's institutions were located in cities and towns where pogroms had taken place, including Kyiv, Uman, Ovruch, Fastov, Berdichev, and Belaia Tserkov'.

Most of the institutions were described as schools (*shkola, ochag*), orphanages (*detskii dom*), and nurseries; only one was a "children's club." Most had been founded between 1919 and 1922, some by new Soviet state agencies, including the Jewish Section of the Communist Party and the Division of Public Education (Narobraz); others were created by the Kultur-Lige and OZE (Organization to Promote Health among Jews). Among the oldest was an orphanage named after the Yiddish author I. L. Peretz, established in 1892 in Belaia Tserkov'.

Forms used to determine the occupations of pogrom survivors were recycled to provide information about children at shelters (*ochagi*). These forms do not indicate the location of the institution. The children's names and ages were listed and their orphaned status, whether they were pogromed, and the reason they were in the institution were indicated. One of these forms indicated that out of seventeen children, eleven had been in pogroms; the circumstances of their orphaned condition included "father left," "mother very poor," "father in Red Army," and "mother died." Children as young as four years gave this information.[8] Schneersohn will ask whether they understood its meaning.

The questionnaire made a distinction between physical illness and a category of pathology subsumed under the term *slabosil'nye* (weak) children. This broad category was a legacy of late nineteenth-century medicine and pedagogy that included mental retardation, behavioral abnormalities, weakness, criminality, "nervousness," and other problems.[9] The types of illness reported on the questionnaires I examined included tuberculosis and the "tendency toward tuberculosis," skin diseases, bed wetting, lack of appetite, epilepsy, and anemia. Nearly every institution reported a significant number of children who fell into the "weak" category. One questionnaire stated that some children were "mentally retarded" and others "defective," another extensive category that included children with disabilities, mental disturbances, criminality, and simply those who had run away from home.[10] Some forms indicated an unspecified "nervousness" among the children. A report to the Jewish Joint Distribution Committee (JDC) described the "nervous" condition of refugee children in Kyiv, who hoarded bread, grew anxious when adults left the room, and constantly retold stories about pogroms.[11] This is the type of child who will be the focus of Schneersohn's study.

An indication of the overwhelming need can be gathered from the answers to the question as to how many children the institution in question did not serve; this number was always higher than the number served. A frequent answer to the question as to what the institution needed was: "literally everything." Shoes, clothing, medicine, repairs to the physical building, more food, and more nourishing food were among the items listed in this category. The questionnaires and forms completed by the staff at children's institutions demonstrate the ongoing crisis of epidemic illness, lack of sanitary conditions, and shortages. The typical answers to the question about necessary items were food, clothing, and medicine and, less often, study materials and libraries. The 1923 JDC report that I mention earlier included a request to support and enlarge the Professional Technical School in Belaia Tserkov'. In one unusual instance, in contrast, the question of the children's potential emerged as a primary concern.

A staff member at a "shkola-klub" established in Belaia Tserkov' in 1920 said that in addition to food above the norm for pogromed children (who constituted all but two of the fifty-four children at the institution), what was necessary above all were teachers trained in the visual, vocal, and dramatic arts; physical education; various trades; and a physician who could teach hygiene. This request indicates that thought was given not only to the children's survival, precarious though it was. The request for teachers who could provide vocational training to the children points to a belief in their capacity to learn so-called productive occupations in the new Soviet society. The request for art teachers also shows the belief in the children's creative potential and its value for their future. Schneersohn will show how this potential could be discovered in the aftermath of catastrophe, in the confrontation with the child's apparent apathy and other pathological signs.

Questionnaires for Children

The Information and Statistics Division of Evobshchestkom designed a set of questions that could provide details about the psychological condition of children brought to Petrograd from Ukraine. The questions as a whole were to offer information about "a group of the population (children), who are now at the center of the government's and society's attention."[12] As Marina Mogilner explains, the 1922 "Experimental-Psychological Survey of Children" divided the child's experience into past, present, and future. The list of questions began with an inquiry into the child's earliest memories, whom the child loved the most in the past and present, and continued:

> 6. Whom did you most fear in childhood and why?
> 7. What did you most fear in childhood and why?
> 8. Whom do you most fear in the present and why?
> 9. What do you most fear at present and why?
> ...
> 21. Talk about the most terrible events in your life.
> 22. Talk about the happiest events in your dreams.
> 23. Talk about the saddest events in your dreams.
> ...
> 30. What or whom do you want to become when you grow older?
> 31. Is it better—to be Jewish or non-Jewish?
> 32. Do you want to be—Jewish or non-Jewish—and why?
> ...

39. Where would you like to be now and why?
40. Where do you want to be when you become an adult, and why?[13]

The tripartite division suggested, as Mogilner aptly points out, "the possibility of programming the future by curing or censoring negative content from the past."[14] The survey also asked the children to name the objects and phenomena they considered "funny, cheerful, frightening, and unpleasant." This is a sample of the categories the investigator was to use. The survey shows an interest in children's well-being as a particularly important segment of the population, not in particular children as individuals. The survey was part and parcel of what Mogilner calls "Jewish biopolitics," and, just as the questionnaires and forms I discuss in chapter 7, it served the interest of a linear narrative of progress and potential for productivity. Questions about which cities and countries were the best and the worst gauged the children's beliefs about the new socialist society. The focus of the survey was not directed at children's emotional responses to the questions or the state of their emotions generally. Although there is a clear concern with the children's future, the tripartite time frame rests on a linear model of the child's psychological state and the belief that the past could stay in the past. The answers to the questions are not available, but something approximating how children might have responded, especially "tell me about the most terrible events in your life," can be gleaned from Doyvber Levin and Fischel Schneersohn's work.

Children's Stories: Levin

Statistics were of no interest to Doyvber Levin. Stories were. Levin was born in Liady, a shtetl in Vitebsk province in Belarus, well known as the place of residence for the Schneersohn Hasidic dynasty (to which Fischel Schneersohn belonged). Levin came to Leningrad in the early 1920s to pursue a university education. He was a member of the avant-garde Russian association, the Union for Real Art (OBERIU), and was a close friend of one of its founders, Daniil Kharms.[15] Only fragments of Levin's OBERIU work have survived. His archive was destroyed in the siege of Leningrad, and the author himself was killed in battle in 1941. All that remains is his short fiction aimed at a young audience—and references to him in the remarks and memoirs of his more well-known contemporaries.[16]

A grotesque, surrealist style was central to the aesthetic of OBERIU's theatrical productions as well as Levin's tale *The Free States of Slavichi* (*Vol'nye shtaty Slavichi*), which tells the story of an anarchist takeover of a town. A gallery of grotesque folkloric and Gogolian figures populate the town, including a pair of anarchists, one tall with a "fat face," the other so short as to resemble a dwarf, a "hobgoblin" with a flattened, hairless face, more a scarecrow than a person. The Jewish houses are like bird coops, built on posts, and "the birds you could meet in these cages—children with bloated stomachs, bald women, and cripples of every kind."[17] The standard trope of the pathology of shtetl life and the emerging Soviet script of the friendship of nations protrude awkwardly from the text. Jewish factory owners and the local priest side inexplicably side with the anarchists, and young people (Jews and peasants), with the Bolsheviks.

In *Ten Wagons*, in contrast, the prose is oriented toward plot, and the description (of people, the surrounding landscape and environment) is kept to a minimum. The grotesque, ornamental stylization of Levin's other work is gone. The only exception in terms of style occurs in one child's description of pogrom perpetrators, who are bare-chested under their coats, "shaggy like animals," and, instead of speaking, produce only an incoherent "drone."[18] Explicit statements of political ideology are largely absent, as are descriptions of the shortages and hardships evidenced in the reports on care institutions previously mentioned.[19] *Ten Wagons* opens with stories of arrival, that of both the children at the orphanage and two friends, Khlopushin (Kharms) and Boris Mikhailovich Ledin (Levin).[20] At the end, some of the children set out for agricultural work at various locations. After a few introductory chapters, which include one child's account of how he became separated from his family during a pogrom, the succeeding chapters group the children's stories by plot line, with titles that include "Flight," "Bandits," Makhno, Denikin, and "Bezprizorniki" (the unsupervised).

The opening chapters explicitly raise the question of how to tell a story correctly, with the emphasis on suspense. The two friends Ledin and Khlopushin stumble into the courtyard of the building where the Jewish orphanage is located to escape a rainstorm. The children invite them inside and one tells an unengaging little tale of how he too escaped a rainstorm. The other children tell the two writers that they know better stories, for example, getting separated from their parents and escaping "bandits." This is the point of departure for the series of vignettes that constitutes the volume.

The new Soviet style known as factography, evident in Shklovsky and Kipnis's work, also appears in Levin's text. A cut-and-dried approach to language, the deliberate restraint from the expression of emotion, and an emphasis on the ongoing present were characteristic features of this antiartistic aesthetic.[21] The focus is on ongoing reality with all its unpredictability. Levin foregrounds the accidental nature of his visit to the orphanage; he discovers its existence by chance. Chaos and contingency are the central, form-giving principle of the work as a whole; indeed, explicit expressions of this principle bookend the work. I've already mentioned the opening gambit of the two friends seeking shelter from a rainstorm. At the end, the Levin character barely makes it to the train station where most of the children are setting off for the next phase of their young lives. He never gives the speech he planned. Uncertainty, tentativeness, and the precarity of the present dominate the work as a whole.

The focus on the present is important for two reasons. Levin's volume of fictionalized children's testimony lacks the memorial ethos—that is, the work does not mourn the world that was destroyed. This is in part because children are the authors of the narratives and because Levin welcomes the new Soviet society under construction at the time. One of the longer narratives concerns gang violence among shtetl children, an instance of violence that predates the Russian Revolution and has nothing to do with interethnic conflict. *Ten Wagons*, however, does not invoke the bright socialist future. There is discussion of the future, but not one to which the experiences recounted in this volume lead. It is disconnected from the present reality recounted in the children's stories. In the future, people will not remain on the surface of the earth; instead, they will fly to the moon and Mars on hot air balloons.[22] The day will come when everyone will have personal airplanes; houses will be spherical and made of glass; swimming pools and fountains will be constructed on their rooftops; and, right outside Moscow, cocoa will be cultivated.[23] This vision may be read as an indication of lack in the present, but it also contains even in its utopian impossibility a belief in a future of abundance, complete personal freedom, and release from all limits, even those imposed by gravity.

Separating the children's stories from the past and future underscores the contingency of their discovery. The author stumbles across the children and reports their stories; he does not invent them. Emphasizing the accidental factor intensifies the sense of the world as perceived rather than merely recognized.²⁴ Seeing things afresh is the goal of art, according to Victor Shklovsky, and the techniques of defamiliarization are key to its success. Estrangement played a key role in both literature and life at this time. It was a key element of the factographic style and the children's experience because they were forced to encounter events and people outside the normal run of their daily lives. Natan Shostak's account is an example. At four o'clock in the afternoon on a summer day, he suddenly heard a buzzing sound from above, "as if a great big bumblebee was flying overhead." Then he saw two birds that "grew bigger and bigger and stopped looking like birds."²⁵ The miller told him to run away, because the "birds" were airplanes. This was the beginning of the invasion of the town, which led to the death of both of Natan's parents. Another inhabitant of the orphanage, a former street child, describes his encounter with mannequins in a shop window when he first arrived in Leningrad. He banged on the glass and tried to get their attention by speaking to them in Yiddish. The first episode is tragic and the second, comic. Both are naive defamiliarizations, the radical alteration of the children's experience, caused by violence and emphasized by the factographic style.

Levin's editorial presence comes across in the lean, minimalist prose of the children's stories. Shamai's description of the invasion of the "Greens" (peasant insurgents), for instance, boils down to a series of verbs. The greens "rush into a village, a settlement, a shtetl, steal, kill, hang the 'Bolsheviks,' hack the 'Soviets' to pieces, fill their carts with stolen goods" and leave. Another child's account from another section of Levin's book describes how the inhabitants of a shtetl started to flee from an incursion. The account also foregrounds action: the townspeople "pour out onto the street.... drag out their belongings.... slam their doors shut... drive out their livestock" (ellipses added). From the same story: "tripping, falling, drifting off, we ran all night."²⁶ The narrative is a study in motion. The succession of verbs distills the chaos of the pogroms into a series of quick cinematic shots. This style of narration also accords with Schneersohn's analysis of children's accounts: children did not understand the meaning of the activity they witnessed, focusing instead on the exterior changes, including the rapid movement of those seeking escape from danger.

The destruction of Levin's archive makes it difficult to say with certainty, but it is likely that the examples above reveal the author's skilled editing, especially in comparison to the testimonies given by children available from archival sources. The repetition of mundane details, including those pertaining to Jewish religious practice, is abundantly evident in the children's testimonies available from archival materials but absent in Levin's stories. For example, Hersh Shapiro, age thirteen, who survived the 1920 pogrom in Minsk province, reports that on Saturday he "got up in the morning, prayed, and drank coffee" and heard everyone talking about the "unfortunate fate" of the Jews. Hersh opens his story of what happened on Sunday in the same way: in the morning, he "got up."[27] Leaving the question of editing aside, Schneersohn, as I show, explains the particularly flat way in which children narrate catastrophic events.

The absence of emotion from Levin's book is consistent with his factographic orientation toward the nonliterary text, including the document, report, protocol, and list. The children's stories of the invasion of their towns and homes by hostile soldiers and neighbors; the deaths of parents, siblings, and friends; and the flight from violence all unfold without the expression of anger, fear, sorrow, loss, or any other sentiment. Consider Natan Shostak's story (the child who thought airplanes were birds). At the age of seven or eight, he saw the shooting of his father and the death of his mother after childbirth (the baby was stillborn). Shostak's comment on these events is simply, "I saw everything." He reports that he was an eyewitness as if the events had nothing to do with him personally. Levin does not provide a description of the child's facial expression, tone of voice, or gestures. One of the children reports an episode in which pogromists cut the *heder* teacher's beard and commanded the children to laugh, to participate in the rabbi's humiliation.[28] As I have shown earlier, ritualized laughter was part of the repertoire of pogrom violence. The child narrating the episode in *Ten Wagons* reports that he and the others did not comply with the bandit's request to laugh, but again, there is no account of what they felt instead. In contrast, the Minsk children's testimonies that I mentioned earlier contain some expression of fear, agitation, and relief. For example, when the Bolsheviks returned to their town, the "Jews rejoiced," one child reported.[29] In both cases, however, the child's own emotion is at a minimum.

Children's Stories: Schneersohn

Schneersohn's clinical and research work at this time focused precisely on the children's apparent lack of emotional response. He reports in the opening pages of his 1923 *Catastrophic Times* that children from the ages of five to twelve appeared as witnesses in Soviet court proceedings, and even though grown women burst into tears after hearing their testimony, the children, without any emotional outburst, calmly identified men sitting in front of them who had murdered their parents and raped their sisters.[30] Schneersohn looked beyond the children's seemingly nonchalant attitudes toward their own experience. He showed that data-oriented methodologies could not track the subterranean forms that emotions assumed. Schneersohn's 1923 study was a groundbreaking work on the effects of intimate violence on the psychology of children, and it was recognized as such in the Yiddish press.[31] Schneersohn also deserves credit for his investigation into the relation between pogroms and the emotions and was thoroughly versed in the science of emotion of his time.[32] As I pointed out in the previous chapter, the social scientists who organized research into and relief work for victims of pogroms did not focus on the question of the inner experience of those who perished in or survived the anti-Jewish violence of revolutionary Russia and Ukraine.

Schneersohn was one of the direct descendants of Shneur Zalman of Liady, the founder of the Chabad movement in Hasidism.[33] A distinction must be made between Chabad in Schneersohn's time and the present day; Chabad in the late nineteenth century was not the global organization that it is today.[34] Schneersohn was ordained at the young age of fifteen but left the Hasidic community and went on to receive a medical degree at the University of Berlin. Schneersohn worked for a time with the Russian reflexologist Vladimir Bekhterev. He founded the department of psychotherapy at the University of Kyiv. In 1919–21, during the time of political upheaval and anti-Jewish violence, and he and his students worked directly with children categorized as suffering from intellectual disabilities, criminal children, street children, and those who had been the victims of pogroms. He relocated from Kyiv to Berlin, where he published several Yiddish novels of Hasidic life and other scientific studies in Russian, Yiddish, and German in addition to *Catastrophic Times*.[35] Among these were the Russian *Psychology of the Child's Intimate Life* (1923) and the Yiddish *Der veg tsum mentsh* (1927). Although the title translates as *The Path to the Person*, it was published in English as *Studies in Psycho-Expedition*; the English version included an introduction by John Dewey. This work was Schneersohn's solution to what Freud would later call civilization's discontents; Schneersohn prescribes the cultivation of religious ecstasy, what Freud called the oceanic feeling of union with the universe. He left Berlin in the early 1930s and settled in Palestine, where he continued researching and publishing on children and trauma. The field of study that focuses on children and youth (in Yiddish, *yugnt-forshung*) received significant development from Schneersohn's work, and Max Weinreich's major study of children and youth, his 1935 *Der veg tsum yugnt* (*The Path to Youth*) refers to Schneersohn's work several times.

Schneerson was familiar with the psychological science of his time, and discussions of William James, Théodule Ribot, Henri Bergson, Alfred Binet, Sigmund Freud, Alfred Adler, and Paul Schilder appear in this work. The scholarship on Schneersohn has focused mostly on his novels and *Studies in Psycho-Expedition*; the discussion that follows, while building on these approaches, introduces his scientific work with children.[36] Schneersohn's religious background is important to his theories of care and recovery.

Methods and Objects

In *Catastrophic Times*, Schneersohn notes with dismay that scientists and educators were paying far too little attention to the problem of the next generation in an epoch of war and revolution.[37] In the case of Jewish children in Ukraine and Russia, where the "front" had invaded the intimate space of the family home, the problem was particularly acute. Jewish children who lived through the pogrom period and non-Jewish children who saw what happened were different from children who had survived war.[38] Non-Jewish children are also victims, because of what they saw; Schneersohn's diagnostic gaze is all-encompassing.

Why was it important to show that the child's indifference was superficial? The failure to respond to stimuli was an indication of pathology, to put it the most general terms, a cessation of the vital sensibility. More specifically, as Schneersohn points out in *The Psychology of the Child's Intimate Life*, psychologists frequently encountered a decrease in overall emotional responsiveness among criminal children.[39] The failure to respond was a sign of the morbid state of the organism, in this case, not only the individual Jewish child but an entire generation of Jewish children who had been exposed to violence. The experience of violence could change everything for the child, and not only in the short term; it could also influence her capacity for productive work. The Jewish social scientists and Schneersohn, regardless of differences in approach, shared a common concern about this very point. If pogromed populations were incapable of work, they would not receive the rights or care afforded by the new Soviet society. The future of Jewish children in Russia and Ukraine was at stake. Schneersohn was frustrated, however, with the limitations of prevailing research and therapeutic methodologies. Children's games, dreams, and drawings were recorded, analyzed, and interpreted; children were asked to describe what they saw in selected pictures, and their reactions were photographed. They had to remember a sequence of numbers, and to take tests.[40] None of these methods, in Schneersohn's view, could penetrate the child's inner emotional landscape and thus the dynamic processes indicative of continued vitality remained obscure. He was opposed to the statistical methods of biopolitics, but he and his colleagues at Jewish relief commissions in Kyiv both shared a common goal: the ongoing and future life of the population in their care.

The questionnaire was the scientific method of choice in this period. It was used not only by Jewish relief agencies, as I discuss earlier and in chapter 7, but also in a seminar at Yale titled "The Impact of Culture on Personality," run by Edward Sapir and his student John Dollard.[41] This method was also flawed, according to Schneersohn. Even if the interviewer managed to obtain an answer about emotions, it was not the emotion itself that the interview subject produced, but instead, a representation or description of the emotion, or, as Schneersohn puts it, a "translation" of the emotion, which always tends to conceal itself. The work of Théodule Ribot (whom Schneersohn cites at length) is clearly important for this claim. Ribot separated the intellect from the emotions.[42] The capacity to form representations and the capacity to experience feelings are not the same, and the former is not necessary for the latter, according to Ribot. Emotion has to do with the vital tendencies, instincts and physical movements of the organism and thus is separate from ideas and representations. Language is an intellectual process, distinct from emotion, and when language dominates, the emotions tend to retreat to the associative stream.[43] A paucity of statements expressing feelings did not mean there was a paucity of feelings. Schneersohn's preferred method, the solicitation of the children's free narration, which included autobiographical and fictitious stories, fantasies, and dreams, could reveal her indirectly expressed emotional responses, which remained hidden from questionnaires, interviews, photography, and the laws of large numbers.[44] Asking children to invent fictions was an innovative departure from the standard methodologies of the time.

Schneersohn's arguments about the delayed impact of catastrophic events will resonate with readers familiar with Freud and the traumatic turn in literary and cultural study. Originally limited to a physical wound, the term *trauma* expanded significantly in the first quarter of the twentieth century, especially after World War I, and is used broadly in the humanities today. The meaning of *trauma* extends beyond medical studies of post-traumatic stress disorder to include philosophical debates about what is posited as the fundamentally traumatic condition of human history, which for some theorists, remains unknowable and unrepresentable.[45] Several distinctions should be made, however, between the current preoccupation with the theory of trauma and Schneersohn's most pressing point. His insistence on the importance of delayed effect stems from a single motivation: to show that pogromed children were still responsive to their environment even though they may have presented another appearance. Only by understanding delayed effect could the outside observer discern the children's *vitality*. The focus is not on the psychic wound, the pathology, but the underlying evidence of health and, as I shortly show, even greater potential growth because of the injury.

Schneersohn's elaboration of delayed effect (to which he devotes an entire chapter), and his explicit reference to Freud, shows that he was conversant with discussions of trauma in his time, even though he did not use the term in this study. The working definition of *trauma* available in Schneersohn's milieu was "a wound to the mind caused by unexpected emotional shock" and the subsequent inability to remember the precipitating event.[46] The wound manifests itself only in the aftermath of the event in a variety of disturbances, including sleeplessness, mutism, nightmares, and other symptoms. Schneersohn's description of the wound to the mind is dramatic and vivid: he writes about the "bloody memory-wounds [*erinerungs-vundn*] of fear, pain, and murder" that could influence the growing generation of Jewish children in Russia and Ukraine.[47] What is not clear, however, is whether he means that in these cases memory ceases to function properly, highlighting trauma as a problem of memory, or whether he means that the events are painful to remember. Schneersohn's analysis of mental disorders in children caused by pogroms, breaks the problem into various phases, beginning with a moment in which the "bio-psychical defense mechanism" is overwhelmed, and transitioning to a later stage in which the initial "shock-effect" spreads itself over time free from episodes of violence.[48] The symptoms of delayed effect in children include epilepsy, hysterical hunger, melancholy, night terrors, insomnia, and "forced memories." For example, Itsik, age ten, gave testimony in court. Pogromists killed his father and severely wounded his mother; "everything was destroyed"; afterward, he entered an orphanage. During the trial, he recognized those responsible, and subsequently, he stopped sleeping and compulsively told anyone he met about what happened. The fact that the child remained seemingly indifferent during the trial is immaterial, because the trial, Schneersohn says, stimulated the delayed effect of earlier impressions.[49]

Schneersohn's account of the delayed effect of catastrophic events rests on the science of his day, including the work of Bekhterev and Freud. Schneersohn conducted experiments in Bekhterev's laboratory that showed that the response to a stimulus was strengthened when a pause was introduced between the first and subsequent stimulus episodes. Latency was a key component of his argument about the emotional health of pogromed children. The complex of images in the child's psyche, Schneersohn writes, changes in the course of time and serves as the source for subsequent disturbances. These experiments provided a basis for the argument about latency and the children's lack of response; however, he did not support the use of stimulus/response exercises in either the diagnosis or the cure of children.[50] Schneersohn does not reference Freud's 1919 *Beyond the Pleasure Principle*, which begins with a discussion of the war neuroses and delayed response. This book, however, was not Freud's first engagement with the problem of *Nachträglichkeit*. Hysteria, according to Freud, also rests on the mechanism of delay. Hysteria depended on a first and then a subsequent event that would reanimate the suppressed desire, ultimately translating it into a symptom. While claiming that children even more than hysterics suffer from delayed influence, Schneersohn, however, explicitly distances himself from Freud's argument about sexuality as the basis for delayed effect, characterizing it as "too narrow." His argument about delayed effect in children, more importantly, hinges on the potential for recovery. Creativity plays a crucial role, both in the diagnosis of children's inner emotional state and in their recovery from what he terms their "memory-wounds."

Creativity and Diagnosis

Whereas direct questioning cannot provide access to children's feelings, the exploration of their fantasies can because fantasies are the embodiment and development of children's emotions. The study of children's play is important for this analysis. Schneersohn's interest in play was not unique, since Russian and other researchers had studied children's violent games in response to their experience of World War I. Schneersohn describes funeral procession games and games in which children pretended to be well-known pogromists, including Struk, for example. He emphasized that what interested the children was movement and excitement, pretending to shoot, running, and hiding, and not destruction in and of itself.[51] They lacked the capacity to understand the consequences of the activities they imitated.

Schneersohn's particular interest, like Levin's, was the children's stories, which he breaks down into three categories: unlimited memory narratives, unlimited narrative (fiction), and unlimited autobiography. He dedicates a significant number of pages in *Catastrophic Times* to the stories and memories of children who otherwise demonstrated a lack of emotion or, as he puts it, "stoniness" in relation to the violence they had experienced. The way he elicited these narratives was often as simple as asking, "Tell me something interesting." Schneersohn's approach was distinct from the prevailing methodologies of working with children who had experienced violence. Not only the Jewish Public Committee to Aid Victims of Pogroms but also Russian scientists and educators working to respond to the crisis of childhood created by World War I relied on "questionnaires on children's reading practices, personal interests, and worldviews, or else they collected and analyzed children's drawings, diaries, and schoolwork."[52] Schneersohn's method, "tell me something interesting" was closer to Doyvber Levin than to approaches used by his fellow scientists. It was more open-ended, less structured, and, in his view, revealed more. The stories the children created in response revealed the inner life of their emotions.

In *Catastrophic Times*, Schneersohn compares the narratives of German Jewish children who had not experienced pogroms to children from Ukraine and Russia who had. The former told him about pleasant train journeys and life-cycle events, including, for example, their bar-mitzvahs; the latter, about being driven first by one group of soldiers and then another from place to place. An eleven-year-old girl describes the invasion of her home by pogromists in the following terms: "A whole night went by as if there were Purim maskers. This was during Sukkot."[53] During Purim, which occurs in the early spring, Jews retell the story of miraculous salvation from the villainous Haman, and they dress in costume and go door to door; drinking is a part of the celebration. The holiday of Sukkot (reenacting temporary shelter during the exodus from Egypt) takes place in the fall. Literary authors working in Yiddish and Ukrainian use a similar motif of temporal disorientation, the holiday out of joint, to describe the experience of occupation by the anarchist Makhno and episodes of home invasion by pogromists. Kvitko's poem "How Many Minutes in an Hour?" shatters a single instant into multiple images and sensations of terror. The autobiographical accounts provided by German Jewish children underscored the regular patterns of their lives; in contrast, those given by pogromed children revealed their profound sensibility of disruption in relation to calendrical order. Time itself was wounded.

A seven-year-old girl experienced the invasion of her home by "bandits," who occupied her town for an extended period. Her family moved to Kyiv, and her parents, concerned about her apathy and depression, brought her to Schneersohn for treatment. After discussing the child's physical condition, which was normal, and discounting the factor of heredity, a common medical concern of the time, Schneersohn turns to his own method of eliciting narratives from the child, including her memories of her experience and her fictitious creations. She witnessed pogromists shooting at a dead body as loud music played, an episode that Schneersohn characterizes as a "cannibals' holiday," again, the motif of the holiday out of joint.[54] The case of the young girl whom Schneersohn cared for in Kyiv deserves particular attention because he uses it to indicate the potential for cure. The young girl played a crucial role in protecting her family during the invasion of their home. She distracted the invaders from their untoward interest in her mother; played cards with them, allowing them to win; sang for them; danced and, in this way, managed to prevent acts of violence. When she was not engaged in this work, her play consisted of digging holes in the courtyard to search for "magic wands."

Among the fictitious stories she provided were the following. Children were playing in a field of flowers when suddenly a spider appeared and ate all the flies buzzing around the flowers. The children felt great pity for the flies and grew frightened for themselves: Would the spider eat them also?

Their mother told them not to worry because a spider doesn't eat people. Another story by the same child involved a brother and sister who ran away from a cruel stepmother to live in the woods. The little boy became ill from the berries they ate, but his sister called a doctor, who cured the child. Then they found a little house made of cookies and ate their fill.

Elements familiar from fairy and adventure tales (the Hansel and Gretel house of sweets) and reflections of historical reality (summoning a doctor) combine in this and other stories. An eleven-year-old boy tells a story about a young hero, a boy-sailor, who joins the crew of a ship bound for Africa, where he saves himself from a lion.[55] A fourteen-year-old tells the story of a boy whose parents cannot afford to educate him. He runs away, and a witch gives him magical tools: a table that provides food and a coat whose pockets are always full of money. The boy studies at a university and becomes an aide to a king; when king dies, the boy takes the throne, but he never forgets his poverty-stricken childhood and does good for others.

Schneersohn sees the reflection of the children's experience of pogroms in their fiction: danger (the lion, living in the woods), cruelty (the stepmother), mass killing (the spider and the flies), becoming an orphan (running away from home). He also discerns the basis for the children's recovery in their representation of their ability to solve problems with knowledge (spiders don't eat people) and autonomous action on their own behalf (the sibling calls the doctor on behalf of her brother). Children who lost their families also discovered their own inner resources. Rive, the young girl who saved her family, suffered from depression that lasted two years. Schneersohn concludes her case history by stating that she learned "the bitter secrets of life, but has achieved equilibrium and confidence." The little stories the children told Schneersohn, any "fantasy" is, in his words an "emotional creation," and these stories, furthermore, reveal the children's potential to live life, their vitality and practical skill.[56] The events that harmed them also spark their creativity and precocious development. Just as the science of evolution shows that the organism adapts to harsh conditions in the environment, so do children, who respond to their environment in new and unforeseen ways.[57] By discovering the enhanced capacity for life from within the injuries the children suffered, Schneersohn transforms the chaos and abandonment of the children's lives into evidence of their potential for a future. The importance of creativity has consequences for care. Schneersohn's model for what he calls "therapeutic education" critically depends on creative activity, which must permeate the child's environment. The child must be drawn into the atmosphere of creative activity.[58]

Schneersohn's approach to the care of pogromed children reveals an interplay between injury and recovery. Catastrophe and creativity both involve what Schneersohn calls the "spherical life" of the individual. In *Studies in Psycho-Expedition*, the English translation of the Yiddish *Der veg tsum mentsh* (1927), Schneersohn discusses mental health in broad terms, prescribing the cultivation of spherical life, that is, emotions, thoughts, and sensations that take the individual out of the rut of daily life experience. He defines the spherical realm as "intuitive and affective, but dynamically connected with the normal mode."[59] Schneersohn derives the concept of spherical psychic life from the psychologist Paul Schilder (1886–1940), whom he mentions explicitly in both *Catastrophic Times* and *Studies in Psycho-Expedition*. Schilder is well known in the history of psychology for his development of the idea of the body image and his innovations in group therapy. The psychical sphere, according to Schilder, responds to both internal and external stimuli. This concept has some parallels with William James's understanding of consciousness; Schneersohn explicitly discusses James in his Russian volume, *The Psychology of the Child's Intimate Life*, and in *Studies in Psycho-Expedition*. James's famous stream of consciousness encompasses sensations and movements of the body as well as emotions and thoughts, Schneersohn says. James's concept of "fringe consciousness" is also pertinent to the spherical realm. Both have to do with the epiphenomena of perception, not limited to the recognition of an object according to a predetermined schema, but other responses to the object, for example in bodily states, associations, the feeling of "affinity" toward or repulsion from the object or word, and other immediate reactions—the "psychic overtones" connected with them.[60] Schilder was interested in analyzing this broader realm, the patient's sense of time, space, materiality, and causality.[61] Schilder's curiosity about the fundamental phenomena of his patients' experience is striking. I argue in previous chapters that the poets Hofshteyn and Kvitko explore their relation to the world through a similar phenomenological lens. The time distortion that appears so prominently in archival testimonies, artistic literature, and Schneersohn's own account of pogroms is an example of the spherical response to catastrophe. In his 1923 study, Schneersohn traces the child's experience of pogroms step by step highlighting the vivid fringe, or "spherical" responses. The child hears grown-ups voicing violent agitation; his mother picks him up and runs; he hears words he does not understand, including *pogrom*; he hears shooting and screams. The unclear words and images are fixed symbolically in the "spherical feeling tensions."[62] A shocking event can directly influence conscious life, or it can "descend into the deep abyss of the soul as a spherical tension complex."[63]

Injury is not the only way that the spherical realm may be touched. Great artists and "religious creators" come to an awareness of "a higher existence," absolute beauty, and spirituality indirectly, by means of "intuitive, suggestive images."[64] Children cannot grasp these concepts, but possess the capacity to blend dream and reality, like artists. Childhood, according to Schneersohn, rather than serving as a mere waystation to adulthood is a unique period in which dream and reality meet. The child touched by violence may break through the limitations of her developmental stage to reach "higher" levels of capacity than would otherwise be possible. The highest, most elevated spiritual ideas and artistic representations of beauty or divinity and that which is the most fearful, violent, and destructive stimulate the spherical realm.[65] Both trauma and creativity involve a psychological process of being overwhelmed, as he explains. The artist's fantasy possesses "tremendous force" and gains in strength to the point when it breaks down the habitual, practical adaptation to ordinary circumstances, which has become "ossified."[66] Both episodes of violence and the creativity of art take individuals out of the ordinary categories of time and space and thus in parallel ways may serve to spur them on to some unforeseen trajectory.

Thus far, I have focused on Schneersohn's engagement with the science and clinical practice of his time, but at this point, it is important to introduce the religious dimension of his work. In an interview given in 1927, Schneersohn said that there was no separation between his scientific and artistic work, on the one side, and the Jewish world, on the other. Chabad Hasidism was his "spiritual homeland" (he uses the German word *heimat*). In answer to the interviewer's question, he declared that in no way had he "left the Jewish world."[67] A brief discussion of the basic elements of Schneersohn's conceptual "homeland" will help clarify the Hasidic concepts and practices that he adapted into new forms suitable for his vision of health, disease, and therapy.

Creation, the first phase of cosmic history, is understood as a concentration and contraction of God into himself; the process is known as *tsimtsum*. God's concentration into a limited space allowed for the dispersion of divine light, which was supposed to be caught in specific containers or "vessels" (*sefirot*), but the vessels shattered. Note that creation and rupture, as in Schneersohn's theory of artistic creativity, are linked. The light, the divine elements, became intermixed with the lower world, with evil. The process of creation itself is inherently flawed. Out of creation came confusion and chaos, and it is up to human beings to restore order, remove confusion, and reunite the scattered divine sparks. The restitution of order constitutes the repair (*tikun*) of the world.

David Freis sees a link between Schneersohn's use of "spheres" and the mystical concept of divine emanations, in Hebrew, *sefirot*.[68] Schneersohn's Hasidic background might well have provided an affinity, to use James's word, for the term *spheres*, which circulated widely in the early twentieth century, including, for example, with the notion of the "bio-sphere." As Freis points out, Schneersohn not only relies on the medical term of his time, *psyche*, but also turns to the religious language of the soul. There are several passages in *Catastrophic Times* in which Schneersohn breaks with his restrained style of scientific analysis and heavily Germanicized vocabulary to bring out the importance of Jewish history and Hasidic religious concepts. One of the most important is the following: "The individual's tribulations are unforgettable moments of the people's history. Each individual self-sacrifice bears the great history of the people. There are no murder victims, only martyrs [*kedoyshim*], who write the intimate bloody story of the people's history. And in the innermost depths of the soul the religious ecstasy of the people bursts forth, the people who more than once went to the fire with their arms lifted in ecstasy."[69] The experience of the greatest pain is also a moment of the greatest and most intimately felt connection with the history of Jewish people and with God. In *Studies in Psycho-Expedition*, Schneersohn described "Hassidic ecstasy [*devekut, dveykes* in Yiddish]," an "intimate ecstatic concentration" as a "source of healing" both for individuals and society. Even though he does not use the term *dveykes* in *Catastrophic Times*, but rather the Germanic *ekstaz*, he is referring to the same idea. In *Studies in Psycho-Expedition*, he prescribes the cultivation of this religious emotion as therapy for routinized modern experience. Schneersohn is not trying to deny the pain that his patients endured but, rather, offering an alternative perspective by means of which pain could be addressed. He embeds their suffering in a larger framework of meaning, bringing Jewish history to bear on the problem of how to care for pogromed children. Jewish history is a resource, not a reservoir of disaster.

There is a direct parallel between the argument of the passage cited and the argument of *Catastrophic Times* as a whole, even though the passage is couched in exalted, passionate language, unlike the rest of the book. The injury contains the seeds of cure, and the isolated individual is part of something larger. The child subject to the catastrophic experience of pogroms may be able to break through to a higher level of development. The "dialectic of ascent and descent in the religious ecstasy of the founder of Hasidism" is central to everything Schneersohn wrote.[70] As I discuss in chapter 4, Der Nister and Kvitko, both of whom refer to Rabbi Nakhman, also engage with the theme of ascent through descent. The religious practice of *hefker k'midbar* reflects a similar idea of kenosis for the sake of progress toward a higher spiritual plane.

The psychological diagnosis and therapy of the traumatized individual in Schneersohn's scientific work borrows elements from the Hasidic journey of the soul. The link between injury and recovery is directly tied to the Hasidic notion of *aliye in yeride*, the Hasidic notion of ascent through descent. A year before *Catastrophic Times*, Schneersohn had published the first volume of his novel *Khayim Gravitser (The Story of the Downfallen One): From the World of Chabad*.[71] Set in the middle of the nineteenth century, it tells the story of the fiery, passionate Khayim, a Lubavitch Hasid, who preaches that God is in everything. A proponent of the acosmic view that there is no reality outside of God, he cultivates a psychological state of the nullification of the self, drinks to excess, and flouts the commandments.[72] At the peak of one of his ecstatic discourses, he learns that his only son, Yossele, has died. Still enflamed by his own words about joy, God in everything, and the overcoming of death, Khayim refuses to recognize that his child has died and fails to recite the necessary prayers. At the height of his ecstasy, he finally acknowledges the tragedy, protesting that it took place without his permission. Reeling from the loss he rejects everything he has previously believed and runs away from the community.

The theme of ascent through descent runs through the entire first volume, particularly in the citation of Hasidic discourses, which Schneersohn says he jotted down from lectures he personally heard in the Chabad community. For example, in one discourse, each fall of the holy man contains the message of a coming "spiritual elevation."[73] The spiritual journey of the individual maps directly onto the cosmological plane of the creation, fall, and redemption of the world. Creativity on a cosmic scale is also linked to descent, fall. The Lubavitsher Rebbe tells the assembled community that "falling contains the secret and source of the creation of the world, because the creation of the world is the first and deepest fall, the descent of God into the world, the soul into the body."[74] Emphasizing the point and adding the dimension of humanity's role in creation, he goes on to say that the tsimtsum, God's concentration into himself, is more a matter of God's descending in the world, thus creating it for the first time, and that this act contains the "luminous ascent" of future world creation, which is given to human beings.[75] Each individual human being can be the creator of numerous worlds.

Schneersohn's therapeutic orientation in *Catastrophic Times* rests on the value of the child's creative process. There is a convergence between this emphasis and the cosmic role assigned to humanity in Hasidic thought as Schneersohn represented it in his novel *Khayim Gravitser*. The flawed process of creation means that the worlds and metaphysical realms left fragmented in its wake are in constant need of repair and re-creation. The rabbi's discourse in the opening of the novel links the "fall" of the divine contraction to a subsequent ascent and the "further creation of the world, which is given to man."[76] There is a parallel between Schneersohn's argument about the creative potential of the pogromed child and the Hasidic notion of the human cocreation and continuous restoration of the world in ruins.

This chapter begins with what was, in the first quarter of the twentieth century, a relatively new diagnostic technology, the use of questionnaires, tests, and other evaluative instruments to assess the state of health and sickness among pogromed children and the institutions created to care for them. Doyvber Levin and Fischel Schneersohn both used an alternative technology, older and newer, "tell me a story." The differences between the two methods are important, but the underlying goal shared by relief agencies and Fischel Schneersohn was the same: rescue, recovery, and the promise of a future, no matter how remote it might seem. It is easy to dismiss as self-deluded or childishly naive the staff member at the care institution who demanded art teachers for the children, the futuristic tale recounted in Levin's *Ten Wagons* of houses made of glass and personal airplanes, and the child who tells Schneersohn a story about a house made of cookies. Yet in these statements and stories, a commitment to the future shines through the landscape of disaster. In his pogrom lament *Troyer* the poet David Hofshteyn, kneeling at the edge of the abyss, asks, "What are you still able to do?" The relief agencies, Doyvber Levin, and Fischel Schneersohn all answer the question in a similar way. Whether by documenting, listing, naming, counting, listening, writing poetry, or telling stories, they were providing care and imagining a future.

Conclusion

This study traces the ways that poets, prose authors, relief workers, and medical professionals experienced, witnessed, poetically reimagined, and investigated the pogroms of revolutionary Russia and Ukraine. I have examined both the violence of abandonment (the hefker condition) and the activity of care expressed in poetic form and registered in documentary lists, reports, and testimonies. Hefker originates in Jewish property law, where it refers to "unclaimed" or abandoned goods. It became associated with waywardness and wantonness and then, in the first quarter of the twentieth century, gained additional meanings and contexts: the freedom of being unclaimed, the freedom to create literature in a new way, and the pain of being dispossessed and politically abandoned. To suffer from violence committed with impunity is different from suffering violence for which there is some possibility of recourse in law. It's not merely that someone wrongs and harms you. It's that no one will recognize the wrong and the harm. To resemble "the dust of the earth" suggests the experience of those who have been disavowed. Dust is part of nature, but as the literature of abandonment shows, it is more often the product of history. In the memoirs and poetry of violence, dust is the material deposit of destruction wrought by humans. Mass public violence, however, is not the only occasion of abandonment. The hefker concept reveals occasions of abandonment beyond the actions of sovereign states. The ordinary conditions of daily life are ripe with possibilities for neglect, as Kvitko's childhood shows. The gap in which abandoned individuals unpredictably find themselves can open even within settings designed to provide care, as in Molodowsky's poem about the tuberculosis sanitorium, "Otwock."

My approach to violence has drawn attention to the phenomena of disorientation and the diminution of the capacity to make sense of the world. Hofshteyn and Kvitko's poetry; Der Nister, Kipnis, Shklovsky, and Levin's prose; and Schneersohn's scientific work depict the destruction of a familiar world, with its accompanying commonsense notions that organize daily experience, and its replacement by an alternative realm, a deathworld. At right angles to normal existence, numerous temporary sovereigns, including state actors, warlords, and local individuals, ruled the pogrom world. They exercised their authority by drawing a line between who would receive protection and who would be subjected to robbery, extortion, killing, and rape. In the realm of mob rule and pogrom violence, the distinction between the living and the dead was blurred, and neighbors and loved ones were strangely transformed into grotesque creatures who could not and did not recognize one another.

Space and time changed their contours in this other world; no one knew what day it was, whether it was a holiday or a weekday. Time was different; its "moments were otherwise," as Kvitko writes in his preface to *1919*. In his pogrom lament, Hofshteyn transcribes the discarded messages left floating about in the cosmos, made ancient by catastrophe. The othering of time is a feature of poetry about disaster, no matter where and when the setting. Carolyn Forché's poetry about atrocities in El Salvador also stage a temporal disjuncture between the suffering of victims and the poets who write about them. In "The Island," for example, she writes, "When we listen / we hear something taking place / in the past." In "San Onofre, California," she dramatically elongates the time it takes for a voice to be heard: "the cries of those who vanish / might take years to get here."[1] Violence shatters the continuity of time. Suffering comes from another place in the cosmos that has already gone dead, but whose sounds have not yet reached us.

Hofshteyn and Kvitko's poetic voices are distinct. The free and easy open road is the central hefker motif of Hofshteyn's debut volume, in which the joyous, sensuous encounter of self and world predominates. Hofshteyn's quivering, sensual experience of natural phenomena reassembles who is acting and who is being acted upon. His aliveness and the world's aliveness unfold together. In contrast, in Kvitko's *First Steps*, abandonment is an intractable primordial destiny that consigns him to misery. Uncanny otherness invades his room, sometimes bringing him delight but more often dread. In *1919*, he deploys sound that both mimes and inflicts pain. Regardless of these differences, Hofshteyn and Kvitko's pogrom poetry shares a common feature of the kenotic reduction of self and a relational opening to others. Hofshteyn stills his own voice—not "demanding," only asking—and the poetic act of transcription, the gathering of others' messages, offers the possibility of comfort. Kvitko listens to violence and reproduces something akin to its sounds in his pogrom cycle *1919*, transforming himself into a vibroscope and listening to the suffering of others to the point of deafness. Hefker, the watchword of Yiddish expressionism, typically refers to poetry that howls. As I show, however, it can also refer to the quiet, raspy sounds of Molodowsky's tubercular poetry, and it names an authorial ethics in which poets quiet their own voices to be able to receive the sounds and voices of others. This is a secular reworking of the religious practice of making the self "hefker like the wilderness."

The poets writing about the destruction of life and the means of sustaining life—the possibility of daily life, the sense of time, space, where I am, and whether I am alive—also pose the question of forgiveness. At the edge of the abyss, at the hefker threshold, a hint appears of the possibility of reconciliation, a way to move from the strange intimacy of neighborly violence to the strange intimacy of neighborly care. "You are all in me," writes Kvitko. Hofshteyn tells Ukraine it was once a place of refuge. Chagall's image accompanying Hofshteyn's poem "Falling" shows the little fox, the hunter's target, crawling up the hunter's face. Kipnis shakes his head over the sight of the children of enemies eating together. Look how strange it is to see the children of the murdered and the murdered pogrom perpetrators sitting at one table.

Catastrophe can lead to poetry and catastrophe can lead to documentation. In "Day Grows Darker," Kvitko describes the work conducted by relief agencies to list the names of the dead: "He will write my dead name / with all the others / in tiny letters on a long list." Jewish relief agencies working with the Ukrainian and Soviet governments collected a vast body of data about deaths, injuries, dislocation, the destruction of property, and children left without parents. They kept detailed records about funds and other items dispersed to survivors and wrote reports about conditions leading to anti-Jewish violence. They relied on the tools of questionnaires and statistics, the new gold standard of relief work. Even though these instruments can be used as tools of oppression, in this case, the goal was to provide some form of amelioration of suffering, to remove the pogromed population from the realm of abandonment to the realm of care.

Sometimes poetry replaces documentation. Bialik, charged with documenting the 1903 Kishinev pogrom, collected information but did not write a report, creating instead "In the City of the Slaughter." No matter what form responses to the civil war pogroms took, whether poetry or documentation, both poets and statisticians faced the hefker threshold, the wild unpredictability that could serve as a catalyst for new artistic forms and ethical relations and could also call into question the very procedures meant to control chaos. As the author of one medical report stated, "The dead do not pursue lawsuits for their ruined lives." The chaos of violence, the use of mass graves, and other circumstances meant that he could not be certain of his numbers. The case of the Yiddish poet Moses Carton, listed as dead in Pechora but in fact alive in New York, is an example of the problem. Poems and statistics have something else in common, besides the edge of chaos. What I try to show is that both writing lists and writing poems are ways of remaking the sense of order necessary to live in the world. The first step is registering that the catastrophe has taken place. Counting and specifying names individuate what violence has undifferentiated.

It is unusual to examine poems and documents in one study. I am not alone, however, in finding a link between poetry and the documentation of mass public violence, and in 1919 the conditions of hefker abandonment were not limited to Jews. Eve Ewing's *1919*, a cycle of poems about Chicago's July 1919 race riot, uses the 1922 report *The Negro in Chicago* as her interlocutor, juxtaposing citations from the document with her poems. The riot began when a seventeen-year-old Black youth accidentally violated the "imaginary boundary" separating Black and White swimming areas.[2] He was killed by a White stone-thrower, and the police refused to make an arrest. In the interracial violence that followed twenty-three Blacks and fifteen Whites were killed, and one thousand people lost their homes.

I show that the strangeness of violence is a central theme in both the pogrom investigators' reports and the artistic literature. Shklovsky cannot make sense of all the strange things he saw in postrevolutionary Russia. Strangeness refers to not only the bizarre features of pogrom violence but also a certain opacity regarding the motivation of those who committed these acts. Regardless of all the economic pressures of the historical

CONCLUSION   233

moment and the force of propagandistic speeches labeling all Jews Bolsheviks, it is hard to understand why people did what they did. In *Months and Days*, Kipnis remarks that his non-Jewish neighbors had undergone a mysterious "transformation." Those who committed violence became unrecognizable, not only to others whom they victimized but also possibly even to themselves.[3]

The authors of the 1922 Chicago report directly comment on the problem. Those they call "sightseers" (casual participants in the riot) and those "included in the nucleus did not know why they had taken part in crimes."[4] In her poem "sightseers," Ewing implicates readers to this day who remain "sightseers at the bridge of history / watching the water go by." The term *sightseer* is of use in categorizing various forms of participation in the pogroms of the Russian Civil War. Trial documents from January 1919 in the case of a certain Shumskaia, charged with looting during a pogrom in Zhitomir, provide some details. Shumskaia, an illiterate non-Jew, had worked as a cook in a Jewish home, the Fefermans. She was found to be in possession of stolen goods (including an umbrella, washing powder, ladies' stockings, and bootlaces) but claimed some soldiers had given these things to her. The Feferman family, whose home was raided and money and property stolen, fired her because they could no longer afford her salary. When asked why she participated in looting, her answer was only that everyone else was doing it. She said that during one of the attacks on her employer's home, she was beaten by the men who thought she knew where the family hid their money. Shumskaia was fined and jailed. The irrationality of her own actions and the injury she did to herself as well as others become especially clear in the final document in her file: a note she had dictated pleading with jail officials to permit her access to her things so that she could change into another article of clothing. She had been wearing the same dress for a month.[5]

Ewing's *1919* transforms violence into hope. One of the most disturbing aspects of the Chicago report has to do with various plans for the alleged solution to the race problem, including deporting the Black population to Africa, creating a separate state for them, and, the most sinister of all, "hope for a solution through the dying out of the Negro race."[6] Ewing reworks this language in her poem "Countless Schemes." The racist scheme for the elimination of Blacks becomes a statement affirming their continued vitality. "Now we are millions," Ewing writes. The fourth stanza begins by citing the report, putting its language in the mouth of an adversary who would wish for the destruction of Blacks: "You said / Hope for a solution through the dying / out of the Negro race." As the stanza continues, Ewing rewrites these lines, arriving at: "you said hope."[7] The last line excerpts three crucial words, changing their meaning so that hope changes direction, not against Blacks, but for them. The poem puts the message into the mouth of the formerly hate-filled speaker.

In chapter 4, I discuss Kvitko's "Geshet" ("It Happens") from his *1919* cycle. The poem offers a strange ensemble of voices and sounds made by people, animals, and objects used to inflict pain, and the poet says they all speak through him. The last stanza switches *I* and *you* to *we*:

> We are we,
> and there are a lot of us,
> and a lot of them.
> Why do they keep coming here
> for so many thousands of years?[8]

The poet affirms the continued presence of Jews as a collective and their right to live where they are. Kvitko undermines the characterization of Jews as aliens in the former Russian empire; it is not Jews who are strangers, but "they," the non-Jews. Both the Yiddish volume *1919*, published a hundred years ago, and Ewing's *1919* reverse the terms of exclusion to which their respective communities have been subject.

The psychologist Fischel Schneersohn, dismayed by the terrible conditions in which pogromed children were living and the lack of appropriate treatment, saw potential where others found only emotional deadness. Instead of using questionnaires and tests, he asked children to tell him stories. These stories—for example, about a wicked stepmother and flight into the woods, a house made of cookies, and summoning the doctor for a sibling who was ill—combined elements from fairy tales with the children's recent experience of danger and violence. Schneersohn's attention was especially drawn to the experience of one young girl, who helped to keep pogromists appeased by entertaining them with stories, songs, and card games. When left on her own during this time, she would search for "magic wands" in the courtyard. This case and the narratives Schneersohn heard from other children revealed their potential and practical skill.[9] The events that harmed them also sparked their creativity and precocious development. In Ewing's *1919*, a little girl also plays a starring role. Taking a line from the 1922 report about the "imaginary boundary" in the water separating White and Black swimming areas, Ewing has her heroine proclaim that "every boundary is imaginary." The girl leads other children on a fantastical exodus out of the dangers of Chicago and into the unclaimed, wild spaces of the desert, the marsh, and the mountain.

Putting experience and emotion into language—albeit strange and wild hefker language, but nonetheless ordered and deliberate language—is a way out of hefker chaos and abandonment. Literature is a heightened form of attentiveness to something that has taken place, not for the sake of escape from the strange and terrible thing, but as a way of being with it more closely. In her poem "Map," American poet Linda Hogan writes, "This is the map of the forsaken world."[10] If the world is abandoned and forsaken, its contours and markings effaced, its landmarks unrecognizable, how do you map it? This book has told the story of how a particular set of individuals and groups mapped the forsaken world of 1919, rewriting hopelessness with glimmers of hope.

NOTES

Introduction

1. "Mir zenen gevorn vi zamd, vos iz hefker, / vos yederer tret mit di fis," from "Zamd un shtern." S. G. Frug and Yaakov Levin, *Oysgeveylte shriftn: Far idishe shulen un heymen; Mit der biografye fun Frugn un a verterbikhl fun di shverere verter* (New York: Hibru Publishing, n.d.), 27. A Russian version of the same poem, "Pesok i zvezdy," was included in the Russian-language collection of his poetry, published in St. Petersburg in 1897. Lacking a single term for hefker, the Russian version reads thus: "v nevole, v bessilii, v nuzhde / Peskom my davno uzhe stali sred' mira zemnogo / Topchet nogami nas vsiakii prokhozhii vezde." This version of the poem substitutes for hefker "lack of freedom," "powerlessness," and "need" (S. G. Frug, *Stikhotvoreniia*, vol. 2 [St. Petersburg: Isidor Gol'dberg, 1897], 212). The earliest available version of the Yiddish appeared in a song collection published a year later and subsequent publications of the Yiddish can also be found in a Hebrew newspaper in 1901. See S. G. Frug, "Zamd un shtern," in *Neginot Yisroel: Liedersammlung*, ed. Abraham Bernstein (Vilnius, 1898), 7. Frug could have originally written the poem in Yiddish and then translated it into Russian or, thought of hefker and searched for a Russian gloss. I am grateful to Joe Lenkart, director of the Slavic Reference Service at the University of Illinois, Urbana-Champaign; Liudmila Sholokhova; and Gennady Estraikh for help with the publication history of this poem.

2. Shalom Albeck and Menachem Elon, "Hefker," in *Encyclopaedia Judaica* (Gale ebooks, 2007). "Chosen Mishpat" (273:13) in the sixteenth-century *Shulkhan Arukh* states that the wilderness, seas, and rivers and everything in them is hefker.

3. Jeffrey Veidlinger, *In the Midst of Civilized Europe: The Pogroms of 1918–1921 and the Onset of the Holocaust* (New York: H. Holt, 2021), 5. I address the problem of numbers in chapter 7.

4. Noam Leshem, "Spaces of Abandonment: Genealogies, Lives and Critical Horizons," *Environment and Planning D-Society and Space* 35, no. 4 (August 2017): 620–36; Veena Das, *Life and Words: Violence and the Descent Into the Ordinary* (Berkeley: University of California Press, 2007); João Biehl, *Vita: Life in a Zone of Social Abandonment* (Berkeley: University of California Press, 2005); Elizabeth Povinelli, *Economies of Abandonment* (Durham, NC: Duke University Press, 2011). Leshem argues for a parallel between *hefker* and abandonment.

5. Leshem, "Spaces of Abandonment."

6. For an exploration of poetic practice that focuses on the no-man's-land between languages, see Lital Levy, *Poetic Trespass: Writing between Hebrew and Arabic in Israel/Palestine* (Princeton, NJ: Princeton University Press, 2014).

7. For more on Jewish biopolitics, see Marina Mogilner, *A Race for the Future* (Cambridge, MA: Harvard University Press, 2022), 204–43.

8. For 1919 and violence, see Elissa Bemporad, "The Pogroms of the Russian Civil War at 100: New Trends, New Sources," *Quest: Issues in Contemporary Jewish History* 15 (August, 2019): vi.

9. The most comprehensive literary study remains David Roskies, *Against the Apocalypse: Responses to Catastrophe in Modern Jewish Culture* (Cambridge, MA: Harvard University Press, 1984).

10. For a discussion of Shklovsky beyond literary theory, see, for example, Svetlana Boym, "Poetics and Politics of Estrangement: Victor Shklovsky and Hannah Arendt," *Poetics Today* 26, no. 4 (December 1, 2005): 581–611, https://doi.org/10.1215/03335372-26-4-581. See also the discussion in chapter 6.

11. For examples, see Sam Johnson, "Pogrom in the Anglo-American Imagination, 1881–1919," in *Jews in the East European Borderlands: Essays in Honor of John D. Klier*, ed. Eugene Avrutin and Harriet Murav (Boston: Academic Studies Press, 2012), 147–66. David Engel discusses the key elements of a pogrom in "What's in a Pogrom? European Jews in the Age of Violence," in *Anti-Jewish Violence: Rethinking the Pogrom in East European History*, ed. Jonathan Dekel-Chen et al. (Bloomington: Indiana University Press, 2011), 19–37.

12. John D. Klier and Shlomo Lambroza, eds., *Pogroms: Anti-Jewish Violence in Russian History* (Cambridge: Cambridge University Press, 1992). For succinct overviews of the history and historiography of pogroms, see Eugune M. Avrutin, "Pogroms in Russian History," *Kritika: Explorations in Russian and Eurasian History* 14, no. 3 (2013): 585–98. See also Eugene M. Avrutin and Elissa Bemporad, eds., *Pogroms: A Documentary History* (Oxford: Oxford University Press, 2021), 3–22.

13. See Avrutin, "Pogroms in Russian History," 592–93.

14. Oleg Budnitskii, *Rossiiskie evrei mezhdu krasnymi i belymi* (Moscow: Rosspen, 2005).

15. I take this language from Omer Bartov and Eric D. Weitz, eds., *Shatterzone of Empires: Coexistence and Violence in the German, Habsburg, Russian, and Ottoman Borderlands* (Bloomington: Indiana University Press, 2013).

16. Georgiy Kasianov, "Ukraine between Revolution, Independence, and Foreign Dominance," in *The Emergence of Ukraine: Self-Determination, Occupation, and War in Ukraine, 1917–1922*, ed. Wolfram Dornik et al. (Edmonton: Canadian Institute of Ukrainian Studies Press, 2015), 76–131.

17. Avrutin and Bemporad, *Pogroms*, 12–13. For a study of rape, see Irina Astashkevich, *Gendered Violence: Jewish Women in the Pogroms of 1917–1921* (Boston: Academic Studies Press, 2018).

18. Henry Abramson, *A Prayer for the Government: Ukrainians and Jews in Revolutionary Times, 1917–1920* (Cambridge, MA: Ukrainian Research Institute and Center for Jewish Studies, Harvard University, 1999), 109–39.

19. See Steven J. Zipperstein, *Pogrom: Kishinev and the Tilt of History* (New York: Liveright Publishing Corporation, 2018); Astashkevich, *Gendered Violence*; William W. Hagen, *Anti-Jewish Violence in Poland, 1914–1920* (Cambridge: Cambridge University Press, 2018); Elissa Bemporad and Thomas Chopard, "The Pogroms of the Russian Civil War at 100: New Trends, New Sources," *Quest: Issues in Contemporary Jewish History* 15 (August 2019): v–xix; Elissa Bemporad, *Legacy of Blood: Jews, Pogroms, and Ritual Murder in the Lands of the Soviets* (New York: Oxford University Press, 2019); Bela Bodo, *The White Terror: Antisemitic and Political Violence in Hungary, 1919–1921* (New York: Routledge, 2021); Veidlinger, *In the Midst of Civilized Europe*. For reflections on the meanings and contexts of the pogroms in Ukraine, see Mayhill Fowler, "Introduction: Ukraine in Revolution, 1917–1922," *Slavic Review* 78, no. 4 (2019): 931–34; Serhy Yekelchyk, "Searching for the Ukrainian Revolution," *Slavic Review* 78, no. 4 (2019): 942–48; Larysa Bilous, "Re-Thinking the Revolution in Ukraine: The Jewish Experience, 1917–1921," *Slavic Review* 78, no. 4 (2019): 949–56. For a sourcebook, see Avrutin and Bemporad, *Pogroms*.

20. Hagen, *Anti-Jewish Violence in Poland, 1914–1920*, 49.

21. Veidlinger, *In the Midst of Civilized Europe*, 375.

22. William G. Rosenberg, "Paramilitary Violence in Russia's Civil Wars: 1918–1920," in *War in Peace: Paramilitary Violence in Europe after the Great War*, ed. Robert Gerwarth and John Horne (Oxford: Oxford University Press, 2013), 21–39; Laura Engelstein, *Russia in Flames: War, Revolution, Civil War 1914–1921* (Oxford: Oxford University Press, 2018).

23. The phrase in Yiddish: "der Yidisher kolektiv als gantser, vos vert ibergelozn af hefker fun dem prat" (Ber Borokhov, *Po'ale Tsiyon shriftn*, vol. 2 [New York: Jewish National Workers' Alliance, 1928], 164, http://books.google.com/books?id=4sMkAQAAMAAJ).

24. Amelia Glaser, "From Jewish Jesus to Black Christ: Race Violence in Leftist Yiddish Poetry," *Studies in American Jewish Literature* 34, no. 1 (2015): 44–69. See also Glaser, *Songs in Dark Times: Yiddish Poetry of Struggle from Scottsboro to Palestine* (Cambridge, MA: Harvard University Press, 2020).

25. Engelstein, *Russia in Flames*, xviii.

26. Stephen Velychenko, *Life and Death in Revolutionary Ukraine: Living Conditions, Violence, and Demographic Catastrophe, 1917–1923* (Montreal: McGill-Queen's Press, 2021), 199.

27. The civil war became the training ground for the perpetrators of Stalin's Terror (Lynn Viola, "The Question of the Perpetrator in Soviet History," *Slavic Review* 72, no. 1 [2013]: 1–23).

28. "Vostsarilos' kakoe-to nedoumennoe sushchestvovanie, besprichinnaia prazdnost' i protivoestesvennaia svoboda ot vsego, chem zhivo chelovecheskoe obshchestvo" (Ivan Alekseevich Bunin, *Okaiannye dni*, 1925, Lib.ru/klassika, accessed July 27, 2023, http://az.lib.ru/b/bunin_i_a/text_2262.shtml).

29. Valeriian Pidmohylny, *Tretia revoliutsiia: Opovidannia* (Kharkiv: Knyhospilka, 1926), 25. I am grateful to Andrii Portnov for directing me to this story and Daria Semenova for helping me with a translation.

30. Robin D. G. Kelley, "What Kind of Society Values Property Over Black Lives?," *New York Times*, June 18, 2020, sec. Opinion, https://www.nytimes.com/2020/06/18/opinion/george-floyd-protests-looting.html.

31. A discussion of this problem can be found in Hannah Johnson, *Blood Libel: The Ritual Murder Accusation at the Limit of Jewish History* (Ann Arbor: University of Michigan Press, 2012), 88–89.

32. Oklahoma Commission, *Tulsa Race Riot: A Report by the Oklahoma Commission to Study the Tulsa Race Riot of 1921* (Tulsa, Oklahoma: CreateSpace, 2001). For the coverage of the civil war pogroms, see Bemporad and Chopard, "Pogroms of the Russian Civil War at 100."

33. The internationalist perspective of interwar Yiddish authors is the subject of Glaser, *Songs in Dark Times*.

34. Zipperstein, *Pogrom*, 82.

35. Zipperstein *Pogrom*, 89. Ellipsis added.

36. "Azoy zaynen oykh di reges andersh" (Leyb Kvitko, *1919* [Berlin: Lutze and Vogt, 1923], 6).

37. For an overview, see Michal Givoni, "Witnessing/Testimony," *Mafte'akh*, no. 2e (Winter 2011): 147–69, http://mafteakh.tau.ac.il/en/issue-2e-winter-2011/witnessingtestimony/.

38. For Agamben, the best witness is the Muselmann of the death camp, reduced to "bare life," the condition of mere biological existence that makes political life possible (Giorgio Agamben, *Remnants of Auschwitz: The Witness and*

the Archive [New York: Zone Books, 1999], 158, cited in Givoni, "Witnessing/Testimony," 157).

39. David Engel, *The Assassination of Symon Petliura and the Trial of Scholem Schwartzbard 1926–1927: A Selection of Documents* (Gottingen: Vandenhoeck and Ruprecht, 2016).

40. Helen Vendler, "The Puzzle of Sequence: Two Political Poems," in *Essays in Honour of Eammon Cantwell: Yeats Annual No. 20*, ed. Warwick Gould (Cambridge: Open Book Publishers, 2016), 119–54, https://doi.org/10.11647/OBP.0081.05.

41. As has been pointed out by, among others, Achille Mbembe, "Necropolitics," trans. Libby Meintjes, *Public Culture* 15, no. 1 (Winter 2003): 11–40.

42. James Oldham, "Insurance Litigation Involving the Zong and Other British Slave Ships, 1780–1807," *Journal of Legal History* 28, no. 3 (December 2007): 299–318, https://doi.org/10.1080/01440360701698437; Jeremy Krikler, "The Zong and the Lord Chief Justice," *History Workshop Journal* 64, no. 1 (2007): 29–47.

43. Tyrone Williams, "Marlene Nourbese Philip. Zong!," *African American Review* 43, no. 4 (2009): 786.

44. Carolyn Forché, *What You Have Heard Is True: A Memoir of Witness and Resistance* (New York: Penguin, 2020), 31.

45. Foucault's definition of the archive is a set of rules governing what can be said, the principles by which statements appear and disappear (Michel Foucault, *The Archeology of Knowledge & The Discourse on Language*, trans. A. M. Sheridan Smith [New York: Harper Colophon Books, 1972], 206–207).

46. For a succinct introduction, see B. B. Lawrence and A. Karim, eds., *On Violence: A Reader* (Durham, NC: Duke University Press, 2007), 1–15, https://books.google.com/books?id=_EBb9bgut74C. For a study that emphasizes contingent factors, see Max Bergholz, *Violence as a Generative Force: Identity, Nationalism, and Memory in a Balkan Community* (Ithaca, NY: Cornell University Press, 2016).

47. Elaine Scarry, *The Body in Pain: The Making and Unmaking of the World* (New York: Oxford University Press, 1985).

48. Michael Staudigl, "Towards a Phenomenological Theory of Violence: Reflections Following Merleau-Ponty and Schutz," *Human Studies* 30 (2007): 235–36.

49. Don Ihde, *Listening and Voice : Phenomenologies of Sound*, 2nd ed. (Albany: State University of New York Press, 2007), 189.

50. This point has been made by Mikhail Krutikov, "1919 god—Revoliutsiia v evreiskoi poezii," in *Mirovoi krizis 1914–1920 godov i sud'ba vostochnoevropeiskogo evreistva*, ed. Oleg Budnitskii (Moscow: Rosspen, 2005), 318–41; Dov-Ber Kerler, "Dos yor 1919 in der geshikhte fun yidisher poezye," *Yidishland* 4 (Fall 2019): 3–11. The same point has been made with regard to Ukrainian literature in the same period and in the same place: Kyiv. See Irene Rima Makaryk and Virlana Tkacz,

Modernism in Kyiv: Jubilant Experimentation (Toronto: University of Toronto Press, 2010).

51. Yankev Glatshteyn, A. Leyeles, and N. Minkov, "In zikh," in *In zikh: A zamlung introspektive lider*, ed. M. Apranel (New York: M. N. Mayzel, 1920), 5–27.

52. David Bergelson, "Der gesheener oyfbrokh," *Milgroym* 1 (1922): 41–43.

53. Meylekh Ravitsh, "Di naye, di nakete dikhtung: Zibn tezisn," *Albatros* 1 (1922): 15–16.

54. Walt Whitman, "Song of Myself," 1892, https://www.poetryfoundation.org/poems/45477/song-of-myself-1892-version.

55. Whitman, "Song of Myself."

56. Ravitsh, "Di naye, di nakete dikhtung," 15.

57. Benjamin Harshav, *Language in Time of Revolution* (Stanford, CA: Stanford University Press, 1999), 68.

58. Interest in sound and listening is undergoing a revival a hundred years later, in the first part of the twenty-first century. The *Journal of Sonic Studies*, which began publication in 2011, is an example. One of the basic books in the field is Ihde, *Listening and Voice*. See also Marjorie Perloff and Craig Dworkin, *The Sound of Poetry/The Poetry of Sound* (Chicago: University of Chicago Press, 2009) and Christopher Cannon and Matthew Rubery, "Introduction to Aurality and Literacy," *PMLA (Publications of the Modern Language Association of America)* 135, no. 2 (March 2020): 350–56.

59. Scarry, *Body in Pain*.

60. Fischel Schneersohn, *Di katastrofale tsaytn un di vaksndike doyres* (Berlin: Yidisher literarisher farlag, 1923), 79. All citations from this edition and all translations are my own.

1. Hefker and Abandonment

1. This is part of the "Bedikat chametz" ritual. For the Hebrew, see Wexner, "Bedikat Chametz," Haggadot, accessed July 20, 2023, https://www.haggadot.com/clip/bedikat-chametz-2. Ellipsis added.

2. Giorgio Agamben, *The Use of Bodies*, trans. Adam Kotsko (Stanford, CA: Stanford University Press, 2020), 207–11. See Adam Kotsko, *Agamben's Philosophical Trajectory* (Edinburgh: Edinburgh University Press, 2020), 73; Andrew Norris, "Giorgio Agamben and the Politics of the Living Dead," *Diacritics* 30, no. 4 (2000): 38–58.

3. Giorgio Agamben, *Homo Sacer: Sovereign Power and Bare Life* (Stanford, CA: Stanford University Press, 1998), 6.

4. Giorgio Agamben, *The Use of Bodies Homo Sacer*, trans. Adam Kotsko (Stanford, CA: Stanford University Press, 2016); Vernon W. Cisney and Nicolae Morar, eds., *Biopower: Foucault and Beyond* (Chicago: University of Chicago Press, 2016).

5. "Itst zaynen mir geglikhn tsu bashefenishn, vos inovnt vern zey ingantsn hefker un hilfloz" (Itsik Kipnis, *Khadoshim un teg: A khronik* [Kyiv: Kultur-Lige, 1926], 92, my translation).

6. I am oversimplifying. See Ben Golder, "Foucault and the Genealogy of Pastoral Power," *Radical Philosophy Review* 10, no. 2 (2007): 157–76.

7. Adi Ophir's distinction between the providential state, which provides care, and the catastrophic state, which governs a population that may be hurt, still relies on the notion of the state. See Adi Ophir, "The Two-State Solution: Providence and Catastrophe," *Theoretical Inquiries in Law* 8 (2007): 117–60.

8. Agamben, *Homo Sacer*, 29.

9. Giorgio Agamben, *Stasis: Civil War as a Political Paradigm*, trans. Nicolas Heron (Stanford, CA: Stanford University Press, 2015). I am grateful to the eminent scholar and translator of Agamben, Adam Kotsko, for discussing this point with me.

10. Agamben, *Homo Sacer*, 109.

11. Agamben, *Homo Sacer*, 28.

12. See the entry for "abandon" in *Oxford English Dictionary Online* (Oxford: Oxford University Press, 2022), www.oed.com.

13. David Bergelson, *Droyb*, vol. 4 (Berlin: Wostok, 1923), 1.

14. Biopolitics in its most extreme form creates conditions in which nature is indistinct from law. See Agamben, *Homo Sacer*, 185.

15. YIVO, Mizrakh Yidisher Historisher Arkhiv, RG 80 Elisavetgrad (Kirovograd, Kropyvnytsky)–Yaruga (Yaruha) (Folder 316).

16. Achille Mbembe, *Necropolitics*, trans. Steven Corcoran (Durham, NC: Duke University Press, 2019), 71.

17. Mbembe, "Necropolitics," 31.

18. Mbembe, "Necropolitics," 31. For a study of Mexico that uses a similar framework, see R. Guy Emerson, Living death in Mexico, in *Necropolitics*, Studies of the Americas (Cham: Palgrave Macmillan, 2019), 22, https://doi.org/10.1007/978-3-030-12302-4_1.

19. Rosenberg, "Paramilitary Violence in Russia's Civil Wars," 39.

20. Serhy Yekelchyk, "Bands of Nation Builders? Insurgency and Ideology in the Ukrainian Civil War," in *War in Peace: Paramilitary Violence in Europe after the Great War*, ed. Robert Gerwarth and John Horne (Oxford: Oxford University Press, 2013), 107–108.

21. For example, Stanislav Aseyev, *V izoliatsi: Statti* (Kyiv: Liuta sprava, 2018), 162.

22. Aseyev, *V izoliatsi*, 210.

23. Sh. Y. Yatskan reviewing Feygenberg in Sh. Y. Yatskan, "Der pinkes fun a toyte shtot," *Haynt*, August 26, 1927.

24. Joseph Sherman, ed., *From Revolution to Repression: Soviet Yiddish Writing 1917–1952* (Nottingham: Five Leaves Publications, 2012), 20. The Yiddish original: "zey varfn zikh mit unz."

25. See the entry for *hefker* in Marcus Jastrow, *A Dictionary of the Targumim, the Talmud Babli and Yerushalmit, and the Midrashic Literature* (New York: G. P. Putnam's Sons, 1903), https://en.wikisource.org/wiki/A_Dictionary_of _the_Targumim,_the_Talmud_Babli_and_Yerushalmi,_and_the_Midrashic _Literature/%D7%94%D7%A4%D7%9C%D7%90%D7%94_-_%D7%94%D7 %A4%D7%A8%D7%94. For an overview see George Webber, "The Principles of the Jewish Law of Property," *Journal of Comparative Legislation and International Law* 10, no. 1 (1928): 82–93. A succinct discussion is found in Albeck and Elon, "Hefker." See also Leshem, "Spaces of Abandonment," 13. A brief note about grammar. Hefker is an adjective; the noun is *hefkeyres*. I am going to use the adjectival form in all instances except when an author I quote uses the noun.

26. Moses Maimonides, *The Code of Maimonides: The Book of Torts*, trans. Hyman Klein, vol. 11 (New Haven, CT: Yale University Press, 1954), 129–43.

27. Gerald J. Blidstein, "Notes on Hefker Bet-Din in Talmudic and Medieval Law," *Dine Israel* IV (1973): xxxiv–xlix.

28. Madeline Kochen, *Organ Donation and the Divine Lien in Talmudic Law* (Cambridge: Cambridge University Press, 2013), 14.

29. Leshem, "Spaces of Abandonment," 13. Jewish anarchists in the first part of the twentieth century developed the concept of hefker for their own political vision. See Anna Torres, "The Horizon Blossoms and the Borders Vanish: Peretz Markish's Poetry and Anarchist Diasporism," *Jewish Quarterly Review* 110, no. 3 (2020): 458–90.

30. See, for example, Oded Lowenheim, *The Politics of the Trail: Reflexive Mountain Biking along the Frontier of Jerusalem* (Ann Arbor: University of Michigan Press, 2014), 79–112. Joy Resmovits, "Two Countries, Two Approaches to Regulating Embryonic Stem-Cell Use," *Forward*, January 28, 2011.

31. For a brief overview of the conflation of the term *hefker* with Epicurus in the writings of Maimonides and others, see B. Netanyahu, *The Marranos of Spain: From the Late 14th to the Early 16th Century, According to Contemporary Hebrew Sources* (Ithaca, NY: Cornell University Press, 1973), 125n107. See also Louis Isaac Rabinowitz, "Apikoros," in *Encyclopaedia Judaica*, vol. 2 (n.p.: Gale ebooks, 2007).

32. Reuben Grossman and M. H. Segal, *Compendious Hebrew-English Dictionary* (Tel-Aviv: Dvir, 1938).

33. Sholem Aleichem's parodical alphabet of curses from his autobiographical novel *Funem yarid* lists *hefker-yung* in the same series as *Haman* and *ne'er-do-well*.

34. I am relying on Gail Labovitz, "More Slave Women, More Lewdness: Freedom and Honor in Rabbinic Female Sexuality," *Journal of Feminist Studies in Religion* 28, no. 2 (Fall 2012): 69–87.

35. For a discussion of the Yiddish poet Malka-Hefetz Tussman's playful use of the Talmudic concept of hefker, see Kathryn Hellerstein, *A Question of Tradition: Women Poets in Yiddish, 1586–1987* (Stanford, CA: Stanford University Press, 2014), 352, 384–86.

36. Tractate Nedarim 55a. See Tzvi Hersh Weinreb and Joshua Schreier, eds., *Koren Talmud Bavli*, vol. 18, *Nedarim* (Jerusalem: Koren Publishers, 2015), 229. I am grateful to Sergey Dolgopolski for discussing this point with me.

37. For the source and for a discussion of the "limits of the anarchic potential" of this concept, see Adi Ophir and Ishay Rosen-Zvi, *One Goy, Multiple Language Games*, vol. 1 (Oxford: Oxford University Press, 2018), https://doi.org/10.1093/oso/9780198744900.003.0008.

38. Shaul Magid, "Ethics Disentangled from the Law: Incarnation, the Universal, and Hasidic Ethics," *Kabbalah: Journal for the Study of Jewish Mystical Texts* 15 (2006): 31–75; Magid, *Hasidism Incarnate: Hasidism, Christianity, and the Construction of Modern Judaism* (Stanford, CA: Stanford University Press, 2014).

39. Harriet Murav, *Holy Foolishness: Dostoevsky's Novels and the Poetics of Cultural Critique* (Stanford, CA: Stanford University Press, 1992). Shaul Magid argues for the significance of kenosis in Hasidism. See *Hasidism Incarnate*, 80–111.

40. Ahad Ha'am, Simon Dubnow, Ben-Ami, Y. Ch. Ravnitsky, and Hayyim Nahman Bialik, "Proclamation of the Hebrew Writers' Union," in *The Literature of Destruction: Jewish Responses to Catastrophe*, ed. David G. Roskies (Philadelphia: Jewish Publication Society, 1988), 157. I am indebted to Ken Moss for this reference.

41. Alan L. Mintz, *Hurban: Responses to Catastrophe in Hebrew Literature* (New York: Columbia University Press, 1984), 132. Noam Pines argues that the conceptual lens of abandonment sheds light on this passage. During the pogrom the Jew is outside the law's boundaries and can be killed with impunity (*The Infrahuman: Animality in Modern Jewish Literature* [Albany: State University of New York Press, 2018], 47–52).

42. My translation of selected stanzas, with ellipses added. For the Yiddish original, see Isaac Leib Peretz, *Ale verk*, vol. 1 (New York: Tsiko, 1947), 268. Peretz's words were put to music and the poem was transformed into a popular Jewish socialist song. For a discussion of the poem in the broad context of Peretz's work on social justice, see Adi Mahalel, *The Radical Years of I. L. Peretz* (PhD diss., Columbia University, 2014).

43. Joshua Fogel, "Shimen-Zev Ayznberg (S. Eisenberg)," *Yiddish Leksikon* (blog), June 1, 2014, http://yleksikon.blogspot.com/2014/06/shimen-zev-ayznberg-s-eisenberg.html.

44. S. Eisenberg, *Milkhome-shtoyb: Zikhroynes fun a litvishn polet, 1915–1917* (Klerksdorf: S. Eisenberg, 1935), 12, http://archive.org/details/nybc201644.

45. For example Eisenberg, *Milkhome-shtoyb*, 37.

46. Andrei Sobol', *Pyl': Roman* (Moscow: Severnye dni, 1917). I thank Marina Mogilner for pointing this out.
47. Harriet Murav, *Music from a Speeding Train: Jewish Literature in Post-Revolutionary Russia* (Stanford, CA: Stanford University Press, 2011), 170. The citation is from Markish's World War II epic, *Milkhome* (War).
48. Dan Seeman, *One People, One Blood: Ethiopian-Israelis and the Return to Judaism* (New Brunswick, NJ: Rutgers University Press, 2009), 150–79.
49. Gil Eyal, *The Disenchantment of the Orient: Expertise in Arab Affairs and the Israeli State* (Stanford, CA: Stanford University Press, 2006), 7.
50. Leshem, "Spaces of Abandonment."
51. Leshem, "Spaces of Abandonment," 16.
52. Nahum Stuchkoff, *Der oytser fun der yidisher shprakh* (New York: YIVO Institute for Jewish Research, 1991), 465, 667, 691.
53. *Dispossession*, as defined by Athenia Athanasiou, offers a counterpart to *hefker*: "processes and ideologies by which persons are disowned and abjected by normative and normalizing powers that define cultural intelligibility and that regulate the distribution of vulnerability" (Judith Butler and Athena Athanasiou, *Dispossession the Performative in the Political : Conversations with Athena Athanasiou* [Cambridge: Polity, 2015], 2).
54. Hersh Bloshteyn, "Gedanken vegn der moderner dikhtung," in *Vispe: Literarisher zamlbukh* (Kaunas: Kultur-Lige Lite, 1923), 26.
55. Discussions of *hefker* as a literary term can be found in Chana Kronfeld, *On the Margins of Modernism: Decentering Literary Dynamics*, Contraversions (Berkeley: University of California Press, 1996), 205; Karolina Szymaniak, "The Language of Dispersion and Confusion: Peretz Markish's Manifestos from the Khalyastre Period," in *A Captive of the Dawn: The Life and Work of Peretz Markish (1895–1952)*, ed. Joseph Sherman Gennady Estraikh, Jordan Finkin, and David Shneer (London: Legenda, 2011), 66–87; Jordan Finkin, "Constellating Hebrew and Yiddish Avant-Gardes," *Journal of Modern Jewish Studies* 8, no. 1 (2009): 1–22; Finkin, *An Inch or Two of Time: Time and Space in Jewish Modernisms* (University Park: Penn State University Press, 2015); Naomi Brenner, *Lingering Bilingualism: Modern Hebrew and Yiddish Literatures in Contact* (Syracuse, NY: Syracuse University Press, 2015), 63–71; Efrat Gal-Ed, *Niemandssprache Itzik Manger—ein europäischer Dichter* (Berlin: Jüdischer Verlag im Suhrkamp, 2016), 31–55; Harriet Murav, *David Bergelson's Strange New World: Untimeliness and Futurity* (Bloomington: Indiana University Press, 2019), 189–91, 214; Torres, "Horizon Blossoms and the Borders Vanish." For a discussion of Moyshe Kulbak's use of *hefker*, see Rachel Seelig, "'A Youthful Rogue Am I': Moyshe Kulbak between Exile and Arrival," in *Strangers in Berlin: Modern Jewish Literature between East and West, 1919–1933* (Ann Arbor: University of Michigan Press, 2016), 79–100, https://www.jstor.org/stable/10.3998/mpub.9223331.8.

56. I am using the translation provided in Kronfeld, *On the Margins of Modernism*, 204. The poem was originally published in Yiddish in Peretz Markish, *Shveln* (Kyiv: Idisher folks farlag, 1918).

57. For a discussion of the political resonance of hefker in the poem, see David Shneer, "'My Name Is Now': Peretz Markish and the Literature of Revolution," in *A Captive of the Dawn: The Life and Work of Peretz Markish (1895–1952)*, ed. Joseph Sherman, Gennady Estraikh, Jordan Finkin, and David Shneer (Oxford: Legenda, 2011), 5. Nokhem Oyslender, a prominent Yiddish critic and contemporary of Markish, read a Nietzschean will to power in Markish's embrace of "barbarism" and his striving toward what lay beyond culture. Oyslender interpreted Markish's use of hefker in this light; Markish was in tune with "hefker harmony." See Nokhem Oyslender, *Veg-ayn veg oys: Literarishe epizodn* (Kyiv: Kooperativer farlag, Kultur-lige, 1924), 113.

58. Finkin, "Constellating Hebrew and Yiddish Avant-Gardes."

59. Brenner, *Lingering Bilingualism*, 63–71.

60. Maks Erik, "Di sphrakh funem yidishn eskspresyanizm," *Albatros* 2 (1922): 17.

61. The point is made by Finkin, "Constellating Hebrew and Yiddish Avant-Gardes."

62. Bergelson, "Der gesheener oyfbrokh," 41. For another discussion, see Naomi Brenner, "Milgroym, Rimon and Interwar Jewish Bilingualism," *Journal of Jewish Identities* 7, no. 1 (January 2014): 23–48.

63. See "The Beginning of December 1919," in Sherman, *From Revolution to Repression*, 61.

64. Moyshe-Leyb Halpern's poem "The Street Drummer" ("Der gasn-poyker") is an example. Halpern proclaims himself as free as a bird, "dancing *hefker* [wildly, with abandon], dancing blind" (Moshe Leib Halpern, *In Nyu-York* [New York: Matones, 1954], 35. The Yiddish: *Zing ikh, vi der foygl, fray, un geshvind, / vi der vint, / tants ikh hefker, tants ikh blind*. For an English translation of the entire poem, see Halpern, *In New York: A Selection*, trans. Kathryn Hellerstein (Philadelphia: Jewish Publication Society of America, 1982), 23–24. For a study of Halpern, see Julian Levinson, "On Some Motifs in Moyshe-Leyb Halpern: A Benjaminian Meditation on Yiddish Modernism," *Prooftexts* 32, no. 1 (2012): 63–88.

65. Efrat Gal-Ed, "Yiddishland: A Promise of Belonging," *Journal of Modern Jewish Studies* 20, no. 2 (2021): 141–169. Manger wrote two poems explicitly dedicated to the Russian Civil War pogroms, including "Petliura's Ballad" ("Di balade fun Petliura") and "Schwartsbard's Ballad" ("Shvartsbard-Balade"); Semen Petliura was the head of the Ukrainian Directory at the time of the pogroms. See also Gal-Ed, *Niemandssprache Itzik Manger – ein europäischer Dichter*. Gal-Ed, *Niemandssprache Itzik Manger*, 31.

66. Gal-Ed, *Niemandssprache Itzik Manger*, 31.

67. Mintz, *Hurban*, 167.

68. For the war experience in relation to the poetry, see Dan Miron, "Uri Zvi Grinberg's War Poetry," in *The Jews of Poland between Two World Wars*, ed. Yisrael Gutman et al. (Hanover, NH: University Press of New England, 1989), 368–82.

69. For a discussion of the journal and its manifestos, see Daria Vakhrushova, "'To Hell with Futurism, Too!' The Metamorphoses of Western and Eastern European Modernism in Yiddish Manifestos," *Quest: Issues in Contemporary Jewish History, Journal of the Fondazione CDEC* 17 (September 2020): 43–74.

70. Uri Tsvi Grinberg, "Proklamirung," *Albatros* 1, no. 1 (September 1922): 3.

71. I borrow the term *enfleshment* from studies of slavery but use it differently. For an analysis of slavery and enfleshment, see Alexander Weheliye, *Habeas Viscus: Racializing Assemblages, Biopolitics, and Black Feminist Theories of the Human* (Durham, NC: Duke University Press, 2014), 99–105. For a detailed discussion of enfleshment as a poetic device in Kvitko, see chapter 4.

72. Grinberg, "Proklamirung," 3.

73. Grinberg, "Proklamirung," 3. Grinberg, "Uri Tsvi farn tseylem," *Albatros* 1, no. 2 (November 1922): 3–4. For more on Grinberg's poetry, see Avidov Lipsker, "The Albatrosses of Young Yiddish Poetry: An Idea and Its Visual Realization in Uri Zvi Greenberg's Albatross," trans. Ruth Bar-Ilan, *Prooftexts* 15, no. 1 (January 1995): 89–108; Neta Stahl, "'Uri Zvi before the Cross': The Figure of Jesus in the Poetry of Uri Zvi Greenberg," *Religion & Literature* 40, no. 3 (2008): 49; Samuel Jacob Spinner, "Else Lasker-Schüler and Uri Zvi Greenberg in 'The Society of Savage Jews': Art, Politics, and Primitivism," *Prooftexts: A Journal of Jewish Literary History* 38, no. 1 (2020): 60–93.

74. Uri Tsvi Grinberg, "In malkhes fun tseylem," *Albatros* 2, no. 1 (1923): 19. The Yiddish original:

> Oy, s'iz a pakhed azoy-ot tsu vaksn af hefker
> Azoy vi a shteyn in der velt, nor der guf iz keyn shteyn nisht.
> Der guf iz fun blut un fun fleysh un fun knokhns, vos filn
> A shnit fun a meser—

75. As Shklovsky writes, "when you fall like a stone," you have no control over your direction. Stones cannot determine their own movement or position (Viktor Shklovsky, *A Sentimental Journey: Memoirs, 1917–1922*, trans. Richard Sheldon [Normal, IL: Dalkey Archive Press, 2004], 133).

76. Alisa Braun, "Kadya Molodowsky," in *Dictionary of Literary Biography: Writers in Yiddish*, ed. Joseph Sherman (Detroit: Gale, 2007).

77. See Kathryn Hellerstein's introduction to Kadya Molodowsky, *Paper Bridges: Selected Poems of Kadya Molodowsky*, trans. Kathryn Hellerstein (Detroit: Wayne State University Press, 1999), 17–60. For a discussion that asserts the correctness of the earlier assessments, see Abraham Novershtern,

"'Who Would Have Believed That a Bronze Statue Can Weep': The Poetry of Anna Margolin," *Prooftexts* 10, no. 3 (1990): 435–67.

78. She describes her experience of one of the Kyiv pogroms in her autobiography. Staying with a friend who lived on Khreshchatyk Street, removed from the Jewish neighborhood, Molodowsky thought she would be safe. A group of "officers" burst in; one pressed a revolver to her heart and demanded all the gold and valuables that the women possessed. See Kadya Molodowsky, "Mayn elterzeydns yerushe," *Svive* 33 (1971): 54. I am grateful to Sheva Zucker for directing me to this section of the autobiography.

79. A. [Shmuel] Litvin [Hurwitz], *Yidishe neshomes*, vol. 3 (New York: Folksbildung, 1917), 152. For a study of the tuberculosis sanitorium as formative for modern Yiddish poetic identity, see Sunny S. Yudkoff, *Tubercular Capital: Illness and the Conditions of Modern Jewish Writing* (Stanford, CA: Stanford University Press, 2018).

80. Molodowsky, *Paper Bridges*, 99. I have modified the translation.

81. Molodowsky, *Paper Bridges*, 103.

82. Kadya Molodowsky, "Otvotsk," in *Varshever almanakh* (Warsaw: Beletristnfareynikung, 1923), 138. Discussions of temperature and weight were common to literary accounts of tuberculosis, but the use of numerical signs was less so in poetry of the time. For a study of literary uses of tuberculosis, see Yudkoff, *Tubercular Capital*.

83. Molodowsky, *Paper Bridges*, 101.

84. Osip Mandelshtam, *The Complete Critical Prose and Letters* (Ann Arbor, MI: Ardis, 1979), 431.

85. Molodowsky, *Paper Bridges*, 101.

86. Kadya Molodowsky, *Kheshvendike nekht: Lider* (Vilnius: B. Kletskin, 1927), 34.

87. Molodowsky, "Otvotsk," 139.

88. Ryan Edwards, "From the Depths of Patagonia: The Ushuaia Penal Colony and the Nature of 'The End of the World,'" *Hispanic American Historical Review* 94, no. 2 (May 2014): 272–302. I am grateful to Amy Kerner for directing me to this source.

89. There is no published English translation; this is mine. The original lines containing the word *hefker*:

> Shvimt di shif antkegn vint, antkegn himl,
> es hobn zi af shutfusdikn hefker genumen ale yamen,
> shvimt di shif af voyedikn umet fun di khvalyes,
> un di levone shvimt ir nokh mit blaykhn ponem fun a mamen.
> (Kadya Molodowsky, *Dzshike gas* [Warsaw: Literarishe bleter, 1933], 19.)

90. The Yiddish critic Nakhmen Mayzel commented that Molodowsky's poem speaks to the epoch in which it was written. Chased from pillar to post, unable to

dock anywhere, the ship resembled "our lives, without purpose or meaning in a sick time" (Nakhmen Mayzel, "Geveyn fun unzer tsayt," *Literarishe bleter*, no. 21 [May 26, 1933]: 334–35).

2. David Hofshteyn Listening

1. David Hofshteyn, *Bay vegn* (Kyiv: Kyiv Kultur-lige, 1919), 11. All citations from this edition, and unless otherwise noted, translations are my own. Yiddish critic Yekhezkel Dobrushin also described Hofshteyn's expression of emotion in terms of the sensory and affective register. Hofshteyn's versification communicates the "innermost modulations of his mood" (Yekhezkel Dobrushin, "Dray dikhter," in *Oyfgang*, vol. 1 [Kyiv: Kultur-Lige, 1919], 90–91).

2. Hofshteyn, *Bay vegn*, 11.

3. Shmuel Charney, *Yidishe shrayber in Sovet-Rusland* (New York: S. Niger Book Committee of the Congress for Jewish Culture, 1958), 49.

4. See, for example, Kronfeld, *On the Margins of Modernism*, 208–15; Kenneth B. Moss, *Jewish Renaissance in the Russian Revolution* (Cambridge, MA: Harvard University Press, 2009), 101–104, 198–200; Glaser, *Songs in Dark Times*, 175–92. There is no book-length English language study of the poet.

5. For Hofshteyn's biography, see Zalman Reyzen, *Leksikon fun der yidisher literatur, prese un filologye*, vol. 3 (Vilnius: B. Kletskin, 1929), 778–82. A useful biographical and bibliographical sketch can be found in Khone Shmeruk, ed., *A shpigl af a shteyn* (Jerusalem: Magnes Press, 1964), 741–44. For an incisive history of Hofshteyn's early years, see Moss, *Jewish Renaissance in the Russian Revolution*, 101–104.

6. David Bergelson, "Belles-Lettres and the Social Order," in *David Bergelson: From Modernism to Socialist Realism*, ed. Joseph Sherman and Gennady Estraikh (Oxford: Legenda, 2007), 342.

7. Kronfeld, *On the Margins of Modernism*, 210.

8. David Hofshteyn, "Yidishe arbet in Erets-Yisroel," *Dos naye lebn*, March 12, 1926.

9. David Shneer, *Yiddish and the Creation of Soviet Jewish Culture* (Cambridge: Cambridge University Press, 2004), 51–52; Gennady Estraikh, *In Harness: Yiddish Writers' Romance with Communism*, Judaic Traditions in Literature, Music, and Art (Syracuse, NY: Syracuse University Press, 2005), 58–60.

10. Hofshteyn, *Bay vegn*, 9. The center three lines of translation are from Bergelson, "Belles-Lettres and the Social Order," 342. The translation is by Lawrence Alan Rosenwald, who only translated what Bergelson cited in his essay; the other parts of the stanza are my translation.

11. Rabbinic controversies regarding the status of property that had been renounced (made hefker) invoked the commandment regarding the unharvested corner of the field. See Albeck and Elon, "Hefker."

12. Oyslender, *Veg-ayn veg oys*, 102.

13. I am using Eric Santner's commentary on "the open" in Rilke as a point of departure. See *On Creaturely Life: Rilke, Benjamin, Sebald* (Chicago: University of Chicago Press, 2006), 1–2.

14. Ihde, *Listening and Voice*, 16–28.

15. "Vi troyerik-zis iz mentsh tsu zayn," in Hofshteyn, *Bay vegn*, 60–61.

16. David Hofshteyn and F. Shames, *Literatur kentenish* (Moscow: Tsentraler felker-farlag fun F. S. S. R., 1927), 4.

17. Hofshteyn and Shames, *Literatur kentenish*, 40–41.

18. The Yiddish: "ruft der klang aroys a bazundere emotsyonele batsiung tsu zikh" (Hofshteyn and Shames, *Literatur kentenish*, 30).

19. Hofshteyn and Shames, *Literatur kentenish*, 30–32.

20. Alexander Blok, "O naznachenii poeta (Blok)," accessed July 29, 2023, https://arheve.org/read/blok-aa-1/o-literature-o-naznachenii-poeta.

21. This motif occurs in the poem "In himl-roym" as well as "Gerekhtikeyt." See Hofshteyn, *Bay vegn*, 43, 91.

22. Hofshteyn, *Bay vegn*, 13.

23. I am borrowing from Veit Erlmann, *Reason and Resonance : A History of Modern Aurality* (New York: Zone Books, 2014), 283.

24. Hofshteyn, *Bay vegn*, 35. I am grateful to Professor Dov-Ber Kerler for discussing this aspect of the poem with me.

25. Moss, *Jewish Renaissance in the Russian Revolution*, 199.

26. The Yiddish: "Un tsvishn veg un onveg nor a shmoln grobn / Nor vies yunge, tsvishn oyg un zunen-shayn— / Vos kon af erd/Nokh shener zayn?" (Hofshteyn, *Bay vegn*, 7).

27. Hofshteyn, *Bay vegn*, 36. This stanza was omitted in subsequent publications of the poem.

28. Hofshteyn, *Bay vegn*, 87.

29. Hofshteyn, *Bay vegn*, 91–92.

30. Charney, *Yidishe shrayber in Sovet-Rusland*, 52.

31. For a discussion of the poetry, see Dror Abend-David, "Gender Benders and Unrequited Offerings: Two Hebrew Poems by Rachel Bluwstein and Dovid Hofshteyn," *Prooftexts* 31, no. 3 (Fall 2011): 211. Abend-David does not point out that one of the poems, "Along the Way," directly recalls the motif of bloody drops from Hofshteyn's earlier Yiddish work *Sorrow*. The second and third stanzas read:

> Drops of blood,
> On the side of the rock,
> Drops of blood
> From the stone's own flesh
> There, there,

> On the northern snow
> Are my drops of blood.

I have slightly modified the translation.

32. David Hofshteyn, "Bayamim ha'hem," *Davar*, December 4, 1925, sec. Supplement; Hofshteyn, "Bayamim ha'hem," *Davar*, November 18, 1925, sec. Supplement.

33. For a discussion of the Caucasus poetry, see Mikhail Krutikov, *From Kabbalah to Class Struggle: Expressionism, Marxism, and Yiddish Literature in the Life and Work of Meir Wiener* (Stanford, CA: Stanford University Press, 2011), 111.

34. Hofshteyn, "Bayamim ha'hem," November 18, 1925. I am grateful to Daria Semenova, PhD, candidate in the Department of Slavic Languages and Literatures at the University of Illinois, Urbana-Champaign, for providing me with a translation.

35. Shmeruk, *A shpigl af a shteyn*, 236.

36. Feyge Hofshteyn, *Mit libe un veytik: Vegn David Hofshteyn* (Tel Aviv: Reshofim, 1985), 66.

37. For a discussion of the crucial role of the images, see Seth Wolitz, "Experiencing Visibility and Phantom Existence," in *Russian Jewish Artists in a Century of Change 1890–1990*, ed. Susan Tumarkin Goodman (New York: Prestel, 1995), 14–15.

38. Benjamin Harshav, *Marc Chagall and His Times: A Documentary Narrative* (Stanford, CA: Stanford University Press, 2004), 302–307.

39. I am modifying the translation found in Seth Wolitz, "Troyer (Grief)—Hofshteyn's Fellow-Traveler Dirge," in *Yiddish Modernism: Studies in Twentieth Century Eastern European Jewish Culture*, ed. Brian Horowitz and Haim A. Gottschalk (Bloomington, IN: Slavica, 2014), 283–309. I have also used Joseph Kerler, "Dovid Hofstein—Our First Wonder," in *The Politics of Yiddish*, vol. 4, Winter Studies in Yiddish (Walnut Creek, CA: AltaMira Press, 1998), 171–85.

40. David Hofshteyn, *Troyer* (Kyiv: Kultur-Lige, 1922), 8. This is my translation.

41. Finkin comments on the significance of the Hebrew term; see Jordan Finkin, "The Consolation of Sadness: The Curious Exile of Dovid Hofshteyn's Troyer," in *Leket: Yiddish Studies Today*, ed. Marion Aptroot, Efrat Gal-Ed, and Roland Gruschka, vol. 1 (Dusseldorf: Dusseldorf University Press, 2012), 21.

42. For another discussion of this work as a whole and this poem in particular, see Finkin, "Consolation of Sadness."

43. Wolitz, "Troyer (Grief)—Hofshteyn's Fellow-Traveler Dirge," 302. I have modified the translation. For the Yiddish, see Hofshteyn, *Troyer*, 14.

44. I disagree with Wolitz that the passage suggests "numbness and passivity." See his *Yiddish Modernism: Studies in Twentieth Century Eastern European Jewish Culture*, ed. Brian Horowitz and Haim A. Gottschalk (Bloomington, IN: Slavica, 2014), 289.

45. Elaine Scarry calls this position "lateralness" and defines it as an ethical element of beauty. Elaine Scarry, *On Beauty and Being Just* (Princeton, NJ: Princeton University Press, 1999), 114. There is a family resemblance between "lateralness," Victor Shklovsky's estrangement, and Mikhail Bakhtin's "outsideness" (*vnenakhodimost'*). For a discussion of the latter two terms, see Caryl Emerson, "Shklvosky's ostranenie, Bakhtin's vnenakhodimost'," *Poetics Today* 26, no. 4 (2005): 637–64.

46. Hofshteyn, *Troyer*, 13.

47. For an approach to the question of the poet's testimony, see Trevor Laurence Jockims, "The Testimony of a Poet: Transcription, Witness, and Poetic Documentation in Charles' Reznikoff's Testimony," *Studies in Testimony* 1, no. 1 (2018): 102–19.

48. See Osher Shvartsman, "In tribn mentshn-land," *Eygns* 2 (1920): 67. Arkadii Shteinberg translated the poem into Russian.

49. Gennady Estraikh, "Shtrom, Der," YIVO Encyclopedia of Jews in Eastern Europe, accessed August 11, 2023, https://yivoencyclopedia.org/article.aspx/Shtrom_Der.

50. Arn Kushnirov, "Azkore," *Shtrom* 1, no. 1 (1922): 28. My translation.

51. Hofshteyn, *Troyer*, 13.

52. Wolitz, "Troyer (Grief)—Hofshteyn's Fellow-Traveler Dirge," 296–97. I have modified the translation; Wolitz has *magical* for *pure*. Finkin translates *hefker un zoyber* as "free and clean" (Finkin, "Consolation of Sadness," 93n11).

53. Hofshteyn, *Troyer*, 13.

54. For discussions, see Wolitz, "Experiencing Visibility and Phantom Existence"; Harshav, *Marc Chagall and His Times*, 307. See also Sabine Koller, *Marc Chagall: Grenzgänge zwischen Literatur und Malerei* (Cologne: Böhlau, 2012), 172–87.

55. Finkin, "Consolation of Sadness," 93.

56. Wolitz, "Troyer (Grief)—Hofshteyn's Fellow-Traveler Dirge," 308. I have modified the translation. For the Yiddish see Hofshteyn, *Troyer*, 21.

57. In another, separate work, not part of the pogrom cycle, Hofshteyn names elements of nature his "pure prayer for the dead" (loytere azkore): "Snows, expanses, clear skies / These are also my first, pure prayer for the dead" (Dovid Hofshteyn, *Gezamlte verk*, vol. 1 [Kyiv: Kultur-Lige, 1923], 11).

58. I am grateful to my friend and colleague Lisa Rosenthal (Professor of Art History, University of Illinois), for pointing this out to me.

3. Leyb Kvitko's Poetry of Abandonment

1. Among his best-known works for children are "Piglets" and "Letter to Voroshilov," see Mikhail Krutikov, "Dos retenish fun Leyb Kvitko (The Enigma of Leib Kvitko)," *Forverts*, June 25, 2016, http://yiddish.forward.com/articles/197215/the-enigma-of-leib-kvitko/?p=all#ixzz5KbCJrYL5.

2. Letter to Shmuel Charney, 1922, in Mordechai Altshuler and Y. Lifshits, *Briv fun yidishe sovetishe shraybers* (Jerusalem: Hebreyisher Universitet in Yerusholayim, 1979), 463.

3. Kvitko himself referred to the book as *First Steps* (*Pervye shagi*) in a Russian-language biographical statement (RGALI fond 631, opis'6, delo 156).

4. As recounted by Gitl Mayzel, *Eseyen* (Tel Aviv: Y. L. Peretz, 1974), 41.

5. Kvitko included a children's poem under this title in a collection published in 1929. See Leyb Kvitko, *Ring in Ring* (Kharkov: Melukhe-farlag fun Ukrayne, 1929), 63.

6. I base my account on Shmeruk, *A shpigl af a shteyn*, 748–51. See also Gennady Estraikh, "Kvitko, Leyb," in *YIVO Encyclopedia of Jews in Eastern Europe* (YIVO, 2010), https://yivoencyclopedia.org/article.aspx/Kvitko_Leyb; Reyzen, *Leksikon fun der yidisher literatur, prese un filologye*, 3:582–86; Joseph Sherman, "Leib Kvitko," in *Dictionary of Literary Biography Complete Online* (GALE, 2007).

7. YIVO, RG 201, Folder 1009, Papers of Abraham Liessin [editor of *Tsukunft*], Letter from Leyb Kvitko to Liessin, August 15, 1922.

8. Catherine Damman, "Dance, Sound, Word: The 'Hundred-Jointed Body' in Zurich Dada Performance," *Germanic Review: Literature, Culture, Theory* 91, no. 4 (October 2016): 352–66, https://doi.org/10.1080/00168890.2016.1223485.

9. Ludmila Shleyfer Lavine, "Vladimir Mayakovsky's Agit-Semitism," *Russian Review* 78, no. 3 (2019): 437–58. For a discussion of the poet's animation of things, see Paul A. Klanderud, "Maiakovskii's Myth of Man, Things and the City: From Poshlost' to the Promised Land," *Russian Review* 55, no. 1 (January 1996): 37, https://doi.org/10.2307/131908.

10. Bergelson, "Der gesheener oyfbrokh." Kvitko was critical of some of this experimentation, insisting that for a Jewish poet content should be as important as form.

11. Gennady Estraikh, "The Kharkiv Yiddish Literary World, 1920s-mid-1930s," *East European Jewish Affairs* 32, no. 2 (2002): 70–88.

12. The Yiddish: "Vu getogt nit genekhtigt. Untern dokh—umru, un in droysn—muradige volkns, shlakregens." See Leyb Kvitko, *Grin groz* (Berlin: Jewish Literature Publishing, 1922), 8. This is my translation.

13. The original Yiddish: "di rut fun oksn-gidn gedreyte, di rut fun shtolik-kaltn tog un elnter naktht in fremdn katsapish-shikorn Nikolaev, oder hungerik-filosofirndn Kherson." See Altshuler and Lifshits, *Briv fun yidishe sovetishe shraybers*, 456. My translation.

14. Leyb Kvitko, *Tsvey khaveyrim: Lyam un Petrik* (Moscow: Emes, 1933), 93.
15. For Agamben and hefker, see Leshem, "Spaces of Abandonment."
16. Leyb Kvitko, "Three Poems," trans. Harriet Murav and Zachary Sholem Berger, in *Geveb: A Journal of Yiddish Studies*, March 5, 2020, https://ingeveb.org/texts-and-translations/kvitko.
17. Santner, *On Creaturely Life*, 45.
18. Santner, *On Creaturely Life*, 47.
19. The pun rests on "Kvitkoaishe," or "Kvitoesque," and chaotic, "khaotishe." See Charney, *Yidishe shrayber in Sovet-Rusland*, 45.
20. Dobrushin, "Dray dikhter."
21. A study may be found in Susanne Strätling, *The Hand at Work: The Poetics of Poiesis in the Russian Avant-Garde* (Boston: Academic Studies Press, 2021).
22. Peretz Markish, "Maskes," *Ringen* 7–8, no. 2 (1921): 101.
23. Kvitko, "Three Poems."
24. Leyb Kvitko, *Trit* (Kyiv: Kyiv Kultur-lige, 1919), 4–5.
25. The poem was also published in subsequent collections of his work. I am using Leyb Kvitko, *Gerangl 1917–1929* (Kharkov: Tsentrfarlag-Kharkov, 1929), 269–85.
26. The first critic to name "In a red storm" as the first Yiddish revolutionary poem was Hersh Remenik; see his "Dikhtung fun revolyutsyonern umru: Leyb Kvitko," in *Shtaplen: Portretn fun yidishe shrayber* (Moscow: Sovetskii pisatel', 1982), 37–49. For a comparison between Blok and Tychyna, see Michael M. Naydan, "Two Musical Conceptions of the Revolution: Aleksandr Blok's Dvenadtsat' and Pavlo Tychyna's Zamist Sonetiv i Oktav," *Journal of Ukrainian Studies* 27, no. 1–2 (Summer–Winter 2002): 93–106. Kvitko and Tychyna lived cheek by jowl in an apartment in Kharkhiv; Kvitko taught Tychyna Yiddish. See Estraikh, *In Harness*, 124.
27. Kvitko, *Gerangl 1917–1929*, 275.
28. I base my account on the following sources. The archival documents include TsDAVO, Fond 3301 opis 2 delo 110, "Dokladnye zapisi Komiteta pomoshchi o pogromakh v Umani" (23 Sept–1 Oct 1919 in Yiddish).
29. Anton Posadskii, "Umanshchina v 1918–1919 gg.: Voina, nastroieniia, zhiznennaia stoikost'," *Historia i swiat* 8 (2019): 163.
30. "Vos heyst ikh shray, az kh'veys nokh nit/ Bay vemen s'iz di shtot haynt?" From "Iz vos, az kloyster glokn" in Kvitko, *1919*, 40.
31. L. B. Miliakova, *Kniga pogromov: Pogromy na Ukraine, v Belorussii, i evropeiskoi chasti Rossii v period grazhdanskoi voiny 1918–1922 gg.* (Moscow: Rosspen, 2007), 118–33.
32. The Yiddish: "Vet a toyes un veytog zayn, oyb men vet mayn bukh—reges af der diner-diner sharf fun zayn un nit-vern—oyb men vet es oyfnemen als dikhtung, als lider vegn pogromen. Vi shoyderlekher kinder-shrek iz din un

mamesh un loyter—azoy iz oykh der payn, dos pakhdones, di zunen-shayn, dos blut-fargosene fun 1919—azoy zaynen oykh di reges mamesh. Vi di luft fun tsar un libe bay di zunen-shtraln in di hoykhn iz andersh,—azoy iz oykh di heym, s'vayb un kind, der seykhl un der viln fun 1919—azoy zaynen oykh di reges andersh" (Kvitko, *1919*, 6). Unless otherwise indicated, all translations are from this edition and are my own. A selection of the poems was published earlier under the title "Folk" in the second volume of *Eygns* in 1920. For a discussion of *1919*, see Sabine Koller, "'The Air Outside Is Bloody': Leyb Kvitko and His Pogrom Cycle 1919," in *Yiddish in Weimar Berlin: At the Crossroads of Diaspora Politics and Culture*, ed. Gennady Estraikh and Mikhail Krutikov (London: Legenda, 2010), 105–22.

33. Review of *1919*, published in the Moscow literary journal *Shtrom*, 1923, no. 4: 83–86.

34. Nokhem Shtif, "Leyb Kvitko, 1919," *Di tsukunft* 30, no. 2 (1925): 128–31. Shtif used his pseudonym Bal-dimyon (Dreamer) for the essay.

35. In the original: "mayn nit oysgeheyltenkayt un nit geshlifenkayt" (YIVO Institute for Jewish Research, Papers of Abraham Liessen, RG 201, Folder 10009, letter dated August 15, 1922, from Berlin, to Abraham Liessin, editor of *Tsukunft*).

36. I take this set of characteristics from Staudigl, "Towards a Phenomenological Theory of Violence."

37. Irina Sandomirskaia, *Blokada v slove: ocherki kriticheskoi teorii i biopolitiki iazyka* (Moscow: Novoe literaturnoe obozrenie, 2013), 13–50.

38. A point made by Scarry in *The Body in Pain*.

39. Kvitko, *1919*, 28.

40. Schneersohn, *Di katastrofale tsaytn un di vaksndike doyres*. I discuss Schneersohn in chapter 8.

41. Sherman, *From Revolution to Repression*. I am using a modified version of Heather Valencia's translation, p. 57.

42. Edgar Allan Poe, "The Coliseum," in *The Collected Works of Edgar Allan Poe*, vol. 1, *Poems*, ed. T. O. Mabbot (Cambridge, MA: Belknap Press of Harvard University Press, 1969), 226–31, https://www.eapoe.org/works/mabbott/tom1p061.htm.

43. Science fiction authors, including Edgar Rice Burroughs, published science fiction novels about reptile people in the early part of the twentieth century (*At the Earth's Core* [1914]; H. P. Lovecraft's *The Nameless City* [1921] is another example).

44. As Sabine points out in Koller, "'Air Outside Is Bloody.'"

45. In contrast to doubting Thomas, who placed his hand inside Jesus's wound. In the original, "Legt s'oyerl tsum vund tsu / Hert zikh ayn" (Kvitko, *1919*, 43–44). For another discussion of the poem, see Koller, "'Air Outside Is Bloody.'"

46. L. L. Bel'skaia, "Ia ukho prilozhil k zemle," *Russkaia rech'*, no. 6 (December 2013): 25–27.

47. B. Kvitko and M. Petrovskii, eds., *Zhizn' i tvorchestvo L'va Kvitko* (Moscow: Detskaia literatura, 1976), 128.
48. Kvitko and Petrovskii, *Zhizn' i tvorchestvo L'va Kvitko*, 128.
49. In her poem "Mayn popugay" Molodowsky writes that her poem wants to make a "sound like glass in a pogrom" (Vi a shoyb in a pogrom). See *In land fun mayn gebeyn* (Chicago: L. M. Stein, 1937), 52.
50. Miliakova, *Kniga pogromov*, 121.
51. The poem is titled "Iz vos, az kloyster-glokn." See Kvitko, *1919*, 45–46.
52. My discussion of sound in Kvitko derives from both Benjamin Harshav and Gaston Bachelard. Harshav argues that meaning and sound lend each other specific qualities in specific contexts (Benjamin Harshav, "Do Sounds Have Meaning?," in *Three Thousand Years of Hebrew Versification: Essays in Comparative Prosody* [New Haven, CT: Yale University Press, 2014], 14–39; Gaston Bachelard, *The Poetics of Space*, trans. Maria Jolas [Boston: Beacon Press, 1994]).
53. Harshav, "Do Sounds Have Meaning?," 32.
54. Oyslender, *Veg-ayn veg oys*, 132. Roni Masel, however, shows that the gothic and the grotesque provide a better framework for Bialik's "In the City of the Slaughter" than approaches limited to a Zionist perspective. See Masel, "National Heroism, Popular Pleasure: Violence, the Gothic and the Grotesque in Hebrew and Yiddish Literatures" (PhD diss., New York University, 2020).
55. A. Leyeles, "Free Verse," in Benjamin Harshav and Barbara Harshav, *American Yiddish Poetry* (Berkeley: University of California Press, 1986), 791.
56. I take the phrase from Bachelard, *Poetics of Space*, 176.
57. Kvitko, *1919*, 12.
58. Kvitko, *1919*, 12.
59. He returned to the theme of words as objects that cause pain in "Vegelekh kalekh" (Handcarts of lime), published in Kvitko, *Gerangl 1917–1929*. A beggar curses him, and the abuse sticks to the poet's flesh. For a discussion, see Krutikov, "Dos retenish fun Leyb Kvitko (The Enigma of Leib Kvitko)."
60. The entire poem can be found in Kvitko, *1919*, 22–24. There is no English translation.
61. Kvitko, *1919*, 22.
62. Kvitko, *1919*, 23. The original: "Kh'hob den nit gebetn zikh / 'Kinderlakh, shpilt zikh, / Hert zikh nit tsu?" / Itst ersht dertsitert, / Zey khapn tsurik shoyn / Di zaydene oyerklakh, / Tseshtokhn, tseblutikt, / Fun prisek tseflamt. / Kh'hob den nit gebetn zikh: / "Kinderlakhn, hert nit, / Kh'veys vos dos poykn batayt."
63. Kvitko, *1919*, 27.
64. Kvitko, *1919*, 156.
65. Kvitko, "Three Poems."

4. Enfleshment

1. Bialik later reworked the poem in Hebrew. For an analysis of the Hebrew version that emphasizes its theological dimensions, see Ziva Ben-Porat, "Disguised Wrath and Hidden Heresy: On Bialik's 'Dance of Despair,'" *Prooftexts* 6, no. 3 (1986): 221–37.

2. Hayyim Nahman Bialik, *Shirim* (Berlin: Klal farlag, 1922), 25. There is no published English translation of the original Yiddish poem; this is my translation.

3. The original: "Ale, ale ayngeshlosn / in eyn groysn festn rung / ayngeflokhtn berd un lokn/shikh un zokn, alt un yung" (Bialik, *Shirim*, 24).

4. This took place in Uman and elsewhere. See YIVO Elias Tcherikower Archive. 369. 103. Khronolohichnyi svit bandits'kikh rukhiv na Umanshchini 1918–20 rik.

5. Wolitz, *Yiddish Modernism*, 274.

6. I borrow this term from Alexander Weheliye's *Habeas Viscus*, but use it in a different sense. Wehilye argues that human flesh and not abstract notions of legal personhood, according to which the flesh is a debased condition, should be the basis for a new politics. Alternative forms of freedom are not recognizable according to the liberal state's notions of the individual, remaining illegible if limited to the understanding of the person as dependent on ownership and the right to dispose of their body. See Weheliye, *Habeas Viscus*, 99–105. For a discussion of "one flesh" in Yiddish poetry see Julia Fermentto-Tzaisler, "Flesh and Blood: The Metaphorics of Meat in Modern Jewish Culture" (PhD diss., University of California, San Diego, 2020).

7. My point of departure is found in Santner, *On Creaturely Life*; Santner, *The Royal Remains: The People's Two Bodies and the Endgames of Sovereignty* (Chicago: University of Chicago Press, 2011).

8. My thinking about sound and the loss of differentiation was spurred by Paul Hurh, "The Sound of Incest: Sympathetic Resonance in Melville's Pierre," in *Novel: A Forum on Fiction*, vol. 44 (Durham, NC: Duke University Press, 2011), 249–67.

9. Elias Cherikover, *Di Ukrainer pogromen in yor 1919* (New York: YIVO Institute for Jewish Research, 1965), 69.

10. For a discussion of a comparable situation see Polina Barskova, *Beseiged Leningrad: Aesthetic Responses to Urban Disaster* (DeKalb: Northern Illinois University Press, 2017), 51–72. Barskova shows that the starving inhabitants of Leningrad were obsessed with their own starvation, and images of "dystrophic" and fat bodies competed in artistic representations of the time.

11. Viktor Shklovsky, *Knight's Move* (Normal, IL: Dalkey Archive Press, 2005), 17. The Russian: "Golodnye govorili s golodnymi o golode" (Shklovsky, *Sobranie sochinenii*, vol. 1 [Moscow: Novoe literaturnoe obozrenie, 2018], 299).

12. From the poem "Red ribbons, green ribbons" ("Royte stenges, grine stenges") (Kvitko, *1919*, 38–39). Unless otherwise noted, all references are to this edition, and all translations are my own. Only a few of these poems have appeared in any language other than Yiddish. For another discussion of this and other poems in *1919*, see Koller, "'Air Outside Is Bloody.'"

13. Kvitko, *1919*, 88–90.

14. For a more detailed discussion, see Murav, *David Bergelson's Strange New World*, 137–40.

15. Samuel Todes, *Body and World* (Cambridge, MA: MIT Press, 2001), 59.

16. Kvitko, *1919*, 83. The Yiddish: "Shpant arum a toyt fun toybenish, / molt un farbt mit toyber toytenish, / mit blutig toybenish / in mayn invelt, in mayn oysvelt."

17. I am grateful to Dov-Ber Kerler for this formulation in an email conversation on April 21, 2020.

18. Kvitko, *1919*, 59. Koller also discusses this poem in "'Air Outside Is Bloody.'"

19. Kvitko, *1919*, 60.

20. Roni Masel shows that the Yiddish translations by both Peretz and Bialik himself multiply the Gothic and grotesque elements of "In the City of the Slaughter," and I am grateful to her for sharing her work. See Masel, "National Heroism, Popular Pleasure." Edgar Allen Poe likely played a role in Kvitko's "Guests." "The Raven," like "Guests downstairs" is also about an unwanted, ominous guest who appears instead of the poet's beloved Lenore. Kvitko takes a page from Poe, using the tropes of Gothic horror to create an effect markedly distinct from the oracular tones of other poets.

21. Kvitko, *Tsvey khaveyrim*, 32.

22. Work on the Gothic that I found helpful beyond Jewish literature includes: Helene Moglen, *The Trauma of Gender: A Feminist Theory of the English Novel* (Berkeley: University of California Press, 2001); Kevin M. F. Platt, Caryl Emerson, and Dina Khapaeva, "Introduction: The Russian Gothic," *Russian Literature* 106 (2019): 1–9; Valeria Sobol, *Haunted Empire* (Ithaca, NY: Cornell University Press, 2020). For a study of the Gothic in Jewish literature, see Karen Grumberg, *Hebrew Gothic: History and the Poetics of Persecution* (Bloomington: Indiana University Press, 2019).

23. Kvitko, *1919*, 110–12. There are parallels between Kvitko and Sergei Esenin's poetry about dogs and other animals. For a discussion of Esenin, see Jessie Davies, "Thematics and Stylistics in Esenin's Poetry," *Canadian-American Slavic Studies* 32, no. 4 (1998): 295–317.

24. For discussion of the image of Jew as dog and other animals in Jewish and non-Jewish literature, see Jay Geller, *Bestiarium Judaicum: Unnatural Histories of the Jews* (New York: Fordham University Press, 2017). Eric Santner discusses "creaturely life," revealed by the exposure to power, as proximate to animal life

in Santner, *On Creaturely Life*. Noam Pines develops an analysis of creaturely life in Hebrew and Yiddish literature, but using his own term, the infrahuman. See Pines, *Infrahuman*. May Barzilai traces the creation of the Jewish monster as a savior for Jewish population in conditions of violence; however, this figure cannot ultimately serve in Jewish nation-building. See Maya Barzilai, *GOLEM: Modern Wars and Their Monsters* (New York: New York University Press, 2020).

25. Mira Beth Wasserman, *Jews, Gentiles, and Other Animals: The Talmud after the Humanities* (Philadelphia: University of Pennsylvania Press, 2017), 99.

26. Kenneth R. Stow, *Jewish Dogs: An Image and Its Interpreters; Continuity in the Catholic-Jewish Encounter* (Stanford, CA: Stanford University Press, 2006).

27. Hofshteyn's extensive citation from *The Merchant of Venice* in his Yiddish-language handbook on literature indicates awareness of Shakespeare's play. See Hofshteyn and Shames, *Literatur kentenish*, 68–70.

28. What Noam Pines calls "the figural construction of Jewish identity as abject animality" plays a role in Kvitko's "They're pushing me" (Pines, *Infrahuman*, 20).

29. The Yiddish critic Bal-Makhshoves (the pseudonym of Yisroel Eliashev) describes Kvitko's two personae as the "simple one" (der tam) and the child. See Yisroel Eliashev, *Geklibene verk* (New York: Cyco, 1953), 305.

30. Charney claims that Der Nister was the only author to have exerted literary influence on Kvitko. See Charney, *Yidishe shrayber in Sovet-Rusland*, 43. For the only collection of essays on the author, see Gennady Estraikh, Kerstin Hoge, and Mikhail Krutikov, eds., *Uncovering the Hidden: The Works and Life of Der Nister* (London: Legenda, 2014).

31. Daniela Mantovan, "Der Nister and His Symbolist Short Stories (1913–1929): Patterns of Imagination" (PhD diss., Columbia University, 1993), 33.

32. *Tales in Verse* (*Mayselekh in ferzn*) was written in 1918 and published in various editions. See Avraham Novershtern, "Der Nister," YIVO Encyclopedia of Jews in Eastern Europe, accessed July 15, 2023, http://www.yivoencyclopedia.org/article.aspx/Der_Nister.

33. Der Nister, *Mayselekh in ferzen*, 3rd ed. (Warsaw: Kultur-Lige, 1921), 33–36.

34. Sabine Koller, "A Mayse mit a hon. Dos Tsigele: Marc Chagall Illustrating Der Nister," in *Uncovering the Hidden: The Works and Life of Der Nister*, ed. Gennady Estraikh, Kerstin Hoge, and Mikhail Krutikov (Oxford: Legenda, 2017), 56.

35. Leah Garrett and Lamed Shapiro, introduction to *The Cross and Other Jewish Stories*, ed. Leah Garrett (New Haven, CT: Yale University Press, 2007), ix–xxxii, http://www.jstor.org/stable/j.ctt1npntv.4.

36. Ruth R. Wisse, "Speaking of the Devil in Yiddish Literature," in *Studies in Contemporary Jewry*, vol. 13, *Jews and Violence: Images, Ideologies, Realities*, ed. Peter Medding (New York: Oxford University Press, 2002), 59–73.

37. Astashkevich, *Gendered Violence*.

38. Lamed Shapiro, "The Cross," in *The Cross and Other Jewish Stories*, ed. Leah Garrett, trans. Jeremy Dauber (Nw Haven, CT: Yale University Press, 2007), 11, http://www.jstor.org/stable/j.ctt1npntv.5.

39. As Leah Garrett shows, the nineteenth-century Russian materialist author Dmitry Pisarev influenced Shapiro, and the so-called scientific approach to the body as consisting of chemical elements is evident in this description (Garrett and Shapiro, Introduction).

40. Wisse, "Speaking of the Devil in Yiddish Literature," 65.

41. Shmuel Charney, *Vegn yidishe shrayber: Kritishe artikln*, vol. 2 (Warsaw: Sh. Shreberk, 1927), 98.

42. Kvitko, *1919*, 147–49.

43. Kvitko, *1919*, 149.

44. For discussions of Africa as a theme in Yiddish literature, see Joseph Sherman, "Serving the Natives: Whiteness as the Price of Hospitality in South African Yiddish Literature," *Journal of Southern African Studies* 26, no. 3 (September 2000): 505–21; Eli Rosenblatt, "Enlightening the Skin: Travel, Racial Language, and Rabbinic Intertextuality in Modern Yiddish Literature" (PhD diss., University of California, 2017), https://escholarship.org/uc/item/8vs7p0bg. I am grateful to Eli for discussing this topic with me.

45. Vjaceslav Ivanov, "Two Images of Africa in Russian Literature at the Beginning of the Twentieth Century: Ka by Chlebnikov and Gumilev's African Poems," *Russian Literature* 29 (1991): 409–26.

46. This and other details are drawn from reports and testimonies in YIVO, Record Group 80, Elias Cherkikover Archive, Folder 369, Uman, Items 103–16.

47. Tsentral'nyi derzhavnyi arkhiv vyshchykh orhaniv vlady (TsDAVO) Fund 2497, opis' 3, delo 300. "Ocherk o travmatichekoi epidemii sredi evreiskogo naseleniia v 1919," Vseukrainskii evreiskii obshchestvennyi komitet po okazaniiu pomoshchi postradavshim ot pogromov (Vseukreobshchestkom).

48. Kvitko, *1919*, 129.

49. Mintz, *Ḥurban*, 134. Another possible source is Matthew 5:29, "If your eye offend you, pluck it out."

50. Kvitko, *1919*, 130.

51. In Isaiah 10:2, the poor are robbed of the judgment that allows them certain privileges, "deprived of their rights." The Hebrew original uses the infinitive of the same root that appears in "nigzl." For the Yiddish usage, see under nigzl in Judah Joffe and Yudel Mark, eds., *Der groyser verterbukh fun der Yidisher shprakh online* (New York: Yiddish Dictionary Committee, 1961), https://www.cs.uky.edu/~raphael/yiddish/searchGroys.cgi.

52. Alex Dubilet argues that experimentation with self-emptying absent a transcendent ideal and for the sake of the affirmation of life can be found both in the early modern and the postmodern periods. See Dubilet, *The Self-Emptying*

Subject: Kenosis and Immanence, Medieval to Modern (New York: Fordham University Press, 2018).

53. Dobrushin, "Dray dikhter," 83. Dobrushin wrote this in 1919, before the publication of Kvitko's pogrom cycle, but his characterization suits the poetic practice of works like "My Eyes," published in 1923.

54. See "Tsu Shmuel Niger," in Altshuler and Lifshits, *Briv fun yidishe sovetishe shraybers*, 463.

55. Zvi Mark, *Mysticism and Madness: The Religious Thought of Rabbi Nachman of Bratslav* (New York: Continuum, 2009), 173, 183, 185, 189.

56. Kvitko, *1919*, 144–46.

57. Kvitko, *1919*, 144.

58. Poetic language uses words in an unexpected way, as Hofshteyn points out in Hofshteyn and Shames, *Literatur kentenish*, 38.

59. Scarry, *Body in Pain*, 144–46, 285.

60. In Kvitko, *1919*, 35.

61. See Erica Fretwell, "Stillness Is a Move: Helen Keller and the Kinaesthetics of Autobiography," *American Literary History* 25, no. 3 (2013): 563–87.

5. Chronicling a Hefker World

1. Kipnis, *Khadoshim un teg*, 11. All references are to this edition, and unless otherwise stated, all translations are my own. The 1929 version of the novel omits the epigraph. A Russian translation of *Months and Days* was published: Itsik Kipnis, *Mesiatsy i dni*, trans. B. I. Marshak (Moscow-Leningrad: Gosudarstvennoe izdatel'stvo, 1930). For an English translation of an excerpt of chapter 8, see Harriet Murav, "Documentary Fiction of the Pogroms of the Civil War," in Avrutin and Bemporad, *Pogroms*, 176–92. For a translation of another part of the novel, see Roskies, *Literature of Destruction*, 323–55.

2. Itsik Kipnis, "Fun der dertseylung Khayele un Pinyele," in *Ukrayne: Literarish-kinstlerisher almanakh* (Kyiv: Kultur-Lige, 1926), 34–52.

3. "Kumt oys di eltere abisl modne ontsukukn azelkhe. Shoyn afile gor modne" (Kipnis, *Khadoshim un teg*, 150).

4. I base my account on Reyzen, *Leksikon fun der yidisher literatur, prese un filologye*, 3:639–45. See also Mordechai Altshuler, "Itsik Kipnis: The 'White Crow' of Soviet Yiddish Literature," *Jews in Russia and Eastern Europe* 52/53 (2004): 68–167.

5. Another discussion of *Months and Days* can be found in Mikhail Krutikov, "Rediscovering the Shtetl as a New Reality," in *The Shtetl: New Evaluations*, ed. Steven T. Katz (New York: New York University Press, 2007), 211–32.

6. For more on Kipnis's later work, see Murav, *Music from a Speeding Train*, 248–58.

7. Kipnis, *Khadoshim un teg*, 8.

8. Rokhl Faygenberg's thinly fictionalized account of the pogrom in Dubovo includes photographs of victims and also uses real-life names. See Faygenberg, *A pinkes fun a toyter shtot* (Warsaw: Akhisfer, 1926). For a discussion of the 1919 Slovechno pogrom that uses Kipnis's novel as a source, see Veidlinger, *In the Midst of Civilized Europe*, 217–31.

9. For examples and discussions of Soviet factography, see Devin Fore, "The Operative Word in Soviet Factography," *October* 118 (Fall 2006): 95–131; Nikolai Chuzhak, "Writer's Handbook," trans. Devin Fore and Douglas Greenfield, *October* 118 (Fall 2006): 78–94. See also Elizabeth Papazian, *Manufacturing Truth: The Documentary Moment in Early Soviet Culture* (DeKalb: Northern Illinois University Press, 2009). A discussion of factography, Tretiakov, and ethnic literature can be found in Steven S. Lee, *The Ethnic Avant-Garde: Minority Cultures and World Revolution* (New York : Columbia University Press, 2015), 83–118.

10. Laura Jockusch, "Chroniclers of Catastrophe: History Writing as a Jewish Response to Persecution before and after the Holocaust," in *Holocaust Historiography in Context: Emergence, Challenges, Polemics, and Achievements*, ed. David Bankier and Dan Michman (New York: Berghahn Books, 2008), 135–66; Jockusch, *Collect and Record!: Jewish Holocaust Documentation in Early Postwar Europe* (New York: Oxford University Press, 2012).

11. For discussions of An-sky, see Gabriella Safran, *Wandering Soul: The Dybbuk's Creator, S. An-Sky* (Cambridge, MA: Harvard University Press, 2010); Eugune M. Avrutin et al., *Photographing the Jewish Nation: Pictures from S. An-Sky's Ethnographic Expeditions* (Waltham, MA: Brandeis University Press, 2009). For a comparative discussion of An-sky, Babel, and Vasilii Grossman, see Polly Zavadivker, "Blood and Ink: Russian and Soviet Jewish Chroniclers of Catastrophe from World War I to World War II" (PhD diss., University of California at Santa Cruz, 2013).

12. I discuss Bialik in the introduction and chapter 4. For an account of the Kishinev pogrom and the worldwide response to it, see Zipperstein, *Pogrom*. For another discussion, see Nakhmen Mayzel, "Itsik Kipnis," in *Untervegns un andere dertseylungen* (New York: International Yiddish Cultural Movement [IKUF], 1960), 13–14. See also Roskies, *Against the Apocalypse*, 84–106.

13. Zipperstein, *Pogrom*, 82.

14. DAKO F3050, opis' 1, delo 123. "Protocol zasedaniia informatsio-statisticheskogo otdela Evobshchestkom from 9/16/1921." Accessed at the University of Illinois Library.

15. "Mit toyznt tatsn heyse tantst di zun" (Hofshteyn, *Troyer*, 8).

16. The most succinct discussion can be found in James E. Young and David William Foster, "Documentary Narrative," *PMLA* 99, no. 5 (October 1984): 998, https://doi.org/10.2307/462149.

17. Kipnis, *Khadoshim un teg*, 92.
18. Isaac Bashevis Singer, "Khadoshim un teg," *Literarishe bleter*, no. 13 (April 1, 1927): 260. Singer used the initials "Yud Beys." to sign his review.
19. Charney, *Yidishe shrayber in Sovet-Rusland*, 134.
20. Kipnis, *Khadoshim un teg*, 10.
21. David Bergelson, "Kipnis's Khadoshim un teg," *Literarishe bleter*, no. 20 (July 19, 1929): 558–60.
22. See Jan Gross, *Neighbors: The Destruction of the Jewish Community in Jedwabne, Poland* (Princeton, NJ: Princeton University Press, 2001); Jeffrey S. Kopstein and Jason Wittenberg, *Intimate Violence: Anti-Jewish Pogroms on the Eve of the Holocaust* (Ithaca, NY: Cornell University Press, 2018).
23. "Ver veyst es nit, as in Rusland iz shoyn a yor nokh der groyser revolutsye? Avade veysn mir. Ober in undzere mekoymes gufe zaynen nokh keyne shum revolutsyes nit forgekumen" (Kipnis, *Khadoshim un teg*, 24).
24. Elias Heifetz, *The Slaughter of the Jews in Ukraine in 1919* (New York: Thomas Seltzer, 1921), 369.
25. According to Kipnis and information in Gosudarstvennyi arkhiv Zhitomirskoi oblasti (GAZHO), f. 270, opis' 3, delo 1. Skhematicheskie plany gorodov i mestechek, "Slovechno," 1910.
26. Kipnis, *Khadoshim un teg*, 52.
27. Kipnis, *Khadoshim un teg*, 50.
28. Testimony from L. Kaplan, in Kievskaia raionnaia komissiia evreiskogo obshchestvennogo komiteta po okazaniiu pomoshchi postradavshim ot pogromov, DAKO, fond 3050, op.1,d. 225, ll. 17-ob.
29. Kipnis, *Khadoshim un teg*, 41.
30. TsDAVO, fond 2497, op. 3, d. 154, "Pokazanie Itsko-Mordakovich Pashkovskii."
31. TSDAVO, fond 2497, op. 3, d. 154, "Pokazanie Moishi Lenderman." See also YIVO Archive, RG80. folder 84.
32. Testimony from L. Kaplan, in Kievskaia raionnaia komissiia evreiskogo obshchestvennogo komiteta po okazaniiu pomoshchi postradavshim ot pogromov, DAKO, fond 3050, op.1, d. 225, ll. 17-ob.
33. TSDAVO, fond 2497, op. 1, d.154.
34. Kipnis, *Khadoshim un teg*, 113.
35. TsDAVO, fond 2497, op. 3, d. 154, "Pokazanie Itsko-Mordakovich Pashkovskii."
36. Kipnis, *Khadoshim un teg*, 89.
37. Kipnis, *Khadoshim un teg*, 103.
38. Miliakova, *Kniga pogromov*, 179.
39. Kipnis, *Khadoshim un teg*, 138.
40. Heifetz, *Slaughter of the Jews in Ukraine in 1919*, 380.

41. Sholem Aleichem, *Some Laughter, Some Tears: Tales from the Old and the New*, trans. Curt Leviant (New York: G. P. Putnam's Sons, 1968), 116–17.
42. Itsik Kipnis, *Di shtub un untervegns* (Tel Aviv: I. L. Peretz Publishing House, 1977), 213. My translation.
43. Kipnis, *Khadoshim un teg*, 11.
44. See for example, Susan Rubin Suleiman, "Pornography, Transgression, and the Avant-Garde: Bataille's Story of the Eye," in *The Poetics of Gender*, ed. Nancy K. Miller (New York: Columbia University Press, 1986), 117–36.
45. Alan Mintz, "The Russian Pogroms in Hebrew Literature and the Subversion of the Martyrological Ideal," *AJS Review* 7 (April 1982): 293.
46. TsDAHO [Tsentral'nyi derzhavnyi arkhiv hromads'kykh orhanizatsii Ukrainy. Central State Archive of Public Organizations of Ukraine] Fond 269, op. 1, delo 262. Voennyi sud, February 22, 1919. For more on this figure and the Ovruch pogrom, see Veidlinger, *In the Midst of Civilized Europe*, 93–104.
47. Kipnis, *Khadoshim un teg*, 62.
48. Heifetz, *Slaughter of the Jews in Ukraine in 1919*, 29.
49. For a sample of the attitudes of the peasantry toward butchers and tanners in Poland, see Hagen, *Anti-Jewish Violence in Poland, 1914–1920*, 31.
50. I take the phrase from Santner, *On Creaturely Life*, 186.
51. Shmuel Gordon, "Y. Kipnis, Oksn," *Shtrom*, no. 5–6 (1923): 402.
52. Dogs, dust, and lice are typical motifs of the hefker poetry of Grinberg and other interwar authors who simultaneously embraced a certain strand of primitivism while also protesting the homelessness of the Jews. For a discussion of primitivism in Grinberg, see Samuel J. Spinner, *Jewish Primitivism* (Stanford, CA: Stanford University Press, 2021), 102–20.
53. Itsik Kipnis, *Oksn* (Kyiv: Vidervuks, 1923), 18.
54. Itsik Kipnis, "Gnod," *Shtrom* 3 (1922): 39.
55. Kipnis, "Gnod," 39.
56. Kipnis, *Khadoshim un teg*, 92. It is not an accident that Sholem Aleichem's short story about a severely disabled girl, "Bashefenish," was published in the year of the Kishinev pogrom, 1903.
57. Eric Santner, a scholar of German literature, characterizes the changes wrought by abandonment as the emergence of "creaturely life" (Santner, *On Creaturely Life*, 47).
58. Kipnis, *Khadoshim un teg*, 93.
59. Kipnis, *Khadoshim un teg*, 135.
60. DAKO, f. 3050, delo 225.
61. Kipnis, *Khadoshim un teg*, 135.
62. For a discussion of the significance of "days" in the work, see Roskies, *Against the Apocalypse*, 183–85.
63. Kipnis, *Khadoshim un teg*, 82.

64. Kipnis, *Khadoshim un teg*, 133.
65. Kvitko, *1919*, 6.
66. Kipnis, *Khadoshim un teg*, 105.
67. Kipnis, *Khadoshim un teg*, 128.
68. DAKO F3050, opis' 1, delo 225. Accessed at the University of Illinois Library.
69. Kipnis, *Khadoshim un teg*, 107.
70. Kipnis, *Khadoshim un teg*, 107.
71. Heifetz, *Slaughter of the Jews in Ukraine in 1919*, 368–72.
72. Kipnis, *Khadoshim un teg*, 67–68.
73. Kipnis, *Khadoshim un teg*, 136.
74. See Mikhail Akulov, "War without Fronts: Atamans and Commissars in Ukraine, 1917–1919" (PhD diss., Harvard University, 2013), 100–101.
75. For a discussion of Chinese participants in the Red Army, see Gregor Benton, *Chinese Migrants and Internationalism: Forgotten Histories, 1917–1945* (New York: Routledge, 2007), 23–25. See also Velychenko, *Life and Death in Revolutionary Ukraine*, 118.
76. Kipnis, *Khadoshim un teg*, 150.
77. Kipnis, *Khadoshim un teg*, 54.
78. Kipnis, *Khadoshim un teg*, 54.
79. Irina Sandomirskaja, explicating Derrida on the "poetics and politics of witnessing," in *Sovereignties in Question*, emphasizes that testimony depends on faith and belief enacted in the relationship between the witness and the listener. See Irina Sandomirskaja, "Derrida on the Poetics and Politics of Witnessing," in *Rethinking Time*, ed. Hans Ruin and Andrus Ers (Huddinge: Södertörns högskola, 2011), 247–55.
80. Kipnis, *Khadoshim un teg*, 103.
81. For a discussion, see Charney, *Yidishe shrayber in Sovet-Rusland*, 132–38.
82. For a discussion of documentary strategies in literature, see Ilya Kukulin, "Documentalist Strategies in Contemporary Russian Poetry," trans. Josephine von Zitzewitz, *Russian Review*, no. 4 (2010): 585. One of the strategies that Kukulin identifies, parataxis, the juxtaposition of contradictory elements, is also characteristic of the love story/pogrom chronicle of *Months and Days*.

6. Victor Shklovsky's Archive of Abandonment

1. I use the terms interchangeably; for a discussion about translating *ostranenie* as "enstrangment," see Benjamin Sher, "Translator's Introduction: Shklovsky and the Revolution," in *Theory of Prose* (Elmwood Park, IL: Dalkey Archive Press, 1990), xv–xxi.
2. Viktor Shklovsky, *Theory of Prose* (Normal, IL: Dalkey Archive Press, 1990), 5. "Iskusstvo kak priem" was first published in Russian in 1917.

3. For the English translation, see Shklovsky, *Sentimental Journey*. For the Russian, Shklovsky, *Eshche nichego ne konchilos'* (Moscow: Vagrius, 2002), 15–266. I cite from this edition, which uses the 1923 version. The 1923 original also appears in Viktor Shklovsky, *Sobranie sochinenii*, ed. Il'ia Kalinin, 2 vols. (Moscow: Novoe literaturnoe obozrenie, 2019).

4. Emerson, "Shklvosky's ostranenie, Bakhtin's vnenakhodimost'," 639n36. For a discussion of the larger context, see Galin Tihanov, *The Birth and Death of Literary Theory: Regimes of Relevance in Russia and Beyond* (Stanford, CA: Stanford University Press, 2019).

5. Greta Slobin, *Russians Abroad: Literary and Cultural Politics of Diaspora 1919–1939* (Boston: Academic Studies Press, 2018); Svetlana Boym, "The Off-Modern Turn: Modernist Humanism and Vernacular Cosmopolitanism in Shklovsky and Mandelshtam," in *Jews and the Ends of Theory*, ed. Shai Ginsburg, Martin Land, and Jonathan Boyarin (New York: Fordham University Press, 2018), 164–86; Harriet Murav, "Technology, the City, and the Body: Bergelson and Shklovsky in Berlin," in *Migration and Mobility in the Modern Age: Refugees, Travelers, and Traffickers in Europe and Eurasia*, ed. Anika Walke, Jan Musekamp, and Nicole Svobodny (Bloomington: Indiana University Press, 2017), 260–75.

6. Il'ia Kalinin, "Istoriia kak iskusstvo chlenorazdel'nosti," *Novoe literaturnoe obozrenie* 71, no. 1 (2005): 103–31. For the argument that the representation of bodily pain and the fragmentariness of the text are nomadic writing strategies, see Anne Dwyer, "Standstill as Extinction: Viktor Shklovsky's Poetics and Politics of Movement in the 1920s and 1930s," *PMLA* 131, no. 2 (March 2016): 269–88, https://doi.org/10.1632/pmla.2016.131.2.269.

7. In *Sentimental Journey*, Shklovsky remarks that he is not a Bolshevik but a Freudian. I am taking this somewhat seriously.

8. Boym, "Poetics and Politics of Estrangement."

9. Shklovsky, *Sentimental Journey*, 22.

10. Shklovsky, *Sentimental Journey*, 78.

11. Shklovsky, *Sentimental Journey*, 78.

12. Shklovsky, *Sentimental Journey*, 148.

13. Shklovsky, *Sentimental Journey*, 165.

14. The English translation gives "out of place." See Shklovsky, *Sentimental Journey*, 273. I am arguing, however, that Shklovsky uses "strange" for a reason. Violence estranges the world; so does intervention that attempts to mitigate it.

15. Das, *Life and Words*, xi.

16. Shklovsky, *Eshche nichego ne konchilos'*, 142; Shklovsky, *Sentimental Journey*, 134.

17. As Cristina Vatulescu points out in "The Politics of Estrangement: Tracking Shklovsky's Device through Literary and Policing Practices," *Poetics Today* 27, no. 1 (2006): 41.

18. Shklovsky, *Sentimental Journey*, 63; Shklovsky, *Eshche nichego ne konchilos'*, 78.
19. Shklovsky, *Sentimental Journey*, 160.
20. This is Vatulescu's translation; see Vatulescu, "Politics of Estrangement," 41.
21. The word for "country" is another source. For a discussion, see Slobin, *Russians Abroad*, 38–39.
22. Shklovsky, *Sentimental Journey*, 175. I have modified the translation. The Russian: "Vse bylo goloe i otkrytoe, kak otkrytye chasy" (Shklovsky, *Eshche nichego ne konchilos'*, 178).
23. Shklovsky, *Sentimental Journey*, 271. I have modified the translation. The Russian: "Glavnoe otlichie revolutsionnoi zhizni ot obychnoi, to chto teper' vse oshchushchaetsia. Zhizn' stala iskusstvom" (Shklovsky, *Eshche nichego ne konchilos'*, 260).
24. Galin Tihanov, "The Politics of Estrangement: The Case of the Early Shklovsky," *Poetics Today* 26, no. 4 (December 1, 2005): 675.
25. Anne Dwyer sees the role of estrangement in the text in different terms, emphasizing the significance of the borderland: "a new and strange view of the body of Russia, its people, and its texts is possible—from its borders" (Anne Dwyer, "Revivifying Russia: Literature, Theory, and Empire in Viktor Shklovskii's Civil War Writings," *Slavonica* 15, no. 1 [2009]: 25). Sergei Zenkin also highlights the theme of strangeness in *Sentimental Journey*. See his "Prikliucheniia teoretika: Avtobiograficheskaia proza Viktor Shklovskogo," *Druzhba narodov* 12 (2003): 170–83.
26. Svetlana Boym, *Another Freedom: The Alternative History of an Idea* (Chicago: University of Chicago Press, 2010), 219.
27. Leah Dickerman, "The Fact and the Photograph," *October* 118 (Fall 2006): 142.
28. Chuzhak, "Writer's Handbook," 91. Victor Erlich's characterization of the whimsicality, "pluck and irreverence" of *Sentimental Journey* is similar. See Victor Erlich, *Modernism and Revolution: Russian Literature in Transition* (Cambridge, MA: Harvard University Press, 1994), 222.
29. Zenkin, "Prikliucheniia teoretika," 186.
30. Shklovsky, *Sentimental Journey*, 184. For the Russian, see Shklovsky, *Eshche nichego ne konchilos'*, 186.
31. Radoslav Borislavov, "Viktor Shklovskii—Between Art and Life" (PhD diss., University of Chicago, 2011); Borislavov, "'I Know What Motivation Is': The Politics of Emotion and Viktor Shklovskii's Sentimental Rhetoric," *Slavic Review* 74, no. 4 (2015): 785–807. See also Vatulescu, "The Politics of Estrangement," 36–66; Vatulescu, *Police Aesthetics: Literature, Film, and the Secret Police in Soviet Times* (Stanford, CA: Stanford University Press, 2010).
32. Shklovsky, *Sentimental Journey*, 244; Shklovsky, *Eshche nichego ne konchilos'*, 238.
33. Shklovsky, *Sentimental Journey*, 140.

34. Shklovsky, *Sentimental Journey*, 16, 17. I have modified the translation. For the Russian, see Shklovsky, *Eshche nichego ne konchilos'*, 29, 31.

35. Viktor Shklovsky, "Boi na Dniepre," in *Sobrainie sochinenii*, 2 vols. (Moscow: Novoe literaturnoe obozrenie, 2018), 1:155–57.

36. Shklovsky, *Sentimental Journey*, 83. I am modifying the translation to reflect the repetition of the full phrase Shklovsky used in the original Russian. See Shklovsky, *Eshche nichego ne konchilos'*, 96.

37. Borislavov, "Viktor Shklovskii," 122.

38. Miliakova, *Kniga pogromov*, 238–39.

39. Shklovsky, *Eshche nichego ne konchilos'*, 217; Shklovsky, *Sentimental Journey*, 221.

40. Shklovsky, *Sentimental Journey*, 221.

41. Miliakova, *Kniga pogromov*, 239.

42. One source indicates a certain S. I. Gorban', active in Ukraine during the Civil War, without providing additional detail (Shklovsky, *Sobranie sochinenii*, 1:958n3). There was a Gubanov active in the Nikolaev region in 1919. See Miliakova, *Kniga pogromov*, 215.

43. Maksim Gorky also writes about the reign of samosud in revolutionary Russia. Wikipedia helpfully pointed me to this text; see Wikipedia, s.v. "Samosud," last modified January 7, 2023, https://ru.wikipedia.org/wiki/Samosud.

44. Shklovsky, *Sentimental Journey*, 140.

45. For a discussion of excessive fleshiness in besieged Leningrad during World War II that also discusses *Sentimental Journey*, see Barskova, *Beseiged Leningrad*, 51–72.

46. Shklovsky, *Sentimental Journey*, 232.

47. Shklovsky, *Sentimental Journey*, 189.

48. Shklovsky, *Sentimental Journey*, 98. For the Russian, see Shklovsky, *Eshche nichego ne konchilos'*, 111.

49. Henri Bergson, *Laughter: An Essay on the Meaning of the Comic*, trans. Cloudesley Brereton (New York: Macmillan, 1914), 29. For a discussion of Shklovsky and Bergson, see James Curtis, "Bergson and Russian Formalism," *Comparative Literature* 28, no. 2 (1976): 109–21.

50. Bergson, *Laughter*, 29.

51. For another discussion of Shklovsky's writings from the 1920s that also uses Scarry, see Emerson, "Shklvosky's ostranenie, Bakhtin's vnenakhodimost'."

52. Scarry, *Body in Pain*, 286.

53. Scarry, *Body in Pain*, 145.

54. Shklovsky, *Sentimental Journey*, 276; Shklovsky, *Eshche nichego ne konchilos'*, 266.

55. Shklovsky, *Sentimental Journey*, 183.

56. Shklovsky, *Sentimental Journey*, 183.
57. Shklovsky, *Sentimental Journey*, 218.
58. Shklovsky, *Sentimental Journey*, 218–19. I have modified the translation. For the Russian, see Shklovsky, *Eshche nichego ne konchilos'*, 216.
59. Shklovsky was working on Tolstoy at this time. See Zenkin, "Prikliucheniia teoretika," 171–72.
60. Leo Tolstoy, *War and Peace*, trans. George Gibian, 2nd ed. (New York: W. W. Norton, 1996), 725.
61. Tolstoy, *War and Peace*, 726.
62. Shklovsky, *Sentimental Journey*, 220.
63. Shklovsky, *Sentimental Journey*, 226. The term in the original Russian is *rodoslovnaia*.
64. Shklovsky, *Sentimental Journey*, 227.
65. Shklovsky, *Sentimental Journey*, 228.
66. Tsentral'nyi derzhavnyi arkhiv vyshchykh orhaniv vlady ta upravlinnya Ukrayiny (The Central State Archive of the Highest Organs of Government and Administration of Ukraine) (TsDAVO) fond 348. Opis 1. Delo 108. Elisavetgrad. Historian Brendan McGeever gives the lower, but still extraordinary, number of 1,526, based on a figure provided by the Russian Red Cross ("Red Antisemitism: Anti-Jewish Violence and Revolutionary Politics in Ukraine, 1919," *Quest. Issues in Contemporary Jewish History*, no. 15 [August 2019], https://doi.org/10.48248/issn.2037-741X/839).
67. Testimony of Abram Markovich Serbin, TsDAVO Tsentralnyi Gosudarstvennyi Arkhiv Vysshykh Organov Vlasti i Upravleniia Ukrainy (TsDAVO) F. 348. Opis 1. Delo 108. Elisavetgrad. For a discussion of gendered violence in Elisavetgrad, see Astashkevich, *Gendered Violence*, 62–63.
68. Shklovsky, *Sentimental Journey*, 228. I have modified the translation.
69. Miliakova, *Kniga pogromov*, 490. For a Ukrainian literary portrait of Makhno's occupation of a town, see the introduction to this study.
70. Devin Fore, "Introduction," *October* 118 (Fall 2006): 10.
71. Shklovsky, *Sentimental Journey*, 80.
72. Shklovsky, *Sentimental Journey*, 78.
73. Shklovsky, *Sobranie sochinenii*, 1:180. My translation.
74. I base my account on John Joseph, *The Modern Assyrians of the Middle East: Encounters with Western Christian Missions, Archaelogists, & Colonial Powers* (Leiden: Brill, 2000); David Gaunt, *Massacres, Resistance, Protectors: Muslim-Christian Relations in Eastern Anatolia during World War I* (Piscataway, NJ: Gorgias Press, 2006); Peter Holquist, "The Politics and Practice of the Russian Occupation of Armenia, 1915–February 1917," in *A Question of Genocide: Armenians and Turks at the End of the Ottoman Empire*, ed. Ronald Grigor Suny, Fatma

Muge Gocek, and Norman M. Naimark (New York: Oxford University Press, 2011), 151–74.

75. Holquist, "Politics and Practice of the Russian Occupation of Armenia."

76. Other scholars come to different conclusions, characterizing the Russian army's policy as a form of ethnic killing. See Joshua Sanborn, "The Genesis of Russian Warlordism: Violence and Governance during the First World War and the Civil War," *Contemporary European History* 19, no. 3 (2010): 195–213.

77. Umit Ungor Ugur, "Paramilitary Violence in the Collapsing Ottoman Empire," in Gerwarth and Horne, *War in Peace*, 164–83.

78. Shklovsky, *Sentimental Journey*, 99; Shklovsky, *Eshche nichego ne konchilos'*, 112.

79. Shklovsky, *Sentimental Journey*, 114; Shklovsky, *Eshche nichego ne konchilos'*, 123. The key phrase in Russian reads: "drug dlia druga oni ne byli volkami."

80. Shklovsky, *Sentimental Journey*, 102.

81. Shklovsky, *Sentimental Journey*, 98.

82. Shklovsky, *Sentimental Journey*, 98.

83. Shklovsky, *Sentimental Journey*, 100–101; Shklovsky, *Eshche nichego ne konchilos'*, 113.

84. Shklovsky, *Sentimental Journey*, 113; Shklovsky, *Eshche nichego ne konchilos'*, 122.

85. Shklovsky, *Sentimental Journey*, 91; Shklovsky, *Eshche nichego ne konchilos'*, 103.

86. Shklovsky, *Sentimental Journey*, 92. I have modified the translation. For the Russian, see Shklovsky, *Eshche nichego ne konchilos'*, 106.

87. Shklovsky, *Sentimental Journey*, 92. I have modified the translation.

88. Shklovsky, *Sentimental Journey*, 100; Shklovsky, *Eshche nichego ne konchilos'*, 112.

89. This is part of the "Bedikat chametz" ritual. For the Hebrew, see "Bedikat Chamtez," Haggadot, accessed July 7, 2021, https://www.haggadot.com/clip/bedikat-chametz-2. Ellipsis added.

90. Shklovsky, *Sentimental Journey*, 92.

91. Shklovsky, *Sentimental Journey*, 133; Shklovsky, *Eshche nichego ne konchilos'*, 142. I have changed the translation.

92. Shklovsky, *Sentimental Journey*, 96.

93. Shklovsky, *Sentimental Journey*, 272.

94. Shklovsky, *Sentimental Journey*, 273; Shklovsky, *Eshche nichego ne konchilos'*, 261. I have modified the English translation to capture the emphasis on the word *strange*, used throughout the text.

95. Mary Lewis Shedd, *The Measure of a Man: The Life of William Ambrose Shedd, Missionary to Persia* (New York: George Doran, 1922).

96. Shklovsky, *Sentimental Journey*, 112; Shklovsky, *Eshche nichego ne konchilos'*, 122.

97. Shklovsky, *Sentimental Journey: Memoirs, 1917–1922*, 184.

7. Counting

1. "Tog vert finsterer," "Day Grows Darker," trans. Heather Valencia, in Sherman, *From Revolution to Repression*, 56. The Yiddish:

> An umgliklikh farblibener
> vet ibertseyln di harugim.
> Er vet mayn toytn nomen
> glaykh mit alemens farshraybn mit klayne oysyeslakh
> in langn tsetl.
> Oy, zol er khotsh nit fargesn dort
> Fartseykenen in langn tsetl
> Vifl ikh bin alt geven!
> (Kvitko, *1919*, 26)

2. U.S. Holocaust Museum Archives, RG-31.057M, held in University Library, University of Illinois at Urbana-Champaign. Copy of Derzhavnyi Arkhiv Kyivs'koi Oblasti (henceforth DAKO), f. 3050, op. 1, d. 240.

3. When I wrote this chapter in November 2020 during the COVID-19 pandemic, public health officials warned families that they would experience the emotions of loss, sorrow, and grief during the Thanksgiving holiday and advised everyone to permit themselves these emotions. I cannot find similar discussions during the 1918 influenza pandemic. Indeed, the emotional script of the day was stoicism. See Mark Honigsbaum, "Regulating the 1918–19 Pandemic: Flu, Stoicism and the Northcliffe Press," *Medical History* 57, no. 2 (April 2013): 165–85, https://doi.org/10.1017/mdh.2012.101.

4. A specific example may be found in Efim Melamed and Gennady Estraikh, "O pogrome v Berdicheve," in *Archive of Jewish History* (Moscow: Rosspen, 2016), 8:162.

5. There is continuity with the aims of OZE, which I discuss later. For the earlier period, see Jockusch, "Chroniclers of Catastrophe." An-sky's *Ethnographic Program* had two thousand questions. See Avrutin et al., *Photographing the Jewish Nation*; Nathaniel Deutsch, *The Jewish Dark Continent: Life and Death in the Russian Pale of Settlement* (Cambridge, MA: Harvard University Press, 2011).

6. For the documents, see Engel, *Assassination of Symon Petliura and the Trial of Sholem Schwartzbard 1926–1927*.

7. For a discussion of Jewish vulnerability in this regard, see Golfo Alexopoulos, *Stalin's Outcasts: Aliens, Citizens, and the Soviet State, 1926–1936* (Ithaca, NY: Cornell University Press, 2003).

8. For a theoretical discussion of biopower's "positive relation" with life, see Catherine Mills, "Biopolitics and the Concept of Life," in *Biopower: Foucault and Beyond*, ed. Vernon W. Cisney and Nicolae Morar (Chicago: University of Chicago Press, 2016), 82–101. A discussion of the use of modern biopower to

marginalize the disabled in the early Soviet period can be found in Maria Cristina Galmarini-Kabala, *The Right to Be Helped* (Ithaca, NY: Cornell University Press, 2016), https://doi.org/10.7591/j.ctv177tj4p. See also Mogilner, *Race for the Future*.

9. Peter Holquist, "To Count, to Extract, and to Exterminate," in *A State of Nations*, ed. Ronald Grigor Suny (Oxford: Oxford University Press, 2001), 111–44.

10. This is the point of Marina Mogilner's project, which she kindly shared in personal communication with me and which is also available, in part, in Marina Mogilner, "ARA Relief Campaign in the Volga Region, Jewish Anthropometric Statistics, and the Scientific Promise of Integration," *Science in Context* 32 (2019): 5–24, https://doi.org/10.1017/S0269889719000012.

11. The center/periphery model has been discussed by Polly Zavadivker, "Contending with Horror: Jewish Aid Work in the Russian Civil War Pogroms," *Quest: Issues in Contemporary Jewish History* 15 (August 2019): 10–11, http://www.quest-cdecjournal.it/focus.php?id=414.

12. For a similar point without the use of the term hefker, see Miliakova, *Kniga pogromov*, xix.

13. Miliakova, *Kniga pogromov*, 290.

14. Mitchell Bryan Hart, *Social Science and the Politics of Modern Jewish Identity* (Stanford, CA: Stanford University, 2000).

15. For the history of Evobshchestkom, see Michael Beizer, *Relief in Times of Need: Russian Jewry and the Joint, 1914–24* (Bloomington, IN: Slavica, 2015), 97–137. For more detail, see also Marat Botvinnik, "Pervye shagi Evobshchestkoma v Sovetskoi Belarussii (1920–1923)," *Independent Israeli Site*, accessed July 11, 2020, https://belisrael.info/?p=832. See also Miliakova, *Kniga pogromov*, xxiii.

16. Heifetz, *Slaughter of the Jews in Ukraine in 1919*, ii.

17. For a study of the work of the JDC in the immediate postpogrom period, see Elissa Bemporad, "Parameters and Predicaments of Aiding Soviet Jews in the Interwar Years," in *The JDC at 100: A Century of Humanitarianism*, ed. Avinoam Patt et al. (Detroit: Wayne State University Press, 2019).

18. A discussion can be found in Zavadivker, "Contending with Horror." Succinct summaries of the various organizations and their documentary paper trails can be found in E. I. Melamed and M. S. Kupovetskii, eds., *Dokumenty po istorii i kul'ture evreev v arkhivakh Kieva: Putevoditel'* (Kyiv: Dukh i litera, 2006). I wish to thank the late Efim Melamed for his personal assistance with this history.

19. YIVO [Elias Tcherikower Archive] RG-80, folder 280: Relief Work, 1919–1921, Part I. Untitled, unsigned document.

20. Mogilner, "ARA Relief Campaign," 17.

21. Ian Hacking, "Biopower and the Avalanche of Printed Numbers," in *Biopower: Foucault and Beyond*, ed. Vernon W. Cisney and Nicolae Morar (Chicago: University of Chicago Press, 2016), 194–242.

22. Sergei Tretiakov, "To Be Continued," *October* 118 (Fall 2006): 51–56.

23. I base my account on Gur Alroey, "Demographers in the Service of the Nation: Liebmann Hersch, Jacob Lestschinsky, and the Early Study of Jewish Migration," *Jewish History* 20, no. 3–4 (2006): 265–82; Gennady Estraikh, "Jacob Lestschinsky: A Yiddishist Dreamer and Social Scientist," *Science in Context* 20, no. 2 (June 2007): 215–37, https://doi.org/10.1017/S0269889707001251.

24. Jacob Lestschinsky, "Nokh di pogromen," *Forverts*, June 9, 1921.

25. Alroey, "Demographers in the Service of the Nation," 277.

26. Jacob Lestschinsky, *Dos yidishe folk in tsifern* (Berlin: Klal farlag, 1922), 14.

27. Lestschinsky, "Nokh di pogromen."

28. Tsentral'nyi Derzhavnyy Arkhiv Vyshchykh Orhaniv Vlady ta Upravlinnya Ukrayiny, The Central State Archive of the Highest Organs of Government and Administration of Ukraine, Kyiv (henceforth TsDAVO) "Instruktsii," f. 2497, op. 3, d. 133, "Instruktsiia dlia vypolneniia anket."

29. TsDAVO, "Instruktsii," f. 2497, op. 3, d. 133, "Instruktsiia dlia vypolneniia anket."

30. Jockusch, "Chroniclers of Catastrophe," 149–50.

31. DAKO, f 3050, op. 1, d.87.

32. TsDAVO, f. 2497, op. 3, d. 133, "Instruktsii," (Statistiko-Informatsionnyi Otdel Vseukrevobkoma).

33. DAKO, f. 3050, op. 1, d. 123, "Protokol zasedaniia Statistiko-Informatsionnogo Otdela."

34. An example of a standard form and examples of completed forms can be found in Miliakova, *Kniga pogromov*, 502–19.

35. DAKO, f. 3050, op. 1, d. 730. Among the personnel documents is the note that he died in September 1921. There was no information about the cause of death.

36. For a succinct discussion of the controversies around the use of the term in modern Jewish history, see Engel, "What's in a Pogrom?" For an account of why the 1903 Kishinev pogrom became paradigmatic, see Zipperstein, *Pogrom*.

37. YIVO, RG80-f287, Part I, "O polozhenii v Kievskoi gub. k kontsu 1920 goda." For a succinct discussion of the destruction in Fastov, see Bemporad, *Legacy of Blood*, 28–30.

38. DAKO, f. 3050, op.1, d. 123, "Protokol zasedanii statisticheskogo otdela," August 23, 1921.

39. TsDAVO, f. 2497, op. 3, d. 133, "Instrukstii."

40. Discussed in the introduction. See also Vladimir P. Buldakov, "Freedom, Shortages, Violence: The Origins of the 'Revolutionary Anti-Jewish Pogrom' in Russia, 1917–1918," in Dekel-Chen et al., *Anti-Jewish Violence*, 74–91.

41. DAKO, f. 3050, op. 1, d. 123, "Doklad zaveduiushchogo informatsionnym otdelom komiteta pomoshchi postradavshim ot pogromov Rosssiskogo

Obshchestva Krasnogo Kresta (POKK)." This and other reports also appear in S. I. Gusev-Orenburgskii, *"Bagrovaia Kniga": Pogromy 1919–20 gg. na Ukrainie* (Kharbin: Izd-vo dal'nevostochnogo evreiskogo obshchestvennogo kom-ta pomoschchi sirotam-zhertvam pogromov, 1922).

42. Eric Lohr, "The Russian Army and the Jews: Mass Deportation, Hostages, and Violence during World War I," *Russian Review* 60, no. 3 (2001): 404–19; Lohr, "1915 and the War Pogrom Paradigm in the Russian Empire," in Dekel-Chen et al., *Anti-Jewish Violence*, 41–51; Budnitskii, *Rossiiskie Evrei mezhdu krasnymi i belymi*; Budnitskii, "Shots in the Back: On the Origin of the Anti-Jewish Pogroms of 1918–1921," in Avrutin and Murav, *Jews in the East European Borderlands*, 187–201.

43. DAKO, f. 3050, d. 1, op. 123. "Doklad zaveduiushchogo informatsionnym otdelom komiteta pomoshchi postradavshim ot pogromov ROKK."

44. Heifetz, *Slaughter of the Jews in Ukraine in 1919*, ii.

45. Miliakova, *Kniga pogromov*, 503.

46. Miliakova, *Kniga pogromov*, 515.

47. DAKO, f. 3050, op. 1, d. 94, "Ovruch."

48. TsDAVO, f. 2497, op. 3, d. 180, Report of Abram Moiseevich Bramson.

49. Heifetz, *Slaughter of the Jews in Ukraine in 1919*, 148. I have modified the English translation, using the Russian account found in DAKO, f. 3050, op. 1, d. 123. The archival document is a translation from the Yiddish, but the Yiddish is not included.

50. TsDAVO f. 2497, op.3, d. 133.

51. As Ann Stoler summarizes Derrida. See Ann Stoler, "Colonial Archives and the Arts of Governance on the Content in the Form," in *Archives, Documentation, and Institutions of Social Memory*, ed. Francis X. Blouin and William G. Rosenberg (Ann Arbor: University of Michigan Press, 2006), 269.

52. Alexandra Garbarini, "Document Volumes and the Status of Victim Testimony in the Era of the First World War and Its Aftermath," *Études Arméniennes Contemporaines* 5 (2015): 113–38, https://doi.org/10.4000/eac.782.

53. Tseli i zadaniia Foto-Biuro pri Komitetakh, DAKO, f. 3050, op.1, d. 87.

54. Protokol zasedaniia pri Evobshchestkome o finansirovanii zhertv pogromov, DAKO, f. 3050, op.1, d. 87.

55. Valérie Pozner, "Pogroms on Screen: Early 20th-Century Anti-Jewish Violence and the Limits of Representation," ed. Elissa Bemporad and Thomas C. Chopard, *Quest. Issues in Contemporary Jewish History* 15 (August 2019): 74–110.

56. DAKO, f. 3050, op. 1, d. 267. The name of the organization providing the aid: Ob"edinennaia komissiia individual'noi pomoshchi. The form indicates gender; this source only included forms filled out by women.

57. TsDAVO, f. 2497, op. 3, d. 133. "Vsem gubupolnomochennym i upolnomochennym po koloniiam."

58. For studies of the Kultur-Lige, see Moss, *Jewish Renaissance in the Russian Revolution*; Gennady Estraikh, "The Yiddish Kultur-Lige," in *Modernism in Kyiv: Jubilant Experimentation*, ed. Irene R. Makaryk and Virlana Tkacz (Toronto: University of Toronto Press, 2010), 197–217. See also Gennady Estraikh, Harriet Murav, and Myroslav Shkandrij, eds., *Building Modern Jewish Culture: The Yiddish Kultur-Lige* (Oxford: Legenda, 2023).

59. DAKO, f. 3050, op. 1, d. 105, Correspondence with Kultur-Lige.

60. DAKO, f. 3050, op. 1, d. 123, "Polozhenie na mestakh."

61. YIVO, RG-80, f. 287, "Evobkom reports, Part 3."

62. TsDAVO, f. 2497, op. 3. d. 197.

63. YIVO, Rg-80, folder 240, part 1.

64. Miliakova, *Kniga pogromov*, 875n 280.

65. Miliakova, *Kniga pogromov*, 164.

66. DAKO, f. 3050, op. 1, d. 240, "Pokazaniia otdel'nykh lits"; YIVO, Rg-80, folder 240, part 1.

67. DAKO, f. 3050, op. 1, d. 240, "Pokazanie syna sviashchennika (Georgii Kul'mannitskii)."

68. YIVO, RG-80, folder 240, Part 1, no author, dated September 12, 1919.

69. YIVO, RG-80, folder 240, Part 1, B. Broytman, October 1919.

70. DAKO, f. 3050, op. 1, d. 240. For material in English about rape in Pechora, see Avrutin and Bemporad, *Pogroms*, 157. For the topic of rape, in addition to Astashkevich, see Elissa Bemporad, "The Female Dimensions of Pogrom Violence, 1917–1921," in Avrutin and Elissa Bemporad, *Pogroms*, 150–75.

71. YIVO, RG-80, folder 240, part 1.

72. In Slovechno, as I discuss in chapter 5, the local priest agitated the local population against Jews. For a discussion of attitudes of the church and bibliographic references, see also Buldakov, "Freedom, Shortages, Violence." Velychenko finds that research on the question is inadequate; see *Life and Death in Revolutionary Ukraine*, 148.

73. DAKO, f. 3050, op. 1, d. 240, "Legenda."

74. I base my account on Reyzen, *Leksikon fun der yidisher literatur, prese un filologye*, 3:559–61.

75. TsDAVO, f. 348, opis 1, d. 108. Elisavetgrad. I am using the numbers provided by Oleg Budnitskii, *Russian Jews between the Reds and the Whites, 1917–1920* (Philadelphia: University of Pennsylvania Press, 2012), 218.

76. TsDAVO, f. 348, opis 1, d. 108. Elisavetgrad.

77. DAKO, f. 3050, opis. 1, d. 632; V. Iu. Gessen, *K istorii evreev: 300 let v Sankt-Peterburge* (St. Petersburg: SPb. RAN Nestor-Istoriia, 2005).

78. U.S. Holocaust Museum Archives, RG-31.057M, held in University Library, University of Illinois at Urbana-Champaign. Copy of DAKO, f. 3050, op. 1, d.123, Doklad tsentral'nomu Evobshchestkomu L. Ia. Ioffe.

79. Zachary Baker, Jonanthan Boyarin, and Jack Kugelmass, eds., *From a Ruined Garden: The Memorial Books of Polish Jewry*, 2nd ed. (Bloomington: Indiana University Press, 1998), 2, 19.

80. Cited by Beizer, *Relief in Times of Need*, 133.

81. The Hebrew-laden phrase in Yiddish: "di heymloze, aroysgeshtoysene fun zeyere khorev-gevorene yeshuvim, hobn zikh durkh yeyesh un hefker gelozt tsu der grenets" (YIVO R80 f 287 part 2, "Di zitsung in Kiever Yidgeskom").

82. TsDAVO, f. 2497, op. 3, d. 300, "Ocherk o travmaticheskoi epidemii sredi evreiksogo naselenii v 1919," M. S. Tarasenko. Gusev-Ortenburgskii cites this line without attribution in his *Crimson Book*.

83. Jean-François Lyotard, *The Differend: Phrases in Dispute*, trans. Georges Van den Abbeele (Minneapolis: University of Minnesota Press, 1988).

8. Children

1. For a discussion of these children as the basis for "normative" reframing, see Andy Byford, "Trauma and Pathology: Normative Crises and the Child Population in Late Tsarist Russia and the Early Soviet Union, 1904–1924," *Journal of the History of Childhood and Youth* 9, no. 3 (2016): 450–69, https://doi.org/10.1353/hcy.2016.0070. See also his *Science of the Child in Late Imperial and Early Soviet Russia* (Oxford: Oxford University Press, 2020), https://doi.org/10.1093/oso/9780198825050.001.0001.

2. Schneersohn, *Di katastrofale tsaytn un di vaksndike doyres*, 79. All citations from this edition and all translations are my own.

3. Nokhem Shtif, *The Pogroms in Ukraine, 1918–19: Prelude to the Holocaust*, translated and annotated with an introduction by Maurice Wolfthal (Cambridge: Open Book Publishers, 2020), 39.

4. I. M. Kovalsky, "Report on Belaia Tserkov," American JDC, Russian Unit, Kyiv, April 26, 1923, NY_AR2132_00403.

5. YIVO-f287-part 2, "Chislo polu-sirot" and "Chislo kruglykh sirot."

6. YIVO, RG80-f287, part 1, "O polozhenii v Kievskoi gub. k kontsu 1920 goda."

7. DAKO, f. 3050, d.1, opis. 248, Kievskaia raionnaia komissiia evreiskogo obshchestvennogo kommiteta po okazaniiu pomoshchi postradavshchikh pogromov, Informatsionno-statischikeskoi otdel, Oprosnye listy k otchetu o meditsinskogo pomoshchi. I examined completed questionnaires from approximately 150 institutions.

8. DAKO, f. 3050, d.1, opis. 248, Oprosnye listy k otchetu o meditsinskogo pomoshchi, RG-31.057M.0022.00000883, Anketa.

9. See Andy Byford, "Professional Cross-Dressing: Doctors in Education in Late Imperial Russia (1881–1917)," *Russian Review* 65, no. 4 (2006): 586–616;

Byford, "Trauma and Pathology"; Byford, "The Imperfect Child in Early Twentieth-Century Russia," *History of Education* 46, no. 5 (September 3, 2017): 595–617, https://doi.org/10.1080/0046760X.2017.1332248.

10. Galmarini-Kabala, *Right to Be Helped*, 79–82.

11. M. Zaslovskaya, "Report on the Work in Kiev during 1919–1920," JDC archives, Collection 1919–1920, NY AR191921 / 4 / 36 / 2 / 255.3.

12. GARF f. 1339, Evobshchestkom. Informatsionno-statischeskii otdel, Op. 1, d. 575, Tsikuliary Mediko-Sanitarnogo otdela o zapolnenii ankety obseldovaniia detskikh uchrezhdenii, January 10, 1922–August 22, 1922. I am very grateful to Marina Mogilner for sharing these materials with me.

13. Mogilner, "ARA Relief Campaign," 19.

14. Mogilner, "ARA Relief Campaign," 19.

15. An introduction to Levin and his work by Valerii Dymshits can be found in Doyvber Levin, *Desiat' vagonov* (Moscow: Knizhniki, 2016), 5–44. For a discussion that takes issue with Dymshits's argument, see Dubravka Ugresic, *Fox*, trans. Ellen Elias-Burcać and David Williams (Rochester, NY: Open Letter, 2018), 193–200.

16. For example, Gennady Gor mentions Levin among other members of OBERIU in Gennady Samoilovich Gor, *Zamedlenie vremeni*, accessed July 7, 2023, http://books.rusf.ru/unzip/add-on/xussr_gk/gor___g48.htm?3/5.

17. Doyvber Levin, *Vol'nye shtaty Slavichi* (n.p.: Salamandra P.V.V., 2013), 209. All citations are from this edition and all translations are my own.

18. Levin, *Desiat' vagonov*, 201.

19. As Valerii Dymshits points out, *Ten Wagons* contrasts the "bad old days" of care institutions in the late imperial period with the positive new beginnings of the early Soviet period.

20. Located on the premises of a prerevolutionary Jewish orphanage on the tenth line of Vasilevsky Ostrov in Leningrad, Orphanage No. 79 closed in 1938. See the introduction by Valerii Dymshits in Levin, *Desiat' vagonov*, 5–44. My discussion uses this edition. I am grateful to Valerii Dymshits for introducing me to this work.

21. For examples and discussions of Soviet factography, see Fore, "Operative Word in Soviet Factography"; Chuzhak, "Writer's Handbook." See also Papazian, *Manufacturing Truth*. A discussion of factography, Tretiakov, and ethnic literature can be found in Lee, *Ethnic Avant-Garde*, 83–118.

22. Levin, *Desiat' vagonov*, 65.

23. Levin, *Desiat' vagonov*, 124.

24. My discussion of this point relies on Dickerman, "Fact and the Photograph."

25. Levin, *Desiat' vagonov*, 95.

26. Levin, *Desiat' vagonov*, 193, 59.

27. Miliakova, *Kniga pogromov*, 612–13.

28. For a discussion of humiliation as a way of restoring social hierarchy, see Stefan Wiese, "'Spit Back with Bullets!' Emotions in Russia's Jewish Pogroms, 1881–1905," *Geschichte und Gesellschaft* 39 (2013): 472–501.
29. Miliakova, *Kniga pogromov*, 614.
30. Schneersohn, *Di katastrofale tsaytn un di vaksndike doyres*, 2.
31. Y. Rubin, "Prof. Dr. F. Schneersohn: Di katastrofale tsaytn un di vaksndike doyres," *Literarishe bleter*, no. 33 (December 19, 1924): 6.
32. The question of pogroms is largely absent from studies that examine the emotions in Russia and Eastern Europe in this period. See for example, Jan Plamper, "Emotional Turn? Feelings in Russian History and Culture," *Slavic Review* 68, no. 2 (Summer 2009): 229–37; Mark Steinberg, "Emotions History in Eastern Europe," in *Doing Emotions History*, ed. Susan J. Matt and Peter N. Stearns (Champaign: University of Illinois Press, 2013); Steinberg, *Petersburg Fin de Siècle* (New Haven, CT: Yale University Press, 2011).
33. For Schneersohn's biography and discussions of his scientific and creative work, see Alyssa Masor, "The Evolution of the Literary Neo-Hasid" (PhD diss., Columbia University, 2011); Eli Rubin, "Traveling and Traversing Chabad's Literary Paths: From Likutei Torah to Khayim Gravitser and Beyond," *In Geveb: A Journal of Yiddish Studies*, October 9, 2018; David Freis, "Ecstatic Expeditions: Fischl Schneersohn's 'Science of Man' between Modern Psychology and Jewish Mysticism," *Transcultural Psychiatry* 57, no. 6 (2020): 775–85, https://doi.org/10.1177/1363461520952625.
34. Freis, "Ecstatic Expeditions," 2.
35. The Yiddish press took notice of his work. A review of his 1935 study on play therapy was published in the Warsaw Yiddish paper *Der moment*. See Y. Gelbfarb, "Prof. Fischel Schneersohn. Intime heyl-pedogogik," *Der moment*, September 6, 1935.
36. The studies by Galmarini and Byford that I rely on in this chapter omit all discussion of Schneersohn as well as the treatment of pogromed children.
37. Scientists and educators in the late imperial and early Soviet period studied children's autobiographies, survey questions, and, to some extent, their creative work in response to World War 1. See A. A. Sal'nikova, *Rossiiskoe detstvo v XX veke: Istoriia, teoriia i praktika issledovaniia* (Kazan': Kazanskii gosudarstvennyi universitet, 2007).
38. Schneersohn, *Di katastrofale tsaytn un di vaksndike doyres*, 6.
39. Fischel Schneersohn, *Psikhologiia intimnoi zhizni rebenka* (Berlin: Grani, 1923), 377.
40. For discussions of methodologies in the late czarist and early Soviet period, see Sal'nikova, *Rossiiskoe detstvo v XX veke*; Byford, *Science of the Child in Late Imperial and Early Soviet Russia*; Schneersohn, *Psikhologiia intimnoi zhizni rebenka*. In his Yiddish study, *Catastrophic Times*, Schneersohn cites the work of

the German researcher Rudolph Schulze, who used photography and cinema to produce and record emotional responses. For a discussion, see Claudia Wassman, "The Science of Emotion: Studying Emotions in Germany, France, and the US, 1860–1920" (PhD diss., University of Chicago, 2005), 226–35.

41. In which Max Weinreich took part; see Barbara Kirshenblatt-Gimblett, "Coming of Age in the Thirties: Max Weinreich, Edward Sapir, and Jewish Social Science," *YIVO Annual* 23 (1996): 1–103.

42. See Théodule Armand Ribot, *The Psychology of the Emotions* (London: Walter Scott, 1897), 1–24. An analysis of Ribot including this point can be found in Wassman, "Science of Emotion," 113–15.

43. Schneersohn, *Di katastrofale tsaytn un di vaksndike doyres*, 24.

44. Sal'nikova refers to the psychologist M. Rubinshtein, who published a study based on children's autobiographies and diaries in 1928, *Iunost' po dnevnikam i avtobiograficheskim zapisiam*. I am grateful to Andy Byford for pointing this out to me.

45. Cathy Caruth has argued for the universality of trauma; see *Unclaimed Experience: Trauma, Narrative, and History* (Baltimore: Johns Hopkins University Press, 1996). Andreas Huyssen describes the "problematic privileging of the traumatic dimension of life" in *Present Pasts: Urban Palimpsests and the Politics of Memory* (Stanford, CA: Stanford University Press, 2003), 8. Ruth Leys provides a historically rich critique of the present tendency to focus solely on Freud and Caruth; see *Trauma: A Genealogy* (Chicago: University of Chicago Press, 2000). For a succinct overview of the field of trauma studies, see Antonio Traverso and Mick Broderick, "Interrogating Trauma: Towards a Critical Trauma Studies," *Continuum* 24, no. 1 (February 2010): 3–15, https://doi.org/10.1080/10304310903461270.

46. I am relying on Leys, *Trauma*, 4. For a study of Russian military doctors and traumatized soldiers during World War I, see Jan Plamper, "Fear: Soldiers and Emotion in Early Twentieth-Century Russian Military Psychology," *Slavic Review* 68, no. 2 (2009): 259–83, https://doi.org/10.2307/27697958.

47. Schneersohn, *Di katastrofale tsaytn un di vaksndike doyres*, 101.

48. He uses the German word *Erschütterung* in Hebrew characters; see 115.

49. Schneersohn, *Di katastrofale tsaytn un di vaksndike doyres*, 100–101.

50. See Byford, *Science of the Child in Late Imperial and Early Soviet Russia*, 70–77, 180–81.

51. Schneersohn, *Di katastrofale tsaytn un di vaksndike doyres*, 25, 49.

52. Byford, *Science of the Child in Late Imperial and Early Soviet Russia*, 144.

53. Schneersohn, *Di katastrofale tsaytn un di vaksndike doyres*, 206.

54. Schneersohn, *Di katastrofale tsaytn un di vaksndike doyres*, 139.

55. Schneersohn, *Di katastrofale tsaytn un di vaksndike doyres*, 172.

56. Schneersohn, *Di katastrofale tsaytn un di vaksndike doyres*, 25.

57. Schneersohn, *Di katastrofale tsaytn un di vaksndike doyres*, 149.

58. Schneersohn, *Di katastrofale tsaytn un di vaksndike doyres*, 223–24.

59. Fischel Schneersohn, *Studies in Psycho-Expedition: Fundamentals of the Psychological Science of Man and a Theory of Nervousness*, trans. Herman Frank (New York: Science of Man Press, 1929), 86n1.

60. William James, *Principles of Psychology*, vol. 1 (New York: Henry Holt, 1918), 261–62. William Reddy's definition of emotion as "activations of thought material" that cannot be subsumed within the ordinary procedures of attention resembles James's definition of "fringe consciousness." Reddy does not discuss James in his study, William Reddy, *The Navigation of Feeling: A Framework for the History of Emotions* (Cambridge: Cambridge University Press, 2004). Maria Todorova's discussion of the history of emotions pointed me toward this parallel. See Maria Todorova, *The Lost World of Socialists at Europe's Margins: Imagining Utopia, 1870s–1920s* (London: Bloomsbury Academic, 2020), 172–73.

61. William L. Roller and Donald A. Shaskan, *Paul Schilder, Mind Explorer* (New York: Human Sciences Press, 1985), 65, https://catalog.hathitrust.org/Record/000577195.

62. Schneersohn, *Di katastrofale tsaytn un di vaksndike doyres*, 71.

63. Schneersohn, *Di katastrofale tsaytn un di vaksndike doyres*, 77.

64. Here and throughout, Schneersohn, *Di katastrofale tsaytn un di vaksndike doyres*, 72.

65. Schneersohn added three layers of consciousness in his subsequent work, *Studies in Pscyho-Expedition*: the spherical intimate, spherical primitive, and normal consciousness.

66. Schneersohn, *Psikhologiia intimnoi zhizni rebenka*, 157.

67. Nakhmen Mayzel, "A shmues mit professor Sniurson," *Literarishe bleter*, no. 13 (April 1, 1927): 244.

68. See Freis, "Ecstatic Expeditions," 8.

69. Schneersohn, *Di katastrofale tsaytn un di vaksndike doyres*, 237.

70. Freis, "Ecstatic Expeditions," 6.

71. Fischel Schneersohn, *Khayim gravitser (di geshikhte fun dem gefalenem): Fun dem Khabadisher velt* (Berlin: Yidisher literarisher farlag, 1922). Two more volumes followed. I am grateful to Ri J. Turner, Maison de la culture yiddish–Bibliothèque Medem in Paris, for discussing this work with me.

72. Scholem's discussion of kabala notes the "well-known Yiddish novel," which describes the acosmic ecstatic union with God, pointing out that it is not typical of Jewish mysticism (Gershom Scholem, *Major Trends in Jewish Mysticism* [New York: Schocken Books, 1971], 123).

73. Schneersohn, *Khayim gravitser*, 17.

74. I am paraphrasing from Schneersohn, *Khayim gravitser*, 18.

75. Schneersohn, *Khayim gravitser*, 19.

76. Schneersohn, *Khayim gravitser*, 19.

Conclusion

1. Carolyn Forché, *The Country between Us* (New York: Harper Perennial, 2019).

2. Eve L. Ewing, *1919* (Chicago: Haymarket Books, 2019), 59, http://www.vlebooks.com/vleweb/product/openreader?id=none&isbn=9780141991986.

3. I am borrowing language about "what makes the other strange not only to me but also to him or herself" from Santner, *On Creaturely Life*, xiii.

4. Cited in Ewing, *1919*, 39.

5. GAZhO, Gosudarstvennyi Arkhiv Zhitomirskoi Oblasti (Zhitomir State Archives), Volynskoi gubnerniia revtribunal, Fond 1820, opis 5, delo 128.

6. Cited by Ewing, *1919*, 54.

7. Ewing, *1919*, 54.

8. Kvitko, *1919*, 146.

9. Schneersohn, *Di katastrofale tsaytn un di vaksndike doyres*, 25.

10. From Linda Hogan, *DARK. SWEET.: New and Selected Poems* (Minneapolis, MN: Coffee House Press, 2014). Used with the permission of Coffee House Press. Published in Poem-a-Day on March 6, 2021, by the Academy of American Poets.

WORKS CITED

Archival Collections

Derzhavnyi arkhiv Kyïvs'koï oblasti (DAKO)
    Fond 3050 Kievskaia raionnaia komissia Evreiskogo obshchestvennogo komiteta po okazaniiu pomoshchi zhertvam pogromov (Documents of the Kiev Oblast' Committee for Relief to Victims of Pogroms)
Gosudarstvennyi arkhiv Zhitomirskoi oblasti (GAZHO)
    Fond 270 Skhematicheskie plany gorodov i mestechek
    Fond 1820 Volynskii gubnernskii revtribunal
Institute for Jewish Research Archives (YIVO)
    RG 201, Folder 1009, Papers of Abraham Liessin
    RG 80, Elias Tcherikower Archive
JDC archives, Collection 1919–1920
Rossiiskii gosudarstvennyi arkhiv literatury i iskusstva, Russian State Archive of Literature and Art (RGALI)
Tsentral'nyi derzhavnyi arkhiv hromads'kykh orhanizatsii Ukrainy (Central State Archive of Public Organizations of Ukraine) (TsDAHO)
    Fond 269 Kollektsiia dokumentov "Ukrainskii muzei v Prage"
Tsentral'nyi derzhavnyi arkhiv vyshchykh orhaniv vlady ta upravlinnya Ukrayiny (The Central State Archive of the Highest Organs of Government and Administration of Ukraine) (TsDAVO)
    Fond 348
    Fond 2497 Vseukrainskii Evreiskii Obshchestvennyi Komitet po okazaniiu pomoshchi postradavshim ot pogromov. [Meditsinskii otdel]
    Fond 3301 Vseukrainskii Tsentral'nyi Komitet pomoshchi postradavshim ot pogromov pri Ministerstve evreiskikh del UNR

Books and Articles

Abend-David, Dror. "Gender Benders and Unrequited Offerings: Two Hebrew Poems by Rachel Bluwstein-Sela and Dovid Hofshteyn." *Prooftexts* 31, no. 3 (Fall 2011): 210–28.

Abramson, Henry. *A Prayer for the Government: Ukrainians and Jews in Revolutionary Times, 1917–1920*. Cambridge, MA: Ukrainian Research Institute and Center for Jewish Studies, Harvard University Press, 1999.

Agamben, Giorgio. *Homo Sacer: Sovereign Power and Bare Life*. Translated by Daniel Heller-Roazen. Stanford, CA: Stanford University Press, 1998.

———. *Stasis: Civil War as a Political Paradigm*. Translated by Nicolas Heron. Stanford, CA: Stanford University Press, 2015.

———. *The Use of Bodies*. Translated by Adam Kotsko. Stanford, CA: Stanford University Press, 2020.

———. *The Use of Bodies Homo Sacer*. Translated by Adam Kotsko. Stanford, CA: Stanford University Press, 2016.

Ahad Ha'am, Simon Dubnow, Ben-Ami, Y. Ch. Ravnitsky, and Hayyim Nahman Bialik. "Proclamation of the Hebrew Writers' Union." In *The Literature of Destruction: Jewish Responses to Catastrophe*, edited by David G. Roskies. Philadelphia: Jewish Publication Society, 1988.

Akulov, Mikhail. "War without Fronts: Atamans and Commissars in Ukraine, 1917–1919." PhD diss., Harvard University, 2013.

Albeck, Shalom, and Menachem Elon. "Hefker." In *Encyclopaedia Judaica*, 8:752–55. n.p.: Gale ebooks, 2007.

Aleichem, Sholem. *Some Laughter, Some Tears: Tales from the Old and the New*. Translated by Curt Leviant. New York: G. P. Putnam's Sons, 1968.

Alexopoulos, Golfo. *Stalin's Outcasts: Aliens, Citizens, and the Soviet State, 1926–1936*. Ithaca, NY: Cornell University Press, 2003.

Alroey, Gur. "Demographers in the Service of the Nation: Liebmann Hersch, Jacob Lestschinsky, and the Early Study of Jewish Migration." *Jewish History* 20, no. 3–4 (2006): 265–82.

Altshuler, Mordechai. "Itsik Kipnis: The 'White Crow' of Soviet Yiddish Literature." *Jews in Russia and Eastern Europe* 52/53 (2004): 68–167.

Altshuler, Mordechai, and Y. Lifshits. *Briv fun yidishe sovetishe shraybers*. Jerusalem: Hebreyisher Universitet in Yerusholayim, 1979.

Aseyev, Stanislav. *V izoliatsi: Statti*. Kyiv: Liuta sprava, 2018.

Astashkevich, Irina. *Gendered Violence: Jewish Women in the Pogroms of 1917–1921*. Boston: Academic Studies Press, 2018.

Avrutin, Eugene M. "Pogroms in Russian History." *Kritika: Explorations in Russian and Eurasian History* 14, no. 3 (2013): 585–98.

Avrutin, Eugene M., and Elissa Bemporad, eds. *Pogroms: A Documentary History*. Oxford: Oxford University Press, 2021.

Avrutin, Eugune M., Valerii Dymshtis, Alexander Ivanov, Alexander Lvov, Harriet Murav, and Alla Sokolova. *Photographing the Jewish Nation: Pictures from S. An-Sky's Ethnographic Expeditions*. Waltham, MA: Brandeis University Press, 2009.

Bachelard, Gaston. *The Poetics of Space*. Translated by Maria Jolas. Boston: Beacon Press, 1994.

Baker, Zachary, Jonanthan Boyarin, and Jack Kugelmass, eds. *From a Ruined Garden: The Memorial Books of Polish Jewry*. 2nd ed. Bloomington: Indiana University Press, 1998.

Barskova, Polina. *Beseiged Leningrad: Aesthetic Responses to Urban Disaster*. DeKalb: Northern Illinois University Press, 2017.

Bartov, Omer, and Eric D. Weitz, eds. *Shatterzone of Empires: Coexistence and Violence in the German, Habsburg, Russian, and Ottoman Borderlands*. Bloomington: Indiana University Press, 2013.

Barzilai, Maya. *GOLEM : Modern Wars and Their Monsters*. New York: New York University Press, 2020.

Beizer, Michael. *Relief in Times of Need: Russian Jewry and the Joint, 1914–24*. Bloomington, IN: Slavica, 2015.

Bel'skaia, L. L. "Ia ukho prilozhil k zemle." *Russkaia rech'* 6 (2013): 25–27.

Bemporad, Elissa. "The Female Dimensions of Pogrom Violence, 1917–1921." In *Pogroms: A Documentary History*, edited by Eugene M. Avrutin and Elissa Bemporad, 150–75. Oxford: Oxford University Press, 2021.

———. *Legacy of Blood: Jews, Pogroms, and Ritual Murder in the Lands of the Soviets*. New York: Oxford University Press, 2019.

———. "Parameters and Predicaments of Aiding Soviet Jews in the Interwar Years." In *The JDC at 100: A Century of Humanitarianism*, edited by Avinoam Patt, Atian Grossmann, Linda G. Levi, and Maud S. Mandel, 41–60. Detroit: Wayne State University Press, 2019.

Bemporad, Elissa, and Thomas Chopard. "The Pogroms of the Russian Civil War at 100: New Trends, New Sources." *Quest: Issues in Contemporary Jewish History* 15 (August 2019): v–xix.

Ben-Porat, Ziva. "Disguised Wrath and Hidden Heresy: On Bialik's 'Dance of Despair.'" *Prooftexts* 6, no. 3 (1986): 221–37.

Benton, Gregor. *Chinese Migrants and Internationalism: Forgotten Histories, 1917–1945*. New York: Routledge, 2007.

Bergelson, David. "The Beginning of December 1919." In *From Revolution to Repression: Soviet Yiddish Writing 1917–1952*, edited by Joseph Sherman, 61–65. Nottingham: Five Leaves Publications, 2012.

———. "Belles-Lettres and the Social Order." In *David Bergelson: From Modernism to Socialist Realism*, edited by Joseph Sherman and Gennady Estraikh, 338–45. Oxford: Legenda, 2007.

———. "Der gesheener oyfbrokh." *Milgroym* 1 (1922): 41–43.

———. *Droyb*. Vol. 4. 6 vols. Berlin: Wostok, 1923.

———. "Kipnis's Khadoshim un teg." *Literarishe bleter*, no. 20 (July 19, 1929): 558–60.

Bergholz, Max. *Violence as a Generative Force: Identity, Nationalism, and Memory in a Balkan Community*. Ithaca, NY: Cornell University Press, 2016.

Bergson, Henri. *Laughter: An Essay on the Meaning of the Comic*. Translated by Cloudesley Brereton. New York: Macmillan, 1914.

Bialik, Hayyim Nahman. *Shirim*. Berlin: Klal farlag, 1922.

Biehl, João. *Vita: Life in a Zone of Social Abandonment*. Berkeley: University of California Press, 2005.

Bilous, Larysa. "Re-Thinking the Revolution in Ukraine: The Jewish Experience, 1917–1921." *Slavic Review* 78, no. 4 (2019): 949–56.

Blidstein, Gerald J. "Notes on Hefker Bet-Din in Talmudic and Medieval Law." *Dine Israel* IV (1973): xxxiv–xlix.

Blok, Alexander. "O naznachenii poeta (Blok)." February 28, 2011. Accessed July 29, 2023. https://arheve.org/read/blok-aa-1/o-literature-o-naznachenii-poeta.

Bloshteyn, Hersh. "Gedanken vegn der moderner dikhtung." In *Vispe: Literarisher zamlbukh*, 26–29. Kaunas: Kultur-Lige Lite, 1923.

Bodo, Bela. *The White Terror: Antisemitic and Political Violence in Hungary, 1919–1921*. New York: Routledge, 2021.

Borislavov, Radoslav. "'I Know What Motivation Is': The Politics of Emotion and Viktor Shklovskii's Sentimental Rhetoric." *Slavic Review* 74, no. 4 (2015): 785–807.

———. "Viktor Shklovskii—Between Art and Life." PhD diss., University of Chicago, 2011.

Borokhov, Ber. *Po'ale Tsiyon shriftn*. Vol. 2. New York: Jewish National Workers' Alliance, 1928. http://books.google.com/books?id=4sMkAQAAMAAJ.

Botvinnik, Marat. "Pervye shagi Evobshchestkoma v Sovetskoi Belarussii (1920–1923)." Independent Israeli Site. Accessed July 11, 2020. https://belisrael.info/?p=832.

Boym, Svetlana. *Another Freedom: The Alternative History of an Idea*. Chicago: University of Chicago Press, 2010.

———. "The Off-Modern Turn: Modernist Humanism and Vernacular Cosmopolitanism in Shklovsky and Mandelshtam." In *Jews and the Ends of Theory*, edited by Shai Ginsburg, Martin Land, and Jonanthan Boyarin, 164–86. New York: Fordham University Press, 2018.

———. "Poetics and Politics of Estrangement: Victor Shklovsky and Hannah Arendt." *Poetics Today* 26, no. 4 (December 1, 2005): 581–611. https://doi.org/10.1215/03335372-26-4-581.

Braun, Alisa. "Kadya Molodowsky." In *Dictionary of Literary Biography: Writers in Yiddish*, edited by Joseph Sherman, 333:188–94. Detroit: Gale, 2007.
Brenner, Naomi. *Lingering Bilingualism: Modern Hebrew and Yiddish Literatures in Contact*. Syracuse, NY: Syracuse University Press, 2015.
———. "Milgroym, Rimon and Interwar Jewish Bilingualism." *Journal of Jewish Identities* 7, no. 1 (January 2014): 23–48.
Budnitskii, Oleg. *Rossiiskie evrei mezhdu krasnymi i belymi*. Moscow: Rosspen, 2005.
———. *Russian Jews between the Reds and the Whites, 1917–1920*. Philadelphia: University of Pennsylvania Press, 2012.
———. "Shots in the Back: On the Origin of the Anti-Jewish Pogroms of 1918–1921." In *Jews in the East European Borderlands: Essays in Honor of John D. Klier*, edited by Eugune M. Avrutin and Harriet Murav, 187–201. Boston: Academic Studies Press, 2012.
Buldakov, Vladimir P. "Freedom, Shortages, Violence: The Origins of the 'Revolutionary Anti-Jewish Pogrom' in Russia, 1917–1918." In *Anti-Jewish Violence: Rethinking the Pogrom in East European History*, edited by Jonathan Dekel-Chen, David Gaunt, Natan M. Meir, and Israel Bartal, 74–91. Bloomington: Indiana University Press, 2011.
Bunin, Ivan Alekseevich. Okaiannye dni, 1925. Lib.ru/klassika. Accessed July 27, 2023. http://az.lib.ru/b/bunin_i_a/text_2262.shtml.
Butler, Judith, and Athena Athanasiou. *Dispossession: The Performative in the Political*. Cambridge: Polity, 2015.
Byford, Andy. "The Imperfect Child in Early Twentieth-Century Russia." *History of Education* 46, no. 5 (September 3, 2017): 595–617. https://doi.org/10.1080/0046760X.2017.1332248.
———. "Professional Cross-Dressing: Doctors in Education in Late Imperial Russia (1881–1917)." *Russian Review* 65, no. 4 (2006): 586–616.
———. *Science of the Child in Late Imperial and Early Soviet Russia*. Oxford: Oxford University Press, 2020. https://doi.org/10.1093/oso/9780198825050.001.0001.
———. "Trauma and Pathology: Normative Crises and the Child Population in Late Tsarist Russia and the Early Soviet Union, 1904–1924." *Journal of the History of Childhood and Youth* 9, no. 3 (2016): 450–69. https://doi.org/10.1353/hcy.2016.0070.
Cannon, Christopher, and Matthew Rubery. "Introduction to Aurality and Literacy." *PMLA (Publications of the Modern Language Association of America)* 135, no. 2 (March 2020): 350–56.
Caruth, Cathy. *Unclaimed Experience: Trauma, Narrative, and History*. Baltimore: Johns Hopkins University Press, 1996.

Cherikover, Elias. *Di Ukrainer pogromen in yor 1919*. New York: YIVO Institute for Jewish Research, 1965.

Chuzhak, Nikolai. "Writer's Handbook." Translated by Devin Fore and Douglas Greenfield. *October* 118 (Fall 2006): 78–94.

Cisney, Vernon W., and Nicolae Morar, eds. *Biopower: Foucault and Beyond*. Chicago: University of Chicago Press, 2016.

Curtis, James. "Bergson and Russian Formalism." *Comparative Literature* 28, no. 2 (1976): 109–21.

Damman, Catherine. "Dance, Sound, Word: The 'Hundred-Jointed Body' in Zurich Dada Performance." *Germanic Review: Literature, Culture, Theory* 91, no. 4 (October 2016): 352–66. https://doi.org/10.1080/00168890.2016.1223485.

Das, Veena. *Life and Words: Violence and the Descent into the Ordinary*. Berkeley: University of California Press, 2007.

Davies, Jessie. "Thematics and Stylistics in Esenin's Poetry." *Canadian-American Slavic Studies* 32, no. 4 (1998): 295–317.

Deutsch, Nathaniel. *The Jewish Dark Continent: Life and Death in the Russian Pale of Settlement*. Cambridge, MA: Harvard University Press, 2011.

Dickerman, Leah. "The Fact and the Photograph." *October* 118 (Fall 2006): 132–52.

Dobrushin, Yekhezkel. "Dray dikhter." In *Oyfgang*, 1:73–98. Kyiv: Kultur-Lige, 1919.

Dubilet, Alex. *The Self-Emptying Subject: Kenosis and Immanence, Medieval to Modern*. New York: Fordham University Press, 2018.

Dwyer, Anne. "Revivifying Russia: Literature, Theory, and Empire in Viktor Shklovskii's Civil War Writings." *Slavonica* 15, no. 1 (2009): 11–31.

———. "Standstill as Extinction: Viktor Shklovsky's Poetics and Politics of Movement in the 1920s and 1930s." *PMLA (Publications of the Modern Language Association of America)* 131, no. 2 (March 2016): 269–88. https://doi.org/10.1632/pmla.2016.131.2.269.

Edwards, Ryan. "From the Depths of Patagonia: The Ushuaia Penal Colony and the Nature of 'The End of the World.'" *Hispanic American Historical Review* 94, no. 2 (May 2014): 272–302.

Eisenberg, S. *Milkhome-shtoyb: Zikhroynes fun a litvishn polet, 1915–1917*. Klerksdorf: S. Eisenberg, 1935. http://archive.org/details/nybc201644.

Eliashev, Yisroel. *Geklibene verk*. New York: Cyco, 1953.

Emerson, Caryl. "Shklvosky's ostranenie, Bakhtin's vnenakhodimost'." *Poetics Today* 26, no. 4 (2005): 637–64.

Emerson, R. Guy. "Living Death in Mexico." In *Necropolitics*. Studies of the Americas. Cham: Palgrave Macmillan, 2019. https://doi.org/10.1007/978-3-030-12302-4_1.

Engel, David. *The Assassination of Symon Petliura and the Trial of Scholem Schwartzbard 1926–1927: A Selection of Documents*. Gottingen: Vandenhoeck and Ruprecht, 2016.

———. "What's in a Pogrom? European Jews in the Age of Violence." In *Anti-Jewish Violence: Rethinking the Pogrom in East European History*, edited by Jonathan Dekel-Chen, David Gaunt, Natan M. Meir, and Israel Bartal, 19–37. Bloomington: Indiana University Press, 2011.

Engelstein, Laura. *Russia in Flames: War, Revolution, Civil War 1914–1921*. Oxford: Oxford University Press, 2018.

Erik, Maks. "Di sphrakh funem yidishn ekspresyanizm." *Albatros* 2 (1922): 17.

Erlich, Victor. *Modernism and Revolution: Russian Literature in Transition*. Cambridge, MA: Harvard University Press, 1994.

Erlmann, Veit. *Reason and Resonance : A History of Modern Aurality*. New York: Zone Books, 2014.

Estraikh, Gennady. *In Harness: Yiddish Writers' Romance with Communism*. Judaic Traditions in Literature, Music, and Art. Syracuse, NY: Syracuse University Press, 2005.

———. "Jacob Lestschinsky: A Yiddishist Dreamer and Social Scientist." *Science in Context* 20, no. 2 (June 2007): 215–37. https://doi.org/10.1017/S0269889707001251.

———. "The Kharkiv Yiddish Literary World, 1920s-mid-1930s." *East European Jewish Affairs* 32, no. 2 (2002): 70–88.

———. "Kvitko, Leyb." In *YIVO Encyclopedia of Jews in Eastern Europe*. YIVO, 2010. https://yivoencyclopedia.org/article.aspx/Kvitko_Leyb.

———. "The Yiddish Kultur-Lige." In *Modernism in Kyiv: Jubilant Experimentation*, edited by Irene R. Makaryk and Virlana Tkacz, 197–217. Toronto: University of Toronto Press, 2010.

Estraikh, Gennady, Kerstin Hoge, and Mikhail Krutikov, eds. *Uncovering the Hidden: The Works and Life of Der Nister*. Oxford: Legenda, 2014.

Estraikh, Gennady, Harriet Murav, and Myroslav Shkandrij, eds. *Building Modern Jewish Culture: The Yiddish Kultur-Lige*. Oxford: Legenda, 2023.

Ewing, Eve L. *1919*. Chicago: Haymarket Books, 2019. http://www.vlebooks.com/vleweb/product/openreader?id=none&isbn=9780141991986.

Eyal, Gil. *The Disenchantment of the Orient: Expertise in Arab Affairs and the Israeli State*. Stanford, CA: Stanford University Press, 2006.

Faygenberg, Rokhl. *A pinkes fun a toyter shtot*. Warsaw: Akhisfer, 1926.

Fermentto-Tzaisler, Julia. "Flesh and Blood: The Metaphorics of Meat in Modern Jewish Culture." PhD diss., University of California, San Diego, 2020.

Finkin, Jordan. "The Consolation of Sadness: The Curious Exile of Dovid Hofshteyn's *Troyer*." In *Leket: Yiddish Studies Today*, edited by Marion Aptroot,

Efrat Gal-Ed, and Roland Gruschka, 1:91–107. Dusseldorf: Dusseldorf University Press, 2012.
———. "Constellating Hebrew and Yiddish Avant-Gardes." *Journal of Modern Jewish Studies* 8, no. 1 (2009): 1–22.
———. *An Inch or Two of Time: Time and Space in Jewish Modernisms*. University Park, TX: Penn State University Press, 2015.
Forché, Carolyn. *The Country between Us*. New York: Harper Perennial, 2019.
———. *What You Have Heard Is True: A Memoir of Witness and Resistance*. New York: Penguin, 2020.
Fore, Devin. "Introduction." *October* 118 (Fall 2006): 3–10.
———. "The Operative Word in Soviet Factography." *October* 118 (Fall 2006): 95–131.
Foucault, Michel. *The Archeology of Knowledge & The Discourse on Language*. Translated by A. M. Sheridan Smith. New York: Harper Colophon Books, 1972.
Fowler, Mayhill. "Introduction: Ukraine in Revolution, 1917–1922." *Slavic Review* 78, no. 4 (2019): 931–34.
Freis, David. "Ecstatic Expeditions: Fischl Schneersohn's 'Science of Man' between Modern Psychology and Jewish Mysticism." *Transcultural Psychiatry* 57, no. 6 (2020): 775–85. https://doi.org/10.1177/1363461520952625.
Fretwell, Erica. "Stillness Is a Move: Helen Keller and the Kinaesthetics of Autobiography." *American Literary History* 25, no. 3 (2013): 563–87.
Frug, S. G. *Stikhotvoreniia*. Vol. 2. St. Petersburg: Isidor Gol'dberg, 1897.
———. "Zamd un shtern." In *Neginot Yisroel: Liedersammlung*, edited by Abraham Bernstein, 7. Vilnius, 1898.
Frug, S. G., and Yàakov Levin. *Oysgeveylte shriftn: Far idishe shulen un heymen; Mit der biografye fun Frugn un a verterbikhl fun di shverere verter*. New York: Hibru Publishing, n.d.
Gal-Ed, Efrat. *Niemandssprache Itzik Manger—ein europäischer Dichter*. Berlin: Jüdischer Verlag im Suhrkamp, 2016.
———. "Yiddishland: A Promise of Belonging." *Journal of Modern Jewish Studies* 20, no. 2 (2021): 141–69.
Galmarini-Kabala, Maria Cristina. *The Right to Be Helped*. Ithaca, NY: Cornell University Press, 2016. https://doi.org/10.7591/j.ctv177tj4p.
Garbarini, Alexandra. "Document Volumes and the Status of Victim Testimony in the Era of the First World War and Its Aftermath." *Études Arméniennes Contemporaines* 5 (2015): 113–38. https://doi.org/10.4000/eac.782.
Garrett, Leah, and Lamed Shapiro. Introduction to *The Cross and Other Jewish Stories*, edited by Leah Garrett, ix–xxxii. New Haven, CT: Yale University Press, 2007. http://www.jstor.org/stable/j.ctt1npntv.4.
Gaunt, David. *Massacres, Resistance, Protectors: Muslim-Christian Relations in Eastern Anatolia during World War I*. Piscataway, NJ: Gorgias Press, 2006.

Gelbfarb, Y. "Prof. Fischel Schneersohn. Intime heyl-pedogogik." *Der moment*, September 6, 1935.
Geller, Jay. *Bestiarium Judaicum: Unnatural Histories of the Jews*. New York: Fordham University Press, 2017.
Gessen, V. Iu. *K istorii evreev: 300 let v Sankt-Peterburge*. St. Petersburg: SPb. RAN Nestor-Istoriia, 2005.
Givoni, Michal. "Witnessing/Testimony." *Mafte'akh*, no. 2e (Winter 2011): 147–69. http://mafteakh.tau.ac.il/en/issue-2e-winter-2011/witnessingtestimony/.
Glaser, Amelia. "From Jewish Jesus to Black Christ: Race Violence in Leftist Yiddish Poetry." *Studies in American Jewish Literature* 34, no. 1 (2015): 44–69.
———. *Songs in Dark Times: Yiddish Poetry of Struggle from Scottsboro to Palestine*. Cambridge, MA: Harvard University Press, 2020.
Glatshteyn, Yankev, A. Leyeles, and N. Minkov. "In zikh." In *In zikh: A zamlung introspektive lider*, edited by M. Apranel, 5–27. New York: M. N. Mayzel, 1920.
Golder, Ben. "Foucault and the Genealogy of Pastoral Power." *Radical Philosophy Review* 10, no. 2 (2007): 157–76.
Gor, Gennady Samoilovich. *Zamedlenie vremeni*. Accessed July 7, 2023. http://books.rusf.ru/unzip/add-on/xussr_gk/gor___g48.htm?3/5.
Gordon, Shmuel. "Y. Kipnis, Oksn." *Shtrom*, no. 5–6 (1923): 402–404.
Grinberg, Uri Tsvi. "In malkhes fun tseylem." *Albatros* 2, no. 1 (1923): 15–24.
———. "Proklamirung." *Albatros* 1, no. 1 (September 1922): 3–4.
———. "Uri Tsvi farn tseylem." *Albatros* 1, no. 2 (November 1922): 3–4.
Gross, Jan. *Neighbors: The Destruction of the Jewish Community in Jedwabne, Poland*. Princeton, NJ: Princeton University Press, 2001.
Grossman, Reuben, and M. H. Segal. *Compendious Hebrew-English Dictionary*. Tel Aviv: Dvir, 1938.
Grumberg, Karen. *Hebrew Gothic: History and the Poetics of Persecution*. Bloomington: Indiana University Press, 2019.
Gusev-Orenburgskii, S. I. *"Bagrovaia Kniga": Pogromy 1919–20 gg. na Ukrainie*. Kharbin: Izd-vo dal'nevostochnogo evreiskogo obshchestvennogo kom-ta pomoshchi sirotam-zhertvam pogromov, 1922.
Hacking, Ian. "Biopower and the Avalanche of Printed Numbers." In *Biopower: Foucault and Beyond*, edited by Vernon W. Cisney and Nicolae Morar, 194–242. Chicago: University of Chicago Press, 2016.
Hagen, William W. *Anti-Jewish Violence in Poland, 1914–1920*. Cambridge: Cambridge University Press, 2018.
Halpern, Moshe Leib. *In New York: A Selection*. Translated by Kathryn Hellerstein. Philadelphia: Jewish Publication Society of America, 1982.
———. *In Nyu-York*. New York: Matones, 1954.

Harshav, Benjamin. "Do Sounds Have Meaning?" In *Three Thousand Years of Hebrew Versification: Essays in Comparative Prosody*, 14–39. New Haven, CT: Yale University Press, 2014.

———. *Language in Time of Revolution*. Stanford, CA: Stanford University Press, 1999.

———. *Marc Chagall and His Times: A Documentary Narrative*. Stanford, CA: Stanford University Press, 2004.

Harshav, Benjamin, and Barbara Harshav. *American Yiddish Poetry*. Berkeley: University of California Press, 1986.

Hart, Mitchell Bryan. *Social Science and the Politics of Modern Jewish Identity*. Stanford, CA: Stanford University Press, 2000.

Heifetz, Elias. *The Slaughter of the Jews in Ukraine in 1919*. New York: Thomas Seltzer, 1921.

Hellerstein, Kathryn. *A Question of Tradition: Women Poets in Yiddish, 1586–1987*. Stanford, CA: Stanford University Press, 2014.

Hofshteyn, David. *Bay vegn*. Kyiv: Kyiv Kultur-lige, 1919.

———. "Bayamim ha'hem." *Davar*, November 18, 1925, sec. Supplement.

———. "Bayamim ha'hem." *Davar*, December 4, 1925, sec. Supplement.

———. *Troyer*. Kyiv: Kultur-Lige, 1922.

———. "Yidishe arbet in Erets-Yisroel." *Dos naye lebn*, March 12, 1926.

Hofshteyn, David, and F. Shames. *Literatur kentenish*. Moscow: Tsentraler felker-farlag fun F. S. S. R., 1927.

Hofshteyn, David. *Gezamlte verk*. Vol. 1. Kyiv: Kultur-Lige, 1923.

Hofshteyn, Feyge. *Mit libe un veytik: Vegn David Hofshteyn*. Tel Aviv: Reshofim, 1985.

Hogan, Linda. *DARK. SWEET.: New and Selected Poems*. Minneapolis: Coffee House Press, 2014. Used with the permission of Coffee House Press. Published in Poem-a-Day on March 6, 2021, by the Academy of American Poets.

Holquist, Peter. "The Politics and Practice of the Russian Occupation of Armenia, 1915–February 1917." In *A Question of Genocide: Armenians and Turks at the End of the Ottoman Empire*, edited by Ronald Grigor Suny, Fatma Muge Gocek, and Norman M. Naimark, 151–74. New York: Oxford University Press, 2011.

———. "To Count, to Extract, and to Exterminate." In *A State of Nations*, edited by Ronald Grigor Suny, 111–44. Oxford: Oxford University Press, 2001.

Honigsbaum, Mark. "Regulating the 1918–19 Pandemic: Flu, Stoicism and the Northcliffe Press." *Medical History* 57, no. 2 (April 2013): 165–85. https://doi.org/10.1017/mdh.2012.101.

Hurh, Paul. "The Sound of Incest: Sympathetic Resonance in Melville's Pierre." *Novel: A Forum on Fiction* 44, no. 2 (Summer 2011): 249–67.

Huyssen, Andreas. *Present Pasts: Urban Palimpsests and the Politics of Memory*. Stanford, CA: Stanford University Press, 2003.

Ihde, Don. *Listening and Voice: Phenomenologies of Sound.* 2nd ed. Albany: State University of New York Press, 2007.
Ivanov, Vjaceslav. "Two Images of Africa in Russian Literature at the Beginning of the Twentieth Century: Ka by Chlebnikov and Gumilev's African Poems." *Russian Literature* 29 (1991): 409–26.
James, William. *Principles of Psychology.* Vol. 1. 2 vols. New York: Henry Holt, 1918.
Jastrow, Marcus. *A Dictionary of the Targumim, the Talmud Babli and Yerushalmit, and the Midrashic Literature.* New York: G. P. Putnam's Sons, 1903. https://en.wikisource.org/wiki/A_Dictionary_of_the_Targumim,_the_Talmud_Babli_and_Yerushalmi,_and_the_Midrashic_Literature.
Jockims, Trevor Laurence. "The Testimony of a Poet: Transcription, Witness, and Poetic Documentation in Charles' Reznikoff's Testimony." *Studies in Testimony* 1, no. 1 (2018): 102–19.
Jockusch, Laura. "Chroniclers of Catastrophe: History Writing as a Jewish Response to Persecution before and after the Holocaust." In *Holocaust Historiography in Context: Emergence, Challenges, Polemics, and Achievements*, edited by David Bankier and Dan Michman, 135–66. New York: Berghahn Books, 2008.
———. *Collect and Record! Jewish Holocaust Documentation in Early Postwar Europe.* New York: Oxford University Press, 2012.
Joffe, Judah, and Yudel Mark, eds. *Der groyser verterbukh fun der Yidisher shprakh online.* New York: Yiddish Dictionary Committee, 1961. https://www.cs.uky.edu/~raphael/yiddish/searchGroys.cgi.
Johnson, Hannah. *Blood Libel: The Ritual Murder Accusation at the Limit of Jewish History.* Ann Arbor: University of Michigan Press, 2012.
Johnson, Sam. "Pogrom in the Anglo-American Imagination, 1881–1919." In *Jews in the East European Borderlands: Essays in Honor of John D. Klier*, edited by Eugene Avrutin and Harriet Murav, 147–66. Boston: Academic Studies Press, 2012.
Joseph, John. *The Modern Assyrians of the Middle East: Encounters with Western Christian Missions, Archaelogists, & Colonial Powers.* Leiden: Brill, 2000.
Kalinin, Il'ia. "Istoriia kak iskusstvo chlenorazdel'nosti." *Novoe literaturnoe obozrenie* 71, no. 1 (2005): 103–31.
Kasianov, Georgiy. "Ukraine between Revolution, Independence, and Foreign Dominance." In *The Emergence of Ukraine: Self-Determination, Occupation, and War in Ukraine, 1917–1922*, edited by Wolfram Dornik, Georgiy Kasianov, Hannes Leidinger, Peter Lieb, Alexei Miller, Bogdan Musial, and Vasyl Rasevych, 76–131. Edmonton: Canadian Institute of Ukrainian Studies Press, 2015.
Kelley, Robin D. G. "What Kind of Society Values Property over Black Lives?" *New York Times*, June 18, 2020, sec. Opinion. https://www.nytimes.com/2020/06/18/opinion/george-floyd-protests-looting.html.

Kerler, Dov-Ber. "Dos yor 1919 in der geshikhte fun yidisher poezye." *Yidishland* 4 (Fall 2019): 3–11.
Kerler, Joseph. "Dovid Hofstein—Our First Wonder." In *The Politics of Yiddish*, 4:171–85. Winter Studies in Yiddish. Walnut Creek, CA: AltaMira Press, 1998.
Kipnis, Itsik. *Di shtub un untervegns*. Tel Aviv: I. L. Peretz Publishing House, 1977.
———. "Fun der dertseylung Khayele un Pinyele." In *Ukrayne: Literarish-kinstlerisher almanakh*, 34–52. Kyiv: Kultur-Lige, 1926.
———. "Gnod." *Shtrom* 3 (1922): 36–40.
———. *Khadoshim un teg: A khronik*. Kyiv: Kultur-Lige, 1926.
———. *Mesiatsy i dni*. Translated by B. I. Marshak. Moscow-Leningrad: Gosudarstvennoe izdatel'stvo, 1930.
———. *Oksn*. Kyiv: Vidervuks, 1923.
Kirshenblatt-Gimblett, Barbara. "Coming of Age in the Thirties: Max Weinreich, Edward Sapir, and Jewish Social Science." *YIVO Annual* 23 (1996): 1–103.
Klanderud, Paul A. "Maiakovskii's Myth of Man, Things and the City: From Poshlost' to the Promised Land." *Russian Review* 55, no. 1 (January 1996): 37. https://doi.org/10.2307/131908.
Klier, John D., and Shlomo Lambroza, eds. *Pogroms: Anti-Jewish Violence in Russian History*. Cambridge: Cambridge University Press, 1992.
Kochen, Madeline. *Organ Donation and the Divine Lien in Talmudic Law*. Cambridge: Cambridge University Press, 2013.
Koller, Sabine. "'The Air Outside Is Bloody': Leyb Kvitko and His Pogrom Cycle 1919." In *Yiddish in Weimar Berlin: At the Crossroads of Diaspora Politics and Culture*, edited by Gennady Estraikh and Mikhail Krutikov, 105–22. London: Legenda, 2010.
———. *Marc Chagall: Grenzgänge zwischen Literatur und Malerei*. Cologne: Böhlau, 2012.
———. "A Mayse Mit a Hon. Dos Tsigele: Marc Chagall Illustrating Der Nister." In *Uncovering the Hidden: The Works and Life of Der Nister*, edited by Gennady Estraikh, Kerstin Hoge, and Mikhail Krutikov, 55–72. Oxford: Legenda, 2017.
Kopstein, Jeffrey S., and Jason Wittenberg. *Intimate Violence: Anti-Jewish Pogroms on the Eve of the Holocaust*. Ithaca, NY: Cornell University Press, 2018.
Kotsko, Adam. *Agamben's Philosophical Trajectory*. Edinburgh: Edinburgh University Press, 2020.
Kovalsky, I. M. "Report on Belaia Tserkov." American JDC, Russian Unit, Kyiv, April 26, 1923, NY_AR2132_00403.
Krikler, Jeremy. "The *Zong* and the Lord Chief Justice." *History Workshop Journal* 64, no. 1 (2007): 29–47.
Kronfeld, Chana. *On the Margins of Modernism: Decentering Literary Dynamics*. Contraversions. Berkeley: University of California Press, 1996.

Krutikov, Mikhail. "Dos retenish fun Leyb Kvitko (The Enigma of Leib Kvitko)." *Forverts*, June 25, 2016. http://yiddish.forward.com/articles/197215 /the-enigma-of-leib-kvitko/?p=all#ixzz5KbCJrYL5.

———. *From Kabbalah to Class Struggle: Expressionism, Marxism, and Yiddish Literature in the Life and Work of Meir Wiener*. Stanford, CA: Stanford University Press, 2011.

———. "1919 god—Revoliutsiia v evreiskoi poezii." In *Mirovoi krizis 1914–1920 godov i sud'ba vostochnoevropeiskogo evreistva*, edited by Oleg Budnitskii, 318–41. Moscow: Rosspen, 2005.

———. "Rediscovering the Shtetl as a New Reality." In *The Shtetl: New Evaluations*, edited by Steven T. Katz, 211–32. New York: New York University Press, 2007.

Kukulin, Ilya. "Documentalist Strategies in Contemporary Russian Poetry." Translated by Josephine von Zitzewitz. *Russian Review* 69, no. 4 (2010): 585.

Kushnirov, Arn. "Azkore." *Shtrom* 1, no. 1 (1922): 27–29.

Kvitko, B., and M. Petrovskii, eds. *Zhizn' i tvorchestvo L'va Kvitko*. Moscow: Detskaia literatura, 1976.

Kvitko, Leyb. *Gerangl 1917–1929*. Kharkiv: Tsentrfarlag-Kharkov, 1929.

———. *Grin groz*. Berlin: Jewish Literature Publishing, 1922.

———. *1919*. Berlin: Lutze and Vogt, 1923.

———. *Ring in Ring*. Kharkiv: Melukhe-farlag fun Ukrayne, 1929.

———. "Three Poems." Translated by Harriet Murav and Zachary Sholem Berger. In *Geveb: A Journal of Yiddish Studies*, March 5, 2020. https://ingeveb .org/texts-and-translations/kvitko.

———. *Trit*. Kyiv: Kyiv Kultur-lige, 1919.

———. *Tsvey khaveyrim: Lyam un Petrik*. Moscow: Emes, 1933.

Labovitz, Gail. "More Slave Women, More Lewdness: Freedom and Honor in Rabbinic Female Sexuality." *Journal of Feminist Studies in Religion* 28, no. 2 (Fall 2012): 69–87.

Lavine, Ludmila Shleyfer. "Vladimir Mayakovsky's Agit-Semitism." *Russian Review* 78, no. 3 (2019): 437–58.

Lawrence, B. B., and A. Karim, eds. *On Violence: A Reader*. Durham, NC: Duke University Press, 2007. https://books.google.com/books?id=_EBb9bgut74C.

Lee, Steven S. *The Ethnic Avant-Garde: Minority Cultures and World Revolution*. New York : Columbia University Press, 2015.

Leshem, Noam. "Spaces of Abandonment: Genealogies, Lives and Critical Horizons." *Environment and Planning D-Society and Space* 35, no. 4 (August 2017): 620–36.

Lestschinsky, Jacob. *Dos yidishe folk in tsifern*. Berlin: Klal farlag, 1922.

———. "Nokh di pogromen." *Forverts*, June 9, 1921.

Levin, Doyvber. *Desiat' vagonov*. Moscow: Knizhniki, 2016.

——— . *Vol'nye shtaty Slavichi*. Salamandra P. V.V., 2013.
Levinson, Julian. "On Some Motifs in Moyshe-Leyb Halpern: A Benjaminian Meditation on Yiddish Modernism." *Prooftexts* 32, no. 1 (2012): 63–88.
Levy, Lital. *Poetic Trespass: Writing between Hebrew and Arabic in Israel/Palestine*. Princeton, NJ: Princeton University Press, 2014.
Leyeles, A. "Free Verse." In *American Yiddish Poetry*, edited by Benjamin Harshav and Barbara Harshav, 791–92. Berkeley: University of California Press, 1986.
Leys, Ruth. *Trauma: A Genealogy*. Chicago: University of Chicago Press, 2000.
Lipsker, Avidov. "The Albatrosses of Young Yiddish Poetry: An Idea and Its Visual Realization in Uri Zvi Greenberg's Albatross." Translated by Ruth Bar-Ilan. *Prooftexts* 15, no. 1 (January 1995): 89–108.
Litvin [Hurwitz], A. [Shmuel]. *Yidishe neshomes*. Vol. 3. 6 vols. New York: Folksbildung, 1917.
Lohr, Eric. "1915 and the War Pogrom Paradigm in the Russian Empire." In *Anti-Jewish Violence: Rethinking the Pogrom in East European History*, edited by Jonathan Dekel-Chen, David Gaunt, Natan M. Meir, and Israel Bartal, 41–51. Bloomington: Indiana University Press, 2011.
——— . "The Russian Army and the Jews: Mass Deportation, Hostages, and Violence during World War I." *Russian Review* 60, no. 3 (2001): 404–19.
Lowenheim, Oded. *The Politics of the Trail: Reflexive Mountain Biking along the Frontier of Jerusalem*. Ann Arbor: University of Michigan Press, 2014.
Lyotard, Jean-François. *The Differend : Phrases in Dispute*. Translated by Georges Van den Abbeele. Minneapolis: University of Minnesota Press, 1988.
Magid, Shaul. "Ethics Disentangled from the Law: Incarnation, the Universal, and Hasidic Ethics." *Kabbalah: Journal for the Study of Jewish Mystical Texts* 15 (2006): 31–75.
——— . *Hasidism Incarnate: Hasidism, Christianity, and the Construction of Modern Judaism*. Stanford, CA: Stanford University Press, 2014.
Mahalel, Adi. "The Radical Years of I. L. Peretz." PhD diss., Columbia University, 2014.
Maimonides, Moses. *The Code of Maimonides: The Book of Torts*. Translated by Hyman Klein. Vol. 11. 14 vols. New Haven, CT: Yale University Press, 1954.
Makaryk, Irene Rima, and Virlana Tkacz. *Modernism in Kyiv: Jubilant Experimentation*. Toronto: University of Toronto Press, 2010.
Mandelshtam, Osip. *The Complete Critical Prose and Letters*. Ann Arbor, MI: Ardis, 1979.
Mantovan, Daniela. "Der Nister and His Symbolist Short Stories (1913–1929): Patterns of Imagination." PhD diss., Columbia University, 1993.
Mark, Zvi. *Mysticism and Madness: The Religious Thought of Rabbi Nachman of Bratslav*. New York: Continuum, 2009.
Markish, Peretz. "Maskes." *Ringen* 7–8, no. 2 (1921): 101–103.

———. *Shveln*. Kyiv: Idisher folks farlag, 1918.
Masel, Roni. "National Heroism, Popular Pleasure: Violence, the Gothic and the Grotesque in Hebrew and Yiddish Literatures." PhD diss., New York University, 2020.
Masor, Alyssa. "The Evolution of the Literary Neo-Hasid." PhD diss., Columbia University, 2011.
Mayzel, Gitl. *Eseyen*. Tel Aviv: Y. L. Peretz, 1974.
Mayzel, Nakhmen. "Geveyn fun unzer tsayt." *Literarishe bleter*, no. 21 (May 26, 1933): 334–35.
———. "Itsik Kipnis." In *Untervegns un andere dertseylungen*, 7–23. New York: International Yiddish Cultural Movement (IKUF), 1960.
———. "A shmues mit professor Sniurson." *Literarishe bleter*, no. 13 (April 1, 1927): 244–45.
Mbembe, Achille. "Necropolitics." Translated by Libby Meintjes. *Public Culture* 15, no. 1 (Winter 2003): 11–40.
———. *Necropolitics*. Translated by Steven Corcoran. Durham, NC: Duke University Press, 2019.
McGeever, Brendan. "Red Antisemitism: Anti-Jewish Violence and Revolutionary Politics in Ukraine, 1919." *Quest: Issues in Contemporary Jewish History*, no. 15 (August 2019). https://doi.org/10.48248/issn.2037-741X/839.
Melamed, E. I., and M. S. Kupovetskii, eds. *Dokumenty po istorii i kul'ture evreev v arkhivakh Kieva: Putevoditel'*. Kyiv: Dukh i litera, 2006.
Melamed, Efim, and Gennady Estraikh. "O pogrome v Berdicheve." In *Archive of Jewish History*, edited by Oleg Budnitskii, 8:156–81. Moscow: Rosspen, 2016.
Miliakova, L. B. *Kniga pogromov: Pogromy na Ukraine, v Belorussii, i evropeiskoi chasti Rossii v period grazhdanskoi voiny 1918–1922 gg*. Moscow: Rosspen, 2007.
Mills, Catherine. "Biopolitics and the Concept of Life." In *Biopower: Foucault and Beyond*, edited by Vernon W. Cisney and Nicolae Morar, 82–101. Chicago: University of Chicago Press, 2016.
Mintz, Alan L. "The Russian Pogroms in Hebrew Literature and the Subversion of the Martyrological Ideal." *AJS Review* 7 (April 1982): 263–300.
———. *Ḥurban: Responses to Catastrophe in Hebrew Literature*. New York: Columbia University Press, 1984.
Miron, Dan. "Uri Zvi Grinberg's War Poetry." In *The Jews of Poland between Two World Wars*, edited by Yisrael Gutman, Ezra Mendelsohn, Jehuda Rienharz, and Chone Shmeruk, 368–82. Hanover, NH: University Press of New England, 1989.
Mogilner, Marina. "ARA Relief Campaign in the Volga Region, Jewish Anthropometric Statistics, and the Scientific Promise of Integration." *Science in Context* 32 (2019): 5–24. https://doi.org/10.1017/S0269889719000012.
———. *A Race for the Future: Scientific Visions of Modern Russian Jewishness*. Cambridge, MA: Harvard University Press, 2022.

Moglen, Helene. *The Trauma of Gender: A Feminist Theory of the English Novel.* Berkeley: University of California Press, 2001.

Molodowsky, Kadya. *Dzshike gas.* Warsaw: Literarishe bleter, 1933.

———. *In land fun mayn gebeyn.* Chicago: L. M. Stein, 1937.

———. *Kheshvendike nekht: Lider.* Vilnius: B. Kletskin, 1927.

———. "Mayn elterzeydns yerushe." *Svive* 33 (1971): 54–55.

———. "Otvotsk." In *Varshever almanakh*, 138–43. Warsaw: Beletristnfareynikung, 1923.

———. *Paper Bridges: Selected Poems of Kadya Molodowsky.* Translated by Kathryn Hellerstein. Detroit: Wayne State University Press, 1999.

Moss, Kenneth B. *Jewish Renaissance in the Russian Revolution.* Cambridge, MA: Harvard University Press, 2009.

Murav, Harriet. *David Bergelson's Strange New World: Untimeliness and Futurity.* Bloomington: Indiana University Press, 2019.

———. "Documentary Fiction of the Pogroms of the Civil War." In *Pogroms: A Documentary History*, edited by Eugene M. Avrutin and Elissa Bemporad, 176–92. Oxford: Oxford University Press, 2021.

———. *Holy Foolishness: Dostoevsky's Novels & the Poetics of Cultural Critique.* Stanford, CA: Stanford University Press, 1992.

———. *Music from a Speeding Train: Jewish Literature in Post-Revolutionary Russia.* Stanford, CA: Stanford University Press, 2011.

———. "Technology, the City, and the Body: Bergelson and Shklovsky in Berlin." In *Migration and Mobility in the Modern Age: Refugees, Travelers, and Traffickers in Europe and Eurasia*, edited by Anika Walke, Jan Musekamp, and Nicole Svobodny, 260–75. Bloomington: Indiana University Press, 2017.

Naydan, Michael M. "Two Musical Conceptions of the Revolution: Aleksandr Blok's Dvenadtsat' and Pavlo Tychyna's Zamist Sonetiv i Oktav." *Journal of Ukrainian Studies* 27, no. 1–2 (Summer–Winter 2002): 93–106.

Netanyahu, B. *The Marranos of Spain: From the Late 14th to the Early 16th Century, According to Contemporary Hebrew Sources.* Ithaca, NY: Cornell University Press, 1973.

Charney, Shmuel. *Vegn yidishe shrayber: Kritishe artikln.* Vol. 2. 2 vols. Warsaw: Sh. Shreberk, 1927.

———. *Yidishe shrayber in Sovet-Rusland.* New York: S. Niger Book Committee of the Congress for Jewish Culture, 1958.

Nister, Der. *Mayselekh in ferzen.* 3rd ed. Warsaw: Kultur-Lige, 1921.

Norris, Andrew. "Giorgio Agamben and the Politics of the Living Dead." *Diacritics* 30, no. 4 (2000): 38–58.

Novershtern, Abraham. "Der Nister." YIVO Encyclopedia of Jews in Eastern Europe. Accessed August 11, 2023. http://www.yivoencyclopedia.org/article.aspx/Der_Nister.

———. "'Who Would Have Believed That a Bronze Statue Can Weep': The Poetry of Anna Margolin." *Prooftexts* 10, no. 3 (1990): 435–67.
Oklahoma Commission. *Tulsa Race Riot: A Report by the Oklahoma Commission to Study the Tulsa Race Riot of 1921*. Tulsa, Oklahoma: CreateSpace, 2001.
Oldham, James. "Insurance Litigation Involving the *Zong* and Other British Slave Ships, 1780–1807." *Journal of Legal History* 28, no. 3 (December 2007): 299–318. https://doi.org/10.1080/01440360701698437.
Ophir, Adi. "The Two-State Solution: Providence and Catastrophe." *Theoretical Inquiries in Law* 8 (2007): 117–60.
Ophir, Adi, and Ishay Rosen-Zvi. *One Goy, Multiple Language Games*. Vol. 1. Oxford: Oxford University Press, 2018. https://doi.org/10.1093/oso/9780198744900.003.0008.
Oyslender, Nokhem. *Veg-ayn veg oys: Literarishe epizodn*. Kyiv: Kooperativer farlag, Kultur-lige, 1924.
Oxford English Dictionary Online. Oxford: Oxford University Press, 2022. www.oed.com.
Papazian, Elizabeth. *Manufacturing Truth: The Documentary Moment in Early Soviet Culture*. DeKalb: Northern Illinois University Press, 2009.
Peretz, Isaac Leib. *Ale verk*. Vol. 1. 11 vols. New York: Tsiko, 1947.
Perloff, Marjorie, and Craig Dworkin. *The Sound of Poetry/The Poetry of Sound*. Chicago: University of Chicago Press, 2009.
Pidmohylny, Valeriian. *Tretia Revoliutsiia: Opovidannia*. Kharkiv: Knyhospilka, 1926.
Pines, Noam. *The Infrahuman: Animality in Modern Jewish Literature*. Albany: State University of New York Press, 2018.
Plamper, Jan. "Emotional Turn? Feelings in Russian History and Culture." *Slavic Review* 68, no. 2 (Summer 2009): 229–37.
———. "Fear: Soldiers and Emotion in Early Twentieth-Century Russian Military Psychology." *Slavic Review* 68, no. 2 (2009): 259–83. https://doi.org/10.2307/27697958.
Platt, Kevin M. F., Caryl Emerson, and Dina Khapaeva. "Introduction: The Russian Gothic." *Russian Literature* 106 (2019): 1–9.
Poe, Edgar Allen. "The Coliseum." In *The Collected Works of Edgar Allan Poe*, vol. 1, *Poems*, edited by T. O. Mabbot, 226–31. Cambridge, MA: Belknap Press of Harvard University Press, 1969. https://www.eapoe.org/works/mabbott/tom1p061.htm.
Posadskii, Anton. "Umanshchina v 1918–1919 gg.: Voina, nastroieniia, zhiznennaia stoikost'." *Historia i swiat* 8 (2019): 163–82.
Povinelli, Elizabeth. *Economies of Abandonment*. Durham, NC: Duke University Press, 2011.

Pozner, Valérie. "Pogroms on Screen: Early 20th-Century Anti-Jewish Violence and the Limits of Representation." Edited by Elissa Bemporad and Thomas C. Chopard. *Quest. Issues in Contemporary Jewish History* 15 (August 2019): 74–110.

Rabinowitz, Louis Isaac. "Apikoros." In *Encyclopaedia Judaica*. Vol. 2. Gale ebooks, 2007.

Ravitsh, Meylekh. "Di naye, di nakete dikhtung: Zibn tezisn." *Albatros* 1 (1922): 15–16.

Reddy, William. *The Navigation of Feeling: A Framework for the History of Emotions*. Cambridge: Cambridge University Press, 2004.

Remenik, Hersh. "Dikhtung fun revolyutsyonern umru: Leyb Kvitko." In *Shtaplen: Portretn fun yidishe shrayber*, 37–49. Moscow: Sovetskii pisatel', 1982.

Resmovits, Joy. "Two Countries, Two Approaches to Regulating Embryonic Stem-Cell Use." *Forward*, January 28, 2011.

Reyzen, Zalman. *Leksikon fun der yidisher literatur, prese un filologye*. Vol. 3. 4 vols. Vilnius: B. Kletskin, 1929.

Ribot, Théodule Armand. *The Psychology of the Emotions*. London: Walter Scott, 1897.

Roller, William L., and Donald A. Shaskan. *Paul Schilder, Mind Explorer*. New York: Human Sciences Press, 1985. https://catalog.hathitrust.org/Record/000577195.

Rosenberg, William G. "Paramilitary Violence in Russia's Civil Wars: 1918–1920." In *War in Peace: Paramilitary Violence in Europe after the Great War*, edited by Robert Gerwarth and John Horne, 21–39. Oxford: Oxford University Press, 2013.

Rosenblatt, Eli. "Enlightening the Skin: Travel, Racial Language, and Rabbinic Intertextuality in Modern Yiddish Literature." PhD diss., University of California, 2017. https://escholarship.org/uc/item/8vs7p0bg.

Roskies, David G. *Against the Apocalypse: Responses to Catastrophe in Modern Jewish Culture*. Cambridge, MA: Harvard University Press, 1984.

———, ed. *The Literature of Destruction: Jewish Responses to Catastrophe*. Philadelphia: Jewish Publication Society, 1988.

Rubin, Eli. "Traveling and Traversing Chabad's Literary Paths: From Likutei Torah to Khayim Gravitser and Beyond." *In Geveb: A Journal of Yiddish Studies*, October 9, 2018.

Rubin, Y. "Prof. Dr. F. Schneersohn: Di katastrofale tsaytn un di vaksndike doyres." *Literarishe bleter*, no. 33 (December 19, 1924): 6.

Safran, Gabriella. *Wandering Soul: The Dybbuk's Creator, S. An-Sky*. Cambridge, MA: Harvard University Press, 2010.

Sal'nikova, A. A. *Rossiiskoe detstvo v XX veke: Istoriia, teoriia i praktika issledovaniia*. Kazan: Kazanskii gosudarstvennyi universitet, 2007.

Sanborn, Joshua. "The Genesis of Russian Warlordism: Violence and Governance during the First World War and the Civil War." *Contemporary European History* 19, no. 3 (2010): 195–213.

Sandomirskaja, Irina. *Blokada v slove: ocherki kriticheskoi teorii i biopolitiki iazyka.* Moscow: Novoe literaturnoe obozrenie, 2013.

———. "Derrida on the Poetics and Politics of Witnessing." In *Rethinking Time*, edited by Hans Ruin and Andrus Ers, 247–55. Huddinge: Södertörns högskola, 2011.

Santner, Eric L. *On Creaturely Life: Rilke, Benjamin, Sebald.* Chicago: University of Chicago Press, 2006.

———. *The Royal Remains: The People's Two Bodies and the Endgames of Sovereignty.* Chicago: University of Chicago Press, 2011.

Scarry, Elaine. *The Body in Pain: The Making and Unmaking of the World.* New York: Oxford University Press, 1985.

———. *On Beauty and Being Just.* Princeton, NJ: Princeton University Press, 1999.

Schneersohn, Fischel. *Di katastrofale tsaytn un di vaksndike doyres.* Berlin: Yidisher literarisher farlag, 1923.

———. *Khayim gravitser (di geshikhte fun dem gefalenem): Fun dem Khabadisher velt.* Berlin: Yidisher literarisher farlag, 1922.

———. *Psikhologiia intimnoi zhizni rebenka.* Berlin: Grani, 1923.

———. *Studies in Psycho-Expedition: Fundamentals of the Psychological Science of Man and a Theory of Nervousness.* Translated by Herman Frank. New York: Science of Man Press, 1929.

Scholem, Gershom. *Major Trends in Jewish Mysticism.* New York: Schocken Books, 1971.

Seelig, Rachel. "'A Youthful Rogue Am I': Moyshe Kulbak between Exile and Arrival." In *Strangers in Berlin: Modern Jewish Literature between East and West, 1919–1933*, 79–100. Ann Arbor: University of Michigan Press, 2016. https://www.jstor.org/stable/10.3998/mpub.9223331.8.

Seeman, Dan. *One People, One Blood: Ethiopian-Israelis and the Return to Judaism.* New Brunswick, NJ: Rutgers University Press, 2009.

Shapiro, Lamed. "The Cross." In *The Cross and Other Jewish Stories*, edited by Leah Garrett, translated by Jeremy Dauber, 3–18. New Haven, CT: Yale University Press, 2007. http://www.jstor.org/stable/j.ctt1npntv.5.

Shedd, Mary Lewis. *The Measure of a Man: The Life of William Ambrose Shedd, Missionary to Persia.* New York: George Doran, 1922.

Sher, Benjamin. "Translator's Introduction: Shklovsky and the Revolution." In *Theory of Prose*, xv–xxi. Elmwood Park, IL: Dalkey Archive Press, 1990.

Sherman, Joseph, ed. *From Revolution to Repression: Soviet Yiddish Writing 1917–1952.* Nottingham: Five Leaves Publications, 2012.

———. "Leib Kvitko." In *Dictionary of Literary Biography Complete Online*. GALE, 2007.

———. "Serving the Natives: Whiteness as the Price of Hospitality in South African Yiddish Literature." *Journal of Southern African Studies* 26, no. 3 (September 2000): 505–21.

Shklovsky, Viktor. "Boi na Dniepre." In *Sobrainie sochineni*, edited by Il'ia Kalinin, 1:155–57. Moscow: Novoe literaturnoe obozrenie, 2018.

———. *Eshche nichego ne konchilos'*. Moscow: Vagrius, 2002.

———. *Knight's Move*. Normal, IL: Dalkey Archive Press, 2005.

———. *A Sentimental Journey: Memoirs, 1917–1922*. Translated by Richard Sheldon. Normal, IL: Dalkey Archive Press, 2004.

———. *Sobranie sochinenii*. Edited by Il'ia Kalinin. 2 vols. Moscow: Novoe literaturnoe obozrenie, 2019.

Shmeruk, Khone, ed. *A shpigl af a shteyn*. Jerusalem: Magnes Press, 1964.

Shneer, David. "'My Name Is Now': Peretz Markish and the Literature of Revolution." In *A Captive of the Dawn: The Life and Work of Peretz Markish (1895–1952)*, edited by Joseph Sherman, Gennady Estraikh, Jordan Finkin, and David Shneer, 1–15. Oxford: Legenda, 2011.

———. *Yiddish and the Creation of Soviet Jewish Culture*. Cambridge: Cambridge University Press, 2004.

Shtif, Nokhem. "Leyb Kvitko, 1919." *Di tsukunft* 30, no. 2 (1925): 128–31.

———. *The Pogroms in Ukraine, 1918–19: Prelude to the Holocaust*. Translated and annotated with an introduction by Maurice Wolfthal. Cambridge: Open Book Publishers, 2020.

Shvartsman, Osher. "In tribn mentshn-land." *Eygns* 2 (1920): 67.

Singer, Isaac Bashevis. "Khadoshim un teg." *Literarishe bleter*, no. 13 (April 1, 1927): 260.

Slobin, Greta. *Russians Abroad: Literary and Cultural Politics of Diaspora 1919–1939*. Boston: Academic Studies Press, 2018.

Sobol', Andrei. *Pyl': Roman*. Moscow: Severnye dni, 1917.

Sobol, Valeria. *Haunted Empire*. Ithaca, NY: Cornell University Press, 2020.

Spinner, Samuel J. "Else Lasker-Schüler and Uri Zvi Greenberg in 'The Society of Savage Jews': Art, Politics, and Primitivism." *Prooftexts: A Journal of Jewish Literary History* 38, no. 1 (2020): 60–93.

———. *Jewish Primitivism*. Stanford, CA: Stanford University Press, 2021.

Stahl, Neta. "'Uri Zvi before the Cross': The Figure of Jesus in the Poetry of Uri Zvi Greenberg." *Religion & Literature* 40, no. 3 (2008): 49.

Staudigl, Michael. "Towards a Phenomenological Theory of Violence: Reflections Following Merleau-Ponty and Schutz." *Human Studies* 30 (2007): 233–53.

Steinberg, Mark. "Emotions History in Eastern Europe." In *Doing Emotions History*, edited by Susan J. Matt and Peter N. Stearns. Champaign: University of Illinois Press, 2013.

———. *Petersburg Fin de Siècle*. New Haven, CT: Yale University Press, 2011.
Stoler, Ann. "Colonial Archives and the Arts of Governance on the Content in the Form." In *Archives, Documentation, and Institutions of Social Memory*, edited by Francis X. Blouin and William G. Rosenberg, 267–79. Ann Arbor: University of Michigan Press, 2006.
Stow, Kenneth R. *Jewish Dogs: An Image and Its Interpreters; Continuity in the Catholic-Jewish Encounter*. Stanford, CA: Stanford University Press, 2006.
Strätling, Susanne. *The Hand at Work: The Poetics of Poiesis in the Russian Avant-Garde*. Boston: Academic Studies Press, 2021.
Stuchkoff, Nahum. *Der oytser fun der yidisher shprakh*. New York: YIVO Institute for Jewish Research, 1991.
Suleiman, Susan Rubin. "Pornography, Transgression, and the Avant-Garde: Bataille's Story of the Eye." In *The Poetics of Gender*, edited by Nancy K. Miller, 117–36. New York: Columbia University Press, 1986.
Szymaniak, Karolina. "The Language of Dispersion and Confusion: Peretz Markish's Manifestos from the Khalyastre Period." In *A Captive of the Dawn: The Life and Work of Peretz Markish (1895–1952)*, edited by Joseph Sherman and Gennady Estraikh, 66–87. London: Legenda, 2011.
Tihanov, Galin. *The Birth and Death of Literary Theory: Regimes of Relevance in Russia and Beyond*. Stanford, CA: Stanford University Press, 2019.
———. "The Politics of Estrangement: The Case of the Early Shklovsky." *Poetics Today* 26, no. 4 (December 1, 2005): 665–96.
Todes, Samuel. *Body and World*. Cambridge, MA: MIT Press, 2001.
Todorova, Maria. *The Lost World of Socialists at Europe's Margins: Imagining Utopia, 1870s–1920s*. London: Bloomsbury Academic, 2020.
Tolstoy, Leo. *War and Peace*. Translated by George Gibian. 2nd ed. New York: W. W. Norton, 1996.
Torres, Anna. "The Horizon Blossoms and the Borders Vanish: Peretz Markish's Poetry and Anarchist Diasporism." *Jewish Quarterly Review* 110, no. 3 (2020): 458–90.
Traverso, Antonio, and Mick Broderick. "Interrogating Trauma: Towards a Critical Trauma Studies." *Continuum* 24, no. 1 (February 2010): 3–15. https://doi.org/10.1080/10304310903461270.
Tretiakov, Sergei. "To Be Continued." *October* 118 (Fall 2006): 51–56.
Ugresic, Dubravka. *Fox*. Translated by Ellen Elias-Burcać and David Williams. Rochester, NY: Open Letter, 2018.
Ugur, Umit Ungor. "Paramilitary Violence in the Collapsing Ottoman Empire." In *War in Peace: Paramilitary Violence in Europe after the Great War*, edited by Robert Gerwarth and John Horne, 164–83. Oxford: Oxford University Press, 2013.
Vakhrushova, Daria. "'To Hell with Futurism, Too!' The Metamorphoses of Western and Eastern European Modernism in Yiddish Manifestos."

Quest: Issues in Contemporary Jewish History, Journal of the Fondazione CDEC 17 (September 2020): 43–74.

Vatulescu, Cristina. *Police Aesthetics: Literature, Film, and the Secret Police in Soviet Times*. Stanford, CA: Stanford University Press, 2010.

———. "The Politics of Estrangement: Tracking Shklovsky's Device through Literary and Policing Practices." *Poetics Today* 27, no. 1 (2006): 36–66.

Veidlinger, Jeffrey. *In the Midst of Civilized Europe: The Pogroms of 1918–1921 and the Onset of the Holocaust*. New York: H. Holt, 2021.

Velychenko, Stephen. *Life and Death in Revolutionary Ukraine: Living Conditions, Violence, and Demographic Catastrophe, 1917–1923*. Montreal: McGill-Queen's Press (MQUP), 2021.

Vendler, Helen. "The Puzzle of Sequence: Two Political Poems." In *Essays in Honour of Eammon Cantwell: Yeats Annual No. 20*, edited by Warwick Gould, 119–54. Cambridge: Open Book Publishers, 2016. https://doi.org/10.11647/OBP.0081.05.

Viola, Lynn. "The Question of the Perpetrator in Soviet History." *Slavic Review* 72, no. 1 (2013): 1–23.

Wasserman, Mira Beth. *Jews, Gentiles, and Other Animals: The Talmud after the Humanities*. Philadelphia: University of Pennsylvania Press, 2017.

Wassman, Claudia. "The Science of Emotion: Studying Emotions in Germany, France, and the US, 1860–1920." PhD diss., University of Chicago, 2005.

Webber, George. "The Principles of the Jewish Law of Property." *Journal of Comparative Legislation and International Law* 10, no. 1 (1928): 82–93.

Weheliye, Alexander. *Habeas Viscus: Racializing Assemblages, Biopolitics, and Black Feminist Theories of the Human*. Durham, NC: Duke University Press, 2014.

Weinreb, Tzvi Hersh, and Joshua Schreier, eds. *Koren Talmud Bavli*. Vol. 18, *Nedarim*. Jerusalem: Koren Publishers, 2015.

Wexner. "Bedikat Chametz." Haggadot. Accessed July 20, 2023. https://www.haggadot.com/clip/bedikat-chametz-2.

Whitman, Walt. "Song of Myself." 1892. https://www.poetryfoundation.org/poems/45477/song-of-myself-1892-version.

Wiese, Stefan. "'Spit Back with Bullets!' Emotions in Russia's Jewish Pogroms, 1881–1905." *Geschichte und Gesellschaft* 39 (2013): 472–501.

Williams, Tyrone. "Marlene Nourbese-Philip. Zong!" *African American Review* 43, no. 4 (2009): 785–87.

Wisse, Ruth R. "Speaking of the Devil in Yiddish Literature." In *Studies in Contemporary Jewry*, vol. 13, *Jews and Violence: Images, Ideologies, Realities*, edited by Peter Medding, 59–73. New York: Oxford University Press, 2002.

Wolitz, Seth. "Experiencing Visibility and Phantom Existence." In *Russian Jewish Artists in a Century of Change 1890–1990*, edited by Susan Tumarkin Goodman, 14–15. New York: Prestel, 1995.

———. "Troyer (Grief)—Hofshteyn's Fellow-Traveler Dirge." In *Yiddish Modernism: Studies in Twentieth Century Eastern European Jewish Culture*, edited by Brian Horowitz and Haim A. Gottschalk, 283–309. Bloomington, IN: Slavica, 2014.

———. *Yiddish Modernism: Studies in Twentieth Century Eastern European Jewish Culture*. Edited by Brian Horowitz and Haim A. Gottschalk. Bloomington, IN: Slavica, 2014.

Yatskan, Sh. Y. "Der pinkes fun a toyte shtot." *Haynt*, August 26, 1927.

Yekelchyk, Serhy. "Bands of Nation Builders? Insurgency and Ideology in the Ukrainian Civil War." In *War in Peace: Paramilitary Violence in Europe after the Great War*, edited by Robert Gerwarth and John Horne, 107–25. Oxford: Oxford University Press, 2013.

———. "Searching for the Ukrainian Revolution." *Slavic Review* 78, no. 4 (2019): 942–48.

Young, James E., and David William Foster. "Documentary Narrative." *PMLA* 99, no. 5 (October 1984): 998. https://doi.org/10.2307/462149.

Yudkoff, Sunny S. *Tubercular Capital: Illness and the Conditions of Modern Jewish Writing*. Stanford, CA: Stanford University Press, 2018.

Zavadivker, Polly. "Blood and Ink: Russian and Soviet Jewish Chroniclers of Catastrophe from World War I to World War II." PhD diss., University of California at Santa Cruz, 2013.

———. "Contending with Horror: Jewish Aid Work in the Russian Civil War Pogroms." *Quest: Issues in Contemporary Jewish History* 15 (August 2019). http://www.quest-cdecjournal.it/focus.php?id=414.

Zenkin, Sergei. "Prikliucheniia teoretika: Avtobiograficheskaia proza Viktor Shklovskogo." *Druzhba narodov* 12 (2003): 170–83.

Zipperstein, Steven J. *Pogrom: Kishinev and the Tilt of History*. New York: Liveright Publishing Corporation, 2018.

INDEX

1919 (the year), 4, 26, 28, 34, 45, 58, 64, 73, 82–83, 94, 101, 130–32, 143, 161, 176, 183, 185, 196, 207, 219; creativity and, 11, 18, 37, 61, 85, 107, 128, 200, 235; pogroms and, 4–5, 7, 25, 57, 84–85, 115, 121–22, 125–26, 129, 131, 134–36, 141–42, 152, 159, 173, 188, 191, 197, 206; violence and, 13, 17, 46, 66, 72, 87, 90, 100, 147, 166, 181, 190, 215, 232–33. *See also under* Kvitko, Leyb: *1919*. *See also* pogroms, violence.

abandonment, 2, 5, 13, 97–98, 107, 121, 128, 136, 142–43, 151, 155, 157, 164, 168, 174, 191, 202–204, 229, 232, 235; artistic literature and, 2, 4, 12, 15–18, 35–40, 59, 61, 73–74, 78–79, 85, 101, 154; children and, 4, 81, 103, 205, 222; governments and, 2–3, 5, 7, 18, 23–30, 34–35, 39, 43–44, 48, 77, 139, 141, 179, 181–82; Jews as abandoned, 2, 4, 7, 36–37, 71–72, 99, 117, 230; pleasure and, 30–31, 37, 107, 136; violence and, 2–4, 8–10, 12, 14, 17, 37, 43, 46, 60, 68, 83, 85, 95, 100, 102, 149, 151, 163, 172, 175–78, 187, 229. *See also* biopolitics, hefker.

Agamben, Giorgio, 3, 23–27, 35, 39, 43–44, 77, 141, 169, 190. *See also* biopolitics.

aid organizations, 104, 128, 148–49, 179–84, 187–89, 193–94; aid workers, 4, 18, 179–80, 182, 185–86, 193–95, 201; All-Ukrainian Committee to Aid Victims of Pogroms, 183, 203; All-Ukrainian Jewish Public Committee: 186, 188, 192, 195–97; All-Ukrainian Relief Committee, 191; Jewish Committee to Aid Victims of the War (EKOPO), 184; Jewish Joint Distribution Committee (JDC), 182, 184, 198, 206, 208; Jewish Public Committee to Aid Victims of Pogroms (Evobshchestkom), 6, 127, 179–81, 183–84, 186–87, 189–90, 192–93, 195–98, 201, 203–204, 206–207, 209, 220; Information Division of Kyiv District Committee to Aid Victims of Pogroms, 140,

187; Kyiv Public Committee to Aid Victims of Pogroms, 166, 179, 188, 193, 196–98, 201–202, 207; Russian Red Cross, 182; American Joint Distribution Committee, 198, 206. *See also* care, relief organizations.
Aleichem, Sholem, 129–30, 134, 148.
animals, 1, 29, 34, 67, 75–78, 83, 89, 100–101, 108–10, 115–116, 118–20, 125, 131, 137–38, 145–46, 148, 158, 161–63, 170–71, 198, 211, 221–22, 234; birds, 13, 48–49, 134, 140, 211, 213; cows, 34, 54, 77–78, 134, 164; dogs, 32, 75, 79, 92, 101, 107–110, 115, 121, 138, 156, 162, 170; foxes, 32, 66–71, 231; hides of, 75–77, 110, 125–26, 131, 137–38; horses, 34, 134, 158, 164, 174, 198; Jews seen as animals, 25, 68, 108, 128, 134, 139, 145; livestock, 25, 33, 139, 213; oxen, 77, 138, 148 (*see also under* Kipnis, Itsik: *Oxen*); pigs, 115–16; wolves, 32–33, 68, 134, 169–71.
An-sky, Shimon, 127, 180.
antisemitism, 4, 151, 169.
archives, 2–3, 5–6, 14, 78–79, 90, 104, 115, 128, 131–33, 166, 179, 182–83, 193, 210, 213.
Armenians, 9, 47, 57, 168–70, 193. *See also* genocide.
Aseyev, Stanislav, 28, 34.
Assyrians, 9, 158, 168, 174–76.

Babel, Isaac, 100, 158.
Belarus, 39, 73, 203, 210; Liady, 210, 215; Minsk, 194, 214.
Bergson, Henri, 162, 216.
Berlin, 19, 37, 47, 76, 84, 89, 99, 110, 114, 150, 179, 205, 215–16.
Bialik, Hayim Nachman, 10, 32, 84, 91, 99–100, 121, 127, 139, 141, 160, 161, 180, 200; "In the City of the Slaughter": 10, 32, 65, 99, 106, 108, 111, 116, 135–36, 232.
biopolitics, 2–5, 18, 23–27, 29–30, 34–35, 38, 100–101, 128, 181–83, 185, 210, 217. *See also* Agamben, Giorgio.
Bekhterev, Vladimir, 215, 219.
Borokhov, Dov Ber, 7.
Bergelson, David, 7, 16, 24, 26, 37, 39, 46, 49, 54, 61, 76–77, 89, 102, 110, 129–30, 133, 139, 140.
Blok, Alexander, 16, 51, 82, 89.
blood, 7, 31–32, 34–35, 38, 41, 66–69, 72, 77, 85, 89–90, 99, 102–103, 110–11, 115, 132–33, 135, 138, 140–41, 144, 152, 160, 165–66, 187, 199–200, 218, 225. *See also* body; flesh.
body, 2, 15, 24, 26, 30, 41–42, 51–52, 69, 74, 84, 91, 106, 110–11, 118, 120, 135–36, 143, 146, 162–63, 172, 181–82, 184, 189, 192, 223, 227; bodily organs, 50, 76, 115, 117, 161, 171; corpses, 55, 61, 115, 140–41, 143, 160–61, 164, 170, 175, 177, 198, 202, 221; hefker and, 34–35, 117, 171; loss of integrity and, 50, 53–54, 76–77, 101–103, 116–117, 138, 157; mass body, 99–100, 121, 141, 171; mutilation and, 8, 13–14, 32, 38, 60, 77, 94, 110, 115, 140, 143, 166–67, 189, 198; pleasure and, 18, 30, 44–47, 58, 74, 130, 135–36; wounds and: 38, 74, 89, 100–102, 110, 133–34, 165–66, 176, 199, 218–19. *See also* blood; enfleshment; flesh; pain.
Bolsheviks, 6, 8, 34, 83, 146, 150, 156–57, 161, 185, 211, 213–14, 233.
Bramson, Abram Moiseevich, 192.
Bunin, Ivan, 8.

care, 2–5, 7, 10, 12, 17–19, 24–25, 31, 41, 78, 126, 128–29, 134, 139, 143–47, 151, 155, 170, 174–75, 177, 181–82, 184, 191–92, 197, 204–207, 211, 216–17, 221–23, 226–32; comfort and, 13, 58, 69, 71–72, 121, 206, 231. *See also* aid organizations; children; relief organizations.

Carton, Moses (Moshe Karton), 200, 202–204, 232.

Cavell, Stanley, 153–54.

Chagall, Marc, 60, 67, 69–72, 205, 231.

Charney, Shmuel (Shmuel Niger), 56, 79, 96, 118, 129.

chaos, 99, 156, 181–83, 212, 222, 225, 235; as theme in poetry, 12, 15–17, 36–37, 45, 56, 59–60, 73–74, 76, 79, 109; pogroms and, 7, 111, 136, 195, 197, 202–204, 213, 232; toyhu-vavoyhu (primordial chaos): 57, 80–82, 97.

Cherikover, Elias, 179, 186.

Chicago, 233, 235.

children, 12, 38–39, 53–54, 66, 68, 73, 75, 77–78, 80–81, 84, 89–90, 94–95, 98, 102–103, 106–107, 109, 114–15, 120, 131–32, 136, 138–39, 141, 158, 162, 164–65, 169–70, 173–74, 183, 200, 231; creativity of, 196, 205–15, 217–18, 220–24, 234–35; infants, 50, 90, 115, 164, 214; orphans, 4, 19, 126, 146, 189, 194, 205–207; orphanages and, 10, 19, 60, 72, 195–96, 205, 207, 210–13, 219; pogroms and, 4–5, 10, 19, 86, 126, 134, 145–47, 151, 195, 205, 208–209, 211, 213, 216, 218–19, 220–21, 223–24, 226–27, 234; "weak" children, 208. *See also* care; disease; pogroms; women.

Chuzhak, Nikolai, 156–57, 167.

clothing, 26, 133, 141, 150, 157, 165, 167, 195, 208, 222, 233; shoes, 78, 99–100, 171, 195, 208. *See also* body; care.

creatures, 32, 58, 74, 89, 100, 121, 134, 138–40, 144, 147, 156, 170, 174–75, 177, 230. *See also* animals; body; enfleshment; flesh.

creativity, 5, 10–13, 16–19, 31, 42, 47, 49, 53, 56, 59, 62, 67–68, 71, 73, 79, 81–82, 85, 136, 163, 177, 182, 196, 206, 209, 219, 222–25, 227, 234. *See also* care; children; poetry.

disease, 40, 42–43, 86, 107, 163, 199, 202, 207–208, 227; cholera, 175; nervous disorders, 185, 192, 208; mental disorders, 192, 199, 204, 208, 218, 228; trauma, 11, 79, 144, 192, 204, 216, 218, 224, 226; tuberculosis, 12, 35, 39–40, 42, 44, 75, 81, 106–107, 192, 208, 230; typhus, 126, 200. *See also* medicine.

Defoe, Daniel, 175.

Der Nister (Pinkhes Kahanovitsh), 39, 75, 101, 107, 109–10, 121, 138, 226, 230.

Denikin, Anton (*see also*: Ukraine): 57, 185, 211

destruction, 3, 16, 26, 54, 56, 58, 60, 69, 71, 92, 127, 129–30, 133, 151–52, 161, 163–65, 171, 177, 188, 195–98, 213, 220, 229–31, 234; khurbn (Jewish national disaster), 56; of property, 5, 8, 84, 188, 231. *See also*: creativity, objects, things, violence)

documentation, 3–4, 9–10, 13–14, 18, 60, 127–28, 148–49, 176, 178–79, 182, 187, 203–204, 228, 231–32; documentary materials, 1–3, 7, 12, 14–15, 18, 27, 147, 229;

documentary strategies, 4, 13–14, 18, 126–29, 147, 149, 156. *See also* factography; questionnaires; statistics.
Dostoevsky, Fyodor, 118, 200.
Dubnow, Simon, 10, 32, 127, 180.
dust, 23, 28, 33–34, 47–48, 138, 171–72, 229. *See also under* Sobol.

emotions, 2, 95, 99, 149, 164, 175, 215, 217, 222–23, 225, 235; anger, 35, 78, 82, 98, 109, 128, 145, 159, 168, 170, 172, 180, 214; despair, 180, 202–203; fear, 29, 38, 48, 57, 75, 77, 84, 86, 90–92, 103–104, 106–107, 113, 136, 144, 150, 155, 166–68, 171, 191–93, 209–10, 214, 218, 221, 224; grief, 59–60, 84, 144, 172, 180; horror, 11, 107, 125, 155, 203; humiliation, 28, 84, 100, 136, 214; in documentation, 197–98, 202; joy, 18, 34, 37, 45, 48–49, 52, 54, 56, 59–60, 72–73, 82, 112, 119, 138, 152, 157, 178, 210, 226, 230; lack of, 128, 156, 158, 171, 180–81, 194, 206, 210, 212, 214, 216, 219–20, 234; poetics and, 15–18, 48, 50–51, 56, 78, 85, 96, 98, 108, 178; regret, 153, 172; shame, 32, 38, 61, 107–108, 115, 135, 172, 186, 194; sorrow, 56, 71, 76, 82, 178, 214. *See also* children; Schneersohn, Fischel.
enfleshment, 99–110, 117–118, 121, 140, 160–63. *See also* body; flesh.
everyday life, 2, 13, 35, 80, 86–88, 134–38, 140, 190.
Esenin, Sergei, 16.
Ewing, Eve, 232–35.
Eisenberg (Ayzenberg), Shimon Zev, 33.

factography, 12–13, 18, 127, 151, 156–57, 167, 171, 184, 212–14.
Faygenberg, Rokhl, 28, 201.
flesh, 16–18, 37–39, 41, 50–52, 60, 77, 82, 90, 93–94, 100–103, 110–111, 116–18, 121, 135, 151, 156, 161–63, 165, 175–76. *See also* body; enfleshment; Kvitko, Leyb; violence.
food, 23, 25, 32, 47–48, 99–100, 108, 114, 116, 126, 131–32, 138, 143, 145–47, 151, 161, 172, 175–76, 201, 208–209, 222, 231. *See also* care; hunger.
Foucault, Michel, 3, 23–25, 27.
Freud, Sigmund, 215–16, 218–19.
Frug, Simon, 1–2, 5, 32, 168.

genocide, 9, 11, 35, 168–70, 193. *See also* Armenians; Holocaust.
Gogol, Nikolai, 211.
Gordon, Shmuel, 138.
Gorky, Maxim (Maksim), 168.
Grinberg, Uri Tsvi, 24, 31, 38–39, 44, 46–47, 50, 100, 114.
Gusev-Orgenburgskii, Sergei, 179.

Ha'am, Ahad (Asher Zvi Hirsch Ginsberg), 10, 32.
Hasidism, 4, 19, 31, 198, 205, 210, 215, 224–27. *See also*: Schneersohn, Fishel.
Hayderabad: 162, 165, 170
hefker, 19, 28, 74, 77, 80, 85, 102, 139, 141, 151, 173, 182, 190, 202, 204–206, 235; as threshold condition, 30, 35, 43–44, 48, 54–55, 59, 81, 137–38, 161, 183, 197, 231–32 (*see also under* Hofshteyn, David); in Jewish property law, 1–3, 18, 23–24, 29, 31, 43, 107, 117, 159, 229; Jews as hefker, 1–2, 5, 7–8, 11, 24–25,

29, 32–35, 37–39, 68, 71–72, 95, 99, 117, 168, 197; kenosis and, 31, 46, 72, 101, 118, 121, 128–29, 226, 231; nature and, 1, 26, 29, 30–31, 43, 49, 55–56, 71–72, 79, 117, 226, 231; poetics and, 1–2, 10–12, 15–18, 24, 36–40, 44, 46–50, 52, 60–61, 64, 67–69, 72–73, 85, 96, 101, 230–31; sexuality and, 2, 8, 18, 30, 43, 101, 107, 135; violence and, 1, 4, 9, 14, 16, 25–26, 32, 34–35, 38–39, 45, 68, 81–83, 99–100, 121, 128–30, 140, 142, 148, 155, 159, 171–72, 229, 232. See also abandonment; children; dust; pogroms.
Heifetz, Elias, 191.
Hobbes, Thomas, 33, 169.
Hofshteyn, David: 4, 39, 95, 141, 196; animals and, 66–71; chaos and, 45, 49, 56–57, 59–60; children and, 10, 53–54, 60, 66–68, 72, 200, 205; comfort and, 13, 58, 69, 71–72, 121, 205–206, 231; emotions and, 16, 45, 48–52, 56–57, 59–60, 62, 72, 98; hefker and, 15–16, 31, 43–50, 52, 59–61, 64, 67–69, 71–72, 230–31; hefker as a threshold condition and, 54–55, 59, 61, 183; "In Those Days: Fragments from My Recollections of the Civil War in Russia" ("Bayomim ha'hem"), 46, 57–59; literary handbook (*Literatur kentenish*), 50–51, 79; nature in, 37, 47–50, 53–56, 60, 68, 72, 230; *On the Road* (*Bay vegn*), 45–47, 52, 54, 57–58, 60, 68, 72; pain and, 56–60, 62–65, 68–69, 71–72, 174; pleasure and, 45–47, 58, 72; pogroms and, 7, 10, 16, 46, 48, 56, 59–61, 68–69, 71–72, 74, 81–2, 121, 127, 157, 173, 205–206, 228, 230–31; sense perception and, 16, 18, 43–45, 50–54, 66–68, 223, 230; *Sorrow* (*Troyer*), 4, 46, 48–49, 59–61, 69, 71–72, 96, 117, 128–29, 173, 205–206, 228; sound and, 16–17, 43, 46, 48–59, 61–66, 69, 71, 90, 98, 126, 200; time and, 55, 57, 59–61, 64, 66, 72; Ukraine as a theme in, 46, 57–58, 60–61, 67–68, 71, 173, 231.
Hokhgelernter, H., 202.
Holocaust, 6, 11–12, 34–35, 100, 130, 203. See also genocide; World War II.
hunger, 77, 89, 101–102, 153, 157, 161–63, 165, 168, 176, 219. See also food.

Ioffe, Lev Iakovlevich, 187–88, 200–201.

James, William, 216, 223.

Kerensky, Alexander, 152.
Kharkiv, 76, 183, 193–95.
Kharms, Daniil, 210, 211.
Kipnis, Itsik, 4, 7; animals and, 25, 128, 134, 137–39, 145; care and, 25, 126–29, 134, 139, 143, 145, 147, 151, 231; emotions and 18, 126, 128–30, 133, 135–36, 144, 146, 149; factography and, 12, 18, 127–28, 148–49, 212; hefker and, 25, 127–30, 135, 137–42, 148; *Months and Days* (*Khadoshim un teg*), 18, 25, 121–22, 125–26, 128–35, 137, 139–44, 146–49, 157, 233; neighbors and, 129–34, 143–47, 151, 233; *Oxen* (*Oksn*), 126, 138; pogrom violence and, 12, 18, 126, 128–34, 136, 138–42, 145–49, 151, 173, 230; strangeness as theme in, 126, 128–29, 133–34, 136–37, 140–47, 149, 151, 173, 231; time and 125, 128, 130, 141–43, 146–49;

Untervegns (*On the road*), 126, 134; witnessing in, 126, 129, 132, 144, 147–49. *See also*: Slovechno.
Kornilov, Lavr Georgievich, 152.
Kurds, 155, 158, 168, 170, 174.
Kushnirov, Arn, 64–66.
Kvitko, Leyb, 7, 46, 56, 105, 147, 151, 161, 164, 174, 183, 187, 193, 196, 202, 204, 221, 223, 226; *1919*, 4, 11, 18, 73–75, 83–85, 89–93, 95–96, 98, 100–101, 107, 110–11, 113, 117–18, 120, 136, 142, 166, 178, 230–32, 234; abandonment and, 8–10, 15–16, 18, 29, 31, 39, 72–75, 77–82, 85, 96, 98, 100–101, 103, 117, 128; animals and, 77, 89, 91, 107–109, 138, 162; body as theme in, 76–77, 91–93, 95, 99–103, 106, 111, 115–18, 121, 160–61; chaos and, 73–74, 76, 79–82, 97, 99, 109, 119; children and, 75–81, 84, 89–90, 94–95, 98, 103, 106–107, 109, 112, 114–15, 120–21, 126, 200, 229; enfleshment and, 39, 100, 102, 117, 121, 160; "In a Red Storm" ("In a roytn shturem"), 73, 82–83; pain as a theme in, 74, 80–81, 84–85, 92–95, 98, 101–103, 115, 117–21; pogroms and, 11–12, 14, 73–75, 78, 81–86, 89–91, 93–97, 100–102, 104, 106, 108–11, 113–15, 121, 162, 178–79, 230; sense perception and: 15, 39, 73–74, 79, 84–86, 90, 115–17; sound and, 17, 74, 76, 78, 81, 85, 89–95, 97–98, 101, 103–104, 106, 112–116, 118–21, 126, 231, 234; *Steps* (*Trit*), 73–74, 78–79, 82, 85, 96–97, 118, 230; *Two Friends: Lyam and Petrik* (*Tsvey khaverin: Lyam un Petrik*), 75, 77, 106–107; violence as theme in, 15–16, 72–75, 78, 82–91, 93–96, 98, 100, 102–107,

110–15, 118–21, 140–42. *See also* Uman.
Kyiv, 4, 39, 46, 57–60, 64, 76, 82–83, 102, 110, 126, 130–31, 150, 152–53, 173, 179, 182–83, 185, 187, 191–92, 194–95, 201–202, 206–208, 215, 217, 221
Kyiv Kultur-Lige (Kyiv Culture League), 46, 60, 76, 182, 196, 207.

Leshem, Noam, 2, 35.
Lestschinsky, Jacob, 184–85, 189, 204. *See also* statistics.
Levin, Doyvber, 4, 12, 19, 205–206, 210, 220, 227–28, 230; *Ten Wagons* (*Desiat' vagonov*): 211–14, 228.
Litvakova, Zinaida, 188, 198, 207.
Lukhtan, Marko, 131–33, 146. *See also* neighbors.
Lyotard, Jean Francois, 203.

Machines, 93, 148, 154, 158–59, 162–65, 171, 173–74, 176, 177.
Makhno, Nestor, 9, 83, 167, 176, 211, 221.
Mandelshtam, Osip, 42.
Manger, Itzik, 37–38, 46.
Markish, Peretz, 36–37, 46, 50, 69, 79, 121, 141; "The Mound" ("Di kupe"), 4, 84, 100.
Mayakovsky, Vladimir, 16, 76.
Mbembe, Achille, 23; necropolitics, 27–28, 115, 181.
Malakhovka, 60, 72, 205. *See also under* children: orphanages.
medicine, 14, 29, 40–43, 86, 106–107, 183–84, 199, 208, 221; medical professionals, 4–5, 179, 192, 203–204, 209, 229; psychology, 192, 202, 204, 210, 214–16. *See also* diseases, Schneersohn, Fischel.

memory, 15–16, 18, 66, 96, 112, 148, 193, 201, 209, 212, 218–22; memorialization, 152, 156, 201, 204, 212.
Mendl, Menachem of Vitebsk, 31.
military, 57, 84, 132, 170, 187–88; Imperial Russian army, 5, 33, 47, 57, 150, 152–53, 155, 158, 162–63, 169–70, 174, 177, 181, 190, 198, 200; state, 27; nonstate, 9, 27; Red Army, 26, 28, 64, 146, 150, 153, 167, 181, 208; Ukrainian army, 6, 27–28, 83; Volunteer Army, 57, 83, 167, 185; White Army, 28, 158. *See also* Russia; Ukraine.
modernism, 15–17, 36, 38, 46, 58, 72, 90, 139; expressionism, 16, 37–38, 50, 84, 231; introspectivists (Inzikhistn), 16, 78; modernist manifestos, 16, 44, 76; New Growth (Vidervuks), 126; Union for Real Art (OBERIU): 210–11. *See also* Grinberg, Uri Tzvi; Hofshteyn, David; Kvitko, Leyb; poetry.
Molodowsky, Kadya, 12, 16, 76, 90; abandonment and, 4, 9–10, 24, 39–40, 42–44, 79, 231; "Chako" ("Tshako"), 39, 43, 79; "Otwock" ("Otvosk"), 40–43, 230.

Nakhman of Bratslav, Rabbi, 118, 226.
neighbors, 31, 57, 91, 104, 106, 143–45, 202–203, 214, 230–31; Jewish-Christian relations: 84, 87–89, 122, 129–34, 146–47, 168, 175–76, 192, 199, 204, 233.
Nourbese-Philip, Marlene, 13, 43.
Nusinov, Isaac, 126, 129–30, 147.

objects, 86, 101, 120, 163–65, 210, 223; as hefker, 1–2, 29, 35, 59, 136; in literature, 50–51, 74–75, 78, 101, 103–104, 118, 135–136, 157, 171, 234. *See also*: property, things.
Odesa, 75, 183, 193–94.
Organization to Promote Health among Jews (OZE), 184, 192, 207.
Ovruch, 131, 136, 143, 146–47, 192, 207.

Pain (*see also*: body, violence): 60, 105, 119, 121, 125, 155, 174, 218, 225–27; of abandonment, 3, 37–39, 69, 74, 80–81, 84–85, 98, 136, 164, 229; of others, 56–57, 64–65, 68, 71–72, 95, 114–115, 117–18; of torture, 15, 102, 120, 163–64, 176; sound and, 58–59, 63–64, 92–95, 103, 231, 234.
Palestine, 2, 7, 39, 47, 57, 216.
Peretz, I. L., 32–33, 68, 207.
Petliura, Symon, 11, 136, 153, 167, 180, 198.
phenomenology, 14–15, 50, 86, 102, 223.
Pidmohylnyi, Valerian, 8–9.
property, 9, 13, 28, 33, 102, 145, 233; destruction of, 5, 8, 9, 13, 84, 177, 188, 231; hefker and, 1–3, 29–30, 32, 34, 43, 107, 117, 159, 229; Jewish property law: 1–2, 18, 23- 24, 35, 43, 229. *See also* objects; things.
Poe, Edgar Allan, 16, 89, 91.
poetry, 3–4, 7, 15–16, 18, 46–47, 55, 65–69, 73, 84, 89, 116, 120–21, 127, 156, 196, 200, 228–32; body as a theme in, 16, 18, 38, 41, 43–44, 49–51, 53, 85, 100, 103; emotions and, 45, 48, 50, 59, 78, 84–85, 91; experience and, 15–17, 50, 69, 79; experimental poetry, 11, 39, 41, 50, 75; hefker as aesthetic principle: 1–2, 16, 24, 36–39, 43–44, 49–52,

59, 61, 64, 72, 74, 77, 79, 85, 96, 101, 117, 121, 231–32; pogroms and, 10, 14, 16, 18, 44, 46, 48, 59, 71–72, 78, 85, 96, 121, 136, 142, 173, 183, 228, 230–32; sense perception and, 18, 44, 50–51, 53, 68, 71, 79, 86, 90, 94, 107; sound and, 11, 17–18, 41–43, 48–52, 54, 57–59, 61, 65–66, 69, 74, 81, 85, 90–94, 97–98, 101, 103–104, 106, 114–16, 119, 121, 228, 231; violence and 10–14, 17, 34, 38, 61, 68–69, 74, 82, 85–86, 90, 106, 119, 229, 232. *See also* Bialik, Hayim Nakhman; Ewing, Eve; Grinberg, Uri Tzvi; Hofshteyn, David; Kvitko, Leyb; Mandelstam, Osip; Manger, Itzik; Markish, Peretz; Molodowsky, Kadya; Mayakovsky, Vladimir; Whitman, Walt.

pogroms, 81, 90, 94, 108, 114, 131–34, 149, 185–87, 201, 217–19; abandonment and, 1–4, 10, 12, 14, 16, 18–19, 25–26, 39, 44, 46, 48, 59, 61, 65, 68–69, 71–74, 82–83, 95–102, 128, 130, 139, 142, 151, 155, 174, 177, 204, 229–30; Belaia Tserkov', 206–209; Berdichev, 195, 207; Cossacks, 33–34, 158, 166; Drohobych, 7; Dubovo, 28, 201; Elisavetgrad (Kropyvnytskyi), 4–5, 26, 152–53, 166–67, 171, 200; Fastov (Fastiv), 188, 207; Horodyshche, 185; investigators, 2–3, 5–7, 10, 18, 35, 90, 140, 144, 147, 161, 177, 179–83, 188–94, 197–98, 200, 202–204, 210, 229, 232; Kherson, 159, 164, 166–67, 177; Kishinev, 5–6, 10, 32, 99, 127, 180, 232; Kosenko (Kosinko), 131–32, 134, 140; Kozyr-Zyrko, Ataman Oleksander, 136–37, 190; Liakhovich, Ataman Evgenii, 198; literature and, 4, 10–12, 14, 16, 18–19, 25–26, 39, 44, 46, 48, 56–57, 59–61, 65, 68–69, 71–75, 78, 82–86, 89, 91, 93, 95–98, 100–102, 106, 109–11, 113, 121–22, 126, 128, 130, 138–45, 151–53, 157, 160, 166–68, 170–75, 178, 206, 213–14, 220–24, 228, 231, 234; Nikolaev, 77, 159, 166; Pechora (Pechera), 197–200, 202, 204, 232; perpetrators, 6, 11, 13, 33, 35, 71, 108, 121, 126, 147, 158, 172, 191, 195, 203, 211, 231; Sokolovskii, Ataman, 198; survivors, 7, 10, 86–87, 90, 115, 128, 132, 178–79, 186, 191–92, 194, 197, 199, 202, 204, 206–207, 214–16, 231; victims, 4, 9–10, 14–15, 17, 33, 35, 68, 71, 84, 100, 104–108, 111, 115, 117, 121, 126, 134, 140–41, 143, 146–47, 158, 160, 162, 170–71, 178, 187–90, 193–95, 200, 203, 205, 207, 215–16, 231; warlords, 6, 25, 27–28, 130, 160, 190, 230; Zhitomir, 233. *See also* aid organizations; children; neighbors; relief organizations; Slovechno; violence; Uman.

questionnaires, 180, 182, 186, 188, 190, 194–95, 197, 199, 206–10, 218, 220, 227, 231, 234. *See also* aid organizations; relief organizations; statistics.

rabbinic literature, 3, 29–31, 43, 71, 79, 108, 118, 143, 151.
Ravitsh, Melekh, 16–17.
refugees, 145, 147–48, 159, 179, 193–94, 197, 202, 207–208.
relief agencies, 2, 9, 12, 25, 85, 104, 127, 181–82, 197, 200, 205–206, 217,

227–28, 231; relief workers, 4, 7, 10, 13, 18, 180, 186–87, 200, 215, 229. *See also* aid organizations.
Reznikoff, Charles, 13.
Russia, 24, 28, 47, 110, 151, 157, 173–74, 192, 201–202, 217–18, 220, 229, 232; 1917 Russian Revolution: 1, 5, 73, 82, 127, 130, 151, 154, 156, 157, 158–60, 168, 173, 176–77, 184, 189, 200, 212; Cheka, 153; Civil War, 1, 6, 8–10, 12, 14, 23, 25–28, 31, 33, 36, 73, 99, 101, 130, 146, 153, 170, 178–81, 184, 190, 194, 200, 205, 232, 233; Jewish Section of the Communist Party and the Division of Public Education (Narobraz), 207; Leningrad, 12, 19, 201, 205, 210, 213; Moscow, 153, 158, 175, 177, 183, 212; Petrograd, 150, 152, 160, 162, 209; provisional government: 6, 150, 152; revolutionary period, 3, 6–8, 11–12, 14, 23, 25, 28, 82, 149, 164–65, 169, 171, 176–77, 215–16, 229; Russian empire, 1, 3–6, 32–34, 154, 160, 234; Saratov, 153; Socialist Revolutionaries, 156, 157, 159; St. Petersburg: 46, 58, 101, 152–53, 158, 160–62, 164–65, 173–75, 177.

Santner, Eric, 78, 157.
Savchenko, Yakov, 71.
Scarry, Elaine, 14–15, 120, 163.
Schilder, Paul, 216, 223.
Schneersohn, Dr. Fischel, 86–87, 230; abandonment and, 19, 205; *Catastrophic Times and Growing Generations* (*Di katastrofale tsaytn un di vaksndike doyres*), 19, 205–206, 208, 214, 215–16, 220, 223, 225–27; children and, 4–5, 10, 19, 205–206, 208–209, 213–16, 218, 220–24, 226–28, 234–35; creativity and, 5, 10, 205–206, 217, 219–25, 227–28, 230–31; emotions and, 206, 209, 216–19, 222–23, 225, 234; Hasidism and, 205, 210, 215–217, 224–227; *Psychology of the Child's Intimate Life, The* (*Psikhologiia intimnoi zhizni rebenka*), 215–16, 223; *Story of the Downfallen One, The: From the World of Chabad* (*Khayim gravitser [di geshikhte fun dem gefalenem]: Fun dem Khabadisher velt*), 226–27; *Studies in Psycho-Expedition*, 215–16, 223, 225; trauma and, 218–19, 226.
Schwartsbard, Shlomo, 11, 180.
Shapiro, Lamed, 101, 110–111.
Shedd, Dr. (William Ambrose Shedd), 153, 164, 169, 174–75, 177.
Shklovsky, Victor (Viktor), 58, 101, 169, 230; abandonment and, 4, 9, 18, 102, 149, 151, 155, 157–59, 161, 163–64, 168, 171–72, 174, 176–77; "Art as Device," 96, 155; estrangement as literary device in, 150–51, 153–55, 161, 166, 170, 172–74, 177, 213, 232; factography and, 18, 127, 156, 212; objects, 157–58, 163–65, 171–72; *Sentimental Journey: Memoirs, 1917–1922* (*Sentimental'noe puteshestvie: Vospominnaniia, 1917–1922*): 18, 149–57, 159–60, 162–63, 166–67, 171–73, 175–76.
shtetl, 4, 25, 33, 54, 66, 75–76, 129, 131, 134–36, 140, 185, 198, 210–13.
Shtif, Nokhem, 84–85, 206.
Shvartsman, Osher, 64–66.
Singer, Isaac Bashevis, 129.
slavery, 10, 12–13, 27, 30, 43, 114.
Slovechno (Slovechne), 4, 12, 18, 25, 122, 125–26, 128–34, 139–41,

143–47, 151, 173, 191. *See also* Kipnis, Itsik.

statistics, 169, 194, 204, 210, 217; as documentary strategy: 4, 178–82, 184–86, 187–89, 191, 196–98, 203, 206–208, 228, 231–32; counts of the dead: 133, 146, 155, 166, 175, 177–78, 202–203. *See also* aid organizations; Lestshchinsky, Jacob; pogroms; relief organizations.

Staudigl, Michael, 14–15.

Sterne, Laurence, 150.

Sobol', Andrei, 34.

sound, 17, 46, 57, 102, 133, 144, 171, 200, 203, 213; human voices, 40–42, 54, 56–57, 75, 90, 106, 114, 118–119, 121, 126, 144, 172, 199, 214, 224, 230–31, 234; listening, 11, 17, 14, 17, 51–52, 59, 62–64, 85, 87, 89–90, 121, 228, 231; pain and, 58–59, 74, 117, 234; poetry and, 11, 17–18, 41–43, 48–52, 54, 57–59, 61, 65–66, 69, 74, 81, 85, 90–94, 97–98, 101, 103–104, 106, 114–16, 119, 121, 228, 231; silence, 54–55, 62–65, 78–79, 103, 106–107; violence and, 17, 54, 57–59, 65–66, 74, 89–98. *See also under* Hofshteyn, David; Kvitko, Leyb.

Sudarsky, Itskhok, 201.

testimony, 5, 10–12, 13, 19, 64, 85, 90, 104, 126, 128–29, 131, 133–34, 139, 144, 148–49, 179–80, 191–94, 197–99, 200, 204–206, 212–15, 223, 229. *See also* witnessing.

things, 13, 15, 40, 45, 48, 59, 67, 76, 89, 101, 103–105, 118, 121, 135–36, 150, 155, 157, 159, 162–64, 233. *See also* objects.

time, calendar, 60, 122, 125, 141–42, 221, 230; hefker and, 8, 11, 17, 55, 82, 142, 148; Jewish calendar, 60, 112, 132, 135, 141–42, 176, 186–87, 221, 225; moments of, 8, 11, 57, 85–87, 91, 96, 113, 167; strangeness of, 7, 15, 57, 59, 61, 64, 66, 72, 74, 80, 96, 125, 149, 154, 174, 223; violence and, 109, 128, 130, 141–43, 146–47, 221, 223, 230.

Tolstoy, Lev, 165–67.

Tretiakov, Sergei, 184.

Tychyna, Pavlo, 82.

Ukraine, 4, 11, 28, 34, 37, 71, 76, 85, 97, 127, 153, 158, 167, 171, 174–75, 197, 203, 209, 217–18, 220, 229, 231; Donbas, 28; in poetry, 61, 67–68, 71, 114, 200, 231; revolutionary period: 3, 6–8, 23, 25, 27–28, 82, 147, 149, 164–65, 169, 181, 189, 199, 215–16, 229; Skoropadskyi, Hetman, 153; Ukrainian People's Republic, 27.

Uman, 4, 11, 72, 83–85, 87, 90, 94, 101–102, 115, 118, 151, 166, 195, 207. *See also* Kvitko, Leyb.

Urmia, Iran (Persia), 152–53, 161, 163–64, 167–71, 174–75, 177.

Violence 14–15, 19, 27, 43, 57, 60, 62, 74, 82–83, 89, 91, 93, 96, 98, 101, 104, 118, 125–27, 129, 135, 138, 145, 148, 153, 157, 159, 161, 170, 173, 179–82, 192, 194, 198, 212–14, 219–21, 224; abandonment and, 2, 4, 10, 17, 25, 28, 37–38, 45–46, 65, 85, 95, 100, 102, 139, 151, 163, 172, 174, 176–78, 187, 229; anti-Black violence, 9, 114, 232–35; anti-Jewish violence, 1, 3–6, 8, 12, 16, 18, 26, 37, 68–69, 84, 130, 131–34, 147, 149, 152, 167, 169, 187–90, 198–200, 215–16, 231; cannibalism, 94, 110,

221; hefker and, 1–2, 31, 38, 45, 61, 72, 95, 121, 128, 139–40, 142, 229; killing, 27, 60, 65–66, 68, 115, 133–34, 136, 139–40, 159, 166, 176, 179, 181, 187–88, 198–99, 222, 230; mass (public) violence, 1, 5, 8–9, 13, 16, 29, 45, 73, 75, 78, 86–88, 90, 102, 106, 121, 147, 149, 154, 222, 229, 232; murder, 5, 13, 34, 43, 68, 84, 87–88, 93, 105, 108, 115, 118, 140, 146, 187–88, 192, 215, 218, 225, 231; mutilation, 8, 13–14, 32, 38, 60, 77, 94, 110, 115, 140, 143, 166–67, 189, 198; retributive, 111, 126, 146, 149; ritual humiliation, 100, 136, 214; self-defense, 188; sexual violence, 6, 8–9, 30, 34, 84, 110–115, 116, 136, 146, 149, 159, 167, 170, 188–89, 195, 198–99, 215, 230; strangeness of, 7, 11, 14, 18, 66, 86, 94, 101, 103, 107, 115, 126, 128–29, 136, 140–43, 147, 149, 151, 154–55, 160, 173, 175–77, 230–32; torture, 8, 15, 28, 58, 84, 102, 120, 142, 160, 163–64, 176. *See also* pogroms; Scarry, Elaine; Staudigl, Michael.

Weinreich, Max, 216.
Wells, H. G., 173.

Whitman, Walt, 16–17, 50.
witnessing, 1, 5, 7, 11–13, 78, 89, 110, 115, 126, 128–29, 132–33, 144, 147–49, 153, 155–57, 183, 186, 188–89, 191, 193–94, 197–99, 203, 213–15. *See also*: testimony.
women, 4, 9, 30, 33, 40, 67–68, 78, 105–107, 111–13, 115, 135, 140–41, 143–47, 159, 166–67, 169–70, 179, 183, 192–3, 195–96, 199, 211, 214–15, 220–22, 233 and pregnancy, 90, 126, 163, 199, 214. *See also under* violence: sexual violence.
World War I, 2, 5, 13, 31, 33, 36, 38, 114, 127, 130, 132, 145, 150–151, 155, 168–69, 173, 179–80, 184–85, 187, 189–90, 200–201, 218, 220.
World War II, 11–12, 39, 201. *See also* Holocaust.

Yiddish journals, *Albatross (Albatros)*, 38, 50, 114; *Current (Shtrom)*, 47, 65, 126, 138; *Dawn (Baginen)*, 82; *Forwards (Forverts)*, 34, 185; *Future, The (Di tsukunft)*, 79, 84, 200; *Our Own (Eygns)*, 39, 76; *Pomegranate (Milgroym)*, 37; *Red World, The (Di royte velt)*, 76–77.
YIVO: 120, 179, 185

Harriet Murav is Center for Advanced Study Professor in Slavic Languages and Literatures and the Program in Comparative and World Literatures at the University of Illinois, Urbana-Champaign. She is author of *Holy Foolishness: Dostoevsky's Novels & the Poetics of Cultural Critique* (1992), *Russia's Legal Fictions* (1998), *Identity Theft: The Jew in Imperial Russia and the Case of Avraam Uri Kovner* (2003), *Music from a Speeding Train: Jewish Literature in Post-Revolution Russia* (2011), and *David Bergelson's Strange New World: Untimeliness and Futurity* (Indiana University Press, 2019).

For Indiana University Press
Gary Dunham, Acquisitions Editor and Director
Anna Francis, Assistant Acquisitions Editor
Anna Garnai, Editorial Assistant
Brenna Hosman, Production Coordinator
Katie Huggins, Production Manager
Darja Malcolm-Clarke, Project Manager/Editor
Dan Pyle, Online Publishing Manager
Pamela Rude, Senior Artist and Book Designer
Stephen Williams, Marketing and Publicity Manager

www.ingramcontent.com/pod-product-compliance
Lightning Source LLC
Chambersburg PA
CBHW021343300426
44114CB00012B/1056